Elizabeth Grant
of Rothiemurchus

The Highland Lady
in Dublin

1851–1856

Edited by

Patricia Pelly and Andrew Tod

With an Introduction by

Andrew Tod

NEW
ISLAND

Published in Ireland in 2005 by
New Island
2 Brookside
Dundrum Road
Dublin 14

www.newisland.ie

Introduction Copyright © Andrew Tod 2005

ISBN 1-904301-94-0

British Library Cataloguing-in-Publication Data
A catalogue record for this book is
available from the British Library

Typeset by Hewer Text UK Ltd, Edinburgh
Printed and bound by Creative Print and Design, Ebbw Vale, Wales

Contents

List of Illustrations

The half-title page and the six part-title pages feature reproductions of engravings from *Heffernan's Handbook of Dublin* (1861); courtesy of the National Library of Ireland.

Introduction

Elizabeth Smith, née Grant, the *Highland Lady*, was in her fifty-fifth year when she started another new year's journalising in 1851. Born to Sir John and Lady Grant of Rothiemurchus, a twenty-thousand-acre estate some thirty miles from Inverness, she had led a rich and varied life before her marriage in 1830 to Colonel Henry Smith of Baltiboys, a twelve-hundred-acre estate twenty miles south of Dublin in Co. Wicklow. Her changing circumstances, as the Grant family fortunes plummeted with her father's obsessive determination to cut a figure in Edinburgh and London legal and political circles to the severe detriment of his estate, provided her with copy for the surviving writings she produced before starting on the diary she began in 1840 and was to write down to the end of her long life in 1885.

She wrote articles for various literary journals in the wretched winter of 1827/1828 when she and her sister Mary's earnings were the sole family income before the by now disgraced Sir John slipped off to India to take up a judgeship to which he had somewhat fortuitously been appointed, leaving his equally unreliable son William (who later in 1852 she believed was 'speculating like any common gambler with money not his own') to take responsibility for no less than £65,000 of his father's personal debts. These early years she described for her family so that they would not forget all the tales of her Highland childhood in Badenoch and early womanhood in Edinburgh, Oxford and London, together with her experiences in India, all of which she had made sure they had all heard at her knee as they in turn grew up. These memories were started in 1846 and completed in 1854, towards the end of the years covered by this volume. They were prepared for publication by Lady Strachey, her niece, in 1898 under the title of *Memoirs of a Highland Lady*, and it is as the Highland Lady that she has been known to succeeding generations who have come to appreciate the enduring merits of this masterpiece of Scottish nineteenth-century literature.

But she is also increasingly well known for her Irish writings. From 1840 she kept a journal, clearly not the first, although her earlier ones have not survived, and an edited version of the opening decade was published in 1992 under the title of *The Highland Lady in Ireland*. The two years she and her family spent retrenching on the Continent at Pau and Avranches followed separately as *A Highland Lady in France*, so this opening spell of her diaries has been well served. They show her managing to make time to write voluminously both in the journal and for magazines like *Chambers' Edinburgh Journal* (its full all-embracing title was *Chambers' Journal of Popular Literature, Science and Arts*) to augment their income during that troubled decade. This was achieved in moments snatched during a busy life that involved playing a large part in the day-to-day administration of the estate, for her husband was a chronic sufferer from asthma, as well as organising a large household and taking responsibility for the upbringing of her three children.

There were other subtler reasons for continuing to write, as she explained in the opening entry for January 1856 when she was tempted to abandon the enterprise:

> I thought for this week past that I would give up this journal. It grows dull on my hands; age and troubles have cast a gloom over a once cheerful spirit; and the sameness of the life we lead is little calculated to revive it. But it was as the loss of a friend to me; for so many years it has been my only intimate companion, the repository of most of my thoughts, my feelings, my cares and such pleasures as have crossed a chequered path, that the want of some such safety valve seemed as evil. So, beginning the new year here I am at the old egotistick work, not uncomfortably balancing one thing against the other.

And she persevered down to her dramatic announcement in October 1856, 'Blind of one eye', that severely curtailed her writings, although she was sufficiently optimistic to write as her last comment of the year 'by care I shall escape total blindness.

And so farewell dear journal for a time'. She continued to keep what had to be an intermittent diary right down to a few months before her death in 1885 but this point in 1856 seemed to be the obvious cut-off point.

This journal of the years 1851 to 1856 has long since departed from the original interests and concerns of the Highland Lady now that she is so well entrenched in her life as the wife of the proprietor of a modest but improving Irish estate. In any case, as her shrewd sister Jane had observed in her travelling diary on a visit to the newly married Elizabeth Smith written as early as 1831, she possessed an 'extraordinary propensity for falling into the ways, the habits, customs, manners and opinions even of those she lives with . . . they have made an Irish woman of you now'. Her Dublin diaries were to be as interesting and valuable as anything she had written earlier.

The Smith family moved from Baltiboys in 1851 and resided in a succession of rented Dublin properties. First they spent a month in Haddington Terrace in Kingstown (Dún Laoraigh), then they moved to Nassau and Dawson Streets before their longest residence in Leeson Street, and 1856 finds them in Hatch Street. The principal concern of the Highland Lady during these years was naturally her family. Her husband was twenty years older and he needed an orderly existence, which was complicated by the arrival of her aunt. This was her mother's sister, Mary Ironside, who had married first the Master of University College Oxford, with whom Elizabeth Grant had stayed as a girl, and afterwards the Professor of Physics and then Clinical Medicine, Richard Bourne, so she was very comfortably off and had made it clear that her considerable fortune was to be left to her niece as her principal legatee, so there was no question of her foibles not being tolerated. She indeed it was who determined that a move had to be made from beloved Baltiboys to Dublin. In addition to the needs of two elderly invalids, the responsibility for the two children still at home fell on her shoulders. The eldest daughter Janey, born in 1832, had to be guided through the Dublin social milieu and her only son Jack ('The poor boy inherits his father's easily depressed irritable temperament and my bilious one') had to be prepared for his proposed career in India or the army at the recently established St. Columba's (where she found the Warden to be a 'pompous disciplinarian'), followed by crammers in London and Edinburgh for a military career.

But it is Annie, with whose marriage *The Highland Lady in Ireland* closes, who is the source of greatest concern. Or rather her spendthrift husband James King. She makes it perfectly clear that although she is well aware of his many fine qualities and what her role ought to be ('Mother-in-law will never advise nor interfere nor dictate'), when she locates that lack of financial probity she associated with her own family, then she must communicate it to her journal. Thus there were ominous signs that their finances were not in good order as early as June 1851, six months after the wedding ('That marriage was half a dozen nails in my coffin'). She was well aware that James' father Captain John King (whom she variously described as an 'odious, mean fool of a man', a 'knave or a lunatick' and an 'unprincipled old maniack') with a prestigious address at no less than 24 Merrion Square had not fulfilled his part of the marriage settlement. And there was general relief when James inherited £1,350 from a maiden aunt which it was thought would 'put him before the world'. Alas, this too was swallowed up and it was estimated that he owed another £1,000 in September 1853. On this occasion he was bailed out by Annie's godfather, George Robinson, the enigmatic Blessington doctor, who had behaved so strangely towards everybody since the wedding that it was commonly believed he had lost all sense of reality: 'There is some feeling deep down in the bottom of that half-broken heart, which perhaps it is best should never see the light'. Next year when a £200 bill was due, the Highland Lady manages to avoid catastrophe by securing a loan from her agent, the John Robinson who was the doctor's brother; this enabled James King to buy essential stock at the spring fairs. Even so, the position is just as disastrous at the beginning of 1855 when his 'ascertained debts' amount to £1,100. His mother (née Tottenham), who emerges as a more realistic parent than his father, observed that 'In four years, since his marriage, he has gone through four thousand pounds and nothing to shew for it but a little furniture, most of it presents, three cows and five horses'. And his mother-in-law evidently thought that he was up to his old tricks right at the end of this selection of her diaries when she notes carefully that in September 1855 he borrowed four pounds to pay the harvesters and promptly spent sixteen shillings of it on a case of *eau de cologne*.

This whole relentless tale is described in these journals, reaching the point in September 1852 when in a characteristic homily she urges Jack to 'avoid any business transactions' with his 'amiable brother-in-law'. Above all, she writes, 'I want to caution you – and to beg of you to make my memory a solemn promise to endorse no bills for him – and not to lend even a £1 unless you feel you can afford it to give it'. She later thought that this whole incident gave her serious concerns and perhaps even suggested that the journals for these years ought to be destroyed. There certainly are points where pages have been removed. In the manuscript for 1853 there are clear gaps where it is plain that deliberate cuts have been made. All the pages are numbered in her neat hand and 27, the second half of 28, 56, 57 and the second half of 58 are all missing. This was, of course, a particularly fraught year as far as relations with her son-in-law were concerned and it is possible Annie, to whom in the end the journals descended, understandably had decided to cull some of the severer criticisms of her husband's financial management. These omissions apart, overall the manuscript (which has been given with characteristic generosity to the National Library in Dublin by my co-editor Patricia Pelly, great-great-granddaughter of the Highland Lady: her influence and intimate knowledge of her family history is reflected on every page of this book) can be seen as a complete unity.

Despite all these family worries and concerns and her own worries about her own health, the family were much involved in the public occasions and spectacles appropriate to their class and position in society. They attended Castle Levées and Balls, Garrison theatricals, entertainments organised by the Colonel's Kildare Street Club and the Dublin Exhibition. There were concerts and regular visits to see celebrities like Fanny Kemble ('the vulgarity of her is beyond endurance') and to the opera where they heard Grisi, Mario, Lablanche and Cruvelli, mingling with their friends and acquaintances at whose homes soirées and parties took place. She naturally took steps to return hospitality, for example in March 1855 at Leeson Street:

It has recalled one to the ways of the world this little party we are giving. I have got so into the habit of living by

myself in my cheerful little room with my books and my
thoughts, and my journal to tell them to, that the dirty
under current has rolled by unheeded, fathoms below my
high philosophy.

It is interesting to note her critical comments on what she heard
in a varied series of concerts and operas. She adored contemporary composers such as Bellini and Donizetti, encouraging
her gifted daughter Janey to sing arias from *Norma* in her
singing lessons and playing transcripts with her on the piano.
She had very definite views on earlier composers, commenting
for example after one particularly full concert that she had heard
'Mendelsohn, Beethoven and Schubert. And last and best,
Mozart, so full, so rich after the more *meagre* compositions'.
Beethoven, indeed, was clearly a problematical composer for her
as she found his 'musick is so incomprehensible to me', describing him as 'a composer I never pretend to know'.

This was the social world of Elizabeth Smith's Wicklow
neighbours like the Downshires and the Milltowns, and the
Countess of Milltown was a frequent visitor who helped keep
her abreast with her accounts of high fashion and gossip around
the Lord Lieutenant's court. Lady Milltown did not have far to
seek her own troubles but they were trivial compared to those
suffered by her poverty-stricken sister Mrs. O'Reilly who regularly came to share her misery with our diarist's sympathetic
ear. Abandoned by her husband and living on the little that
could be afforded by her sisters and friends, her wretchedness
was summed up by the predicaments of her family. One son
Henry had been murdered and the profligate Jos. died in 1855.
That left the flighty Pysie and the remaining son Eyre who
turned out to have pretended to have married a pretty servant
girl Margaret and then heartlessly abandoned her. This is a
completely different stratum of Dublin society, reminiscent
more of that occupied by the hordes she saw from her windows
heading off for the 'Saturnalia' at Donnybrook; as she wrote:
'there have been no murders owing to the efficiency of the
police more than to any improved habits of temperance'.

Temperance and servants were a constant problem. She
frequently had to resort to the agencies after disasters in the
household ranging from almost ritual theft to an unforeseen

pregnancy of a housemaid who gave birth on her way to the lying-in hospital. She tried to minimise these problems by employing youngsters from the estate but they often turned out to be as bad as the unreliable housekeepers, alcoholic butlers and light-fingered cooks. In the end it always seemed to return to the demon drink; as she observed: 'what can bewitch the people so with drink – clothes, food, fire, shelter all bartered for whiskey punch'.

All was not gloom, however, and from her vivid and entertaining descriptions it is clear that there was a range of characters, occasions and events that she took great pleasure in confiding to her journal. Visits to Edinburgh to her mother and sister Jane were opportunities to comment on the changes she saw both in the development of her other favourite city and in some of its distinguished citizens she had known in her earlier existence. She comments on the ravaged appearance of an old friend Mrs. Cockburn, wife of the famous judge who wrote the classic *Memorials of his Time*: 'so handsome as she was and now a sort of drunken looking cook or fishwife, red and bleared and bloated, from want of care they say and over-eating, porter etc.' And in Leonard Horner, one of the founders of the University of London, she found 'another shock, a fat, red-faced, red nosed man'. Dublin contained lots of characters to whose eccentricity her pen did full justice such as Colonel Layard, the obsessed mesmerist later to commit suicide whose demonstrations so completely convinced Richard Whately, the protestant Archbishop of Dublin. He in his turn was described as a 'huge, queer, shapeless monster of a man with his giant's intellect yet simple credulous as a child . . . mad certainly but such a good man'. Naturally she was not out and about as much as she had been when she was so involved in the running of Baltiboys, but she took advantage of what she saw and experienced in her walks and drives around Dublin to write witty, moving anecdotes about, for example, her visit to the Salthill baths, and a railway accident close to the estate ('the first that has ever happened in Ireland'). On her voyage back from Greenock after a visit to Edinburgh she speculates on the relationship between an elderly military roué sporting a fez and his much younger companion she thought might be a seamstress.

Politics, moreover, continued to invite comment. In the

aftermath of the repeal of the Corn Laws in 1846, these were changing times and she provides interesting opinions on the fluctuating ministries and politicians of the day. There is no-one earning the unqualified admiration she had bestowed on Sir Robert Peel during his 1840s ministry. For her Lord John Russell is 'a gutta percha body', Gladstone is dismissed as 'a rank Puseyite', Palmerston is seen as 'a brilliant goose' and she dismisses Aberdeen and his 'ricketty cabinet' out of hand. The great event of these years is, of course, the Crimean War and she comments on every stage of the lead-up to hostilities, the course of the war and eventual peace. Much of her information is derived from what she learned from the Dublin papers and the *Times* so, for example, she is able to appreciate the 'graphic detail' of the Dubliner W.E. Russell's innovatory reporting from the front. Florence Nightingale, whose father had been a friend of her family during her childhood, she thought 'an excellent, benevolent, active minded girl . . . devoting herself to doing good works in the wandering friar style'. Lord Raglan, who she believed to be 'an amiable man but no sort of capacity for active service', naturally does not emerge with much credit: 'one would suppose he did not read the lists of the dead he signs so coolly'. But the hero of the campaign for her was Napoleon III, 'the only head there is'.

And as ever she read widely once her two invalids had finished with their newspapers and completed their game of whist. She did not appreciate Boswell ('no favourite of mine') or Sidney Smith ('vain, trifling and a glutton'), and although she appreciated Dickens's *Household Words* and his novels, she was not impressed by him as a person, describing him as 'a little, handsome, conceited, pompous dandy'. She got confused about a possible relationship between Dickens and Charlotte Brontë but she enjoyed the Villette of 'Currer Bell'. She drew a fascinating comparison between her own writing and the 'Letters to a Female Friend' of Wilhelm von Humboldt ('that amiable philosopher') when she observed that 'what Charlotte was to Humboldt, this odd journal is to me'. She had little time for Tom Moore ('wretched literary trifler') and she was extremely dismissive of both Goethe ('that he was crazy I have no doubt') and Macaulay ('so clever, so accomplished [but] a slave to the bottle'). Perhaps her most interesting comments initially were directed at 'the wretched, flippant, egotistical diary of the celebrated Miss Burney . . . I really never read such odious stuff', someone with whom perhaps she had quite a lot in common and with whom, as she read successive volumes, she felt increasing sympathy.

She does not neglect Blessington, where there were social occasions organised by the Downshires, let alone her beloved Baltiboys, because she went down twice a year to keep a watchful eye on her schools and supervise the collection of the rents from a tenantry, whose characters and idiosyncracies she knew so well, in the company of the agent and latterly a good friend and neighbour, John Hornidge of Tulfarris. There is grief as well when the plan to install James and Annie in the old house predictably produces further financial complications that lead to yet another deterioration in their relationships. Once they have been persuaded to remove, other problems arise with the difficult clergyman who decides to rent the property, Augustus West.

There were more serious problems amongst the tenantry. The journals for the 1840s make it clear that she knew them and their situations intimately and she was genuinely but realistically concerned about their interests, as the occupiers of Baltiboys House change in these six years. This is best illustrated perhaps in what she had to write about her visit in 1851 to collect the December rents from a tenantry just beginning to emerge from the horrors of the famine years:

All yesterday was too busy a day for any poetical regrets etc. The tenants began to appear at eleven o'clock and it was past six when the last retired. I cannot say they pleased me. They did not on the whole pay badly, but some of them paid grudgingly, tried to impose on me, believing me to be weak, which I call dishonest and mean and therefore I rejoice that they have met their match. All justice they shall have, proper allowance for the time – help – time – every encouragement, but what they ought to pay they must pay and without taking the liberty to squabble with me and occupy their time with their nonsense. There is a bad spirit on one or two of them, on whom it will be well to keep a watchful eye.

It is plain from the evidence in *The Highland Lady in Ireland* that Baltiboys deserves to be placed in that category of estates which, despite the scale of the problems even in Co. Wicklow, managed to emerge battered but able to contemplate positive change on the scale of what had been achieved since the Smiths returned in 1830. This was so obviously dependent upon regular payments of rent and, although there were doubtless different views of what the landlord's wife meant by 'justice' and perhaps it might have behoved her to pay more attention to what might have been 'nonsense' to her but matters of some significance to them, it would have been surprising if, when there was a difference of opinion, someone with her strength of character did not prevail.

But all was not harmony and it turned out that she was correct to emphasise the 'bad spirit' that certainly existed. She was well aware of the existence of Ribbonism and commented several times on its existence elsewhere in Ireland. Nearer home, however, there were examples of the sort of outrage she equally condemned elsewhere. There was a failed ambush of James King with tree trunks laid across the road to sabotage his carriage; copses on the hill behind Baltiboys House were burnt; and in March 1852 there was a carefully planned attempt to set fire to the front door in the hope that the whole house would be destroyed. It is interesting that amongst the names of those she suspected of being involved in this 'great crime', this 'fiendish revenge', was the same 'queer, discontented, self-sufficient radical' she suspected was involved in the *cause célèbre* of the accidental murder of Pat Flood in November 1832 shortly after the Smiths had arrived to improve the estate ('every tenant in Baltiboys consenting with two or three honourable exceptions').

However, during these years her life was firmly based in Dublin. It was here that she organised the lives of the two elderly members of her circle, Janey's social life and the education of her son for whom the journals were intended as a guide and perhaps also something more useful, as she wrote in June 1852:

Goodnight my own dear Jack, for all this is for you – you might find a friend in need some day – sell it – have it abridged or weeded – then publish like the rest of the world nowadays, and fund the proceeds.

Abridging or weeding what she wrote during these years is something which presents comparatively few problems because of the orderly and efficient way in which she recorded her thoughts. No matter whether she was writing in a few snatched moments in a busy day or seated in her room with its comforting view of the distant Wicklow hills which enabled her to fancy that she was still at Baltiboys, her pen flowed fluently across the carefully cut paper with hardly a correction or second thought.

Naturally there are occasional sentences which, taken out of context, seem somewhat odd ('The Colonel is sky high since the monkey ran upstairs') but invariably her stylish, elegant and interesting prose acts as an effective vehicle for the communication of her thoughts, as well as being the safety valve and oldest companion with whom she could share her feelings.

It is clear from the *Memoirs* (Chapter 17) and her other published writings that the broken romance with her brother William's college friend left a scar that was still present over half-a-century later as she keeps her Dublin journal. It is this that lies behind otherwise nondescript but interesting comments such as those of September 1852 when she is reflecting after another downturn in her husband's health:

> Ever since I first set seriously to the work of subduing all that was rebellious in me, ever since my first sorrow, now a lifetime ago, than which no other has ever been so sharp, I have kept the tight rein over feelings, and elevated duties into their right place, and been all the happier, certainly the more useful.

Nevertheless, the strong, individual voice that emerges from her Dublin journals is one which does from time to time show that 'feeling' does quite understandably break through.

She was possessed, for example, of a certain vanity. She observed at Dublin Castle one time that 'The Colonel and I found several acquaintances as we marched about together, he much stared at, I most audibly admired', and later she commented that 'my girls have been saved from my dangerous beauty, and their wit, their *mother* wit is well ballasted by the common sense of their excellent father'. One of Janey's admirers was Hamlet Thompson, whose company they all appreciated so that 'We begin to notice the days that Hamlet does *not* call; his attentions are all to me; he makes no secret of this admiration!' She was well aware of her proper place in society, observing at one Vice-regal Ball that 'I am not going to sit apart out of my own proper sphere while all the impudent pushing *little* bodies elbow their way to the top'. And near the end of this volume of her journals in July 1856, she had to be taken in to the wedding breakfast at the Milltown wedding by *Miladi*'s nephew, Jos. McEvoy, because she was 'seated on account of my toe, and so was overlooked in common with a cluster of desolates of more account than myself'. However, she was consoled by the Lord Lieutenant having 'the civility to speak to me . . . perhaps because he had seen me made one of the family'. She does not hide either that she is well aware of her abilities. One of the older tenants, for example, John Fitzpatrick, 'is not dying, as reputed, he only wants a little of my care', and at the charity opera production she organised Lady Downshire 'played well, as well as I used to, in the same good style, but no better'. She certainly saw her basic common sense as the commodity with which to deal with the absurdities of Annie's godfather, Dr. George Robinson; she noted at the beginning of 1851 that 'The Doctor is civilising slightly. Being obliged to speak to me he does it humanly; he is also losing that uneasy manner which the dislike of my clear, calm, grave eye produced in him'.

Editorial interference with what the Highland Lady wrote has been kept to a minimum. She wrote in a regular flow on carefully cut sheets of paper measuring eight by six inches in her meticulous hand with very rare corrections. The only major change has been to break up the sometimes relentless flow of her narrative with modern notions of paragraphing. Her characteristic spelling has been retained so that as much as possible of the authenticity of her individual voice can be discerned. Thus one of the maids descended into 'hystericks', Disraeli is seen as 'meteorick', her son-in-law as 'despotick' and Irish priests as 'fanaticks'. 'Gossipping', 'connexion', 'horrour' and 'duett' are all regular parts of her vocabulary. She distinguishes between the Drawing-room at the Castle and her own drawing room. Christian is sometimes written Xian. She is consistent in her use of Blesington and Milltown but interchanges Sebastopol and Sevastopol and refers to Wirtimburg and St. Petersburgh.

Other occasional Scotticisms creep in with bairns, wifie, anent, manie, guid, beldam and place names like Cannie mills and Porto Bello but otherwise she writes as she had done throughout the 1840s, like an educated, intelligent and strong-minded commentator whose journals faithfully reflect her class, prejudices and times.

There is, however, a great difference between the Dublin writings and her earlier journals. The first decade was much more energetic and physically demanding. Estate, neighbourhood, husband and family all required her very considerable powers of organisation and there was still time to write about the political and religious issues of the day that attracted her probing mind. Her two invalids, Aunt Bourne and the General, necessarily as their differing but demanding routines ate into her day, meant that these years in Dublin could never allow her to lead as full a life as she had been accustomed to at Baltiboys. She still had thirty years of a long and fulfilled existence ahead but she felt that her own health meant that her hold on life was as precarious as that of her husband or aunt. She may have been more housebound, keeping control over the affairs of the estate by remote control, but her writing still has the zest, interest and importance of anything she wrote before and it helps to support her growing reputation as an important commentator upon her life and times in Ireland. The Highland Lady's status is well established. The Dublin journals in the 1850s go a long way to establishing that there is an Irish Lady who has an equal claim to be recognised as an individual and important voice casting light on the fashions, public events and continued history of the Smith family in a somewhat neglected period of Dublin and Irish history.

1851

The year opens with daughter Annie and her new husband settling down to married life at nearby Humfreystown. Although the Highland Lady was displeased with arrears of rent on the Baltiboys estate, her journal suggests that Blessington and its neighbourhood had emerged from the worst of the Famine. Her unmarried daughter Janey enjoys the Dublin social scene and son Jack, on whom her hopes for the future are pinned, is sent off to boarding school at the recently established St. Columba's at nearby Rathfarnham, a venture that was made possible by the generous contribution made by her well-off sister Jane Gibson Craig in Edinburgh. When her mother falls seriously ill in the summer, she makes an extended visit to the city of her birth ('these Scotch people live in noble style'). Later she travels to London to see the Great Exhibition, en route for Oxford to assist her mother's sister, rich Aunt Bourne, to come and spend her declining years with them. This necessitates a move from the country to a very different life, first at Kingstown (Dún Laoghaire) and then to Nassau Street in the heart of Dublin, but she continues scrupulously to keep her daily journal

Illustration: Kingstown from Killiney

TUESDAY, JANUARY 1. Papa, Janey, Annie and I spent our New year's day alone together. We were very happy yesterday evening but we quite forgot to drink the old year out. We had no fun of any kind. James [King] came back today early [from Humfreystown] bringing *Chambers', Household Words*, Newspapers and Almanacks. Mince pies for dinner.

3. We dined alone for the first time for many years, and I don't think the Colonel liked it, but we were very cheerful in the evening, I making tea as of old. We read Dickens, played piquet and talked about our children. How anxious and fretful I have made myself without excuse either, for our children are as yet near us and all happy – they don't want *us* once they are grown up unless in need of our assistance at an odd time. Our regrets are then merely selfish. If they are happy, so should we be, and I will try and teach myself to put off self, to rejoice that I have lived to see one dear child established and to be thankful that she lives so near and that her husband makes himself one of us.

I fancy I was afraid of [James'] prudence. I believe I need not be – he is beginning very economically, and will I think avoid all debt in future; he has had so much annoyance from his former thoughtlessness. The inside man is given up – a neat parlour maid instead – a scrub by the day under Mrs. Mack. The marriage just causes the one additional servant. The fine carriage is packed up in its coverings. She goes out in the car; they sent their boxes here and took them away again in a donkey cart. She is to have an allowance for herself and her household expenses paid her in advance in portions every time they receive their allowance. Thus, they will do well, and they love each other so well, so wisely, why should I fear evil reaching them? The perfect confidence existing between them is their safeguard. Into this I shall never pry. Mother in law will never advise nor interfere nor dictate. When they want me they will find me just as I have ever been, a help in difficulty. Our aim as parents should be to cause our children to be sufficient for themselves – to walk alone, and early.

5. A very beautiful Sunday. There are many mornings I can hardly see, my defective eyes requiring a strong light to be of any use to me. The work of the past week has not been much: setting the house in order, writing some necessary

letters, a little mending, reading for the Clans, piquet every evening, and *Chambers'* and the *Household Words* for a treat occasionally. These last are quite delightful and they are spiriting up my friend Mr. Ritchie, for the Journal is progressively improving. Some really good writers are appearing of late, and he himself always puts in some spirited articles. What a curious book is MacCulloch's [*The Highlands and Western Islands of Scotland*] – so full of learning, ferretted out, God knows how or where, and retailed after a gossipping fashion that makes it the more remarked, I think. My Clan will be all the better of him. I am plagued to death with bad pens, having got such horrid soft quills and hard steels – dreadful. This is the Colonel's gold pen – pleasanter to write with than the steel, but the same nasty pin-point nib, no stroke that can be seen. Now this is Mr. Chambers' steel pen and very good it is at first, but after using it a while it seems to grow stiff – perhaps they require smooth paper.

6. We have been to the raffle. All the world was there and Lady Milltown and her daughters and a man so amusingly in love with Lady Barbara, a Mr. Trewell from the other side of the county – old family and good fortune, still hardly enough for my Lord.* We came home ourselves, the Colonel driving, for poor John has one of his bad headaches. I have never had one since I cut off my long hair.

8. How very uncivilised we still are here, more than half way through the nineteenth century. Marianne Watson, poor little body, was married yesterday to a man she don't care a farthing about, rather dislikes indeed – Tom Delaney, a queer-looking bit of a body certainly but both respectable and industrious – but that is a common thing in this country, a marriage without affection on either one side or the other. The Bridal party was large – thirty to forty people. And in the midst of them all the Bride was sent to bed, undressed by all the women, and then her groom was beat by all the men round and round till he was either hunted into or took refuge in the inner chamber! The door was then closed on the happy couple and the company then danced on the remainder of the night, the Bridegroom having a good house of his own to which he might have repaired with his Bride quietly and decently.

10. Jack talking *gravely* on the necessity of going to School. I believe it would be an advantage to him – how to manage it is the difficulty, so many *conflicting* circumstances interposing between us and any scheme for the family benefit. [The Doctor] has paid a visit, looking peaceable enough, even remaining a few minutes with me on passing through – very few, not quite five – and only speaking on professional subjects. He is much to be pitied – a proud spirit in the wrong, and too weak to own it.* Lady Milltown called today, most particularly gracious, and Cecilia. No house in town – a lodging when necessary *if* it can be managed – hotels too ruinous. Russy forced to sell out [his commission in the 68th of Foot] – returns to farm. Is she not to be pitied, poor woman – what are my little troubles, about which I fret so foolishly, compared to her serious griefs? She sat much above an hour commiserating our loneliness.

11. A godsend, we hope, from India – a legacy left to the Colonel which he never claimed; not too late now, but the papers vouching it being all in native writing, they have to be made out by the learned in Orientals, and so we are not sure yet.

15. We have done a piece of business of some importance. The Colonel has remade his Will, an act rendered necessary by the settlements on Annie's marriage. Mr. Cathcart drew it up in exact conformity to the intentions of the former one and John Hornidge and Tom Darker witnessed it on Monday last the 13th. Many, many years I hope and believe it will be before we have to look there for directions.* I always believe that I shall go first, for though I am so many years younger and so much more active-minded, my constitution is not near so strong in any way. He eats and sleeps well and he has not one unsound tooth in his head. My Clan, which don't interest me, and which is really very troublesome, involving a good deal of research, occupies two good hours of my every morning, besides a third on a rainy day and attentive reading in the evenings.

20. Such a wretched a day is this that we have persuaded James and Annie to remain, the rather that tomorrow is the meet at Blesington. Next day they go to Dublin for a week's gaiety or more; the Drawing-room is not till the 29th, but there are some

concerts they wish to go to. Messrs. Chambers furnishes funds, so there is no drawback on my part to happiness. Their dresses will be very pretty – Annie her Limerick lace over white satin train made out of her white brocade silk wedding gown – her own plume of last year. My Aunt's *point lappets* and my pearls as they are the handsomest, and besides they have a diamond centre – Janey white tarletan over white satin, white tabbinet train, my plume, extracting the third tall feather from it, my Mother's *point lappets* and her sister's pearls.* The Colonel had to go to Blesington to get some carters fined who would go on the wrong side of the road – found Mr. Armstrong very angry at being the only Magistrate upon the Bench.*

SUNDAY, FEBRUARY 3. Ogle Moore called on us on Friday and sat quite a long while. Busy with schools and parish and curate and a pamphlet upon education which he hopes will get him a better living.*

4. The Colonel and I very cheerful last night, talking over the Dublin doings, Mr. Sheehan's delightful dinner and the Drawing-room which was so pleasant. Everybody there the girls knew, and they extremely admired, James whispered. But the sensation they made was at the Ball.

11. This is my dear Jack's birthday, he is thirteen – and we had no fun for him, no pleasure of any kind. I believe that I am worn out, fairly worried out of all energy, for I care for nothing and can hardly rouse myself to go heartlessly about mere duties.

16. Sunday. After all I sent off the Clan thinking Mr. Ritchie could judge better of the whole than of a part. It was a long job requiring careful study, but latterly it interested me. *Beaux* are to be at dinner every day till Thursday when our trio go up to the *private* ball at the Castle – this will be a nice happy week for dear Janey who must find this invalid house very sadly dull. Luckily I have little, cleanly, active Mary Anne back in it, steadied by a servitude in Dublin and by a poor enough marriage, which makes her anxious to earn a little money. She is a very nice servant and so good about the Colonel. By the bye Russy called at Humfreystown yesterday while we were there; more to say for himself a good deal than he had – really pleasant but with very queer lounging manners.

Well now, about the Pope [Pius IX]. Lord John [Russell]'s speech in bringing in the bill was excellent, temperate and very firm and as protestant as the most stern calvinist could desire; his speech in reply to some very cutting observations on his change of feeling towards the R. C. priesthood was equally admirable – he honestly acknowledges that his opinions are altered because he found his confidence misplaced – that's the way to take the whole movement. But then the Bill itself is a miserable mouse out of such a mountain. The assumption of titles is forbid, in Ireland as well as Great Britain and no act is legal in which these titles are employed, and that is all. The synods may meet and churchmen may meddle and Bulls may be promulgated setting all the world by the ears just as now. In no other country is such a nuisance tolerated, not even in R. C. countries, with the exception of Austria, and nowhere should it be tolerated, priests from the beginning of time all the earth over always requiring the tight bridle of civil law over their preposterous pretensions. If Rome takes the hint and is quiet, Lord John hopes nothing further will be requisite. If she goes on plunging she must be further shackled. Why not do it at once and be done with it?*

I have been reading loads of amusing books by the corner of the fire all the rainy weather – Mrs. Trollope's *Paris*, so good* – *Sir Philip Hetherington*,* a novel quite delightful – Miss Austen among better people so very natural and the moral so excellent; still I feel the heroine was not plain – those eyes, and little hands nicely gloved, and neat feet, a pretty figure, and dancing to perfection. She would become very handsome when happily married. After all, beauty is a whim; no two people agree on it luckily. *Household Words* continue to be very good.

23. The Doctor is civilising slightly. Being obliged to speak to me he does it humanly; he is also losing that uneasy manner which the dislike of my clear, calm, grave eye produced in him. He is less nervous certainly, but not happy and quite impenetrable. To me, my old friend George Robinson is dead and buried. He died of brain fever, and as had he lived his intellects would have been permanently affected. I am the better able to bear his loss. In his stead here is a very

skilful and a very attentive Dispensary Doctor of rather singular manners perhaps, but what matter? We need only see him professionally. I fancy I have a queer mind, whether it be strong or weak I declare I don't know

During this long illness of my poor Colonel's coming after my own little fit when during the rainy weather I could not get out, Miss Macdonnell has been exceedingly neglectful of her business at school. She is busy doing needleworks, some for Mrs. Moore, some for sale – Nelly sells them for her – the school is therefore hurried over, no lessons prepared, no work settled, the children sitting listless, lolling about, no life, no business, no tidiness. In short all most discreditable. I have been there twice and shall go there at every opportunity, and make short work of it with this young lady unless she mind what she is doing. There is no principle in the country I believe, and I can't be ever watching, neither do I like to be for ever changing. How hard it is to meet with a really conscientious character in the lower classes in this country at any rate.

25. The Colonel is reading the newspaper now, quite interested in the resignation of the Ministry; it will be a patch up just for the present. Lord Stanley* could not make up a cabinet without Mr. Gladstone, a rank Puseyite, which would not do in these times. Lord Aberdeen was not prepared, so the poor little Queen after ever so many long conferences had to send for Lord John again near mid-night. I long to get the paper into my own hands, being about the greatest political gossip in the world. Really these are exciting days.

SATURDAY, MARCH 8. Little Janey singing away like a little syren; how much I do wish she could hear some good musick. Jack full of school; I, busy marking new shirts and reading *Pendennis* – excellent, clever, deep, interesting, not a pleasant picture but I am sure a true one, and one which ought to make us think of how ill we perform our duties, how improperly we educate our sons, even in these improved days.* What depraving influences surround them from the moment they leave their mother's upright care, and how herding together in the season of passion, before principle is confirmed, reason fully awakened, *sufficient* occupation provided, they continue to corrupt one another in an unceasing career of mistakes. We are beginning to recognise this; I hope beginning to correct it, but the reform is slow.

9. I am reading *Pendennis* – it is so good! and poor Patrick Tytler's *History of Scotland** shewing deep research, good judgement, fair and liberal feelings. When I and others like me avoided dancing with him and Archy Alison,* we little thought the day would come when we should be so proud of being recognised by them; and the butterflies whom we preferred in those giddy days, where are they all? My poor Clan! Mr. Ritchie has taken a world of pains, kind goodnatured man, to let me down easily, but he and Robert Chambers both think it a failure evidently, though they civilly call it only unsuitable to the work it was intended for. They say the sketches of the various Lairds have the air of an *apologue*. I have just looked out the word and find it means 'a fable invented to exhibit some moral truth'. Well, – I see nothing wrong there. They wanted nothing so laborious – they wanted the reality of highland *modern* life in contradistinction to the *conventionalism* of the novelists. I am sure I thought I had done it all and a deal more, and I still think so, but probably my views are unlike theirs – at any rate they won't do for them. But I shall keep the returned paper, read it by and bye with less prejudiced eyes, and if I still like it some other firm shall publish it; and no time is thrown away that has been employed in reading it and thinking, though the fruit may be long in ripening.

10. Richard Hornidge sat an hour talking very pleasantly and the conversation got quite naturally to our dilemma with Tom Darker – I think he gave sufficient reasons for our leaving the farm with him on condition of holding it only from year to year and to be given up on Jack's coming of age should Jack wish it. The plan suits my wish to get rid of the home farm. But the reduction in the rent of other tenants he don't approve of, neither does Ogle Moore, though they can hardly, unskilful as they are, manage to make it. So we have compromised by agreeing to give an allowance for bad markets – so much percent of a reduction for *this year*, keeping the old rent in the Book, having it paid up and giving a receipt in full for it, and then making a present of what we remit. Probably that is the best way.

11. Grand hunting – the black horse borrowed by Miss Janey to take herself and Mrs. King to the meet at Holywood. Jack drove in from Kilbride, breakfasted with John Hornidge and came home to his Papa and me tired enough at four o'clock. The Colonel was quite alive to all the news. Annie amused us with the result of her intercourse with her cousin, the Marquis of Drogheda.* She has now had two conversations with him. The first was at the Castle Ball. He came up to her all smiles. 'It's very hot', he said. Today at Holywood he rode quickly up to the car and in the kindest voice called out 'It's very cold'. Both she and Janey burst laughing – they could not help it.

14. The Lynchs called yesterday. She grown an old fright, he quite recovered. They are so fond of religion and politicks, we hold both a synod and a parliament when they come. Evidently they consider the Pope and John Tuam indefensible,* but as for Lord John they like every one else consider *him* indefensible. James and Annie have just called. Both James and his father are low about the Castle Daly property, the sale of which is put off till June. A purchaser has, however, presented himself inclined to take the whole estate at a price that pays the mortgages in full, so that is consoling. In the meantime outstanding accounts must wait.

    We have I think resolved on sending Jack to St. Columba's.* After due enquiry everything considered there don't seem to be any other school so eligible. The very best Irish boys go there, and only the very best, the terms being high for this country, though cheap as compared with England. The education is acknowledged on all hands to be first-rate and the alleged Puseyite fudge just what we of the Church of England have been brought up in – not the least like Mr. Bennet* and Co. though the Irish Calvinists object to it. The Irish Church is the English Low Church – as opposite as they can make it to the Roman Cath.

15. Tom Darker went to Dublin on business of his own and ours, and took our two worst stallfeds with him and sold them in Smithfield for fifteen pounds. Our oats last market fetched ten shillings a barrel, and we are selling all the turnips we can spare in small quantities at one shilling a

barrel, that is ten shillings a ton – forty ton to the acre – for it was a very fine crop.

Friday the drive up was delightful. Dined in Merrion Square. All sunshine. Warm welcome, good dinner, such wine! Annie so made of. Mama King really very nice. Papa speechifying in praise of us!* Sunday both Cathedrals. Monday the Ball. Dear little girls! they are so happy. Everybody is kind to them, and James is so indulgent, so careful of them. These are their bright days, poor things. And our humble Brides here at home, in their humble way they are equally happy. Catherine and Pat with their savings, their odd silver, they would not break their two pounds! *walked* off in the rain to the fair to make their little purchases. A bundle of rubbish I gave Catherine for help towards the baby linen has enchanted her. Mary Anne is gathering too. Saving her wages and buying bedding, and receiving with thankfulness trumpery which she mends up to look as good as new. We sold our cattle very well. Prices are up a little.

19. A letter from Jane enclosing one from our Aunt Bourne, which inclined Jane to hope her pet scheme may be realised. I fear not. If my Aunt would consent to live *here* nothing would make me happier than to have her [see 6 April]. But we cannot leave this. We have now no agent, neither can we afford to have one. The tenantry require to be personally superintended. Annie must not be deserted. Jack's interests in all ways must be watched. We wish Janey to marry in Ireland. Above all, *this* house, and the Doctor used to him, are necessary to the prolonged life of the Head and Front of all. We must not desert our duties, and Providence having given us our position and a most happy and a useful one, we must faithfully discharge the offices connected with it. Sometimes these are a wear upon the spirits for it is a disappointing country to work in.

20. A letter from Janey full of pleasure. Monday the ball! which was delightful, so crowded as to be quite a crush, one thousand seven hundred people. Squally weather all the time, yet I have always got out. Yesterday only as far as John Fitzpatrick, who though very ill is not dying, as reported, he only wants a little of my care. I left proper advice and brought his little Annie home with me to carry back

necessaries. Recollecting what cabins we found here it is pleasant to find this poor man reared in such a hovel, lying now in a good bed with fit bedding in a bedstead, blankets, sheets, frilled pillow-cases, good white shirt, clean cotton cap, table beside him with his drink and medicine, foot*board* by the bed, large window curtained, chairs, pictures on the walls, chest for clothes, and his kitchen well furnished, his turf-stack large, and sacks of meal standing near the dresser. Yet is he discontented, and thought of America because life is such a struggle here.

21. James and Annie dropped Janey, sat awhile, then went on home, after telling us of a bit of Castle impertinence which unless explained as a mistake reminds one of Lord Normanby's [Lord Lieutenant, 1835 – 1839] day. Janey is much admired. She is new. There are no decided beauties, her dancing is charming, and her general partners worthy of her. She was much noticed by the Throne set on Monday night while dancing with a Captain Bethune, an eminent performer – Scotch. Next day they were all in Merrion Square, when a Castle footman brought an invitation to a private ball there to Miss Smith alone. James then took the card to the Chamberlain's office – all right. It was *the* Miss Smith intended and if she could not go without her chaperone she must write and say so. We will wait; if Annie's card comes we will pocket the flattery and the affront together and let the young things spend a happy evening, but if that is forgotten we are not likely to remember either to ask for the one or to decline the other. The Colonel seems quite glad to have his little Jane back and I am revived by her cheerful countenance. Ogle Moore's pamphlet is out. It is extremely good – beautifully written. Must be read again.

22. Such a lucky hit – Janey thought *Sir Philip Hetherington* might amuse, read aloud – and it did. We all entered into the fun and the sense of this really admirable novel which with many faults is about the best produced at any rate *this* season. Mr. Moore's little pamphlet also much interested our whole party. It is so wise, so temperate, so plain, that only the perverse can misunderstand it, or those devoid of intellect fail to see the consequences painted out in it so clearly, of a bigotry as pernicious to the welfare of the

country as is the superstition these zealots in good faith desire so ardently to enlighten. The world is awakening – a little. Intercourse with others is doing much. It never answers for mind to be chained to a clique, kept to one set of ideas. A very satisfactory answer from St. Columba's. I have now written to enter my boy there.

24. A letter from Jane wishing, nay, insisting upon sharing the expense of Jack's education. What a generous creature! But it must not be. By giving up a luxury or two more we can afford to perform this duty ourselves. The stable expenses are over or nearly so. I can so order them in future that they will never again overwhelm us. Horses and Clubs are delicate subjects, particularly under peculiar circumstances. A riding horse my dear Colonel must have whether he be ever able to ride it or no. So I will not replace poor worn-out Grasshopper. She is quite done up except for field work. We are to get a second hand jaunting car, plenty to be had as good as new nearly these times, and thus we can spare another servant. Either John or Pat must go. We shall need all our economy these difficult times to make the two ends meet. And poor James can't get a sixpence from his father who is hard up himself, and will remain so till the sale of the Castle Daly property, now postponed till June. They are declining gaiety because they can't return the invitations as they used to do. The Castle invitations have all come in proper course. Janey got hers before the general cards were issued.

I have had to write to Mr. Craddock [Blessington R.I.C. Sergeant] this morning about the most annoying set of petty robberies inflicted upon us all in this neighbourhood by, we suppose, two gangs of vagrants, one of them swarming in a hovel belonging to a bad charactered pair of the name of Carr, the other established in the empty house where poor Robin Carney the mason once lived, which they broke open. What are the police about! The first loss I heard of was Marianne's two geese, my present to her; the next my own two, taken last night. Then comes a string! Four or five hens from the Darkers, clothes from several places, potatoes from our seed heap, and no notice taken. But I noticed – in quick time too – for I have no notion of delay in these matters. So

the note I have written to Mr. Craddock I have sent in by
Tom D. to be shown first to Mr. Owen [the Marquis of
Downshire's Agent], who will not let the grass grow under
his feet. The roads were quite infested by these trampers,
dangerous-looking men and most horrid women. Such a
state of things, and little hope of better times yet awhile.
Our own poor law affairs are very comfortable. No rate
struck for this year there being sufficient balance in hands
for our needs. While we have Mr. Owen, Mr. Wolfe, and a
Darker among the Guardians, we can keep our own sturdily,
in spite of all the wretched jobbers at Naas.*

25. The Colonel out walking. A visit from Dick, and a fine
Popish story in the papers about a Miss Talbot and her
eighty thousand pounds. She has been inveigled into a
Convent and there was condemned to the veil, but fortunately for the poor girl and for the cause of reason in
general, just at this particular time, her step-father, one
of the Berkeleys, has brought the matter before the Commons and the Lord Chancellor, whose ward she is, has
ordered her out of the Convent, directed her to come to
London, and in very plain terms without mincing the
matter, said in his Court that the Abbess, the priest and
the self-styled Bishop of Clifton had uttered falsehoods,
both as regarded himself and the young lady. Her Uncle and
Aunt, Lord and Lady Shrewsbury, are frightfully to blame.
They got leave to take her abroad, instead of which they sent
her to this Convent, and then the Abbess and the Bishop
began quarrelling about the spoil which will fall to neither
of them now but to some fine man who will however make
her life happier whatever way it passes than it could have
been within the living grave of those Convent walls. Those
dreadful penitentiaries should not be tolerated.*

26. Rainy night, fine morning. Janey all ready for the drive to
Dublin. They dress early, dine at Mr. Sheehan's and go from
his house to the Ball. Tom Darker is going up with cattle,
and to buy a good second-hand car, offered to us for ten
pounds, which we have descended to instead of buying a
horse at fifteen pounds, to replace Grasshopper, now quite
done up. The car will eat no corn, and even should the
Colonel go for a riding horse *one* man will do in the stable –

another saving – for save we must. The drains on our small income are so many, there is very little left for ourselves.

27. Our plunderers, five of them, went off to jail in the morning. They have been busy this fortnight, though no one thought it worthwhile to inform against them. The English world quite mad about that poor girl, Miss Talbot, whose protestant uncles have come forward to say she has been systematically denied all intercourse with them or any relations of their faith. 'John Tuam' has prohibited every school in his diocese, even merely industrial ones, where a protestant teacher or pupil or book is found. I do not think the exercise of such despotism should be permitted in a free country. What a frightful superstition it is!

28. All came home yesterday. Janey had a delightful Ball, the pleasantest possible dinner at Mr. Sheehan's – all enchanting! James never went to bed, took off his dress boots to put on his riding ones and away by railway with other such like to Sallins.

   Dublin full and busy, and people in good spirits, so pleased with their new Lord Mayor [Benjamin Lee Guinness]. A Beetroot sugar factory really preparing, ditto for chicory. The first steamer direct for America to start next week from Galway, and we sold our cattle pretty well, but here comes Egyptian flour for the merest trifle, so good too. Second reading of the Papal Bill, carried by a larger majority than the first, minority dwindled down to ninety-three, thanks to Miss Talbot's history which is making quite a ferment. We have been reading Mr. Dickens this evening with great pleasure. Nothing escapes his caustick pen. If he can clear off one abuse out of our million we shall owe him no small thanks.

30. Sunday, I have a touch of Influenza in consequence probably of having to go to school to instal William Grindon, a fine intelligent lad likely to answer. All right in the Girls' school and really a very fair attendance considering the horrid kind of weather we have had and the pitiful rags that cover so imperfectly half of these poor children. One don't know what to do. There's the poor house and they will be near death before entering it. Then if we help them we assist in keeping them on such misery out of their proper asylum.

Still I cannot see such deplorable objects in a manner belonging to me, so bundles of old clothes find their way to the naked as does soup, milk and bread to the hungry. Political economy in all its severe details is too harsh a subject for women to enter into perfectly. My boys' school will cost little, the Master having a home with his mother and, making this but a stepping-stone, is only to receive the salary given by the Board this first year, not even the fees; they are to be spent in replacing the maps and such other repairs and improvements as are necessary. Mr. Moore has settled all this and has had William Grindon during the last quarter training under Mr. Clarke in Kilbride. The young man is to continue attending Mr. Lecamp every evening. The needlework is going on nicely since the lecture.

We are all made dull by this odious weather. We have Dickens though to enliven us, brace us indeed, for an hour in the evening. On he marches in his task of exposures, surely certain of effecting some good. Two volumes of Lamartine's frippery I cannot even smile at. *Geneviève* both contradictory and inconsistent, also ridiculous. His own *Memoirs* more absurd still – tedious and egotistical beyond endurance. Yet a love tale in the middle is wrote with fire, hero and heroine crazed too. All this is called poetical, the poetry of Bedlam then.*

Miss Talbot rescued. A poor French teacher seized on his deathbed and robbed by priestcraft of his all. The relations have gone to law and got back half of his miserly life; the rest has vanished into substantial comfort I fancy, not 'thin air'. Such things as these are of weekly occurrence with us here in Ireland, little thought of, never noticed, but when they take place yonder in England they do make a stir about them. It will all work for good, nothing like letting the ultra liberals see and feel that popery is now just what it always was. To get rid of it is our plain duty – but how? Not by persecution certainly, neither by undue fostering – a weak cringing to a clamour unreal and unsafe. The R. Cath.s are being converted to our purer faith by hundreds just now, in Ireland, in Dublin and elsewhere. What is doing among them in England? The thraldom the professors of that melancholy creed are kept in is absolutely frightful, only to be understood thoroughly in all its enormity by such as have the misfortune to live in a popish-ridden country.

31. Little to say this morning, and less will to say anything, for I really am annihilated by influenza. What a horrible feeling it is. Such a headache. A fine day for a wonder. The Census is taking. I have filled up our sheet which is much more particular in details than the one furnished ten years ago. We had a week of *Chambers'* last night, not a very bright one, but one fact announced is comforting. Since 1836 the population has encreased four million, and the consumption of intoxicating drinks has decreased by forty millions of gallons. That is certainly a *fact* worth recording.

Jack has brought home bad news of St. Columba's – a fight, set on by two boys, one of whom is expelled, the other flogged, while the victims are in bed with a broken nose and swelled eyes; and a boy got drunk on St. Patrick's day!

THURSDAY, APRIL 1. Jack off to town very early, 6 o'clock with Tom Darker to finish his equipment and bring home the new car. I am much annoyed at this account of St. Columba's: where is the careful superintendence that was by way of rendering this new college so superiour to the old-fashioned, ill-regulated schools? Harry Leeson wrote the tale to Edward Moore, adding that in the opinion of the boys injustice had been committed by treating the two boys differently. Both were equally to blame, he says, but the commoner was expelled and the nobleman's son only flogged. The boy expelled was named Shawe. If he be the Recorder's son, his father told me that he had sent him there a blackguard and got him back a gentleman – outwardly only it would seem – the taint must have remained.* There is a great drawback to an Irish school even with English masters – the boys are Irish; and the innate vulgarity of the Irish character is such that their companionship is if possible to be avoided. Fights used to go on in all schools. I thought such odious doings were over. Remnants of barbarism truly – how much we have yet to learn! *Chambers'* is so stupid this month! Very good, but dull, and a whole history of mesmerick phenomena quite laughable.*

2. Really quite *floored* yesterday from Influenza. Jack and Tom Darker returned quite late, under such rain as must have

wetted them through and through several times over but for their frieze wraps. The things bought for Jack were certainly cheap to a miracle. Wellington boots for nine shillings, a hat for seven and six. The boy looks like other boys too, with his hair cut. This morning we have seen the car, a very nice one, nice-looking, strong, light and easy! and we have heard of a riding horse for the Colonel. William Boothman's mare, which taught Jack to ride. The first leap he ever took as he ought was on her back. She is as gentle as a fawn! and not timid! plenty of nerve – perfectly steady! etc. In fine, all the qualities wanted in an old gentleman's hack, said invalid well understanding and only enduring the style of a hunter. We must now see whether we can get her – her price will not be high, owing to a scar on one leg. She goes well in harness too.

3. Something quite exciting in the insolence of the trampers. They won't leave our doors or windows, demand rather than ask food, and take all they can lay their hands on. John Fitzpatrick has lost his two beautiful wedding shirts – just whipt off the hedge during the momentary absence of his Wife, who had been watching them drying. I must take these matters into my active hands. The very first of these sturdy vagrants that comes I am determined upon sending for the police and have them off to jail at once, like those fowl-pilferers, who will be transported, two of them, Ody Tyrrell having sworn to a pot found with them, as one of several things stolen at the same time with his ducks from his yard. I can't understand such creatures being let to infest a neighbourhood. There were two impudent men here yesterday, it would not have been at all agreeable for unprotected women to meet on our retired mountain roads, such big sticks were wielded by such strong arms belonging to such savage countenances.

6. My dear Aunt Bourne has written to propose our joining families – she to come and board with us. She is tired of housekeeping – tired of the loneliness of Oxford – tired of life without interest in any thing about her. But I doubt Ireland answering her ideas, and we can live no where else. Edinburgh she would like but for the cold in Spring. In short it is a subject all beset with difficulties. I should so like

to have her with us, and that quite independant of the *purse* part. Poor dear old woman, just eighty! She should not be left to end her days alone.*

7. A friend of Mr. Fitzgerald preached yesterday and very well; it was evidently near about his first sermon, so gives good promise of better things to come. The sermon interested the whole church – it was plain enough for the meanest, satisfactory to all, but such an unfortunate subject – those ten virgins again. A smile was on every countenance, more than a smile on some. Read some more in the evening about Mesmerism and the old force, and wondered how far a credulous imagination can carry clever men. The idea of any one believing in the foreknowledge of accidents which are themselves perfectly uncertain, depending entirely on events which may or may not take place, nothing of this sort being predestined further than the relation of cause and effect! Such a belief as this strikes at the root of all religious feeling, all trust in the Great Power in and through Whom we live. Every age some such folly distracts the mob.

The Lady Leesons being in church I asked about St. Columba's. The boy expelled on account of backing the boxing match was Joy, not Shawe, the son of Mrs. Joy of the Mountains. The boy *not* expelled for drunkenness is Chief Justice Blackburne's son* – he is otherwise ill-conducted. The school, indignant, sent him to Coventry. The Warden insisted he be spoke to. Nine boys refused obedience, so were sent home to their parents – the rest are punished by the loss of their few days' holiday at Easter. There is some insubordination at work certainly, which of course must be checked, but there is something wrong with the management. The Warden will probably soon be superseded; he can't possibly be a firm, judicious, clever man, such a little scribble of a hand as he writes, and rigmarole style of note. The storm in the College may, however, do good, and there are a great many new boys going there in spite of it.*

10. We are putting a stile in the wood and another in the Grove that we may avoid the dirty farm-yard when setting out in that direction. Walks will be made to them, which will greatly improve the grounds; very pretty this place is becoming. I am to have poor John Fitzpatrick to potter about

tidying for a month or two to see to get him stronger – then he can go to America if he likes, that is, if he still continues discontented. We may not be able to afford to keep him, though times may mend.

15. We had visitors yesterday for a wonder. Mr. Fitzgerald to receive the miserable remains of our Lending Library, which, however, he is glad to get to add to his own little Stock, most of it bought with his own money, though he has managed to get a few Subscribers to his fund for keeping up some healthful literature among his flock. He has his church very full in the mornings now, almost equally full in the evenings, a great change; sixty pupils in the Sunday schools regularly classed under voluntary teachers, and it is for these principally that he has set up his Lending Library. Mr. Duffy flew upon him the other day, accused him of an intention to proselytise, called him a new light, all in the open street round Murphy's car, on which they were both preparing to return from Dublin to Blesington. I understand that Father Duffy 'got it' in a way that made a great impression for good on the mob of bystanders collected. The people are all upon the turn, and that the priests know full well.

22. Tom D. has returned with wretched news of the fair, cattle *down* thirty shillings a head, one-third less sellers than last year, three-quarters less buyers; land a drug, thrown up on all hands though offered in some places for little beyond the taxes. We really know nothing in this favoured spot of the condition of other parts of this ruined country. God help those who have no other dependance than their acres.

23. I have begun to read the new edition of Boswell's *Life of Johnson*, which as yet I am far from admiring as it is the fashion to do, but then I have only just finished the first volume. This was the first biography of the gossippy kind, so of course a surprise as well as a pleasure. So many *good* have appeared since that we of this brighter age are not fair judges of it. There is a *narrowness* running through and over all things and all people of those prejudiced ages that frets me to death in the company even of their cleverest minds. The King set I can't tolerate. Minds shut up in a box three hundred years ago and never had the fresh air on them since.

I am quite sure I could not live in the world again; the affectation of all belonging to it would make me sick and their childishness would sadden me.

24. Janey's ankle will be a tedious business. There is a weakness in it that must be summarily dealt with. Just punishment to me for fretting about money difficulties, and annoying myself about a few infirmities of temper. She dear child has brought this upon herself by neglecting her bowels, and the consequence will be a long confinement if no worse. She is to take an airing every day, to keep her spirits up; this I must do for her, and a succession of blisters with careful regimen will we hope cure her. I had to go to Blesington on business yesterday. The caravans, long and short cars etc., came through the village while I was there, loaded. One wonders what the people can have to do running up and down the country in such shoals.

25. Took Janey her airing yesterday. Called with her at Russborough leaving Jack there with the boys and Ned Moore and *Smith O'Brien's* son, a *little* creature of fourteen, Captain of the school.* The two girls came out and talked with their usual frankness. My Lord and Russy were at the Curragh. My Lady in bed, not well. We then went on to Humfreystown, brought Annie back to lunch at our dinner. James soon joined us, and we were very merry hearing all the Dublin news – tea-party at the Lady Crichtons, dinner in Merrion Square, Flower Show and Agricultural ditto.

27. I have been so busy this morning completing business I hate, housekeeper and butler affairs. In Ireland everything not in daily use must be locked up or it would never be forthcoming when wanted. Bedding must be *seen* at the fire, *turned* before sharp eyes; nothing can be trusted to the ready 'never fear' which really means that it will never again be thought of. Also Jack and I have been sorting clothes, books, desks, making lists etc., and so on. Dear boy, it will be a change from the loving atmosphere of home, a trial of the sharpness of life. Heighho, 'all has their trials,' said that respectable schoolmaster in *Nickleby*.*

THURSDAY, MAY 8. We are getting on very comfortably in our lonely life. Here it is. Dressed by nine. Get the Colonel's breakfast, get Janey's, both in their rooms, take my own.

Send for the post, the bread, any other messages; tidy the rooms; order the dinner; give out what is wanted; see any one waiting on business. Then write letters, journal, accounts, or whatever I have time for. On fine days I go out – to the grounds, garden, yard, school or tenants as may be needful. On wet days needlework. Dinner at two, all meeting, and sometimes a visitor joining. Then Janey and I our drive. The Colonel, having walked before dinner, stays at home with the Newspaper. On our return I sometimes take a second walk with him; read till tea; after tea I read aloud till ten, then read or write or sew or knit for a quiet hour before my *bed*, if there is time after preparing the two patients for theirs.

I miss dear Jack sadly but am so glad he is safe off [to St. Columba's]. Home would have ruined him had he remained longer with us. He went away in very fair spirits: his three companions lunched here one day that they spent with him and Lady Milltown was so good as to let him go to school with them, the Colonel being too unwell to take him and Mother's going causing a laugh at the boy's expense sometimes. Dear Jack when you read this, and I am gone, will you remember my love for you and how well we have both borne our parting – our real parting – for you have begun life now, and every year will add to your independance, my *children* are no more – but my son and my daughters, my dearest earthly friends and treasures, are clinging round the declining frame which did its best to rear them rightly. I shall often think of our last two days – our lists – our accounts – our packing – our conversations – and our calmness – and then your little full heart – no breakfast, no dinner – and my good thick sandwiches bundled into the pockets to be eaten on recovery! Our drive on the car to the Burgage gate, your little figure beside your portmanteau first waving your hat, then kissing your hand as John drove you from my sight; how I wept as we walked homewards. 'Poor little fellow', said Papa. Then I thought of your merry journey with the two Leesons and the little O'Brien and then I felt we had done right and I repeated to myself all the proper things I could collect in my foolish head. There was no selfishness in my sorrow, not a grain. I probed my heart well – it was fear, that my darling boy who had been nurtured so lovingly might miss the atmosphere of affection he had hitherto breathed – and he will, a little, and I wish I could have saved him from it, finished his education more naturally, carried it on without thus severing family ties, for I am persuaded this School education is at the bottom of the vice on which our present form of manly character is raised. To counteract the egotism, the selfishness, the idleness, the other evils produced by these, shall be my earnest endeavour while I live. An attractive home, plenty to do, and an early marriage are the best antidotes.

9. St. Columba's, though not perfect, appears to be one of the best schools going. The Warden, a pompous disciplinarian, is unpopular and will probably soon be removed, as he was unwise about the late *émeute*. That is all settled, however, for the present – the discarded boys have returned, and the Chief Justice has taken his unfortunate boy away. 'That lad', said Augustus West to me, 'was ruined by his Mother. She could deny him nothing; he was her youngest, her pet, and slept in the room with her until he was thirteen'.

Janey and I in our drives generally pay off our visits. We have been several times to Humfreystown, to Kilbride Lodge, where is such a look of misery – furniture so shabby – Ogle away – Ned lounging about idle – Nelly dressed up very fine – none of the younger children visible. Mrs. Moore very neat but in old clothes, just going to ly [sic] in of her twelfth child, no nurse as yet to be had, and only two servants in the house, a girl of all work in the kitchen and a protestant orphan in the nursery. I never saw any thing more wretched and with their peculiar oddities there is no way that I know of to help them. There is no chance of preferment for that imprudent man. At Rathbally we saw the new baby, and heard that they have resolved on selling their interest in the place – advertised it already; the want of society and the ill condition of the neighbourhood have determined them to leave it. We need some help to raise our spirits; mine in spite of all exertion are very low. A sort of apathy is creeping over me that there is no dispelling – diet, regimen, exercise, and abundant occupation are all most systematically pursued, and yet nothing interests me. All is done as duty without any pleasure resulting.

Politicks very tiresome. Majorities against the ministry perpetually, for no purpose, as they must remain in till the Exhibition is over. London is full of foreigners. I hope they will eat *our* beef. Miss Talbot shewed there one day with her Chaperone, Lady Newburgh, one of the *perverts*, who won't be long troubled with her charge, the Lord Chancellor has just given his consent to her marriage with Lord Howard. They will have to go without the new R. C. Cathedral at Clifton. I got £6.15.0 yesterday for the three last papers of the Calcutta Journal [*A Twelvemonth in Calcutta*], *making for the whole* £41 odd – very fair pay. Mary Holland has had her gander and three geese stolen, leaving forty orphan goslings behind them. Another gang to be routed out. And my School is really flourishing – fifty-eight *in attendance*.

10. When we first settled to send Jack to School, Jane wrote to me to say she meant to contribute a share of the expense, in fact pay the extra cost of this arrangement. Properly grateful as I truly was for this kindness, I declined it, because I knew that if our means were properly managed we could perfectly afford to perform the duty of educating from our own funds. She wrote again putting forth a host of reasons stronger than it was easy to resist, and I promised to consider of it, mentioning that I had already made some retrenching arrangements in preparation for these large half-yearly Bills. Yesterday I received her answer written on the 7th, my birthday – fifty-four! An order for twenty-five pounds, on the Bank of Ireland, and an intimation that every half year the same sum would be remitted while Jack remains at St. Columba's. I don't deny that is a comfort to me, a certainty of my boy's receiving a fit education to make him independant of all but his own powers and to confirm in him the habits and the feelings of a gentleman while making acquaintance with the very best of the society he is to live amongst. God knows I have no pride, no vulgar pride – my only fear is taking what might be otherwise employed, as I *could* do without it. Yet this timely help does relieve me much. We have such a slobbering way here in Ireland of getting on – so untidy, immethodical – beginning fifty

things, finishing none, idling, shoving off business, unable to resist a love of pleasure and the pursuit of it regardless of circumstances. It is very difficult to keep matters even tolerably in order when the system of all around is so loose. Janey had a very happy note from Jack yesterday. I am quite at ease about him, and very glad indeed that he is away. Annie's two young cousins, the little sons of Lord Erne,* are going this week to St. Columba's – nice little boys. She wrote to Jack to look after them – they are but nine and seven.

18. Our foolish unhappy Doctor is making himself very disagreeable everywhere; he is dictatorial, interfering almost to impertinence, churlish, quite rude even, and therefore people are giving up his company – wisely – or he would treat them all as he has treated us. I can explain it all; he regrets his ill conduct and the proud temper will not allow of his repairing his mistake. Poor man – clever, kind-hearted, full of energy, anxious to do good, all is nullified by temper and extreme self-sufficiency – he has been spoiled among us – and the brain is affected, there is no doubt of it. It is in the family and of course excuses much.

23. Mr. Rutherfurd off – bolted before daylight with wife and bairns, having quietly disposed of his small remnant of stock. An old woman is left in the house to keep possession. Tom Darker was going up to Dublin today to transact various pieces of business, so he will enquire what we can do in this case, which I have long prepared for but had no means of averting. Writs were out against the poor weak old man for the debts owed by his worthless sons to the poor law Guardians. Every body knew that his paying rents or other debts was impossible – he had nothing to pay with. I had hoped, however, that he would have courageously said so and taken advantage of the Colonel's liberal offer to be forgiven all arrears on giving up the land.*

The new mare was sent back yesterday, Tom Darker undertaking for the Boothmans, to whom he had spoken, and though it is a disappointment, they will submit. This morning she is returned! I have sent Pat home with her, begging of them to keep her till Tom Darker comes from Dublin. I am afraid that in his anxiety to help his friends he has been hardly just to his master. I desired him not to pay for her, as the Colonel did not like her. *Wrote* this to him, on the understanding that we were to have a month's trial. I am afraid he has paid for her, which was very wrong after I forbade him, and there will be no chance of getting the money back in that case.

24. The mare was paid for, regularly bought and sold, and has come back accordingly. It is the last transaction I will ever trust out of my own hands, money matter or other business. The honestest amongst them is not to be trusted, so many under-currents there are to sap the principles of an unenlightened people; and yet we may not call them dishonest, Dr. Johnson says, if all the members act up to the standard of their society! The only feeling we can indulge in this case therefore must be regret at having our lot cast where the standard is so low. I must see how best to get out of this hobble.

30. A stop must be put to these absurd doings of Tom Darker. Here he has been since Friday last at fairs with John Hornidge and we have never set eyes upon him again until today. Friday again, and all sorts of business accumulating that cannot be settled without him, and he is by no means in good humour either, which is to be expected after doing wrong.

SATURDAY, JUNE 7. Unable all this while to think of Journal. Rent day and a bad one. Accounts to prepare, books to settle. Allowances for bad, *bad* times to arrange. T.D. slow, idle but so upright. To Dublin with Hal and the money, left the head rent and the rent charges with J.R., paid all bills. Saw dear Jack at St. Columba's: all so nice, he looking so well. Hal upset rather with his little journey though he enjoyed the change much. Bad times but I trust that we may struggle through them. I'll try and get as strong as I can to exert myself in earnest for the good of the family, some one *must* do it, and there is no other. I am really well at last.

15. Sunday. A storm of rain in the morning which quite prevented our going to church. I have been writing so irregularly I hardly remember how so much of this month of June has passed. My occupation has been ordering the house, teaching the new maid, nursing Annie, watching Janey,

reading some novels, Dr. Johnson and Horace Walpole, mending, receiving the rents, and getting through a smart little bit of bilious fever. How much better my health is than it used to be, but I must be careful for the constitution is but middling. I am ordered back to my old airy room, which certainly this summer season is preferable to the very close neighbourhood of my dear Colonel's oven. How he can live in such an atmosphere from which, too, air is so carefully excluded, is a marvel. He thrives in it.

We had a bad rent day, for which private reasons were given me, and I understand more money will be forthcoming during the progress of the summer. James came from town to-day, his rent will be settled on Thursday, yesterday was only the first hearing – examination of books etc. The Castle Daly sale will not take place till November!!

17. A note from Jack this morning has put us all in commotion. The Measles has broke out at St. Columba's. Edward Leeson has the complaint badly, and another boy. Worse again than that is that the best boys do not return after the holidays, and the nice masters go too. Mr. Tripp [the last of the original Fellows] has gone. Mr. Seymour and Mr. Glover have resigned, and also it is believed Mr. de Burgh, leaving only the new Fellow with the Warden.* All the consequences of the Warden's wrong-headedness about the Blackburn business. The Recorder has published the correspondence concerning the whole affair, including letters from himself, the Primate, Lords Hatherton and Ellenborough* and the Warden. We have the pamphlet, and the Warden was wrong – it is the opinion of everybody. He will not acknowledge this, will not give up, will not resign, and by extra harshness, vexatious regulations of every sort and a system of flogging, not approved by parents or proprietors, he tries to secure his own power over a community, which can only be managed by love. All we saw there that is independant of this weak person's direction is so admirable that it will exceedingly annoy us to have to remove Jack, which we shall assuredly do if the Warden remains, as the merits of the school will cease while he commands. We have the holidays before us, time to wait a while before deciding on what will in that case be best to do with Jack.

The House is a fine one situated in a large park beautifully placed on the brow of the line of hills overlooking the City and bay of Dublin, Kingstown, Bray, Howth, Ireland's eye and the plain around. The park is well wooded, of some extent, with fields in it, and thickets, and a brook which fills a plunge bath in the wood. A pretty bit of shrubbery near the bath is laid out in flower-beds for such of the boys as encline to gardening. The House is occupied by the Warden, the Fellows and the Matron, from whose parlour the Infirmary opens. All so handsomely furnished, so extremely comfortable. The Corridor is a Museum. The Common room contains the Library, four thousand books already. Servants' apartments behind. Stables where the Fellows keep horses if they like to ride, a jaunting car for the Warden. And a long strip of ground at the back of these offices is laid out in kitchen garden beds for those boys who prefer vegetables to flowers. There is a cricket ground, ball alley, fine garden with greenhouse and hothouse, a swing, a pole. Two new wings have been added for the School, or one doubled rather, for I hardly remember how the building is managed. The School-room is very large, lofty, light. Each boy has a desk in it. The Hall is a fine room, a cross table at the top for the Warden and fellows, two long tables down the sides for the forty boys. There is an ante-room to each for hanging caps etc. The Dormitory is beautiful, all open above, each little bed and dressing-stand enclosed screen high. All so clean, so airy. Two large fireplaces, plenty of washing; an ante-room for shoes, and Mr. Glover's room opening out of the Dormitory. A pretty Chapel and a good organist who teaches musick. The choir is composed of the boys.

They rise at six, three-quarters of an hour for dressing, chapel, *drill*, breakfast. As much bread and *good* tea as they like and a large pat of butter to *each* boy; half an hour to themselves, then School. Luncheon at twelve – huge lumps of bread and butter. Dinner at half-past three – no head work afterwards, musick, drawing, light reading etc. Chapel at half past seven. Tea, bed at nine. No learning of lessons at night, no cold, freezing toilettes. Warm water and good fires in winter. The tea is like the breakfast; the dinner roast and boiled beef and mutton, plenty of vegetables, puddings or pies Sundays and Thursdays, fish Tuesdays and Fridays. A delicate appetite looked after. Always a pudding for a poor sickly West. Wine for Chrichton [sic]. Beer, good beer, for the rest. Mondays and Fridays five hours work. Tuesdays and Fridays seven. Wednesdays and Saturdays three, so they are half holidays. Whole holidays on Saints days, when at this Season there are picnics to some point or other, drives to the sea to bathe, visits to any show, etc. Would it not be a pity to have such an institution as this done up?

The day we were there, the disagreeable Warden being in England, Mr. Tripp did the honours. We thought him particularly nice, and the boys quite love him: he is gone. Mrs. Brown, the Warden's sister, has just come as Matron – a vulgar sillyish Englishwoman, but apparently good natured and good humoured, likely to be kind to the sick boys. She knows the Freres well, thinks highly of them, and Dr. Wordsworth* and the *Church* and poor John Frere was the intimate friend of Mr. Williams from College days and much esteemed by him. That's the set. Jack has evidently been the better of this connexion, but indeed all spoke well of my boy, he is a general favourite. Masters like Smith minor, and the boys like *Griddles*, their form of pronouncing John Graydon Smith. The lucky monkey has found a real friend in the Wardrobe woman, who had often seen him when a baby at Kilbride, where she lived as nurse to the Ogle Moores in their richer days.

Altogether the whole thing is so very near what School should be that having it at our door and so in all respects suited to us, I can't say how annoying it would be to have to take Jack away. I must brace up my poor silly nerves however to bear this and many other things. There is old Mr. King won't give his son a penny, says he can't till these properties are sold. Never has, since the marriage, promised the wedding expenses on the Bridegroom side, never paid them, promised one hundred pounds in May, we undertaking to pay our *whole* year before that for the young people to live on, which we have done at some inconvenience, he undertaking to do his part from May, and now he says it was only conditional *in case* these estates were sold, but he is wrong and must be told so. We declined the security of these encumbered estates and had the young people's income settled out of a property in the King's County, I think, with a lien* on the funded property should these rents fail. He persuades his son he can't borrow, he has for himself but he can't for the son, and the cranky and *cracky* old man may run restive if teased and make a new Will! disagreeably! here's a fix. James must get some friend to speak.

The tenants it seemed feared there would be no allowance made for them for the times, so resolved to keep all the rent back they possibly could; finding themselves justly dealt with they are all pacified, quite in good humour and will do their best again. They paid only about a third, but are bringing in driblets which will soon make it half at any rate.

19. Got such a fright. The measles has broke out at St. Columba's and Edward Leeson was reported to be dangerously ill of them. A note from Jack confirmed this. On calling at the Doctor's we found he had been to see the boy with Lady M. and had left her there to nurse him. So fearing for the whole school, we sent the car off yesterday morning for our precious piece of goods. It did not bring him back, however, three very kind notes came instead, one from the Warden assuring us there was no danger. The separation between the invalid and the rest was complete. No other boy had caught the infection. Dr. *Stokes,* who had been brought out express, said there was no need for alarm, and the Examinations coming on it is most desirable Jack should stay for them as his place in the next half year will depend on his answering. Mrs. Brown dilates on all this and promises to look after him and to send him home at once should he sicken, and kind Lady Milltown in the midst of all her anxiety sends me a few words to say that there seems to be no risk in leaving Jack, she is leaving Harry. No other boy is ill, and Edward is better. The fever ran very high with him and his head is so easily affected it is impossible not to be very uneasy when any complaint attacks it. There never was anything more good-natured than his Mother writing this note. I returned grateful answers to all this morning, and so this commotion is over.

James and Annie were off early to-day to Dublin. She to prepare for the Waterloo Ball tomorrow given on the 20th so as not to shock the feelings of some French strangers. He to hear his cause decided today. Richard Hornidge, Tulfarris, who valued the land in the dear times for the Cotton interest, has volunteered to go up now to give evidence for the necessity of a reduction. This will be important. Old Mr. King's character cannot stand very fair with the world for, on James saying he had called on business, Richard Hornidge supposed he was to be consulted in his capacity of *Trustee* as to the manner of squeezing out the money due now to his son from the close fists of this shuffling body who tries to persuade James that he has not a penny, is borrowing for himself, has but a few hundreds a year in the funds, was not to be called on for any allowance until these properties were sold, that we had pushed on the marriage, not he, and must pay for it, with other discreditable assertions. There is no getting at the man's brains for he has none, nor probity either it would seem; he is inaccessible to reason and might if irritated still further, and more deeply, injure his son. I shall keep myself out of it; let them manage their own affairs their own way and lend no helping hand they may depend on it. We have kept faith honestly with them, paid the son during the first six months of the marriage £75, all we are bound to give for the whole year on the understanding that the father was to step in [in] May and begin his payment from that date by £100 down and the remainder before Christmas. We also made a present of £50 on the marriage, while he gave nothing, not even the wedding expenses. It is said of him that when driven to the wall he will pay, but kicks as long as he can. He is an odious, mean, fool of a man, and the less we have to do with him the better. His children, of course, bear with him; he has just as much wit as would suffice to injure any that offend him.

Annie will be sure of a plentiful house, no fear of want of comforts. She keeps herself wisely out of all business, all responsibility, and for her own little private purse it will go hard with me if while I live she is not looked after; her husband is kind and generous and may not have very long to wait to be out of thraldom. I never met with such unjust people. The dread of exposure may work upon the father for I showed no inclination to mince matters to him or the family or the world when James made his statement to me. All will be repeated and we shall see whether with any good effect.

I advised James to speak to Mr. Verschoyle the clergyman, the other Trustee who has influence over the father. I declined moving in any way myself, said I had no right to interfere, nor wish, that if he could not get the money from his father, he must mention this to the Receiver and his tradesmen and say so to his father, that *we* were quite unable to give or lend being in considerable embarrassments ourselves, and therefore he must expect no assistance from us, nor any Baltiboys pound-notes till January 1852. This will reach the father too. So there all ends as far as we are concerned.

I grieve for poor James, he deserves better treatment, he does his very best to earn his living and pay his way. I see no extravagance in any respect, but I declare I wonder at his having turned out so well with such bringing up, and his good temper and good spirits amaze me, now I know how severely both are tried. If he could borrow a small sum anywhere just to carry him on till these sales, the old oddity might be in better humour when he sees his thousands once more available, for he is hampered of course by the loss of so much of his income, fretted by difficulties he has been hitherto unused to. We must be just to his weakness though we blame his parsimony, his selfishness I believe: the whole family have a pretty fair share of that amiable commodity.

21. A note from Annie yesterday announces that in his application for a reduction of rent James has been unsuccessful. What they will do is more than I can say. This is a beautifully fine summer's day, on which I have had warm work trying to keep my small household in order. Our fine cook, and she is really excellent, is so tricky, I have to weigh out or count everything she gets, to keep as little in the larder as possible and to give all to her myself; and even with all this watching she cheats me, or cheats the poor rather, the bits and scraps and drops all going home. £3 or £4 will pay all the damage, and she is worth that for the present, but I fancy I will look out for another by the winter, as with fires and short days the present arrangement will not answer.

Then there is such jealousy among them all. So many sets, so many parties, just like the great world. I think between lectures and soft sawder [flattery] I have them all on civil terms for a while.

22. Sunday and fine. The crops look quite luxuriant, the whole landscape rich. Pray God we may have a fine harvest. We had to make an allowance equal to twenty-five per cent on the year's rent to all our tenants who paid beyond twenty-five shillings an acre for their land, a quarter of our income. Add the poor rates to that and what a loss of revenue – much more than equivalent to cheap bread and sugar. How to turn land into profit puzzles our wisest heads.

We have each our little experiment. James is trying the dairy line, so are many more, for butter has fallen to a mere nothing, seven pence a pound grazing is no better, one pound a head less than when he took his very dear farm. We are going on rearing calves, and we have encreased our stock of sheep, finding the trade in young cattle falling. Also we have sowed more green crop, and we have a small experiment in flax – not enough to ruin us should it not succeed – a mere two acres. These hopes, and no expense we can avoid, not an upper servant, not a luxury that can be done without, are leading us on through another struggling year. The difficulty is to keep up the spirits with so much to depress them on every side. However the course of duty is very plain, and when there is no self-reproach to add to trouble we can all bear a good deal.

24. We dined at Humfreystown yesterday and brought our host and hostess home to tea. Annie slept here, for James has gone to town today to try and borrow some money, the father having consented to be the security. It is all I believe that he can do, but he should have done it at once, and so kept faith with his son and us. Annie is looking wretched. She must keep very quiet, be done with her rackettings or we may miss the heir to the Longford property. My Mother has had a fall, is much shook, and though not hurt as far as they can see, feels pain when moved. It is not a pleasant accident.

27. James and Annie spent another pleasant evening with us. A nice pair. Really all these young people are very first rate. How superiour to us of a former day; how immeasurably

superiour to the race around us here. A low style of feeling, a
want of all that is ladylike or gentlemanlike lays deep at the
bottom of even the best of the Irish, speaking generally,
making intimacy with them quite undesirable and any
business transactions with them particularly disagreeable.

29. We got the posts, and I was struck by getting *two* letters from
Jane. My Mother is given over. She is sinking rapidly. I may
or may not be in time to look on her once more. I have taken
an evening to consider the journey in all its bearings. The
Colonel is not fit to be left with only Janey, lame, delicate,
and no nerve whatever, not active enough attend to him nor
resolute enough to bear with him. She would cry or take
hystericks, and Jack coming home, he would be made frantick, and the servants could never stand it all, and then he
would eat and drink everything, worry himself and everybody, and be half killed in two days. I feel so weak myself, too.
My body is so feeble, my head so confused. Often I think my
senses will some day leave me. Unless my poor Mother is
perfectly sensible and asks for me, my place is here.

My not being at dinner to-day, the Colonel ate everything,
ordered wines and drank them, and beer and cream; has had
Asthma all the evening, been so ill-humoured as to be a
perfect plague to the whole household; it is always the case
they say when I am absent. The diet good for him don't suit
Janey, her milk and vegetables kill him. He won't dine by
himself, he won't let her dine by herself. How little do people
thus giving way to their own fretfulness and self-indulgence
comprehend that they reduce all around them to victims.

Those they love and would die to serve, yet actually
cruelly tyrannises over. My poor dear old Mother, whom
while children we did not love but who became very dear to
us when we grew to understand her worth and to make
proper allowance for her difficulties. My firm persuasion is
that at this moment she is no more. How many will grieve
for her – and poor Jane – all she will feel, and so unfit for it.
God help all in need. I would give a great deal to be with her.

30. A better account from Jane today. Our dear Mother had
made a wonderful rally by means of stimulants, however.
Her mind quite right, but no power of muscle whatever. Dr.
Gillespie says she may go on this way for a week or two.

Then she must either get better or sink. Dr. Robinson *thinks* there may be no danger for three weeks, so I have a little time. The inconvenience of leaving home just at this moment is beyond idea afflicting. I hardly see how it can be done ever, all things considered, unless Janey were with me and Jack at School. I am tied by the leg here. I had so little rent in money – had to give such large allowances, that though we had no poor rate this year, I don't feel a bit richer. I am always saving, seem to spend nothing, but there are such heavy drains on our small means I feel at my wits end for cash to pay all, and in some things beyond.

I have gone back to Boswell's *Johnson* of which I had tired, for it is no favourite of mine. Odious men, odious manners, by no means such talent and horrid society. I have been living with ladies and gentlemen, true wit and sound sense too, in the letters of Horace Walpole – once again.

MONDAY, JULY 14. I can hardly tell how we have been passing these last days. My Mother continues much the same, and all are so urgent for my going over that this I find must just be done. I have thought it over and decided – tomorrow, perhaps, at any rate Friday, per Steamer to Glasgow – to stay one week. It is more for Jane's sake than our poor Mother's, and with fear and trembling do I make my few preparations, not well knowing what may happen here.

15. At half after three left home. At six took tea with Mrs. Haughton. At eight went on board the steamer *Herald*. At nine she started. We had had a rainy morning – very showery indeed – heavy and long continued – still I ventured and the afternoon cleared up.

16. At eleven o'clock made Greenock – in fourteen hours. The *Herald* is a new vessel on the American construction. Saloon on the deck, the roof available for walking. Sleeping cabins below, well ventilated. The feather and float attached to the paddles prevents all that trembling motion so very disagreeable. I would have landed at Greenock but for the plague of shifting from ship to railroad first and railroad second, so not being hurried I went on to Glasgow, reached the terminus before three and got to Edinburgh at half past five. They expected me.

18. Jane and I walked again today, another tour of inspection

among the improvements of this very beautiful city – there are more fine buildings, new and grander shops, and additional gardens every time I come here; new banks in particular starting up every where, the Bankers are all vying seemingly as to the appearance of their buildings, some trying height, others width, a third class outside decoration, a fourth class inside, none uniting at all, but all exceeding propriety, as a plain house of a fit size with suitable accommodation is surely sufficient for business purposes, and the Shareholders in these times had better have divided the *rentes* among them than have squandered such sums on vanities.

19. There has been one continued bell-ringing here all morning. First Mrs. Cockburn to change our day to Wednesday and shew what beauty comes to; so handsome as she was and now a sort of drunken looking cook or fishwife, red and bleared and bloated, from want of care they say and over eating, porter etc. We went in the carriage to-day, not a cab, to Musselburgh, Porto Bello and drove along the sea shore to Leith where we walked for near a mile on the new wooden pier, turning only for fear of being late, as the pier extended further, and the walk was delightful with the fresh sea breeze blowing all round and the little steamers rushing out through the narrow opening to the firth, for a second pier is forming, like two long arms they will be, embracing a strip of sea sufficient to hold *in quiet* half the navy.

21. We [went] out early to Donaldson's Hospital [for the deaf], where we spent two hours most agreeably. We took our luncheon at Aitchieson's – ices and buns, and then Jane and I drove to the Deane cemetery. It is very pretty – laid out with great good taste along the steep banks of the water of Leith. Lord Jeffrey and his dear wife were laid simply under the sod; nothing whatever done to their last resting-place, which might have been soon forgotten had not James [Craig] quite lately had a curb-stone laid along upon the grass on either side as if in preparation for a railing. The subscription to the Memorial being beyond what is required to erect the statue fixed on in the Parliament House, the residue is to be employed upon a monument over their remains.

22. This morning my Mother had appeared stronger than at any time since I came. She slept well, looked well, had her mind

quite clear, and this has lasted all day in a degree: neither was she as tired this evening as I have seen her.

We had luncheon rather early and then called *in the carriage* for James and proceeded to Lauriston, the really most beautiful villa of Lord Rutherford.* We met him driving into town with his Irish brother-in-law, Sir James Stewart, and thought him looking better than could have been expected; he is still however very ill. She was at home, a nice kind frank person. She shewed us over the pretty house and the grounds. These Scotch people do live in noble style. Such rooms! such furniture! such pleasure grounds. My *poor* Irish heart sinks at seeing it all; yet their homes are truly enjoyable. All that wealth and taste can add to natural beauty. We then went on to Cramond, a place more to my mind than Lauriston. Still on the firth with much the same sea view, but a simpler house, magnificent trees, more left to nature. The sea, the undulating ground, the grass below and trees above, all quiet, grand and in repose instead of the pretension of the other with its terraces, stone steps, vases, statues and a sort of market gardener's display of flowers so brilliant and in such masses as quite to fatigue the eyes.

23. We had no walk this morning because we were going to Bonally where we found luncheon at two o'clock – none but the family including two nice little grandchildren from India. The walks are very beautiful, the situation on the side of the hills very fine – grounds more to my taste than any I have seen – people very kind. Lord Cockburn reminds me in a degree of Lord Jeffrey, whose life he is writing [see 11.4.1852]. We talked of it and him. Something like the conversation of old times, of which little remains now in the guid town. The lights of other days are quenched and there are none succeeding them; the young do not fill the place of their fathers – the style is different. This generation is probably better educated than the one preceding, but we find little genius, no brilliancy – nothing like Craig Crook and the society once collected there.

25. We called at the Chambers where James joined us and went with us to the Botanical and Horticultural gardens, both close together, a little beyond the water of Leith at the Cannie mills. They are kept in excellent order, are most

agreeably laid out, and all the plants seem healthy, which is the sum of my knowledge in the matter. The glass at the Botanick gardens is extensive, the palm house really a sight, but though so lofty it is too small for its tenants which having outgrown their Castle of Otranto* are turned adrift upon the world to die while younger giants take their place.

26. The Doctors were punctual and they did their business well. The operation itself was soon over, and to the operator there is no doubt the insensibility of the patient is a great point because there is no fear of giving pain, no need to hurry, but the convulsive movements caused by the chloroform, together with the frightful jabbering and the heavy breathing which follow before the state of quiet supervenes, make the scene most distressing to witness. I got quite faint and had to leave the room to recover, otherwise I should have been the reverse of useful. It was difficult to rouse her again. Open windows, salvolatile [smelling salts], fanning and at last brandy were all required and she was dreadfully sick, vomitted for hours. Neither has she recovered yet. She could not sleep nor is she sleeping yet – ten o'clock at night – too much excited still. She describes the sensation as first a swimming and next a deadly sickness. She knew nothing that intervened – had no visions – felt no pain. At four o'clock the doctors came again and found all right, all in a fair way of giving little further trouble. Dr. Gillespie alone came tonight, and is satisfied. He is a kind attentive creature, interested in all belonging to my poor father, his old schoolfellow.

27. Sunday. My Mother had a good night, was quite well on waking, made good breakfast and was asleep again when I came in just now from evening chapel. She is treated just like a child, early to bed, late up, sleep in the middle of the day. A proper portion of proper food brought to her. Dressed, undressed, washed. Such an existence. Yet she seems content, and not to have the slightest idea in the world that there is any chance of her soon leaving it. Seventy-six she is, and what has she not come through. Always too indulging in habits the most prejudicial to health.

29. Left them, good kind James with me as far as Glasgow, where missing the steamer by five minutes, he had to leave me after seeing me safe in the train for Greenock. Civil

porters, calm sea, good passage, crowded cabin, again finding a companion who had known the Freres in Wales.
30. Landed at nine; breakfast at Mrs. Haughton's; home just too late for post. All of them here.
31. Still in a whirl to end July.
SUNDAY, AUGUST 3. All the time of my absence the weather here has been most wretched, rain almost without intermission. The ground is saturated, the air loaded, the hay soaked, flax laid, turnips bad, but corn and potatoes look well and cattle hereabouts. To the feelings it is very dispiriting.
7. Dear little Jack left us yesterday – in true Irish fashion. James King's car, Lord Milltown's horse, our driver, to take both himself and Harry Leeson back. My boy felt the going, he is so happy at home, but he never displays his feelings. I have brought them all up never to annoy others with *themselves*. The ill regulation of temper is the bane of Ireland, the excessive egotism of the people about the greatest of their vices; for one moment consideration for another never enters the head of Irish man or woman. This makes it impossible to trust them, to count upon them or to find a friend among them. A total want of discipline pervades the whole character of the nation, which it will require many generations and much chastening to produce. The course has begun, God knows, and seems likely to continue, for a grub has appeared in all the turnip fields which they say is destroying the crop, certainly hurting it and the potatoes are decidedly touched in many places. The smell of a field going to Humfreystown is horrid.

Emigration will quicken again, and so let it, for we hear that a society is formed in Scotland for assisting farmers there who feel overburdened to pass over to this country where rents are low and taxes few, rather than proceed to the Colonies. Mr. Armstrong has had a letter from a Mr. Thomas Millar of St. Andrew Square, Edinburgh, accompanying very business-like papers on the subject and Ogle Moore, who much desires such an importation, has made me write to enquire as to his respectability. A colony of these Scotch has already settled in Mayo and are so far reported to be doing well. Mr. Armstrong has also let Kippure to a Northumbrian sheep farmer who arrived in spring with his family and servants. We just want some of this sturdy, steady, honest kind to improve the quick, unprincipled *natives*, whatever name may be given them – Celt or Moor. Lord Downshire had another of his Galas last night. Bonfire, fireworks and drink. Our maids sadly annoyed at not being allowed to join the revels. We have had experience enough of his parties to keep decent people out of them. We met Lady Downshire riding with a very queer-looking little man dressed as a game-keeper, an English Croesus, we understand, come over to invest some of his funded thousands in encumbered estates. She is rather in beauty, very agreeable, but I don't intend responding much. I don't like their style, the set they live with or *his* temper and feelings.*

10. Sunday – hay-making is nearly over and the crop seemingly well saved, all at least that was later cut, but the potatoes are without a doubt infected, and turnips in a poor way and Tom Darker yesterday was in great fear about one of the bullocks who was certainly ill, something very like the distemper. I have a theory on this subject which facts hitherto have supported, that we owe this dreadful disease among the cattle to the over-greed of the farmers. This beast is one of the Humfrystown lot, the fourth we have lost, proving that skim milk and buttermilk rearing will never turn out healthy animals. It is like spoon-feeding babies who never can resist severe illness and generally die off or declines before reaching maturity.

The Doctor, who will do nothing himself, yet took the state of our affairs as partly witnessed by him to Ogle • Moore, who came here on purpose to help me; his advice is to get away to the sea as quickly as possible where complete change of scene with amusement may efface present impressions, to remove the irritating cause by paying for the same and to trust to old affection and *habit* to reinstate poor Tom Darker. He has spoken to poor T.D. and tried to convince him that he must *bear* all that is put upon him. There is temper there unluckily with many faults too, but in our peculiar circumstances the man is invaluable to us besides being an excellent creature, *spoiled* not a little – had he been well held up in hand he would have been a better servant. As he is however, he is my last stay, all others have been thrown off, and with all the desire in the world thoroughly to do my duty I could not do his work – I have neither skill nor health nor time for acting Steward and Bailiff. These clouds may blow over, yet I doubt. After such angry words I dare not hope that master and man will ever get on comfortably together. All that is left will be to leave this dear pretty place, settle near a town where perhaps the little sights and sounds and movements might divert a vacant mind, and where we might get up an evening whist table.

13. Monday Janey and I drove to Sallins where I took the railway to Dublin – found Mrs. Haughton so well and Mary ready to accompany me to Kingstown where for five hours we marched about hunting most unsuccessfully, not a hole or corner to be had at present, nor a set of rooms that would hold us to be had by and bye except at an extravagant rate which we must pay.

20. Janey and I have been all the morning preparing for Kingstown, putting away nick nacks, china, plate etc., and we shall have another morning of it packing. There are bills to pay, servants to dismiss etc., for I mean to leave as little expense behind as possible. The school affairs were settled yesterday.

24. 1 Haddington Terrace, Kingstown.

25. Saturday morning we had a deal to arrange. Our lodgings seemed very cramped, rooms very small, staircase very narrow, so we had a deal of squeezing to get into them, but like ship cabins they grow, and so we feel very comfortable today. We have a cheerful little parlour on the ground floor with nothing to interrupt the view of the sea but a narrow strip of garden ground which runs all along in front of the terrace. We could throw a ball into the water. The pier, one pier, runs out just in front. We have the open sea on one side of it, the harbour full of merry-looking little boats on the other. Our dining-room we have to give up to the Colonel being on the ground floor; he is too asthmatic to mount the stairs. Janey a mere closet, I a little half furnished room at the back. All very clean. The servants are accommodated below, and Antoine is really a luxury, so civil and attentive, and knows his business so well. He has brisked up poor stupid Margaret with his *galanteries* and

made her quite good enough for this sort of life. I went to market; found out the good shops, made a few indispensable purchases, enquired the hire of a carriage, looked about us, in short conducted us with the wisdom befitting the heads of the family. On returning unpacked our plate, linen, pie, ham, goose, butter, eggs, wine, small stores; had a capital dinner by the help of fish and cheese, four fine mackerel for fourpence.

26. Nothing particular yesterday save the sight of a white-robed Carmelite friar on board the Holyhead steamer, blessing in a very summary manner the crowds of kneeling penitents thronging the deck and the pier. Among the poor and the women this mummery still succeeds, but the priests have been left in the lurch by the lay*men*.

THURSDAY, SEPTEMBER 4. It is so hard to get the Colonel dressed after his uncomfortable nights. He always took a long time at his *toilette*: it is now doubled, and the packing, always a serious affair, is now quite a business. We got all accomplished, however, and were off by the two o'clock train.

At Sallins we found Annie's pretty carriage which conveyed us to Humfreystown by half after six. The Colonel had had a very asthmatick night and we had to go to the flower show without him. A stupid affair. May do good, perhaps, but in a very dull way. No two people anxious to do good ever set more unwisely about it than this excellent and noble pair [the Downshires]. Neither of them has any manner. She takes no trouble about anybody. I don't think she spoke to any of the crowd assembled to oblige her – high or low. She had not dressed even. He just called out numbers, heard the names, presented the money prize digging into a bag of silver held by Mr. Owen as he wanted it. Only those quite close could hear or see what was going on. Though we all subscribe to the funds, only those on the Lordship appeared to me to be the successful competitors. They came forward in rags most of them, and with dirty shirts and dirty faces, many of them, a crew to be ashamed of rather. I stood between the Marquis and Marchioness, and so could observe all. By the bye, the Darkers got several small prizes for fruits and flowers, and Marianne got the second prize for a tidy house. She would have got the *first* had her husband made a neat flower garden of the bit of waste ground before his door. There were luncheons at the two houses, the Lord's and the Agent's, and so the tame affair concluded.

On Monday morning, the 1st September, we packed up, wrote Mem.s, went all over James' neat offices. Saw all his active, orderly ways and were quite satisfied he and his servants are doing their best to make the rent. It is all most business-like, admirably conducted, and just as well within. Annie is as neat as he is. They have a good Cook and a very good parlour maid. No other house servants now, Mack and his wife being in the yard and all their assistants being hired by the day.

We were resting after our little survey in her little drawing-room when Dick and the Doctor drove up together. It is another move in the right direction. Alas! how different is the agitated manner, the sheepish countenance, the air of depression of the present unhappy-looking elderly *beau*, from the gay bright *friend* of not very long past days. He has sunk in his own esteem and never will rise again, but perhaps he may feel it less by and bye. To me the man is dead and buried, and this is a disagreeable body in whom I have no interest.

7. I must scribble down my recollections of that happy day at the College. It was a long drive, made longer by our Coachman's ignorance of the proper road, but we went through such beautiful scenery that we were quite resigned to lose ourselves beneath such stately trees. We arrived at two, were received by the Warden and Fellows in full dress and joined by the boys as soon as they had dined, by whom the guests were taken over the house and grounds. We were then invited to the Hall where a very handsome dinner awaited more than sixty people. Healths were drunk and speeches made, so indifferent that surely if all orators puzzle out their want of meaning so incoherently, it must be a dreadful task for the shorthand writers to have to listen to such daily labour. The only fluent one was very short and very neat given by a plot to Colonel Smith! He did it remarkably well and proposed the Warden's health.

This over we repaired to the Cricket Ground. No very

first-rate artists there; and then the rain sending us inside to the house I spent an hour with that antiquarian oddity Dr. Todd,* listening to his explanation of the objects in the Museum. We were then summoned to the Chapel – delighted by the excellent chanting of the boys – and then we had coffee and tea, the boys waiting on us. After that was a concert; the first part Catches and Glees, the second part sacred, all by the boys, and between the Acts the Warden gave the prizes. There are only five – one in each department, and so worth gaining – once a year. It is all very near what should be. A little too much of Classick lore and rather too little of more useful knowledge, but it is coming, and the accomplishments which add such charm to home life are not neglected, and the whole atmosphere of the place is so evident that I thank God my boy is receiving his education there. Dear good little fellow, well thought of by every one.

Lady Louisa Chrichton and her *little* brother were among the company, a plain under-bred girl, quite unlike her graceful brothers. Poor Lady Milltown, how happy she looked when her handsome Harry came up to receive his prize for Mathematicks. So modestly too he stood to hear the high praise of his general good conduct. She could not have had this great pleasure at a better time, for poor Russy has at length sunk as we have, all but her, long dreaded. He had betted at the Phoenix Park races, lost and cannot pay, besides having solemnly passed his word to his father not to gamble there. He feared returning home, so where he was she knew not. A few days after he wrote from Boulogne to the Doctor he had plenty of money borrowed on *Post Obits*.* At such a place, with his habits and in despair, for what has he to look forward to; there is everything to fear; his father is at present implacable, the person in the world who has the least right to be angry. His example, his teaching and the ruin he has produced should make him lenient, but alas we all know that the contrary effect is generally produced on an evil nature by these evil courses.

8. The Colonel and I walked on the pier yesterday afternoon to enjoy the sight of all the trades-people with their families so decently dressed and looking so happy thronging along that healthy sea walk on their day of rest. Curious that these

very persons should be so easily roused to what would in the end put an end to all their comfort. Still only a few of this rank have responded to the madness of their priesthood and none of the higher ranks at all. Neither have the most reputable of the R.C. Clergy joined this mischievous agitation, which after all the noise they have made is likely to have a widely different result from what the insanity of the Italian Conclave expected. The Duke of Norfolk has publickly renounced the errours of Romanism. Appeared at his parish church with his protestant wife and daughters.* We are told that very many others will follow this sensible example. Indeed it is wonderful that men of education could have so long endured the subservience they were constrained to submit to. In Ireland the Converts are now only to be counted by thousands. Give rope enough and the vile will hang themselves.

14. We have a fright about Jack. They had treated him very judiciously, very kindly, and we felt sure that the gray powder pill I presented him with would put all to rights . . . so were quite unprepared for his appearing here yesterday. The Warden and Mrs. Brown brought him over on the College car and paid us a visit. We are to keep him till tomorrow, when he and the de Robecks* will return together. The measles are in the school. Well, another day will show us whether he have caught them or no. There is worse news than that would be amongst us. Dear kind old Miss King is dead.

18. Visitors we have not many. To our surprise yesterday morning in walked Lady Downshire. She had come to the Anglesea Arms with her children for sea-bathing; tired of Blesington but had been frightened by a report of scarletina in this place, which she thought we should know about and luckily the little Doctor being in the house, he satisfied her that it was quite unfounded, so she stays.

Sir Gilbert and Lady King who live here also called on Annie. Lots more of the relations live hereabouts but this mourning to the family keeps them all quiet. She died without a Will, at least none can be found though they have ransacked every repository and Russell her maid declares there was one and that she had had it in her hands and read a part of it. James continues to search for the Will; [he] bears his disappointment beautifully. The poor Aunt had told him she meant to make a new Will and leave him everything. She told his father the same. So it is a trial.

19. Will found in an imperial [carriage case] ten years old. Still better than nothing, for it sets all to rights at once, though not quite satisfactorily. There was £20,000 in money not £12,000. About this latter sum will fall to James's father and his family. James gets £1,200 for his share directly, and by a codicil, not witnessed unluckily, merely signed, £2,500 more. The father, who is residuary legatee, may or may not pay this, but the lesser legacy will be enough to produce comfort. It will pay the few remaining debts, the rent due at Christmas, leave a little capital for the trade – in short put him before the world. He is I think I understand to have all the father now gets at the father's death. I must be off to Dublin directly, for there are just ten days left for house-hunting as I shall explain to posterity again.

22. Two days of house-hunting, and there must be a third, for it is a very difficult matter to *fit* all things together. Rents are still very high in good situations, and with our *mixed* family so many tastes and habits have to be consulted that it makes it more perplexing.

That charming Warden spent Friday evening with us. He came to meet Dr. Wordsworth who is on some educational tour, I suppose, for he has been at Radley and is going to Armagh. Janey and I were invited to meet him yesterday at St. Columba's and gladly accepted. We meant to be in time for Chapel but in this house it is so impossible to be early that of course we set out late and, the man not driving quick, we found the 'door shut' – nor would it open! So we said our prayers under the schoolroom porch, hearing the musick perfectly and following even the lessons with the aid of our books, but we could make nothing of the sermon. So we strolled into the grounds taking beautiful nature for our text and dreaming our own comments as we wandered over what really felt as holy ground. All was so clear, so still, and the organ when it pealed forth from the little chapel touched the most spiritual chord in the heart. We sat an hour after the service talking very pleasantly and then drove home quite revived!

30. 14 Nassau Street. We came here last night to nice clean quiet lodgings. Civil people with attentive servants and no draughts of cold air. That corner-house at the sea-side was charming in summer weather, but it was never meant for winter time.

FRIDAY, OCTOBER 17. Oxford. What I have been about can hardly be told. Everything everywhere. We were able to move into the house we have taken in Dawson Street, which fell into our hands quite suddenly after I was worn out hunting through all the town for what seemed impossible to find. Annie came in from Kingstown to stay with us. She was well through the measles and then miscarried, poor child, as I found the day I went to see her. All Tuesday 7th I was taking inventories – such tiresome work! six hours of it. In the evening James and I drove up to Baltiboys where they had been told to expect me. He went on home and I went to bed in the Colonel's uncarpeted room – dull enough. Next day the servants gave good help in packing a large cart-load of supplies. I looked over everything; sorted, arranged, chose out furniture to be sent again, gave directions etc., interrupted by Lady Milltown and Ogle Moore, we sat an hour. After four James came for me and we carred it back to town. Next morning the 8th he and I breakfasted at seven, went to Kingstown by rail, crossed the water, travelling by the Express, and reached London after midnight, being delayed two hours beyond time by the extreme length of the trains carrying people up to the close of the Exhibition. [Brother] William had been waiting for me and took me to his lodgings where Sally had a nice supper ready. After a good night's rest in poor Henrietta's deserted house, waited on by Mary Cameron, Jane and James Craig took us to the Exhibition and to see the Freres, and then they carried me to the Paddington Station from whence we started for Oxford. Our doings here would fill many pages. Thank heaven the job is over, and tomorrow my dear Aunt and I set out for Ireland. We have a time of it certainly, and how that wonderful old woman has borne all the fatigue she insisted on going through, I can't tell.

19. Sunday. We left Oxford yesterday. We left with two heavy trunks, two boxes, two carpet bags, two large baskets, three

work-bags, two clokes and a set of umbrellas. What they will think in Dawson Street of that wagon load I am sure I do not know, the Colonel will be quite frightened.

They need not envy my wanderings, nor my peep at the Exhibition; it was not worth crossing the street to see. Even the *coup d'oeil* was not striking. The building is a fine observatory. The shew of goods viewed in detail most interesting, but I thought paltry as to general effect. The statuary quite the contrary, grand as a whole, in fact redeeming the flat character of all else and as separate works of art worthless. Our little Dublin Exhibition strikes one more because more cognisable; the spectator gets at the things better, can see them, compare them, examine them, and in an ordinary room they shew better than in that great glass house, the peculiar surprise of which is just the crowd pressing its enormous weight of atoms through such space. From the galleries this has the effect of an ant-hill in the Rothiemurchus forest – wanderings as *purposeless apparently* – hum as indistinct. The crystal fountain is a mean affair, malachite gates just like painted iron deed boxes. What a minute inspection might have created I cannot say, but the cursory view is disappointment. Nothing to make a fuss about. I wish we were at home for I am beginning to feel that rest is needed.

22. Dublin. We left Chester a little after three on Monday. We had two civil gentlemen in our carriage. One rather uncouth, but so alive to all the beauty of the scenery and all the barbarism of the Engineers who have carried their iron rails right through the courtyard of Conway Castle, new-faced the ancient gateways, built up the ruined walls, placed rows of locomotives beneath the battlements. I could admire no tubular bridges in such a situation, and think the offer of knighthood too good for Sir John Stevenson,* no indignity is misplaced on the head of such a Goth. Poor Conway, so beautiful in Uncle Griffith's sketches. How are the mighty fallen. One other companion, a handsome Irishman, paid us most agreeable attention. We reached Holyhead at six, Kingstown not till eleven, passing five miserable hours in a cabin full of sick women with the eternal bang of the engine at our very ears. Dark and dreary was the deck and

fruitless my search for luggage. Lanterns were scarce, bags and boxes numerous. At length over the confusion came the blithe tones of James' voice. He had so kindly come down to help us and after his arrival we had no more difficulties. All the servants and the Colonel and the girls were in the hall. Tea ready. Seventeen packages arrived, and my wonderful Aunt neither done up by her journey, nor frightened by her jolt in the *inside* car; went to bed and slept well after a refreshing cup of tea.

FRIDAY NOVEMBER 7. The sort of quiet bustle we have been living in ever since my Aunt and I returned home has prevented me from having one moment altogether to myself. There has been too much to do that must be done to leave any extra time for private employment. The household to arrange; all new servants, the man too to be hired, involving the examination of about fifty candidates for the place. The Colonel to settle with all his old comforts collected about him, his wardrobe to unpack, prepare etc. My Aunt to settle in her *rooms*, for we give her up the *filling* and managing of the drawing-rooms as well as of her own room. The sorting of all our united plate and linen. Visits to pay and receive. Letters to read and write – long gossips about the past. Drives. The dentist! and a heap of Baltiboys business besides. I think as they say hereabouts that 'the weight of the work' is now over and that in future we shall sail smoothly on, very happily.

We are quite pleased with our house [63 Dawson Street]; quite satisfied with our household. For myself I have not for years been so free from care. The air agrees with me. I am neither over-worked nor kept so anxious, the Colonel being really well and therefore easily pleased: he is much at the Club, a good deal at the Billiard rooms amusing himself looking on at the good players generally, but sometimes trying a game himself with the less skilful hands. He keeps to his habit of breakfasting in his room. He then dresses, sometimes walks or drives with us or goes our messages. Always comes home to our five o'clock dinner; except when he forgets! and passes the evening with the newspaper or piquet, or now and then a rubber at whist. He sleeps all night, has no asthma, nor other ailment, in spite of occasional imprudence; and with these few occupations and the little society belonging to them his mind has wakened up wonderfully. Indeed, it has proved to be a good move, this move to Dublin. I don't wish ever to leave it. Life is so much happier here.

My Aunt, six years older than my husband, gets up at half after seven every morning. Dresses without fire. Is often the first in the breakfast room, where she and Janey and I meet a little before nine. She makes an excellent breakfast – two rounds of brown bread and butter, a bowl of milk coffee, a cup of tea with a raw egg beat up in it. The newspaper or her book, settling the drawing-room tables, the flowers, the nick-nacks, and *writing* a letter or so, fills up her busy morning hours. She then has a little light luncheon, bread and butter, or cold pudding! her favourite *treat*, and drives or walks till dark. Alters her dress, dines with good appetite, takes her part in the employments of the evening, and never cares to go to bed till half-past ten. We are told of sleepless nights, but can discern no sign of them. Janey is bright-looking once more. Always doing something. Very attentive to my Aunt who is quite pleased with her, and to her father, who thinks her a better girl than she used to be.

In short, at present the sun never sets in this house. It is so unlike the gloom of dear Baltiboys, where for so many years we were so happy, but which certainly had become unsuited to the infirmities of our advancing years. We have not yet let that once pleasant home. The offers already made do not suit us. There is a chance, however, of a good tenant, Augustus West having made enquiries concerning it. We shall easily come to terms with him. Tom Darker thinks he can make more of the farm for us than we would get in rent. We can try for a year, Mr. West not wishing for land. Any way we live as cheap here with my Aunt's help as we did there without it, and no plague to *me* of any kind. I hope I am not getting selfish in my old age, this relief to myself coming so often across my mind. It is so great, I can't help feeling it.

8. Our house has four windows in front with a balcony running along the drawing-room floor; very handsome large house within a few doors of Nassau Street, giving us the advantage

of a side view of the College gardens. Inside and underground are kitchen with a most complete range etc., scullery, wash-house, large light closet, footman's pantry, and the best arranged housekeeper's room with all accompaniments that I ever almost saw in town or country; plenty of cellars, meat-safe, bottle rack, pump, open areas, large back green and stables. On ground floor very fine entrance hall and broad easy staircase in one, occupying two of the front windows; hall well furnished; staircase hung with pictures; study with two windows, good bookcase, library table etc. Large dining-room behind, Turkey carpet, etc., all handsome but rather a gloomy room. The staircase leads to a wide corridor with sofas, arm-chairs, pictures, flowers, out of which open three drawing-rooms and the way to the back stairs. This floor is really imposing, the rooms are so good, so well furnished, and *en suite*. On the second floor we have four good bedrooms with all essentials, but we have had to bring up some essentials from Baltiboys. Janey and I share the largest front bedroom. The Colonel's room, a little smaller, opens from ours as well as from the passage. My Aunt has the largest back bedroom. The other is our only spare room, into which James and Annie pack well enough, and which is very comfortable indeed for a single person. Upstairs are a large double-bedded maid-servant's room, housekeeper's ditto, manservants' ditto, and I forget that on the ground floor next the dining room is a capital Butler's pantry with plate closet and all else, and upstairs a large lumber-room and china closet. In fact it is a house fit for people of large fortune, and once would have let for £300 a year. We have it for £160, and used as we are to space and other luxuries we do not find it one bit too big for us. My Aunt is quite pleased with her quarters. My only objection is to the narrow street which gives a gloom on dark days we should not have in a square.

10. Our household consists of Mrs. Russell, my Aunt's maid and my housekeeper, an excellent woman who lived in these capacities for fifteen years with good Miss King. A housemaid belonging to the house and so to be trusted with the handsome furniture in the drawing-rooms, an active obliging woman. A cook made over to us by Annie. A Butler, an

admirable servant if he only go on as he has begun. These four servants having plenty to do in this large house, a charwoman comes every Saturday, and an old man pumps daily and cleans the door-steps and the bit of street belonging to us for 1/- a week. Our washing for the present goes home to Baltiboys, from whence it returns accompanied by butter, cream and vegetables. We have determined on not keeping horses while here. Their keep and the man's keep and wages would amount to more than the hire of a carriage at such times as we may require it, particularly when there is only a lady to manage stable affairs. Besides when jobbing, we get close or open carriage, pair or single horses as we wish, and often a car for 1/- will answer our purpose. All this settled we have sold the black horse with his harness to our Riccarton sisters [Jane Craig's sisters-in-law]. The car to Tom Darker. The carriage and double harness are coming up to be sold. The frightful mare is turned over to farm work. Pat dismissed, more ditto for we mean to get rid of every possible expense at home in the meanwhile and hope before long to let the house, and by and bye the ground too, if during this ensuing year of fair trial we do not find it pay us better to keep the little farm. I have not felt so at ease for years. Really we are as happy here now as we used to be long ago at dear Baltiboys, which I shall ever love like Rothiemurchus. My Aunt seems equally comfortable with ourselves. She is invariably cheerful, always occupied and very great deal more up to fun than I am.

11. We have taken my Aunt four drives since she came to us. The first was round the full extent of the Phoenix Park on a most brilliant day when the streets were clean, the scenery at its best. She has had two or three shopping mornings, and was several times with Mr. Maclean [Francis and Samuel McLean both practised in Stephen's Green] about her teeth. She has four false ones fixed in, a great improvement, and say what I would the same good office must be done for me, the Colonel backing the scheme. So I am very uncomfortably beautified. No pain, but much annoyance, and very much more difficulty in eating than before. She delights in our many visitors. We have had a constant flow hitherto though our acquaintance is small.

13. I don't know how many old friends we are seeing here. But the sun shone too bright to last. I said to them all that our new Butler Halloran must have some serious fault unknown as yet, otherwise no Master would have parted with him for, above all servants ever met with, he appeared to be the Chief, and little by little out came a habit of drunkenness, so inveterate that latterly he was not sober in the day. The necessity of parting with such an unfortunate creature has bustled us all about again, but he is gone this day – very penitent – yet I doubt, unreformed. He had *sober* in all his discharges – saying much for the rate of Irish principles.

16. Sunday night and a chance of a quiet half hour, everybody else being gone to bed. In the evening John Robinson called for me and took me to hear a very eloquent but a half-methodistical Mr. Craig at the Molyneux Asylum for blind females, who preached extempore for near an hour and really without fatiguing the hearers. 'A pin might have been heard to drop on the floor,' as the saying is, among a crowd of quite the tradesman class or even lower, all deeply interested in the discourse addressed to them – a little highly seasoned maybe, but perhaps all the better to make a first impression on unreflecting natures.

27. I don't wish to grumble, but I am done up with all this nursing, so much anxiety, and should feel very much re-lieved were we once more in the old jog trot. I have had to get Dr. McMunn screw me up a peg, and I do feel lighter in hand! Perhaps £90 odd paid by the Rutherfurds very un-expectedly has something to do with the improvement of my 'delicate health'! James has been paying all his debts with his good Aunt's legacy. He and dear Annie are so happy; happy in their little fortune and in each other. My Aunt and I agree that nothing could be better. She sees him as he is now. I see his improvement. *So do his people.*

SUNDAY, DECEMBER 7. All much more comfortable with us. Annie steadily recruiting. The Colonel better behaved than usual under the circumstances of not being only and alone the object of all care. Jack wrote in great spirits after the visitation of the Primate. The old man made a speech that affected the boys extremely, alluding to his own School days, his Eton days, adding good fatherly advice with his

Blessing and saying how he rejoiced in the good report made of their conduct by the Warden.* Tuesday week our boy comes home to us, and we shall be this Christmas all together with our dear Aunt presiding.

Annie is to stay with us another month. I am satisfied now that she is thoroughly happy in her marriage. So kind, so attentive a husband few women have the luck to get. His few faults of character are gradually wearing away. All the good in his disposition is developing in this better atmosphere. His abilities are excellent, his temper amiable, and the manners are even more attractive, now that we are so intimate, than they were on slighter acquaintance. I am quite attached to him – no longer grudge him Annie. His family seem to be now thoroughly satisfied with his marriage. Father, Mother, Sisters, all acknowledge him to be immeasurably improved since it took place. They love and admire his young wife – value her and *us* properly. So the old Papa informed Janey during one of their rides. This satisfaction don't open the purse however, but as the Aunt's legacy has been paid in full, £1,350, they can get on very well for the present. All the debts are paid. There is a floating capital for the business, and a little in *each* purse besides.

We are quiet enough just now; a few morning visitors merely. Janey being away I took no trouble about Concerts. Plays there are none – an interregnum there, Calcraft having retired and the new Lessee not being ready. Parties very few and quite private. Nothing gay but the Lord Mayor's Ball upon the 10th, to which Janey must be taken – by her Papa alone I believe, for down to Baltiboys I must go tomorrow, and I doubt getting away so soon as Wednesday.

There is another revolution in Paris, or attempt rather, for they have got their master among them, those absurd people. Louis Napoleon knew the whole plot and on the eve of its outbreak marched off all the conspirators to Vincennes. The troops being with him he has it all his own way, destroys the barricades etc., etc. For though the middling classes appear to take little interest in the scramble there are plenty of the lowest orders always ready for mischief. At present the President shows well. A calm front to the danger, prompt, firm but not despotick – at least not *seemingly*. He will appeal to the People. At the appointed time resign the supreme authority to the People. Till then he will maintain order. This is the man who played the fool for ever so many years, talking as well as acting sillily, so sillily that he was let out of Ham as too trifling to be dangerous.*

8. This evening I am at home in dear old Baltiboys, all alone in this big house, solitary in my poor Colonel's room except for *Fright* who is stretched out on the hearth rug. James and I left Dublin at near three in a covered car and reached this at six, the last hour driving by moonlight. A beautiful sunny day and mild evening. Mr. Darker and John Fitzpatrick were at the door and little cheerful Catherine opened it. All warm within. *Fright* . . . <u>trotted before me</u> to the Colonel's room, took up her old position on the rug and every now and then till she fell asleep she looked up and wagged her tail. The alteration of the furnace makes it quite easy to heat the house thoroughly at small expense on fuel. All looks very clean, very cheerful, it is such a pretty house.

How unreasonable we are, ever wishing for what we have not, never satisfied with what we have. Ungrateful for our many blessings. Discontented with our lot. We did not make this world, we cannot change this world. We *must* go through it; yet we find it hard to pass on though we know to what exceeding joy the right road takes us. We linger, we look back. I look back! regretfully! Coming up the avenue tonight I thought of little Jack who used to live there, not the fine, manly schoolboy he has grown [into], but the pretty child with his dogs and his penny bugle playing his games by himself and watching for the evening and my fairy tale; and all night memory has been wandering back to Jane and Annie in their short frocks dancing to my old tunes, marching with their baby brother, running about this pretty house, their father gay, the Doctor with us, Jane Cooper or good Miss Clerk beside us. I love a house full of children; I love a country life – anything I suppose I can't have. How has this mind of mine become so ill-regulated?

10. All yesterday was too busy a day for any poetical regrets etc. The tenants began to appear at eleven o'clock and it was past six when the last retired. I cannot say they pleased me. They did not on the whole pay badly, but some of them paid grudgingly, tried to impose on *me*, believing me to be weak, which I call dishonest and mean and therefore I rejoice that they have met their match. All justice they shall have, proper allowance for the times – help – time – every encouragement, but what they ought to pay they must pay and without taking the liberty to squabble with me and occupy my time with their nonsense. There is a bad spirit in one or two of them, on whom it will be well to keep a watchful eye.

We were two hours at work after these gentry left us and then I read Dr. Johnson till bed-time. We finished our agency business and then looked over the farm accounts. He has made a deal of money, near two hundred pounds within the last four months, but the most of it seems to have gone in labour – such a sight of wages and extra work for this bad harvest as is really frightful. I have bid him keep the labour book separate for the future and at the end of every week enter the gross amount in his cash book. Tomorrow the schools, the house, garden etc., will occupy me nearly all the day, I think. I shall hardly get away, the mornings are so short. A lot of visitors this afternoon. Mrs. Dodson with money. Miss Merrey [Blessington milliner] for money. Marianne looking ill and unhappy. Miss Macdonnell in great spirits. She staid to help cut out Annie's sheets and carried them off to her school.

I am very comfortable by myself, so quiet, very busy all day, and then the stillness of the evening is agreeable. Perhaps the feeling that there is money enough to pay our way is in itself soothing. More we can't expect these times. As for this farm, if he does not do more with it than he has done, it must just be let. I have told him so – he has now no family, no stable, to eat up its profits, so if he don't pay me a good rent out of it some one else must.

14. Sunday very gloomy without but bright within, for dear Annie seems really well – weak and thin and pale – but no ailment and with improved appetite. My Aunt pulled down too, yet well, with all her active habits resumed. The

Colonel better than he has been for many years. Janey in high glee. James back last night after three hunts and other gaieties – so we shall be all right by Christmas, the accounts being all satisfactory; and, after all, the tenants collectively don't owe the back half year, so in these bad times we should be thankful to escape so well. Liabilities and charges and allowances all reckoned, we ought to have better than two hundred pounds a year out of our land; poor enough, but even for little matters these times let us be thankful.

The French affair still fills the papers. They have got their master among them, those crazy fools, and so best for 'tis plain they a'n't fit to manage themselves. Louis Napoleon is really great – a Despot very likely, and so he must be to rule over a nation so deranged. Clever and prompt and firm he has done his part well and if the Army remains with him he will soon reign in good earnest. What does it matter under what name? Though *king* be out of fashion, President is surely as good as Emperour.

21. Sunday. Yesterday Annie and I drove out – her first drive. She was only as much tired as is good for her. We went to call on Mrs. O'Reilly* in her shabby lodgings, in good air however, a row of houses in Jones's road. Poor woman! her rents badly paid, her husband exacting his annuity, her two remaining sons stopt in their career for want of funds. Pysie miserably married, and her mourning for her murdered boy never laid aside; it is a wonder amidst such grief and such penury to find her so cheerful still. Her rich sister, Mrs. McEvoy, has refused distinctly several times to help her. Her *poor* sister, Lady Milltown, has saved out of her scanty purse, sold privately her Castle Coote ornaments, vealed a few calves etc., *to give* where it was so needed, and Barbara and Cecilia who never see a penny, and are very shabbily dressed often, having each received £3 from their father for winter bonnets, brought the whole sum up to their cousin Pysie. I don't ever mean to think even of Lady Milltown's temper more. As for her daughters, they are half angels, though of the *Dutch school!*

Christmas Day. The Warden drank tea here on his way home from the Smith O'Briens*, where he had been very happy. He spoke very kindly of Jack – nay, warmly. 'Dear little fellow – honest, manly boy, so well dispositioned and with higher abilities than he at first supposed him to possess'. The best Christmas box I could get, though plenty have been showered over us all in both houses. Our breakfast table was covered with pretty things, dressed up with holly.

27. We had several amusing visitors yesterday, Mrs. King, Mrs. O'Reilly and her daughter, and Sir Philip Crampton.* He certainly must have been a lover! there can be no doubt of it, and it is creditable to the heart of such a man of the world to find at the end of such a career this young, pure feeling still remembered – for it can be no more. On his first visit I was not in the room, but Annie was. He entered quickly, seized [my Aunt's] hands, folded her in his arms, kissed her cheeks, and then placing her in her chair sat down beside her, both so agitated that neither of them for some minutes spoke. At length tender voices talked of other days – rooms, windows, views, hours! Annie wished herself away.

They were very intimate once most certainly, and equally sure it is that such another pair, seventy-six and seventy-eight, meeting after fifty four years would hardly be as like their youth as this old couple. In looks but little altered, they would have known each other. In spirits, energy, activity of mind, and indeed of body, almost as they were. Yesterday Sir Philip was dancing here! Laughing with Janey about an object at the Lord Mayor's Ball all covered up with finery, and exhibiting steps in the Doctor [Robinson] style, he got up to place the figure before us, and with all the suppleness of a young man he ducked and rose with pointed toes, went in and out and round about, like a harlequin. His dancing *was* beautiful – riding, fencing, all active exercises ditto; his figure symmetry – still good though he is now stout – and *vain*, and very pleasant – really clever. We were sorry when he went away. I think I shall succeed my Aunt in his good graces for we had quite a flirtation, talking politicks amongst other wise subjects, and Lord Palmerstown [sic] is out; his foolish speech to the Poles or Hungarians or some rebels of that sort is the immediate cause but his career of folly has been making him generally obnoxious.

31. Farewell to 1851. A happy year upon the whole, at least

there has been much enjoyment scattered through it. As far as we can yet judge, it has prepared no evil for its successor. Private matters, which after all are our world, are all comfortable; publick matters, change what will, little disturb our real position. We have much to be thankful for – a quiet home, a fair share of health, wealth, friends, comfort. Our children good above all – Jack turning out well, Annie happy, Janey satisfied, our dear old Aunt with us. We are no richer for her dear money, the £200 a year she gives us being fully absorbed by the rent of this house and the wages and keep of her maid. So that she herself is a visitor, but so very agreeable an inmate, and 'tis such a blessing to watch over her and keep her so well and so cheerful: and by giving up a little we spend no more than we used to do. If we could rent our pretty country house we should be really easy in circumstances, for as it is, it is an expense additional of £50 a year. To save that and receive £100 as rent would be a most pleasant arrangement.

Then as to the farm, we have talked it over well and think it would be best to let it too. Tom Darker is not up to the times, he is dawdling beyond idea – wasting precious moments, so much cash, and in many respects mismanaging so as to be really an unprofitable Steward. Even this last year he has had a good deal of money from me under the pretence of all the produce served to the house. That is over so he shall make the farm pay for itself while he has it, and the sooner we get rid of him the better. He is a bad Bailiff, but we could not there replace him so must only keep him tight. Since he got that unfortunate farm with the consequent threatening letters, he does not dare do his duty among the tenantry. He is not aware of his cowardice, but I am. Also the family failing of extreme rapacity, disinclines him to an honest estimate of a farmer's capability. However, in this capacity we must endure him, watch him, and make the best of him.* A very bad spirit is now shewing itself with us up in the mountains. Discontent, dishonesty, night meetings, rebellious talk; all proceeding from a few ill-conditioned men who unhappily have influence over the rest. I must go there for a few days to put matters as straight as I can, and to gather up the crumbs of the rent due, always delayed so unpleasantly.

These changes in the Cabinet which must end in its downfall, and joy go with it, may very much improve the condition of the country. The numerous mercantile failures in England are beginning to tell upon general feeling. Lord Palmerston,* a brilliant goose, would appear to have been very unfairly treated, at least he has a strong party to say so – even among the ministers. The *foreign* Secretary replacing him, Lord Granville, is married to either a French or an Italian *R. Cath.* of high lineage, great connexions, and great attractions. Her Confessor will be busy enough. Can any choice have been more ill-advised – more fraught with dangerous consequences, more distasteful to John Bull's newly awakened protestantism? This great mistake, Lord Palmerston's threatened revelations, and the critical state of the Colonies, the Continent, and the *working* interests at home will prepare a fine mess for Parliament.

1852

Under the inspiration of the new Lord Lieutenant, Lord Eglinton, whom she had known in Edinburgh days, the early months see a succession of glittering balls, levées and operas enthusiastically attended and recorded in her journal by the Highland Lady. Changes in Government and Church affairs renew her interest in political and religious affairs, as she organises her invalid household and keeps a firm grasp on everything at Baltiboys, despite the anxiety of an attempt at arson ('a bad spirit stirring').

Doubts appear about the effectiveness of James and Annie's stewardship of Baltiboys and later it is plain she has little confidence in her son-in-law's business acumen or ability prudently to manage his own affairs. Meantime her close friend the Countess of Milltown is increasingly in despair at her husband's profligacy ('utterly ruined'). By way of contrast, the H.L. keeps a tight grip of family finances, supplemented by her fees from Messrs. Chambers but there is little comfort to be derived from her mother's will as it appears that her father's 'negligence' has led to most of the estate being claimed by his creditors.

Illustration: Dublin Castle

FRIDAY, JANUARY 2. Before leaving my bed this morning I felt the pleasant change of weather. Without thinking why, I began to dress without cough or headache when the feeling of relief struck me and I said to Annie that surely that dry frosty fog must be gone, and it was – a peep behind the blinds showed wet streets – so I can write today and having leisure will set down the events of yesterday as a sample of our town life. First the newspaper – *Saunders* – 1d. for an hour's reading. Next letters – the post is going all day. About every two hours or so comes that welcome double knock. Then Jack off in a car for his new clothes, bought at Todd and Burns and forgotten to be sent home – and on to Polston's for a Scotch bun to carry down with him to Russelstown. After this the Lord Mayor's Show – a very pretty sight. The street was crowded from an early hour, the mob gathering in a very orderly manner composed too of respectable people well dressed and good humoured. A strong body of Police was on duty – a sight in themselves – being such a very fine set of men and so perfectly disciplined. Before noon the Dragoons arrived – two troops with their bands. The procession left the Mansion House at 12 – thus: a line of police walking – 2 mounted ditto – a troop of Dragoons, band playing – more police – 2 Sheriff's carriage, very handsome – the state coach less ugly than usual – the two very beautiful carriages of the new Lord Mayor [Rt. Hon. John D'Arcy] – police attending – then dragoons and band – then such a string of carriages, the corporation, and I should suppose their friends, for from the length of time it took for them to pass there must have been 200 at least of the queerest old post chaises, things never seen in these days, and one would have fancied not to be had for the seeking even in all the hiding holes. All passed on to the Castle where the one great citizen resigned his authority and the other was invested with it, and then to gladden all hearts up and down and round about thro' all streets passed the throng till they reached the Mansion House again. In the evening we played whist, which being hungry work we sent out for half a hundred oysters, our Aunt was pleased with the fun as the rest, and so went merrily to bed after Porter and Hollands! and Magnesia!!

18. We have been reading too at home among ourselves the most singular books, wonderfully impressive, by an American Mr. Hawthorne – *The House of the Seven Gables* I like best, but *The Scarlet Letter* is cleverer. This town life is very idling – the morning seems away before I can catch an hour out of it – then exercise and visiting, our early dinner, and the day is done, for were I to omit house management we should be in a nice fix. Tom Darker has been so indescribably stupid or so *cowardly* as to have let Mick Doyle depart leaving James and Helen Quin in his house, and they refuse to go, which will put us to some trouble [see 8 March]. He is quite unfit for the responsible situation he fills – credulous, prejudiced and very inactive. We must set about getting rid of him or things will get too wrong in Baltiboys to be easily put right again.

19. Jack and I have just finished our holiday work, a rather full abstract of St. John's Gospel and a sketch of the Acts of the Apostles. He has also a summary of the Grecian History and some Latin and Greek to have ready for examination – for they don't like the pupils to be idlers. At tea time Dr. Robinson arrived. I was sure [the Colonel] was going on well – as well as any person so utterly imprudent can be expected to do – and it turned out that all was right. The poor Doctor looked uncomfortable of course – would neither eat nor drink, nor take the bed ready for him, but *medically* he was very kind. I suppose he regretted his want of manner, for by and bye he came again, sat awhile, stood longer, and undertook some business for us in the country. The post brought a letter from Annie full of *him*. He and she have made up their quarrel after a four hour conversation. She says he is less to blame than we think him.

24. Last night Vance and Louisa [Hornidge] called for Janey and me. Though we were early we did not get good seats owing to a private door and new regulations reserving one half of the benches numbered for the select – however as 'tis all a free gift on the part of the members no one has a right to complain – we beyond the pale can only envy! It was Elijah/Mendelsohn – the Orchestra excellent in the most precise order – the choruses the best I have ever heard, very fine voices – in tune – in order – not too many – like one instrument.

28. A grand day of fun. Papa dressed up for the *levée* [an afternoon assembly for men only, held by a representative of the monarch, *O.E.D.*], quite content at going, and the old uniform reburnished to look very nice. James and Annie arrived in time to admire him. The town was alive with equipages – our busy street in a fret – carriages at the door of every lodging – Morrison's [Hotel] besieged – every window too filled by persons in the act of adorning. The Colonel was back much quicker than we expected, for there was an immense crowd which he managed to get thro' very cleverly.

29. My dress was a white silk petticoat, dark ruby brocaded tabbinet body and train, the whole dress trimmed with quantities of point, my sister's and mine put together. Janey was all in white – Louisa white petticoat and blue *glacée* train, point lace, pearls and *diamonds*, all most prettily arranged so as to make her look extremely well.* We left at 9 – soon reached the Castle where we took up our station at the end of a short train of carriages – but on reaching the Crush room, a very large room, we found ourselves part of such a crowd. Till a quarter past 10 it kept increasing – without losing one member – at length the folding doors opened for the admission of the first batch and on we moved – thro' such stifling heat, no window open. We got into the Ante room batch No. 3 and, being in our turn attended to and our trains spread, we entered the presence and moved on. There was a large *Entrée* party standing behind their Excellencies [the Earl and Countess of Clarendon]. The Drawing room beyond was quite crammed and remained so, altho' St. Patrick's hall was soon opened, the refreshments being served in it, but the company had not all passed till just one o'clock, till when we were all jammed up unmercifully. The Band at length struck up the old Anthem and soon down along the Drawing room came the little Court released – first of all the gentlemen of the household two and two – then their Excellencies – then all the privileged ladies, a pretty enough sight. It then became pleasant with three additional rooms to wander in. The Colonel and I found several acquaintance as we marched about together, he much stared at, I most audibly admired.

30. James' old fox of a father . . . is either a knave or a lunatick, perhaps the two combined – however he has met his match. By help from my Aunt I have *written* him the answer! an admirable document! in which he is told in the civilest manner in the world that we are not to be humbugged. I decline to quarrel, and to keep to this wise rule refuse again to enter upon these subjects. He and the Trustees to the Marriage Settlement!! can arrange them. He wanted to decline paying his son one farthing of the promised allowance *until such time as some estates are sold*. Who can tell how long that may be – and when I asked how our son and daughter are to live till then he said he expected Colonel Smith would support them!! The mean old body – or the madman which you please.

SUNDAY, FEBRUARY 1. One of the pleasures of living in Dublin is the power of going to the Cathedrals to listen to that delightful Choir – and one of the drawbacks to the full enjoyment of the Choir is the miserable style of sermon uniformly to be heard at St. Patrick's. The Anthem was beautiful, but a long maundering prose from Dr. Todd of fifty minutes length by Mrs. Finnemor's watch was really an infliction.

6. We were idled all the morning by a woman with Limerick lace very much superiour to that sold in the shops. We bought a little and selected a good deal for Madame. This Mrs. Leo – curious name – has 28 young women working for her at from 3 to 5 shillings a week, constant employment, many of them children almost – two and three of a family some times. What good this must do.

11. I have passed some pleasant evenings with two books, Dr. Arnold's *Life and Correspondence*, from which I am making notes, and a very engrossing tale by Mrs. Marsh, *Time the Avenger* – as usual inconsistent, the characters not preserved – incidents unlikely – much of the whole unnatural, yet on the whole most interesting and very clever, a treat, for it sets one thinking on worthy things. What a deal of writing can be picked up out of the load of trash by those who have the means of search. Lady Emily Ponsonby and others, yet all so fail in my idea that I know that if I were to try myself I should fail too.*

12. We had 1,400 at the Ball – the seven rooms open – Dancing in two – refreshments in two and a handsome supper in a third, to which we went through a grove of hot house plants. All grades there – a little row of peeresses in diamonds, Lady Caledon's suite worth £7,000 – then officials, country gentry, professions and *trades*. Two of the finest girls in the room, and decidedly the best and most tastefully dressed, being the daughters of Hodges the hardware shop. They were by no means alone in their glory – other girls of the same grade, very pretty and very nicely dressed, were pointed out to me, and with this class the 'Household' prefers to dance on account of the liberties they can take with such partners, and the 'fun' they get out of them. Good this, for young gentlemen of condition, and the future wives and mothers of decent citizens, whose mates-to-be look woefully ill beside their present elegant attendants. The men are many degrees beneath the women in look, air, size, dress, manner etc., this is always so – every country – as far as I have seen. Our sex is quicker at the 'up take'.* Janey had plenty of partners – Louisa a few – and I found a good many people to speak to. It is really extraordinary how Louisa Hornidge at 39 can be so anxious to go out, to have *Beaux*, to dance. I had to stay a full half hour longer than I intended to give her an unexpected waltz with her fourth partner. Russy was speaking *very thick* to me. Little Janey is spoiled by the rightful way my Aunt and Lady Milltown have made her dress her hair – no becoming curls – but all taken back off her face – she looks younger but certainly not so pretty.

16. We had a long visit today from Jos. O'Reilly, really a very fine young man – I like him, he makes himself so one of us, unfolding all his schemes as if he were with his best friends. Lady Milltown opened the way for him certainly by consulting me for him. He hopes to get out to Australia where he has one friend and we have many – his friend could have given him employment had he been able to go out now – funds were wanting. I suggested an insurance office which will advance him a sum on the £1,000 which must be his at his Mother's death. But the sacrifice is great, she being just 50 her life is worth 24 years, so all they can offer him is £250 – £200 he wants to relieve her of a pressing debt of his

father's which she is paying off by instalments, so that little would remain for his outfit, passage and purse on landing. They had to bribe the wretched father to go off to America and so leave them at peace. The £200 a year from the Kilkenny property has, between free trade and the poor laws, dwindled down to whatever it now and then pleases the tenants to spare. They are living, the Mother, two sons, Pysie, her baby and a maid and a little help on the interest of £3,000 in the funds – £97.10.0 a year, and a few pounds now and then from Kilkenny and Lady Milltown who is in penury herself. Mrs. McEvoy with £900 a year – her two daughters each with £7,000 – Edward with £1,200 a year and Jos. with £600 are none of them able to assist the O'Reillys – not even to send the outfit to Australia, their own requirements are so large. We want our young *protegé* to write for the press, he is very clever, to begin with Miss Cooke, then *Chambers* – to feel his way – then to fly higher if he can. He inclines to try.

17. That abominable Chamberlain [George L'Estrange] has never asked poor Janey and me to the select Ball at the Castle tomorrow. It is really provoking for the little body was ever so deeply engaged. It never entered my head he would overlook us, as last year he asked James, Janey and Annie to everything. He is not to blame poor man – who knows me – hardly one in a hundred – and as I shew very little to the top of the crowds, tall as I am, 'tis no wonder he thinks us rubbish. I thought of writing to ask for a ticket as others do in like circumstances, but I did not do it. Lady Milltown, with whom I spent an hour, said it would be well to do it – however one Ball is no loss.

26. Lord Clarendon goes on Saturday, to the regret of nearly everyone. We are rather grieved for the change on personal motives. We were not asked to the Select Ball, were advised to ask for a ticket but did not do it. Lady Milltown most kindly asked them how they came to leave us out. 'Who are they?' says the vice Chamberlain. She explained. 'God bless me', says Captain Bagot, A.D.C. to Mr. Willis [Captain Frederick Wills was the Gentleman Usher] 'the gentlemanly man who always gave us such good luncheons when we hunted – his family should be down for everything.' And

so a private mark was prefixed to our names. Lord Clarendon, hearing the chatter, asked the subject. 'You should have written direct to Lady Clarendon,' said he, 'she would have sent you a ticket at once'. We may not have so good an introduction to Lord Eglinton, yet we *should* get on both with him and her.*

I have besides a wonderful affair upon hands – nothing less than the settling of Baltiboys to a tenant who will do the land justice and the people good and preserve the house and grounds in order, and whose wife is an improved edition of poor old me. If we did not get a penny of rent from these respectable people we should be gainers by getting quit of it. About £100 a year I have always had to give to Tom Darker for one thing or another, not quite so much this last year though not far from it, and we not living there since August, nor having any horses. He is not up to the times at all – then his salary – Co. Cess – half of poor rate and many an odd expense for repairs &c. Besides we have a claim on the rent of the new tenant who is our dear son James – the annuity we give him, and to secure the rent we propose that Father should pay so much of the allowance he makes his son over to us at once. Whether said father will agree to this can't say – it will be one way of getting so much out of him at any rate. We shall not ask a high rent for the land – nor anything for the house, as we shall require the furniture probably. We shall often some of us be there – it will still be the home house – so happy for everybody, but in particular for Jack who will be wild with delight when he hears the news. Annie will be in heaven in her old haunts, among her own people, near her old friends. There never was a happier scheme, liked by the Colonel, approved by John Robinson, very, very pleasant to us all.

29. Sunday. Christchurch and a long sermon but a good one. Janey and I fell in with the whole of Dublin, Sackville Street filled from end to end, crammed – all other streets on our way ditto. Took shelter and saw glimpses of the procession. Good old Archbishop Murray's funeral.*

WEDNESDAY, MARCH 4. We are all taken up with the new men and law appointments everywhere are excellent – all parties agree – and the others generally better than the men displaced, one or two exceptions maybe – Mr. D'Israeli one. Lord Eglinton is too *racing* to please me, his lady a good little vulgar woman is a *pill* on account of her base birth, but a rich Cockerell son and two well portioned Cockerell daughters will help her down.*

6. Night – at Baltiboys in my old room, for James came up yesterday and we took a covered car together, the Doctor having said I might safely leave the Colonel. Annie is quite herself – the house very clean and she has got it all settled up as nicely as possible, it is a most comfortable house so suited to people of domestick and business habits, so convenient in all respects. We were the whole morning going over every room looking through every cupboard, making lists, and locking up and giving out. I took up every thing from Catherine, made over everything to Annie and then went outside to do the same by the garden, and to see the lots which had been sorted for the Auction on Monday, very tidily arranged by T.D. That over we took a walk, having by the bye sent to Blesington for meat and bread and drink for the mob that will gather here. Our people seem pleased to have James rather than a stranger, and delighted to keep Annie among them. James will take some of our servants – Miles and Luke Byrne, John Grace, Pat Quin and John Fitzpatrick. He does not take Cairns, Moore or Paddy, who was very indignant, quite excited, expressing himself very improperly, as if determined to give all the trouble possible, however he seemed to have thought better of it for he was very calm with me today. Will leave on Tuesday – no nonsense – but be thankful for a good discharge. They think him frightened, for by one assent he appears to be thought guilty of a great crime.

On Tuesday morning I think it was, the maids smelt a singular smell of resin as they fancied – resin or paint burning and then the house suddenly filled with smoke. Just as Catherine was making her way through it, voices sounded at the front door – Mr. Darker was there and Johnny Grace and others busy putting out a fire most artistically constructed against the door – a live turf covered with dry chips, 7 turf around it, smothered with sprigs – quite a large bundle of them, the whole kept in its place by the heavy scraper moved from the other side on purpose. The door is much burned, a large hole in it and a crack a good way up. How many fortunate circumstances combined to save the lives of four innocent people and the little baby sleeping securely they fancied, and this fine house full of furniture. It was a fiendish revenge, for what or by whom we know not, the person whoever he be knew the place well, avoided the ground, stept only on grass, and yet was tracked thereby the frost, but the marks vanished. Nobody who saw them doubts the feet, their shape and the walk is peculiar, also the old shoes commonly worn have disappeared and a bran [sic] new pair are on. It may be all wrong, no one likes the queer, discontented, self-sufficient radical, and he is not a fool, and this is certainly the action of someone deranged in his wits as well as evil disposed, for it could much hurt none. The Colonel would recover the full value from the Barony, which indeed would suffer, for it would be half ruined raising the money, and Mr. King would not have been injured for it was not his. There was a meeting of magistrates, police &c., but nothing has come to light. I shall see Mr. Owen and others tomorrow, for this indeed brought me down as much as the Auction, one precaution we must use, not to give a hint of it to the Colonel. It would break his heart at once to find all his trouble and kindness and money so thrown away – rewarded by such ingratitude – such dreadful temper! high and low alike have this dreadful curse – modified in the better educated certainly, so we may hope to see it wear away.

8. Talking over the burning with Mr. Owen, we can neither of us see any grounds for accusing poor Paddy – I rather incline to accuse lame James Quin,* as a piece of poor spite for being turned out of the house he had no right to stick himself into – particularly as we hear this morning that the fox covert is burned down – last night this happened – and only for the police who discovered it, the plantation on the top of the hill would have shared in the flames. It is very wretched having such a wretch on the property and unable speedily to get rid of him, he may go on till he does some irreparable mischief. We must see if these law proceedings

cannot be expedited and the man sent off to gaol at once. Then the wicked sister [Helen] is worse than himself.

The Lord Lieutenant enters tomorrow, *Levée* announced for the 16th, Drawing-room 17th, St. Patrick's Ball the 24th, presentations all over again, Janey quite happy. How things will go on who can say, I don't like the *corps dramatique* behind the Age, and all that rubbish of nobility, and Court fudge, and entertainments with horse racing &c. which from the very style of people sent here will of course be all the go again, is just the style of folly one wants discountenanced among this idle, semi-barbarous people.* The Law appointments are excellent everywhere – this is the redeeming point – but really the rest don't look like permanence. Do the *heads* of society ever read about the tails – or more properly the *feet*, the supporting feet. Cobbet's pot with scum and dregs had clear sound soup in the middle. The signs of the Times are many and striking – no one will read them.*

Night – the Auction went off remarkably well – very lively and good prices – everything sold, James thinks. Almost all our neighbours attended it, for they dearly love the fun, altho' I do believe they had a wish to help the Colonel, in whom one and all expressed extreme interest. We had a good luncheon in the dining room – cold meat, a beef steak pie and an Irish stew – wine and porter. In the barn there was cold roast beef and cold boiled beef, ale and whiskey – too much of the latter, for reeling and tottering and very thick speaking got into fashion afterwards among the barn company. Our company was very pleasant: Mr Owen, Ogle Moore, Richard Moore, John Hornidge, Hugh Henry, Mr. Verschoyle, Archdeacon Agar, grown very aged. Three more, Dick, Richard Hornidge and John Finnemor did not shew to the ladies – Annie is sure they were not shaved! Fine as the day was we did not stir out on account of the crowd outside.

10. I was too sleepy after writing a long letter to the Colonel last night to journalise. We did not do much yesterday either. Tom D. thinks the Auction realised near £450 – half or rather more must be waited for as James cannot carry on the business without what he purchased, and though his father

owes him double what he owes us, there is no getting much from him till these weary estates are sold. He thought himself very generous in sending him just today the last half of a £20 note. It will all come in the end but we must needs have patience. John Hornidge came to the door yesterday, Dick came in and afterwards when Annie and I were driving, we came upon them and others looking rather dismal for lack of foxes, all the coverts they had drawn being blank. Our covert was burned down here last night, the following evening the one near Greyhills was burned. What next – there surely is a bad spirit stirring. I sent for James Quin hoping to show him his folly, but he would not come, so there is no help for him, he may be more reasonable after the ejectment is served on him. James Ryan is now mending the door.

15. A long pause – back again in Dawson Street and as idly busy as ever. We found my Aunt and the Colonel hardly so well as we expected, they had stood too long at the window the day before watching the very fine triumphant entry of our new Lord Lieutenant, he was well received – quite cordially, so fond is this mercurial people of change – they parted with that excellent Lord Clarendon with perfect indifference, yet now are beginning with their nonsense showing green and orange posies and fighting about them. We were all bustle after arriving – the girls had to go a hunting! for a *beau* to attend us to the garrison play next day, and I had to start for Mr. Toomy the Attorney to see whether he had sent the ejectment for those Quins.

20. We found a *beau*, Robert Hornidge, we went early, still the crush was dreadful, we got good seats, front seats, and were on the whole amused. We saw a good many people we knew and our new Lord and Lady Lieutenant. They were cordially received – I was quite in a fidget about *her* first appearance before the fastidious women of Ireland, recollecting her style of dress when I saw her in Edinburgh – the ruby bracelet across her forehead, the exuberance of frill and furbelow and ornament, but she was perfection – gown, hair, shawl, all was according to rule. She is a pretty woman and he a fine handsome man.

There have been a few tiny attempts at riots, but they

were soon put down. An address from the College today, 1,000 strong, was answered by his Excellency in plain manly terms. Such crowds accompanied it that the floor in the presence chamber gave way, but no one was hurt. An address from the Corporation followed, answered even more boldly. Every one seems pleased with the warmth of Lord Eglinton's manner, he has dissolved the Castle clique, a boon incalculable. The town is in a state of rejoicing, houses taken on all sides – streets fuller than ever – shops so busy – will it last.

Such a busy week, yet somehow these bustling times figure less in the Journal than do quieter days. When fewer facts and more feelings occupy us. The first event was the *Levée* – 1,700 persons, 40 of them Peers. The hour was 1 – the streets began to fill an hour earlier, and it was 6 before they emptied. Next day was the Drawing room, above 2,000 – 60 odd peers and peeresses – 300 had the *entrée*. We left this house at 10, got easily into the Castle yard and without much delay up to the door way. The hall was clear enough, but the whole wide two-branched staircase one moving mass of human beings. It took us a considerable time to reach the top where we found the gallery equally crowded – pushing slowly along the well packed throng after a struggle we reached the door of the long corridor – this was only opened at intervals to allow of certain number to pass, but this did not keep that great extent of passage free – the same pressure surrounded us – just at the ticket table it was fearful. The door of the crush room was in like manner kept closed and in like manner occasionally opened, and what a sight presented itself there.

An equal crowd, before, behind, all round, a mass of human beings heated to a very unbecoming and most exhausting degree – there was no going back, or faint hearted I would have returned, but to push against that stream would have been impossible. Seven gentlemen fainted, though the seven windows of that long room were all open. Mrs. King had to give it up – she turned deadly sick, luckily near a sofa where we left her, and by and bye, by the help of a policeman, she was shewn down a back staircase and *escaped*. The rest of our party pushed on, and at half past twelve we succeeded in rushing thro' the door of the Anti-room – it was a frightful moment – I owed my safety to a tall hussar whose strong right arm sent me forward while Janey crept under it – and as quick as we could decently step we passed before the Viceroy.

She stood beside him brilliant with diamonds, beautifully dressed, two pages holding out her train! very pretty and very young for the mother of nine children. Wonder of wonders! the Withdrawing room and St. Patrick's Hall were as crowded as the Anti-rooms – a dense multitude – and not a vacant seat – after enduring more squeezing we got some refreshing ice – there was plenty of everything and champaign – plate so splendid – such an array of attendants, and at last I got a seat. We met numbers that we knew, for indeed I suppose all Ireland was there, and should have found it very pleasant but for the pressure and the heat. We came away at 2, the crowd very little thinned in the hall, but in the other apartments it was easier to move. Such a demonstration! resounded on all sides. The whole town remained alive till day break. The Kings all came here on their way to shew themselves and a most creditable party they formed. The handsome father in a militia uniform as young looking nearly as his son. The very handsome mother in her diamonds and a train of silver brocaded silk, Arabella blue, the little girls maize – Annie had pink trimmed with silver, Janey and I our old friends, but I took off the point and replaced it patriotically with Limerick, thinking this a delicate attention due to the piece of parchment sent to me after the last Drawing-room with the thanks of the Irish Society for my tabbinet train.*

The Lord Lieutenant had an official dinner on Monday, a select one on Tuesday – on Thursday 70 of all sorts, and before midnight most of his company adjourned to the Subscription Ball. It was really a good one – the Committee were, as they had promised to be, very particular. We placed ourselves well and I was better off than usual, my few acquaintances being mostly of the red benches [that is, Peers], but the poor girls had none of their *Beaux* there – the lawyers are on circuit and the Regiments have been changed and they don't know the Castle set.

The town is still very full though numbers have left it. It is
difficult to walk the streets between the unusual number of
foot passengers and carriages. It is like the dead coming
alive, all so busy, every face so bright, hope in each countenance and no regrets. Poor Lord Clarendon quietly consigned to oblivion, and for the late ministry contempt and
aversion are poor terms to convey the feelings with which
they are remembered. Their conduct since their fall has
certainly been the reverse of dignified, a nest of hornets, or
the spite of vulgar women. Lord Derby and Mr. D'Israeli
have quite disarmed opposition – [they] mean to tide it over
this session and dissolve in summer, then an appeal to the
country will decide the future. Another R. Cath. will get in
for Cork tho', the priests are so busy – not one of them has
been near the Castle, but there never was a better attendance
of the better sort of their flocks. Here's a screed of politicks,
I have not been in such a vein for many a day – there was
nothing to say but to string on a set of miseries – we have
hopes now to cheer us.

I forget whether I set down here that James got a little
money from his father, who also presented him with his
Court dress. I gave Annie her train, the last of my brain
money – I must set to work and write again, but town is a sad
idling place and the ways of our house are quite anti-
industrious. Between my Aunt's early hours and the Colonel's late ones, a little business and a good deal of trifling,
and an invalid room – and the necessary overlooking of an
Irish household with poor Janey's few gaieties, time slips
away in a wonderful manner. I really must pull up a bit and
work in earnest, even the Journal is neglected, very many
interesting things left out of it, not set down at the time and
then forgotten, so that Jack's children will hardly get a *full*
account of their Grandmother's days. Said Jack is well and
happy, learning to spell at last and to write a decent hand.
William and Sally are at Brighton with Lady Byron.*

21. In yesterday's *Saunders* was an account of the perfect success
so far of the Scotch settlers in different parts of Ireland,
farms of 40 acres with suitable dwellings much in request,
from 100 acres upwards with good offices readily taken. The
names are given of all already rented, labourers and landlord

equally satisfied as yet with the result. Nineteen more farmers have come over from Scotland this last week, purchasers of small properties too are beginning to come forward. Pray heaven the wheel have turned.

28. We have been reading *Ravenscliffe*, very good and we *are* reading D'Israeli's *Life of Lord George Bentinck* which so far seems very bad.* We are expecting Lord Jeffrey's *Life* daily, Jane having so kindly sent it as a present to me. It is very highly reported of, as delightful in itself and very creditable to Lord Cockburn. And now our domestick misfortunes – Russell is gone, the most comfortable servant that ever was, neat-handed, obliging, willing – not a good housekeeper, too weak in character, but a really useful person for all that. Well – she cheated, drank, swindled, had her son here for ever, McNamara ditto, and was in plain English his paramour – a married man – a low vulgar dissipated vagabond. Mrs. McNamara came up to Town to accuse her. A Court of Enquiry brought a hideous system of vice and villainy to light. Henceforth I trust nobody – 15 years with Miss King and a regular . . .

29. John Robinson called with the Broker's ticket for Janey – I was so glad to be able to repay her £100, the Auction enabled me to do that. It is invested in the 3 per cents and I hope she will always try and add to it, she may find the little gathering quite a Godsend some day. I had hoped to put by £50 for ourselves but it can't be done just now. The Auction brought £460 or so – Tom Darker required £20 for bringing up his books! – and all that James King bought we are to wait awhile the payment of – as he had nothing left of his Aunt's legacy after paying his debts, including the £500 advanced by the father for the marriage which none of us had any idea he would ever ask for again. He had not given the cash either then, endorsed bills drawn on D.C. Latouche,* and when they become due James was told he must now, having money, take them up. As he still puts off giving his son any allowance, the young couple would be in serious difficulties but for us. We thought the best way of helping them was to assist him in his business, which he understands and really does manage well. This increase of farm will put him before the world

as the stock is on it, but certainly it is a sacrifice on our part for we badly wanted that £260.

Newspapers very interesting, Lord Derby very great, D'Israeli wonderful because sounder, calmer, more carefully painstaking than one could have supposed that meteorick sort of man could ever rise to. Every passing day strengthens this wise ministry all whose component parts are so well filled. Lord John has withdrawn his factious opposition after further damaging his poor remains of reputation by his petulance. In this country we are sailing before the wind, yet it may not last – the Whigs are very sore – the Democrats very furious – the Papists quite unscrupulous. Still I think our Pilot will weather the storm although the breakers are in numbers ahead. All we know here is that our City that was dead is alive.

THURSDAY, APRIL 1. The Ball was the best, the merriest I have ever seen at the Castle – 700 people in good humour, admirable musick, quite beautiful. Janey danced every dance but two, with four partners only – she knew no more. Captain Grange, an elderly *Beau*, but a very agreeable man, was her most devoted – he has been in India – knew there all my family – seemed glad to talk them over – and was most anxious to bring Lady Eglinton and me acquainted, as she likes to gather her old friends round her and she was very intimate with all my people. I must manage this somehow, for I am not going to sit apart out of my own proper sphere while all the impudent pushing *little* bodies elbow their way to the top.

4. Sunday. This following week being Passion Week, and nothing of course doing, our gay trio departed yesterday for the country, there to remain in retirement until Tuesday the 13th – Lady Blakeney's Ball. It will do them a deal of good, they have been so much out of late – Balls, dinners, plays, concerts, the conjuror, &c. When they were fairly off I took a car and went round to pay all bills, my quarter's accounts. It is hard enough to make ends meet – I hope this will be our last *tight* year. The Doctor will be paid off – Tom Darker done with – no little sums varying from £10 to £100 wanted for that absorbing farm – and no £75 allowance to James King. It would have been a very great comfort to me

to have received all the Auction money, but we have done right in giving it up for the present – £240 odd in stock will carry James on till these weary estates are sold. One of them will really be put up next month – and by not asking him for any of the money for a twelvemonth he will be put we hope before the world. Certainly we make a great sacrifice and that old oddity of a father will make none – but if everybody did wrong where should we all be – and as my dear good husband would have this marriage he must abide by the consequences. I thought it over in all ways before acting in this matter of the Baltiboys farm and I do not see how we could have done better.

One or two very pretty anecdotes of that good unaffected little Lady Eglinton deserve recording. A Miss Grove outfitted her for India, who mentioning this said she was too humble to be remembered by Lady Eglinton, though Mrs. Cockerell had ordered dresses from her – but she was wrong for her Excellency has visited her and employed her. And this wicked town, this wicked country I may say, is full of odd evil tales of *her* and every one – Lady Milltown is said to drink, a woman whom to my knowledge of beyond twenty years seldom takes a glass of wine – her red face and excitable spirits are to be accounted for as maliciously as possible. So she laughing immoderately on the Chancellor's arm, who is just out of a fit of the gout, happening to *sway* on their way downstairs, were at once set down as too free with the champaign. It makes one quite angry to hear such horrid falsehoods, but that's Ireland, all mean and low and false and hollow and vile. An odious people to know well, charming to know a little.

11. Sunday. Jack comes to us tomorrow for two days – the last report was not a good one – conduct troublesome – Classicks backward – Arithmetick mediocre. Some mischief had been going on in the Class for [Brownlow Villiers] Layard was equally evil spoken of. I never lecture, I took no notice of this unpleasant missive, wrote as usual all our news, some fun, and then touched on home subjects, Papa's failing health, the weight of business on me, my hopes in *him* who is to be my help, my stay, my comfort, that our separation now, the discipline of his school life &c. are

all necessities, the steps leading to his manly career &c., and the various difficulties, the temptations, trials &c., all a preparation for the graver assults of maturer years, which I felt he would courageously throw off &c. The Warden in granting the leave is 'quite happy' to inform me that no boy can be doing better – Conduct as it used to be, marked improvement in all studies, the same 'dear little fellow' as before.

Politicks distracting people, Ministry quite firm, Priests very busy doing all the mischief in the world – disgusting the educated, driving away the lower orders, for emigration was never so rife. Lord Beaumont* has soon followed the Duke of Norfolk's wise example and separated himself from that intolerant church. A perfect fever of reformation is proceeding, driving the R.C. priesthood to despair, they should join in it, otherwise they will lose their flocks.

A note from Jane yesterday does not give a good account of my Mother – three weeks ill, the disease still there – her weakness great and increasing – restless nights – ideas wandering – seventy-six – years of suffering, years of anxiety, all will tell. Lord Jeffrey's *Life* does *not* satisfy me. It reminds us well of him we who knew him – it does not place him in the least before a stranger – his career – his writings. Many of his sentiments are chronicled accurately – he is faithfully described as to character, acquirements, qualities, but we are not introduced to the *man*. In his social relations we know him not. Craig Crook need not have existed for all we hear of it. He and his wife and his child and his friends and his walks and his conversations and his habits are unknown to any readers but those who had themselves the means of learning of them – a woman would have done this part better. The 'Letters' probably will repair this grave omission but it ought to have been avoided. It would have lightened a heavy work, still deserving of the utmost praise, and Lord Cockburn shows *himself* most favourably throughout it, not only clear headed as we knew he was, but right headed and right hearted, less brilliant than the friend he worshipped but quite his equal in intellect – they were a clever set.*

12. My darling Sprat has just come in, looking so well, quite a fine robust handsome boy and with such gay and natural

manners. He is perfectly happy at school, all is harmony there now. The Colonel is sky high since the monkey ran upstairs, and he neither well nor in spirits yesterday. My Mother better, had slept well. Lord Cockburn's *Life* of Lord Jeffrey is too didactic a performance to please my taste – I like a *Memoirs* style better and to draw my own inferences from details. Jeffrey and the society he lived in, and his home, and his habits have yet to be described – I wonder if I could do it in a paper for *Chambers'* – I fear not. There is an admirable article in this *improving* journal by Leitch Ritchie this week on the affected revival of the tastes of the mediaeval ages, exposing such follies with considerable ability, discovering at the same time a very accomplished mind of his own. He and Dickens are improving each other, *Bleak House* is opening well – against my rule I am reading it as it issues, so I shall be teased once a month and have to go through it all again, no penance certainly. One has little time for quiet occupation in a town life.

29. A day in my Colonel's room nursing him thro' another attack of bronchitis gives me leisure to go back the fortnight. In the gay week we had two Balls, one at Lady Blakeney's,* the other at the Rotunda given by the 5th Dragoons, to which Captain Grange was so good as to get us invited, the cards coming at teatime to Janey's great delight. Both were excellent in their different ways. We also had a small musick and dancing party at the Gledstanes, indeed dined there, and a dinner at the Augustus Wests, very stupid.

This was also the week of the mesmerism, an exhibition at Major Layard's who was the operator upon two of his servant maids. We found in his drawing room his wife and Sir Philip Crampton and his two daughters. Sir Philip came to disprove. Well, it was a most extraordinary scene – the women were soon sent to sleep and in that condition answered every question their master asked them – obeyed every order, believed all he told them, acting most absurdly in consequence – and nobody could wake them – neither by gentle whispers nor shouts not blows nor other ill usage. His voice roused them in a moment, neither did they seem to hear any other – still collusion was possible, though we are not to imagine a *gentleman* would resort to it, so that this, though strange to see, was no proof that to awake was impossible.

Then Sir Philip went out and bought the strongest spirits of ammonia and held it to the nose of one victim. She held her breath which he hailed as a partial victory – but when she had to draw it she coughed very slightly and was not roused, on which the Major applauded. She also drank half a tumbler of strong vinegar as water without a flush or grimace. The women feel no ill effects from their constant practice of obedience to this subduing power – on the contrary it rather enlivens the sluggish character of one and has improved the health of the other. The mesmeriser gets very faint after any lengthened exertion of his powers. I myself don't believe in the business at all – the rationale of the business can't get in to my head in the least – still the exhibition is staggering. It is impossible to doubt the reality of the sleep or trance, but how far imagination or nervousness may have to do with the rest of the performance we must leave to be decided by more accurate investigation. If it be a true power it is a fearful one.

The day of this affair James and Annie went off to the country – there they fell into Lady Drogheda's grand Ball to the Excellencies and a bit of a morning at the Curragh. On the Friday I went back with them to dear old Baltiboys which they have made so neat inside and out all in high order, but I think him expensive for his means and doubt his making the two ends meet even should the father pay him the allowance regularly, which hitherto he has not done. However the old oddity has sent him £100 so I relent and dine with him.

Saturday I went out alone, called on Peggy – then on to school, only in tolerable order, wants a little whipping up and not so many children as should be – staid two hours and examined every one present. Annie then drove me to Farrell's – he has set up a huckstery which I am not sure the Colonel will approve, yet there is certainly no whiskey there, and one almost admires the industry which on the failure of one business tries another. Then on to Jack Byrne, looking ill but good humoured – offered me luncheon – spoke favourably of the times. Red Paddy Quin all right there,

Widow Quin poorly but comfortable – the half blind daughter as clean as possible, but in such misery I had to leave a little help, only a little for I have not much to spare just now. Also some was wanted at Tom Keogh's where poor unfortunate Harry Keogh's corpse was lying, starved out of life I do believe. His widow may go to the poor house or where she likes, worthless body, the good little daughter the Tom Keoghs will take, they have none of their own, and the boy is in service. Then to Garret Doyle, thriving – Dempsey, low, untidy. Widow Byrne with a house full of grandchildren which cannot be allowed – lamenting Peggy Mary's death, comforted on receiving leave to remain rent free in the house and to inherit her large property!

Upon the whole of this day's proceedings I can remark that the tenantry appeared more cheerful, more hopeful, much more satisfied, agreeable they themselves call it, than they have been for many years. A better spirit among them – and certainly no increased love for their priesthood.

Sunday of course went to church. Every body there and staid so long gossipping with Miss Henry that the congregation had all dispersed when we descended our gallery stairs. A bald headed elderly man, slovenly, dressed like Lord Downshire, and in Mr. Owen's pew, turned out to be Mr. Corbett. After luncheon we wandered over the hill calling in all the labourers' cabins. There is no doubt of good ensuing from this introduction of a few strangers among them. We were all too much in a clique like the late ministry, and with equally ill results, general weakness, particularly improprieties, jealousies &c. The Steward seems thoroughly to understand his business, working well himself – no idle moments – no puttings off or shortcomings or dawdlings. The ploughman very good also. Miles Byrne did not long bear the new measures, he removed bodily to the Hyland home, where I forgot to mention one of my errands was to call on Saturday to warn him out. The whole crew were civil enough, humbled amazingly – high times.

I was tired in the evening yet resumed my labours next day – a long round – Widow Ryan – Tom Kelly and then down to Phil Tyrrell's where wonders awaited me. That man has done an immensity, all the little bits of fields down by the

riverside thrown into two large ones – 10 acres and 8 acres –
10 ditches [Irish banks] levelled and a flow dike raised
against the floods. He is just on the point of marriage with
a most deserving young woman, a rustick heiress and in high
glee. Pat Fitzpatrick has a third handsome wife, dull clod as
he is of whom we shall never make anything, he has no
notion of farming or anything else. The old Cullens look
badly, it is very different living under Tom Darker and
under his honour, as their poor remnant of a wretched hut
but too plainly shows – help left there. Jim and Nelly Quin
'made their disappearance' on the issuing of the decree
against them – the house is down – Garrett Doyle is in
possession. We then drove to Humfreystown where I had 14
calves to see – 16 big pigs – 22 little ones – stores, sows, and
all manner of things our own stock, cattle, sheep and horses
sent over to that fine grass while that at Baltiboys is springing. Tuesday we went up to the Moat to pass sentence on
the planting, fences &c., and to see a bad farmer, Carney the
mason, who with his mortar work in hand, neglects his
ground*.

30. The poor Milltowns have not staid for this week's Balls –
something has gone amiss with them – she was very hoity
toity one day – had red eyes with weeping the next – and in
the afternoon they all left Town. I heard the usual account
of my Lord, no longer concealed by anyone – and Russy,
poor fellow, is ill reported of – the girls all alike – and *she* in
spite of all her rudeness, really pitied everywhere. What will
be the end

SUNDAY, MAY 2. Yesterday John Robinson was so very good as to
give me an hour at my agency accounts which had not been
kept quite properly – the few omissions can all be inserted
and he was so very kindly *instructive*, I don't think I shall go
wrong again. He says the people are so crafty it is impossible
to be too exact in all dealings with them – they will swear
black is white with composure so that there must be writing
for every transaction.

5. I have a note from Mr. Ritchie this morning accepting my
Sisters of Charity, which we all here liked. Every body and
every paper is full of the Budget of our wonderful Chancellor of the Exchequer. A man till now, though known to be

eminently clever, yet considered more as a brilliant, biting eccentrick, slap dash, flash in the pan sort of person than as a profound one – he turns out to be the most serious thinker of the age, masterly in conception – calm – comprehensive — full of his subject – oblivious of self. The world is astounded – all parties by acclaim place him at once at the head of all finance ministers – greater than Peel greater than Pitt – opening a new and enlarged view of the science of taxation. He has amazed us all – truly Lord Derby has chosen his working partners well.

7. I *must* go to the Kildare Club Ball tonight – I hope my last, for really besides being unable just at present to enjoy these gaieties, the extra fatigue is too much. Disturbed nights, a very hot room to sit in, perpetual running up and down stairs with plenty of work in the sick room are enough for a poor body, and the whole night in a hot assembly besides is rather beyond my little strength, for I can't sleep in the morning, I must always get up at my usual time, which of course tells against me. James and Annie have sent me a clever *jeu d'esprit* upon the subject of Janey's admirers – a hurdle race for *the prize* – the horses named after the gentlemen and commented on in jockey style – the odds also calculated. It really is a pity we dare not show it, 'tis so good.

8. Such a Ball – never was there such a one seen in Dublin.* A canopy of light blue with silver fringe hung over the two raised arm chairs prepared for their Excellencies – immediately opposite was a stage for the orchestra. A *bush* of flowering shrubs and statues out of which issued the enlivening sound of Hanlon's band – the folding doors all round were concealed by the red cloth drapery, one opened on an ornamented passage leading to a beautiful drawing room, full of lights and flowers and busts and statues and sofas. Another admitted us to a tent superbly fitted up – another to a *garden* where were ices among the plants. Another led to the long room which was also carpeted, well lighted, with plenty of seats in it, and where was such a supper! on dozens of long tables – every thing in the world that could be thought of. All the Club servants in full dress waited, and many others besides. The Club wore white

tablet linings and waistcoats – the Committee in addition a blue and white favour – all the gentlemen lined their coats, a fashion that should be generally adopted.

Janey danced the whole night, partners in plenty, many of them twice over. I found it dull at first all alone in the crowd, but after a while I found out my few acquaintance and got on comfortably – the gentlemen civilly coming to talk and to conduct me to the refreshment rooms. There was a grand peerage display – lots of tiaras – Lord Clonmel tipsey – nobody else, late as we staid, even unsteady. We were home before five. I was ready by nine for my Aunt's breakfast – then had the clothes to do when the cart came in for Janey was done up – then the storeroom work – then some bills to pay – and now here I am at my post in the sick room, setting down my *stuff* while the Colonel sleeps. I should say that the respectability of the company was one of the reasons of the success of our Ball – we had none of the 'lower spear' present.

9. Morrison's deserted – all the great Balls are over – Castle gone out to the Park – most persons have left town. Lady Milltown and those dear nice girls left yesterday dull enough. I went over to sit the last hour with them, found the girls all heart and my Lady very gracious tho' talking nonsense poor soul about her intentions or her wishes rather – for acts she is denied – so ends their season. She and the girls have been for a few months happy at any rate. My Lord is no worse any way than he was – nor poor Russy, of whom I will not think so ill. Evil may have been thrust on him but it is not *yet* in *him*.

17. If the Tenants pay well all will be right – if they do not we shall be short enough, as the savings on Baltiboys will not tell this half year. Tom Darker must get his salary for the last six months – the Cess and poor's rate and the Kings' annuity have been paid – another gale will see us better off. We are no richer with my dear Aunt than without her while we have the house rent to pay. We are much happier which is worth the odds. I try to manage well but I am not an active housewife, should be a fool in a market, and don't scrimp the servants and so on, then *two* invalids – old and *difficult* both of them, all their lives accustomed to luxuries require

more delicacies than my scanty purse can well afford to give them – then Janey's gaieties, horses &c. I am beginning to feel frightened sometimes – must try and get a cheaper house – there again they can't live in a small one, but £160 makes a hole – heighho.

25. Yesterday my Mother died, 'passing away' my brother says 'as if merely falling asleep', just four years after my father.

29. This bright Saturday is her funeral. All her descendants within reach are there, Mr. Gardiner, Tom, John and Trevor, James King and Jack. We have heard twice from Jane who was quite bewildered at first by the suddenness of the shock, for her death was totally unexpected.

31. My poor Mother, her troubled existence is over, and with the exception of her very early youth, probably the few years just passed were among the happiest of her long much vexed life – no – India was her heaven, she really had a happy life there. The last year here was nothing for she was barely conscious of existing.

FRIDAY, JUNE 4. Poor Mrs. O'Reilly was here a few mornings ago with Pysie. The wretched little baby has had the smallpox and very badly – it was that kept them so long away. Pysie was at Russsborough for a week and looks all the better for it. My Lord has gone to London to try to negotiate a loan at four percent to pay off his heavy debts at six – and finds it difficult – the loans being obtained by his man of business from his friends or himself maybe, therefore he don't assist the probability of a lowered interest. John Robinson has offered to go with me to Baltiboys to receive the rents – so very kind in him as there may be disagreeable business to do – also it will keep all the tenants in better order to find him still at the head of matters.

6. [My mother] lies in hallowed ground, not in the wild graveyard of our beautiful Rothiemurchus but yet in her adopted country, on the banks of the pretty stream she often looked at from the windows of the first house she ever called her own, the one in Charlotte Square where Jane and I were born. And he – what rocky cave holds his remains, or are they tossing still around that stormy Cape – an ocean grave – appalling – I never thought so shudderingly of it before. He that thought the rude corner where lie his ancestors too

publick, and chose a little knoll among the lochans seen through the birch trees on Aunt Mary's walk as the spot he should like to be deposited in. And Mary, the child, the only child they lost. She lies at Avranches, in the English corner of the cemetery with none belonging to her near her – *her* children, one at Bath, one in Blesington churchyard – what does it matter.

We do not lose them, they are more ours often than while they live. Old age need not be dreary, yet when I think of happiness I think of my children young, in the nursery days, then is their Mother's paradise. As they grow, they grow *from* us – naturally – I now in the silent night go back in thought to Baltiboys – my girls upon their donkeys, Jack with his little plays – or to Pau where all six danced together. And now Janey a staid wifie in far Calcutta, Johnny at Hobartstown in his *Fantôme*, my baby a school boy – Annie married – only Janey still ours – the home circle gone, but the dear young people composing it are happy, their turn for action has come and we old bodied are nearly ready to retire to leave room for them. I am dull tonight and yet I should not be, for how many blessings surround me and mine.

They are shutting up at Morrison's, I hear the great doors bang – announcing midnight. Mr. Owen is there with Lord Milton* who is canvassing Wicklow County with Mr. Hume. He ran over tonight to secure the Colonel's vote and the votes of his tenantry, and amused me by having his *list* all ready for me to take with me tomorrow. I am sick of politicks. Goodnight my own dear Jack, for all this is for you – you might find it a friend in need some day – sell it – have it revised and abridged or weeded – then publish like the rest of the world nowadays, and *fund the proceeds*. Always en-crease your Capital my boy, and do with your income what you like, 'in all honesty'.

8. John Robinson and I went and came in a downpour and had a downpour all day yesterday, yet we made out our journey well. We started before seven, got home easily in three hours, none of the tenants being ready we were detained, sending here and there and waiting between awhiles. People all hopeful and paying well, the *reduced* rents. Better thus than a nominal rental grudgingly paid, kept back, uncertain.

A few have small sums yet to bring and Rutherfurd brought nothing.

10. Yesterday we drove in the Park, the day and the scenery equally beautiful. We could have fancied ourselves miles and miles away from any town while in the wild upper end of that immense space of ground. We paid a short visit to the little soldier boys who were all at play so merrily and came as tamely up to the carriage as the deer had done, looking up at us with bright intelligent faces, all of them healthy. It is a fine institution that Hibernian school. The Serjeant on duty told us they were not all obliged to enter the army afterwards – those disinclined to military service were provided for in trades more to their liking.

Jane has written daily in improving spirits – she is very busy setting my poor Mother's affairs, whose kind intentions in our favour we must be grateful for as showing her affection for us. There will be much less to divide amongst us than she supposed, owing to some negligence on my father's part. She really leaves in money £600 and a claim for £550. Of the £600 it is supposed that the expenses of her funeral, doctors, mourning &c. will take near £200, and the remainder may be claimed by my father's creditors owing to this mistake. Of the £550 also she will only be allowed a proportion so that her kind legacies will be much reduced in amount.

13. Friday we all went down to Kingstown by the train and had a fine fresh walk on the jetty, which quite revived my Aunt, but I fear was rather too cold for the Colonel as he was hoarse again in the evening and very thirsty, longing for champaign, bitter beer &c., which I attributed to his abominable pickles, and messes of liver and vinegar and so on: perhaps all these imprudences together.

Unfortunately the ways of my two patients do not *dovetail* – she is early, he is late – she likes bracing, he must have coddling, she is all alive and he is much asleep. Both expect me always at their side, it is difficult to manage between them sometimes. The Doctor came up Thursday morning. He is perfectly civil in manner now, an improvement to this *Irishman* all over. Clever brains and warm heart and impulsive temper, and an egotistick self-sufficiency beyond idea – in his case increased by hereditary mental infirmity, capital good Doctor however. How foolish I was to imagine him more than this. Now it is little matter, my play is very near played. I shall soon be the old lady on the shelf of little more use to any one.

16. Parliament to be dissolved on the 29th. Poor Lord John making another miserable exhibition of his mortification. Feargus O'Connor*, whom they have put up as a lunatick, is only more offensive because more noisy – there is as little judgement shown by the one as the other. It must be very distressing to his friends if he has any. Our Irish affairs are doing very well – Rome has *helped* us. It is I hear a fact that the emigration is as much to be quit of the priests as for other reasons – and we know that on reaching America the people turn Protestants in great numbers in some cases writing home to their friends to come out *ready turned* as better for them. The Altars are now fulminating rhapsodies against Emigration – it has diminished clerical incomes not a little – some priests emigrated with their flocks – turned with them – married! and set up farming. The conversions are going on steadily to a wonderful extent aided by this new piece of Romish tyranny. *Educated* men will not bear slavery.

20. News none – all going well, particularly in Ireland where people have not been so content, so quiet, so prosperous since Sir Robert Peel's days. There are several reasons for this – first a strong government that it is well known is afraid of nobody and won't be trifled with – composed *throughout* of men of talent, of influence, of a higher grade in every point, than are to be found on the other side. Second an honest Lord Lieutenant, no politician – rich and very hospitable – with a kind frank manner and a very clear head. Third – the Papal movement which has disgusted all sects. Fourth – the sale of the Incumbered Estates: so one with another the Times mending. *Our* estate is not sold yet though – the King concern, Castle Daly, is and the promised £100 paid to James – but for want of his regular allowance it was forestalled of course. The O'Brien sale is put off until November, and foolish James *will* live like a rich man. Baltiboys will therefore not assist him – *If* it don't further

incumber him! I don't make myself uneasy – he don't – there are no children – and Annie will always have a home. And James will always have the world on his side – his father's conduct being indefensible, living most luxuriously himself – denying himself and his daughters nothing – however expensive their whims may be. Giving his only son, his married son, whose marriage he approved and attended, never a penny unless it be actually squeezed out of him, and worse than all resorting to quibble to justify this. An odious old man – Deranged undoubtedly – A family weakness increased by ignorance and most inordinate vanity. What on earth are such idiots good for.

We have such a clever book just now – tiresome rather too, but so full of good sound common sense, wittily brought forward that 'tis quite a sunshiny reading – by Mr Haliburton, Sam Slick – *The Old Judge* 'tis called, and describes a year in Nova Scotia in an odd rambling way, with such a clever undercurrent of wise notes fully as applicable to Ireland as to N. America that I can't but wish much of it were used as a text book by our rising generation*. I do think we do want the practical men in high places – and let the Peerage go to the Opera. They can't be much longer tolerated where they are by this awakening world.

27. [My Aunt] don't like a country life at all – she has set her heart on Merrion Square. Still I must not encumber the family finances.

For your sake dear Jack, I shall some time set down the particulars – you must never trust your kind and agreeable brother-in-law in money matters, nor ever let him usurp authority – he does it too readily and makes a mess of it. I steadily keep him from all interference in our affairs – utter ruin would be the consequence otherwise. Remember this – he means no harm, but – he has a hasty temper as well as a meddling disposition – he will always be in money difficulties whatever his income – and *intending* some fine day to put all right, on a stormy one would, I fear, not scruple to set all wrong. I may judge him too severely, yet while wishing to excuse, there rise up grave doubts, all unwillingly too. You and I were talking on this subject so lately that my head is full of it.

How happy your poor father looked as you stood by the side of his sick bed, and what a contrast – the pale worn fading form of the old man extended on what had just been the couch of pain – the gay school boy all alive with health and spirits, standing erect as preparing for the race his father has nearly run. You will remember this meeting – my own dear boy be but as good a man – I can wish no more for you – and you will.

29. Might be worried to death if I were to mind all the whims I meet with – but I won't – I'll do all that can be done to make all happy, but I'll always think well over all demands in the quiet of my own room before consenting to fresh demands. Catherine Hyland was here yesterday about emigrating to Australia, and the Widow McNally this morning about getting poor little Sarah Jane into the Protestant Orphan Asylum. They want females in Australia, and will give a free passage to all they can get who are decent. I must go to the office and make more particular enquiries.

THURSDAY, JULY 1. Rainy – went about the orphan, saw Mr. Wolseley who was very obliging. At the too celebrated St. Vincent's hospital, the Sisters of Mercy had made a Roman Catholic of James McNally during the last week of his life.

2. Fine. Mrs. O'Reilly and Pysie came to stay the day. Pysie went with me to verify McNally's death. We went over some of the sick wards, the Institution seems to be admirably conducted. One can fancy nothing more perfect if they would but let their proselyting alone. A very happy set of nuns, they seem fat, merry, well fed, and not a bit more truthful that those of their faith generally are, fond of news – quite dissatisfied with their new Archbishop, a proud, pompous, disagreeable man*. But what matters this opinion, supposing it universal – there he is and there he must stay – to work as much mischief as possible. That trial of Dr. Achilli should open some eyes – what vile secrets are unfolded.

3. Nice riots at Stockport between the two faiths. Those silly or wicked priests would march about in procession with all their mummeries directly in the face of the late proclamation forbidding such shows on account of the danger of a riot in consequence. There has been some loss of life – great

destruction of property, wounds &c. The lower orders never can stop short of murder when their bad blood is up and just now these Popish attempts are maddening John Bull*.

4. Sunday – very hot – Church suffocating. A Circular private and confidential, begging for money of course, from Sir Edward Kennnedy's Committee. He is up for the County Kildare, such an absurd representative. However, he will vote for Lord Derby – that means in these times for rent, and quiet and good faith and property, so I suppose one must squeeze out a few pounds. One or two names to humble sums give me courage, otherwise £25, £50, £100, £200 looked alarming.

These aggressive movements on the part of the R. Cath. clergy oblige people to look about them. We shall be obliged if their follies continue to settle the point at once and let them understand again that this is a Protestant country in which they are only tolerated – on conditions – and they will never be permitted to reign. They are helping our cause in all ways by their assumptions, by their bigotry, and by the revelations of their own witnesses in that trial, forced on by their own spirit of vindictive persecution. Dr. Achilli, long imprisoned by the Inquisition for his heretical opinions, on regaining his freedom left their church, professed himself a Protestant, married, took pupils, and laid himself out to proselyte his countrymen wherever his wanderings carried him. His success in London was so great that Dr. Newman, the celebrated Oxford pervert, equally zealous on his part for the faith he had gone over to, lent himself out of jealousy or enthusiasm to the plot of Rome to destroy this very clever revealer of her secrets. The Pope's Secretary Cardinal Wiseman and some unscrupulous Roman Catholic attorney are understand to have been the principal movers of this most disgusting business. The man's life from his earliest days was scrutinised hour by hour almost as no man's could well bear sifting – and to support the odious accusations, twenty-nine in number, brought forward against him. They raked up from the stews [brothels], the wine shops, the galleys even, a cloud of witnesses such as have not polluted a court of justice since the days of Queen Caroline* – whose evidence no *reader* of it could believe. Neither did the Jury – every charge but one they found not proven – that one relating to the sentence of the Inquisition they allowed.

It has been, fortunately for the world, a most damaging issue to the Papist cause. Supposing the charges true, they prove a degree of profligacy among the priesthood utterly frightful to contemplate, joined with the fact that these crimes are winked at, connived at, concealed, and never punished – and dare not be brought forward against them by their victims. Supposing them false, as an English Jury has found them, it reveals the startling fact that perjury is neither scarce nor dear in Italy, and that for its own purposes her own church will buy it wholesale. Is it not the same here – a Roman Catholic on a jury frustrates all hope of justice in political or polemical matters. I don't myself believe that Dr. Achilli was purer in his manners than other monks, though far from being so vile as they would paint him. Probably too he may affect great Protestant zeal – most converts do – and they find plenty to applaud their enthusiasm. But he has certainly come out of the mud less defiled than have any of those who pushed him into it, or who 'for the love of the Mother Church' invented such atrocities against him. This is the universal judgement.*

5. Summer weather – Jane off tomorrow to Castle Leod to be out of the way of the Election. Mr. Macaulay has been asked to stand – after a little coquetting he consented – so they wish to bring him in with a large majority.* James Craig of course remains to help the Committee.

7. Mrs. McNally has been successful, so our trouble has not been for nothing. She has to appear again with the child on the first Tuesday in August when a number of necessary forms will be completed, but she says the name was written down yesterday and 'admitted' after it. If my emigration affairs succeed as well as this we shall have really done a little good.

9. Here we are at dear Baltiboys – came down yesterday – and though somehow my dear old Aunt was the least inclined to move, she seems about the best pleased to be here. The drive was very pleasant though hot enough, the country in great

beauty, this pretty place never looked prettier. My Aunt is in real truth quite charmed with it, so much exceeding any ideas she had formed of our mountain scenery. I don't think she will be so anxious to dismantle the house here now that she finds it so worthy of admiration. Nothing can be nicer than the management, neater, more tasteful, more comfortable, more economical. Our host and hostess shine at home. Poor James, it was a shame to bring him up so badly and 'tis a pity he belongs to such a wretched set – a whole lot of people without half a quarter of an ounce of brains amongst them. It feels odd to be visiting, but so happy to have our children here, not strangers, and to be *all* together once more – during these bright summer days in our own home. Let me rejoice in the present with a grateful heart, and leave the future to the Direction of the Almighty. Hal is so happy here, his spirits during the drive, his delight on arriving, his whole air this morning – it is as if he were young and strong again. And the Doctor has just been to see him which has pleased him so – queer as usual, where I am concerned, ashamed and not knowing how to get out of his scrape, though we do all we can to help him – poor, good, foolish, ill-tempered Doctor, I made him shake hands with me!! Goose and a half.

10. Now Jack and I are off on a lounging walk to Russborough – all in good humour there – I had two hours full of confidences before the rest arrived, and then my Aunt had to see the house, the trinkets, the millinery – and was made a present of a purse! I fear the wonderful loan is humbug. It was announced as settled, and now there is a hitch. My Lord's journey too was curiously timed to suit Ascott. He squandered on the trip a couple of hundred pounds between his own expenses and the many costly presents he brought back to his ladies. Senseless to the end, *she* says. A quarter of the money would have filled Russborough three or four times with eligibles among the company, some one of whom might have continued a profitable acquaintance with his daughters – or, thought I, it would have helped to redeem the honour of his son. I believe the whole property will be put up for sale out and out immediately – the best way perhaps – the only way probably – the creditors being worn out.

11. A quiet country Sunday – all at peace – no sound but the rippling of the little river or the buzzing of a fly, here where I sit at the open window of the end room, now mine. I am not accustomed to this view – it surprises me with its grave beauty – the ground falling to the water – green covered with fine old trees – the wooded banks beyond – the fields rising again on that other side up to the ridge which separates us from Kildare. What a lovely summer – all the crops look well – most of the hay is made – the fruit only ripening but abundant – all looking well – even the elections – spite of the bullying of the priests on *both* sides. The R. C. clergy are like maniacs – from the hustings, from their altars, from cabin to cabin, raging, threatening, *lying*, and Tresham Gregg's [an extreme evangelical clergyman] display at the nomination for Dublin equally disgraceful to a Christian minister. That laymen should show themselves in earnest is all right – and in the struggle between the creeds which will convulse Europe for a while we must permit the clergy of each party to use all influence with their flocks, but they should be prohibited from these outrageous exhibitions by which really the peace of the publick is endangered. Now for Blesington Church where the service is performed so much more to my mind than anywhere else I know of. There is Annie singing all over the house – dear happy child – her lot is all sunshine.

12. If I were asked to define happiness just now, I should say the life we are leading – 'tis a touch of heaven! By the bye, everybody else is in heaven – such a victory in Dublin – Reynolds sent to the right about – Vance and Grogan elected – Liverpool was a victory, but Dublin is a grand victory – out and out – the two Protestant candidates coming in with a very large majority* – a turn in the tide certainly which must lead to good, as it will influence all the other elections, and as it proves that the Irish mind is at length progressing – emancipating itself from the tyranny of the priesthood. Oxford is the next point of interest – to rescue it from the Tractarians – and it is feared their numbers and their artifices may succeed.

16. John Fitzpatrick is very busy getting his preparations forward for Australia – I hope he may succeed, for he will much

benefit all his family, and he is a discontented peevish sickly creature, unfit for hard work in this climate.

17. Miladi here yesterday. A bright thought struck all, to lend her our town house for the three last days of next week when there are two parties at the Park, and so save her nine guineas. There is a hitch about the loan – something beyond *her* ken, and now the story is that *all* will be sold under the incumbered estates Act – Russborough and pictures, as many as are left, and all. Jack has made up his mind to go to India if we can get him a Writership. I have nothing to say against this, nothing better to propose to him instead, since the happy life of a country gentleman farming his own land is distasteful to him. He has no objection to this in the end, to return to this pretty place which he dearly loves, but young like he must see the world, not vegetate – wander abroad – view – learn – earn a little addition to his patrimony. So many relations in India – his cousins &c., he thinks he should like to pass his working days there. If the plan disappoints him he can return, for by the new regulations Pensions are now awarded in the East India service for *terms* of years – he would get £500 after ten years – and that may do if he be prudent and avoid all debt. He is to consider this scheme well for another year and then we must prepare to act – my indolence must get a shake and my selfish affection be concealed.

23. The Colonel up early, and at ten o'clock he and his son and his son-in-law off to Naas to vote for Sir Edward Kennedy. There are great fears the little body will be beat, the priests have been so very busy, no clergy should be allowed to interfere – one can't prevent their influence in private, but certainly these publick displays of ultra zeal, priests leading up strings of voters with shouts and gestures to the polling booths as pigs are driven along the roads to market is quite a scandal.

25. We depend on the newspapers . . . and just now they tell of nothing but Elections. How these will turn out who can say, there is no calculating upon votes in these days of changing opinions. One thing seems clear enough, that a grand religious struggle is approaching and time for it – the result

being very certain once the determined Protestant feeling is aroused, but the contest will be troublesome. The Irish Election riots are disgraceful to civilisation. Useless, barbaric – one thing they most surely demonstrate that this fine *pesanthry* are as yet unfit for power of any kind and should not have it given to them, and that the priestly system should be a little looked after. What scandals it causes. Dublin County is reported to be safe, the majorities for Taylor and Hamilton very large, four or five hundred, and Kildare 'tho lost by votes, will be regained by an accident, some requisite formalities having been forgotten by poor Henchy*. He is out of pocket £2,000 and can ill spare it.

27. Lady Millown and her girls were here yesterday to thank for her lodgings. She was charmed with the comfort of the house and the excellence of the servants. She is however in very low spirits, the whole property is advertised for sale. She don't like showing herself, so sends the girls with Mrs. Lawless to next week's entertainments. 'Utterly ruined' were her words, he having encumbered her jointure, and deeply, unknown to her. Of course she could set aside these arrangements, but would it be well to do so – it is a balance of evil either way.

29. Janey and I dined at Russborough and found it pleasant as in old times – Him in his most courteous mood, Her very gracious. The girls had gone off to [Castle] Lyons in great glee – alone for the first time in their lives. We had Ogle Moore and wife, Walter de Burgh and wife, John Hornidge and the Warden – a very agreeable party. Mr. and Mrs. de Burgh called here on their way and staid above an hour. She is really very nice, most cheerful and amusing. He is clever – very gentlemanly, but odd, very odd. All the family are eccentrick – he has however once or twice gone rather beyond that. I have just finished an interesting book, a Swedish tale *The Birthright*. Besides an agreeable introduction to a society quite differently constituted from ours, the story is well managed, the characters well brought out, the moral tone good. We have sent for another work by the same author, Isabella Carlen, liking this so much.

31. I sit here in my dear end room catching all the moments to myself that can thus be gained this holiday time. The view

from the window always beautiful, always varying – I lose hours were all my stray minutes of gazing added up honestly, just sitting beside it lost in thought, trying to prepare a much tried heart for coming trials. I read a good deal too, brought my dear *Lord Jeffrey* with me, and dream while reading his letters with dim eyes that my ears still listen to that mind pouring out its treasures as in old sunny days, when he and Jane and I wandered through the woods of Corstorphine hill, or sat on the benches he had placed along his walks, or lay upon the grass beneath the beeches.

We were favoured in our youth, we grew up in an atmosphere of talent and liberal feelings and kindly ones too. Have we profitted as we might have done – Alas no! It may be all right within, but is it practically carried out into the working day world to the benefit of all around us. It seems that we require two natures – the contemplative and the active. A fair union one can hardly look for – how necessary both – each quality requiring the spur and the check of the other – and after all not much can be done in a lifetime – 'tis here a little and there a little with a throwback often. The millennium is very distant – I wonder dear Jack whether you will find the world any nearer to it when you are reading this.

THURSDAY, AUGUST 5. Here we are in dirty dusty Dublin and find it less disagreeable than we expected. I do think the Colonel's cough better, but I don't think he will stay long to try the change for he is packing his portmanteau already. Dr. Robinson wishes him to remain in the hills till the end of the month and then go to the sea, which I can manage as I have sold the little carriage for £20 only. Little Sarah McNally admitted to the Asylum, Mr. Latouche so very kindly wrote me word of this himself, this is a great comfort.

9. Jane was to dine on Thursday at Aviemore where she and Mr. Craig will spend a few days for the purpose of reconnoitring at Rothiemurchus. They seem to have much the same to do there that occupies us here. Remove the squatters, idlers, overplus, who as here are very much disinclined to make way for their betters. It is well we have the safety valve of Emigration – they are resorting to it in Scotland fully as much as we have done, and really I believe un-

necessarily. Could we but make the upper classes rational and the lower classes intelligent.

11. Heard from Jane today from Aviemore – a rough sketch of first impressions – very interesting – details will follow. She never saw Rothiemurchus looking so beautiful. The Duchess [of Bedford] is there* – all kindness – wants them to live with her- will make them dine with her – they accepted twice, but it is painful somehow – besides they are tired after wandering about all day, and prefer a quiet evening in their inn. The dear old Doune, what a happy family once dwelt there – how much wit and fun and learning and elegance and ease once found a bright home there. Of the early set, our dear Aunt Bourne alone is left. Of the late set how few remain and how they are scattered – poor William a wanderer, almost outcast – John so far away – I here – Mary and my father and mother gone – only Jane to stick by the Duchess – and well she does her work – her self imposed task. What would have become of place and people but for her. Will Johnny ever earn his beautiful inheritance, he knows its price well. I shall be a very prosy old woman by and bye, that's plain. Dear Jack, when you read these old journals on your Indian couch you'll smile at your mother's many follies, as you do now sometimes, you monkey. You are three impudent brats and I'm going to give up caring for you.

17. So – *I* think [the Colonel's] strength failing – but all is going right. As no one will see this but you dear Jack, I will mention your father's condition correctly that you may understand what he has gone through, and may know how little chance there could be of his bearing up long against such a complication of complaints. Asthma for years has affected the chest, one lung is gone, a rupture on each side, a tenderness where he sits, kidneys wrong, and now a complicated stricture*. There might be a thousand such like cases and not one as bad as this. Men of fifty have sunk under less – [James William] Cusack [Surgeon to Queen Victoria] gave him but five days of life – Dr. Robinson says weeks. He will come again on Friday when he can better judge how he is going on, and then we shall decide on the best plan for ensuring him most comfort for the rest of his life.

19. I heard from my dear sister Jane saying all that is most kind. I have plenty of money, the pay due now – sold the little carriage and all the harness, and £20 forced on me by the Doctor, poor man, and which, tho' not exactly wanting, I took under all circumstances. The fees are not quite as high as I expected – Mr. Porter takes but £2 – no medicines – and not much expense of any other kind, still money goes – if it could bring us health, what matter.

22. A great racket in the street this evening – 'tis the first day of Donnybrook fair which lasts a week from *Sunday* to *Sunday*. To judge from the singing, shouting, screaming emanating from all the merry carloads of the returning company, Father Matthew is forgotten* – no quarrelling however, good humoured folly so far. I have been finishing today a very clever novel, *The Wilmingtons*, of a very charming writer, Mrs. Marsh, well and powerfully written in many parts and deeply interesting.

WEDNESDAY, SEPTEMBER 1, Baltiboys. My Colonel is sleeping after his breakfast. My Aunt is in a novel in her room. My children are off on an open car to join a Downshire picnic at the Seven Churches. All alone, therefore, I may have time, dear Jack, to set down a few hints that I much wish to give you. They may catch your eye here should my journal be all the mother left you when you will be acting for yourself. Were you not to know my honest opinion of a connexion very likely to influence you, consequences might ensue which would hurt your character and perhaps embarrass your circumstances. I have not formed this judgement hastily, long and careful observation and a good deal of experience personally of the effects of the very serious faults of your really amiable and very agreeable brother-in-law oblige me to warn you against having any business transactions with him. Meaning well to everybody, and very likely to us, he offends perpetually from two or three causes not likely at his age to admit of a cure.

Before alluding to these faults I shall mention the excuses to be made for his possessing them, as only fair, for naturally his dispositions are the best. He has been all his life subject to evil influences. His father, a vain and weak and narrow-minded, ill-tempered man, far from being a guide or an example to his children, can only have been feared by them, never respected, and filled with absurd notions of his own consequence from a connection by the maternal side with some families recently ennobled, and destitute of any sterling qualities, he as it were poisoned the moral atmosphere around him. His mother, of a higher nature rather, is still an uneducated woman, without energy to take or keep her own place or exert herself in any way for the well being of her children. They appear to have no acquaintance, this pair, either with books or men – formed no society to belong to – have no friends, few acquaintance. Poor James King had thus no *home* – worse than no home – it was a home he hated, and took occasion to leave for one hardly better, his good aunt's. Her easiness and kindness and overstrained piety without counteracting principles, completed the mischief. The wonder is that a boy so badly brought up should have turned out anything short of a scapegrace – his affectionate temper saved him and, perhaps, the discipline of a publick school.

His marriage has much improved him – the constant companionship of such a mind as his young wife's is hourly improving him. Also the tone of our family and friendly circle has had its effect, and I think were his affairs, his money affairs, more settled, he would with his abilities and natural love for the right, avoid going so far wrong as I now think he does. The seeds of many of his father's vices are there, he is vain, ostentatious, prejudiced, supercilious, despotick and not delicate in some of his assumptions of authority in this house, lent to him with its furniture. In this place he is managing with near £300 worth of stock still unpaid for – and not in my mind upright in his money dealings. His father is to blame certainly, he never gave him any money generously or even justly – he never made him a fixed allowance – sums smaller or larger were coaxed or cajoled or bullied out of him, according to the temper the son found him in. The Aunt too when she adopted him pursued much the same plan in her gentler manner. She gave uncertainly, she lent without requiring repayment, endorsed bills she had afterwards to take up herself.

Now this is where I want to caution you – and to beg of

you to make my memory a solemn promise to endorse no bills for him or anybody. Here is where I find most fault with my son-in-law – he lives beyond his means, he borrows from you or me when in a hurry for money without being sure of repaying us – without caring very much whether he does repay us provided we don't dun [ask for payment] him. He tells us he lives within his promised income tho' beyond his actual one. Then I say a high-handed man would contract his expenditure till his means improved. I hope that you, my own dear upright boy, your honest, manly father's son, would under such circumstances keep no hunters, no carriage horses, no man servants, rather than owe the money for their food to your tradesmen, and the loose silver in your pocket to your mother-in-law. I do not like that want of rectitude in any matter, and I cannot avoid fearing it may lead to serious evil.

To prevent this evil ever reaching you is my sole reason for setting down these cautionary hints – remember this – no one can help a spendthrift, the spendthrift may ruin others with himself, but you know all the water in the Liffey will never fill a sieve. So my dear Jack be wise – help your kind – help even the less worthy if you can really advantage them, but don't let them meddle with you. In all your affairs be guided by the great principles of truth and justice, which is truth in action. Think for yourself – decide leisurely and peremptorily so that all may understand you are Master of your own. Never act till after deliberate consideration – always for reasons, never from prejudices, and keep out of debt and independant. Now is this not a prose and a half from poor dear over-anxious mammy.

4. Another quiet morning gives me leisure to read over my 'warning'; though it may appear harsh it is nevertheless true. There is in truth a want of sterling quality in the character I have dissected. Who can say at what stage may come the stop, a little moral courage at the beginning, the stern determination to *do right*, to make no compromise with evil, would save the happiness of many families.

Your poor Grandfather Grant and your Uncle William are cases in point. To seem what they were not they sacrificed their own respectability and ruined those they loved best. It began in both with debts contracted almost in their boyhood for the merest nonsense, to redeem which without *self* sacrifice they plunged on year by year deeper into difficulties, betraying trusts, deceiving friends, and your Uncle speculating like any common gambler with money not his own. Had anyone foretold this when young and gay he bought what he could not pay for, how he would have scouted the idea of *his* honour being ever tarnished. He had the same habit I so much condemn in James of taking a few pounds or a few shillings from any of us – never dreaming of repayment nor always employing these accidental supplies wisely. Both knew that we who lent could ill afford the loan, but *self* predominated and an action I call mean, if not dishonest, resulted.

In the case of my son-in-law I do not mean to encourage such improprieties. What I have already lent him, the small sums I mean, has been out of my own private funds – what I had saved from my purse and my brains money. Your father's trust in me has never been deceived, I scrupulously respect his confidence in my worthiness. The larger sum, what James owes for his purchase of stock at our sale, I have entered regularly in my books and in a private account with him. If he do not repay it now by degrees as he promised, you will be no loser, for it will be deducted from what I shall have in my power to bequeath by and bye to Annie of my own. As to the inconvenience of this arrangement, and the loss on the whole transaction, your father made this marriage himself totally against my opinion, and therefore he must lay his account with suffering a little from the consequences.

I am rather annoyed with James just now, so perhaps too hard on him. He has with rather indelicate precipitation made several changes in the disposition of the grounds, not only unauthorised by me but disagreeable to me, and in one instance in direct opposition to my strongly expressed will. He has cut down several trees – one group of Scotch fir in particular which your father planted in fun, close to the window that I might always see my countrymen.* This has exceedingly hurt me, as have also some slighting expressions with regard to our taste, our style, the shabby furniture, the bad soil, the poor stock, vulgar servants &c. &c., of all of which I take no outward notice, having a horrour like the French of any family *scandale* - but I can't avoid being impressed unfavourably by the want of good feeling, and good breeding, thus exhibited. There is a deal of the odious old father in the son, but we will weed the good soil yet.

Janey quite shares my opinions, and shows it rather warmly too at times – her young nature firing up a little at ingratitude. My Aunt thinks Annie slightly affected by her husband's low standard ideas, I do not. I think her less rational, less domestick, less of the active poor man's wife, and more taken up with the names of those noble relations, she don't see much of the bodies belonging to them, than she ought to be who has so many of her own of a much higher grade – but she will 'right again' like the well built ships, and so I leave them to earn their own experience, once again cautioning you to avoid any business transactions with her husband.

5. Matters went a little wrong last night so it was lucky the Doctor came out early this Sunday morning. How strange it seems in me to write so calmly of all the ins and outs of this lingering tragedy. I don't feel the less, it is in my nature to be calm, patient, composed – to set facts before me – to get at the truth, and to do the best I can under the circumstances. Ever since I first set seriously to the work of subduing all that was rebellious in me, ever since my first sorrow, now a lifetime ago, than which no other has ever been so sharp, I have kept the tight rein over feelings, and elevated duties into their right place, and been all the happier, certainly the more useful.*

I read a good deal in our sick room, not much aloud, he don't remember well enough, a bit from here and there or a few verses from the New Testament suffice for him, but to myself I can often read while sitting beside him. We have had since my last Review *Margaret Maitland,** very pretty quaintly written in the peculiar style of an elderly Scotch maiden gentlewoman, yet unnatural too, and the first number of *Uncle Tom's Cabin* – a slave story now making a very great noise – 50,000 copies sold in eight weeks in America and going off in the like rocket style here. It is so far admirable.

12. We are in hope to get Joshua O'Reilly out to Australia before Xmas. My Aunt will give him £20 – Lady Milltown has made £10 for him by selling her butter – I have been this twelve month saving all the Colonel's old clothes and can give a trifle towards one best suit, so I do trust the poor young man may get away to begin life well in that better field at this time when labour of every sort is at a premium there. The younger brother Eyre, who is articled to an Attorney, will be out of his time this summer and will probably follow, and then they can send for the poor much tried mother, Pysie and her two destitute boys, and all meet again more happily. That at least is our vision.

Those most abominable Irish priests, wretched, ignorant fanaticks. The two who figured at Sixmile Bridge are proceeded against, their transportation will probably quiet their class. It has become a tyranny insupportable, unendurable, not to be borne at any rate by England, this systematick interference in secular matters, this growing attempt to grasp at power – unlimited power. The respectable R. Cath.s are as much annoyed by it as we are, but most of them are such very poor creatures they dare not openly rebel. In the meanwhile Parliament meets and Lord Derby settles how to deal with these gentry, let us look with thankfulness on our fine harvest. Markets are good, people are prosperous – times fairly mending.

Our Lord Lieutenant has taken a house on the hill of Howth, he offered Mr. King £100 a month for St. Fintan's and was refused! He might have given this unexpected windfall to his son, our good kind father – no, he has only purse enough for a trip to England – Harrogate, Cheltenham and so on – a little tour of health all by himself, alone. How happy the mother and the twins will be without him. All this scribbling time the Colonel has been dressing – he is now dressed and I must go – goodbye dear Jack.

19. Sunday again, for I have had no writing time all this week. Our sick room very comfortable. Our nights are now unbroken, I and my machinery only being required now twice a day, morning and evening, to keep matters in order. He has to lay a good half hour each time, at which season I read to him – at night in the Bible, in the morning some

serious book, we have begun with my old favourite Mr.
Wilberforce [see *The Highland Lady in Ireland* pp.1–2].
There is no medicine given beyond a rhubarb pill when
necessary, lime water and soda or potass with milk when
wanted. A very careful diet – a very strict regimen –
cleanliness – cheerfulness – and as much fresh air as we
can insinuate into our rather warm apartment do the rest.
And perhaps the want of the hired nurse tender – the
predictions of the Doctors might possibly have been verified
already had he been confided to the care of that evil branch
of the profession. Our spirits have really risen he is so much
relieved, I almost hope he will thus continue.

We have had our little neighbourhood roused by a Ball
given in the Court House by Mrs. Owen on Friday last – a
gallantry of Mr. Owen's to Miss Cotton. Between forty and
fifty people, band from Dublin, capital supper, and all very
pleasant, though there were disappointments about the
company, the Opera having carried away both *Belles* and
Beaux. My two looked remarkably nice in black lace, their
heads were we thought the prettiest in the room with
garlands of white flowers hanging back from their braided
hair, and Janey named the best dancer by no less a judge
than Lord Downshire – she never missed a dance all night.
They came home at four and gave us all their news before
retiring to repose!

My best news is that Jane promises a visit next month,
really means it – my worst that the poor old Duke of
Wellington is dead – eighty four – epilepsy kills slowly.
Lord Combermere 'tis said succeeds him, *if so* Lord Downshire told Janey he could get Jack a commission, should that
suit his father's views for him. Were there ever such kind
people in the world as we have the luck to fall in with. The
Doctor quite inspired by all the fun of this Ball, staid
chatting about it for an hour! beginning with the Colonel
and me! Our laughter attracted the others, and all entering
and joining, did we not make a scene of it! I have got £1.7.6
for my *Sisters of Charity*, not bad for such a scrap, and some
help to poor Mrs. O'Reilly, it reads very well too.

I walked in to evening church this afternoon, afternoon
service being now at five o'clock. Mr. Fitzgerald came on

with me home as far as the bridge, always agreeable he is and he and I agree on so many subjects. At home all was commotion, the flighty housemaid having got quite tipsy – in that condition she had hurt herself, and she was besides like an insane person. Mr. Payne [the Blessington apothecary] had to be sent for, advised she should be watched and soothed and got quit of in the morning, so she was sent off quite early before her master set out for the fair. 'Much learning seems to have made her mad' for she preached away by the hour like a printed book, giving her opinion on all subjects in a string of the longest words she could cull from the dictionary – all well applied. She had her scheme for regenerating Ireland, and to improve herself seems to have applied to the whiskey bottle, or sometimes to the parlour barrel of bitter beer, as a stomachick. I can't believe she was a good girl, her language when excited was so grossly indecent, some fallen sister, poor creature, who seems to have had better days and has been lost thro' the want of a kindly hand to arrest her downward progress.

24. Tuesday the young set went to town. Every day since we have heard from them, all so happy – that Tuesday they dined at Mr. Sheehan's and then took him with them to the opera – *Don Pasquale*, I think by Donizetti. Grisi a little the worse for wear but still charming, Mario in his zenith, young Lablache very good, several good supporters, orchestra in fine order*. We stay-at-homes have been busy putting the house *in* order after the tipsy housemaid's departure. Janey has got a very nice house indeed for us, furnished comfortably and cheap considering the situation – No. 1 FitzWilliam Place – almost in the square, £170 per annum. We can move into it immediately only having a cook to look for. I have hired Mary Delaney as housemaid. This affair of the house has been a great worry to me, we had quite settled upon an unfurnished one when the Colonel stept in with his veto – he would not have Baltiboys dismantled, so we had to disorder our orders.

The Duke of Wellington has been dead this week and will be buried at the meeting of Parliament publickly, like Nelson; not bad men either of them, not good ones certainly, created by their times, efficient in their day, of use to

their poor generation, nothing to make a fuss about, that
hero style required once, now happily at a discount. The
Duke however was a clever man, a long headed hero, and
passing honest as the world goes.

TUESDAY, OCTOBER 4. 63 Dawson Street, Dublin – some little
matters going rather crooked at Baltiboys, I decided on
bringing my division of the family up to town. On Thursday
the last day of September therefore we left the hills which
the Colonel had begun to find too cold. The atmosphere of
the *house*, however, was *warm* enough, that foolish James
having managed to offend my Aunt by certainly very in-
decorous behaviour.

Monday was Lady Downshire's Ball – the best ever given
anywhere! All the countryside, a few from Dublin, officers
from Naas and Newbridge, about sixty people, good musick
– plenty of lights – quantities of refreshments – excellent
supper, the kindest host and hostess – altogether quite a hit.
Matilda and Emma [King] are disgusted with the Dublin
Balls by comparison. They danced all night, a new thing to
them, poor girls, and none of the party got leave to go home
till 5 o'clock in the morning.

Wednesday night James behaved shockingly – got out of
temper at whist and was so rude to me, so rude to her [Aunt
Bourne] that we ought both of us to have left the table.
James is very silly, he has made an implacable enemy out of a
sure friend. He has also lost me, all for the mean desire to
appear what he is not – a rich man – and 'tis this has soured
his naturally good temper. He must be in difficulties – and
for want of the courage to set himself right he flounders on
into deeper mud. All this made me quit the dear old house
with less reluctance.

We had a fine day, he bore the drive well and has I think
been more alive since returning to this 'dingy' house which
is so very comfortable. We were quite at home in it in a
moment, and though without a cook, get bravely on, invaluable Jane doing everything. The new house is very
cheerful, clean, light, airy, with every convenience, plenty
of water, a pretty garden behind, and on every day of the
year a dry walk on the flags all the way down from Merrion
Square to Leeson Street, sheltered from the east wind too,

but it is small, the rooms are good enough but there are few of them, and the Colonel and I have to put up with indifferent accommodation. The dining room is given to him, a good room but no bedroom comforts in it, and I can be no nearer him than the little return on the stairs, an inconvenience with his peculiar ailments, and I doubt my keeping well there, however it can't be helped. Every one else is well off. We pay £10 more for that house than for this, and have to keep the garden in order besides, and last night says my Aunt 'the house in Dublin I wish to live in is 20 Merrion Square North' – £175 a year unfurnished.

10. Another busy week has glided by, and here we are in No. 1 FitzWilliam Place. A good move on the whole I well believe, but to me troublesome, expensive, and so far uncomfortable. However each returning day improves our position – we unpack, put away, change and so in time shall settle. Last Sunday and last Monday I had to lay up, having overdone my strength standing for five hours taking up the inventory of this house. Tuesday we moved – such a job – two drays of John Robinson's made two journeys, Morrison's porter helping to load and unload.

20. Poor Journal – no news publick or private I can now remember so that nothing very interesting could have happened. We have all got fixed down in our places and feel at home – the pure air and the dry street and the plenty of light, together with the good storeroom and the excellent accommodation of all kinds in that department having reconciled me to the change of house. When we get a little more taste applied to the air of our apartments I shall feel quite satisfied. On Saturday last we were revived in earnest as dear Jane arrived, earlier than we expected having a fine passage in the *Herald*, that swiftest of steamers.

29. All alone again – Jane and her best of husbands started at ten o'clock yesterday morning for Belfast, where they would dine and rest and then steam off at night with the mail. I could not enjoy their visit though I felt very grateful for it, I really was too ill to feel anything on earth but languor in the intervals of pain, nor shall I be well for some little time, though thanks to Jane I am certainly in the way to be better.

Miladi and the girls came over one morning to call and,

My Lord being in Dublin, they staid to dinner – were as merry as crickets and wrote a glowing account of their pleasant evening to the poor 'Aunt Fanny' [Mrs. O'Reilly].

Poor indeed just now in purse and spirits, for a relation who always promised her a legacy has died and left her £10 – a new will made during his last sickness by the advice of his heir – a former will not destroyed assured her £500. Poor Jos. and I talking over the disappointment agreed that maybe it is just as well – had this little sum of money come to them they might have been induced to stock the Kilkenny estate and muddle away at farming all there together. As it is he must exert himself and start for Australia, where the field for all labour is so open at present. He has made up his mind to do this, and as soon as he has arranged his Mother's affairs as satisfactorily as is in his power, he will sail for the gold regions.

I often wish for one week, one day, of Miss Coutts' purse* – not having that I must exert myself too – spare to spend, and spend with prudence. We shall lose some income when Kinloss is sold, the mortgage thereon pays 4% – more than 3% is difficult to get in these days, and the funds is nonsense – above par now and expected to yield but two and a half percent next year. Our small household is very economically conducted just now, few servants – none at high wages – no gaiety. Still, all of us being invalids in separate rooms, many luxuries in the eating way are required, and there is very great expenditure of coals and candles – also separate breakfasts, separate luncheons, an immensity of little items to swell the whole. So as the two ends of the year meet I don't much care – debt I never will get into.

My brother John is the Secretary for Bengal, the chief in that department, indeed I fancy the most influential man in the Government, £5,000 a year, leading to Council, which is 10,000 for five years – he surely must make money now. The younger brother thus fairly on the road to affluence, the elder is now employed in securing the little fortune of his wife, on feus in Glasgow – some £7,000 – and hoping to buy the income up for his own life at her earnest desire – the outside £300 a year, poor William, who began so well. But this is a subject I must not think of – we know not *how* he was tempted – we who were never tempted ourselves.

31. There will be a little money [from her mother's estate] which shall be left in brother [in law] James'[Gibson Craig] hands for some rainy day – or for you, you monkey, when you make your start in life. Jane is so wise as well as kind, her superiour character never struck me more than at this meeting when business matters of very great importance had to be discussed amongst us, and she has got poor Uncle Ralph's money secured to him at once. It has made me happier than I well can tell to have seen this little business thus happily settled.

We mean to take care that Mrs. Cottam [his daughter] shall know it – and shall know that we know that she knows it – in order that she may check her propensity to falsehood in this direction at any rate, and not have it in her power to inform any friends of ours that our father ruined her father and that our brother owes them a fortune, thus causing them their straitened circumstances, so different from the style in which she was bred! She lives so completely in a world of her own imagining, acting so to herself the heroine of her own romances that 'tis very probable she believes these dreams and inventions and merely utters them as she thinks them, meaning no evil – for without a doubt she is flighty, a low selfish character full of cunning – with some cleverness, nonsense and cracky.

WEDNESDAY, NOVEMBER 3. A letter from Jane, safe home. A little dull at first all alone in that large house, but our brother William's voice cheered her, full of politicks and Mr. Macaulay, and she revived. Those dreadful servants – since I have had my breakfast in bed it seems that *Mesdemoiselles* Marianne and Maria waited for my remains and held high festival up in their bedroom with a stray bit of bacon and odd drop of cream, dawdling a full precious hour over their gossipping repast. They have also a comfortable fire up there and their tea at any hour before midnight, eschewing the kitchen altogether – and I had quite a fit of the sullens on forbidding such airs. No wonder that coals and candles went and work remained undone.

14. Parliament has met, the Queen's speech more to the pur-

pose than usual, cavilled at of course, but there is no opposition. Lord John made a claptrap speech at Perth, Mr. Macaulay a clever and very eloquent but quite a hustings oration at Edinburgh, both displays much applauded by their partizans, rather a diminishing crew luckily. I thought there was nothing to the purpose in either, no statesmanlike views – no dignity – no rational exposition of affairs – a deal of self-praise, a whole load of squibs, good natured enough, but very satirical, not coming either with a good grace from persons such good targets themselves. However we must allow a little license to the discomfitted.

Louis Napoleon, clever *Buonaparte*, is to be *Empereur*, not by a *coup d'état* not by any intrigue, but by waiting patiently till this climax of his ambition is actually forced upon him by the voice of the people. He seems in no hurry to accept the honour, that is to be invested, crowned – the day is put off from week to week, the clamour rising with every disappointment. How well this man has played his part – over the rest of Europe the R. Cath. sovereigns by the help of their priesthood, are riding rough shod – thousands imprisoned for their opinions political and religious – the millions submitting, and while they submit who can help them – help to be of use must be self generated and rise from the masses – So we can only wait – 'tarry the Lord's leisure'. And perhaps elsewhere as here in Ireland the dawn may gradually brighten. The reformation is spreading here regularly – a weekly increase in the Converts – a general enlightening proceeding, very much owing to the elections, where the violence of the vulgar priests disgusted all ranks – and certainly with the spread of education, minds accustomed to be exercised will begin to think for themselves. Education, what a wide word, how much all classes want it.

Witness the Duke of Hamilton's exit from this 'stormy world' – his occupation during the last few months of his life was the weighing out with his own noble and feeble hands all the spices, resins and other requisites necessary for the embalming of his precious body after death. He had for some years been busy building for his remains a fine mausoleum in his fine park, at a cost of £50,000 – the inside hung with mirrors of unexampled size. In the centre a

porphyry tomb brought at great expense from Egypt, lined
with red velvet padded inside of which are other coffins to
hold the mummy. He had a sort of counter with little dishes
on it and his scales and weights and measures, before which
he sat for hours a day compounding his mixtures*.

21. Now for publick matters to smile at in after years. Mr.
D'Israeli in his speech to the Commons introducing the
subject of the Duke of Wellington's funeral was more
eloquent than can be described – short, simple, truthful,
seizing on all striking characteristicks with a justness worthy
of a statesman. The hearers are described as enthralled – no
one spoke afterwards. Today out comes a facsimile of half of
this quite splendid oration – from the work of Guizot's
which they say the plagiarist has not read this ten years.*
Most likely not, or he would have varied his extracts. I can
understand the mistake, but it is unfortunate.

The funeral itself must have been very imposing – the
military part predominating as of right. The procession took
three hours to pass Apsley House, it was increased afterwards – everybody in the world was there except the French
and *Austrians** – so many troops with Bands, Artillery,
banners &c. must have made the whole pageant wonderfully
imposing as horse and foot, carriages and crowd slowly
wended their solemn way to St. Paul's, inside of which must
have been *the* scene worth seeing. All would have been
spoiled to me by the Herald in his fantastick dress advancing
to the open grave, where dust had been consigned to, there
reciting in a string the titles of those worldly honours so
unsuited to the feelings excited by the solemn rites that had
closed the earthly passage of an immortal soul. Well – I am
peculiar, no one has found fault with this dull farce – and all
the world was entranced with this same funeral – for weeks
before little else thought of – for days before nothing –
business of every kind suspended – even pleasure – and from
the farthest points, from foreign lands, people crowded to
London. It is over now, a great moral lesson.

We in Ireland are getting on gallantly. We were never so
quiet since I remember. The magistrates have fined several
priests for assaults on scripture readers, converts and older
Protestants, which seems to have brought them a little to

their senses. Certainly the Christian community is in an extraordinary state of commotion everywhere – the priest-hood of all sects so grasping at power. To what brutal lengths the Roman Catholics carry their struggle our Elections in Ireland and those imprisonments and butcheries in Italy testify. *We* only hurt with bitter words – how bitter though. The Free Kirk having dissevered from the state in Scotland, there is to be a corresponding secession in England, headed by Bishops and other tractarian dignitaries. I really believe the Colonel is right – we want a good stiff war to bring us all to our senses. It will all work together for good – that's one point we may be certain of.

24. A carriage stopt at our door yesterday – a knock and ring quite aristocratick heralded merely a letter from old Mr. King – ridiculous, impertinent, vulgarly underbred – furious at having had the truth told to him by his son through that sly mischief-maker, his eldest daughter. I have answered it in a few lines, beginning with 'Mrs. Smith's compliments' – the card style – being most justly offended, entered into no particulars, acknowledged the receipt, and expressed in a very dignified manner my surprise at the *tone* assumed. The man is mad, vexed that his mean deceits have been discovered and commented upon, and that he cannot continue to draw money from us to maintain his son. I never read so ungentlemanly a production, in a novel it would be thought 'too bad'. James came to town this morning, of course I showed him his father's letter, and I also told him my grave opinion that the man's intellects are deranged, as well as his temper execrable, and that he would do well to keep eyes and ears open on this unprincipled old maniac. An agreeable set for poor little Annie to have got amongst – they won't bully me however, and if they don't mend their behaviour James will just have to compel them.

29. James remained four hours in rather warm controversy with his reputable father, who has after all done him out of £110 – as thus – two years having elapsed since the marriage, £450 should have been paid by the old man to his son. The first year he gave him £12, the second year £78, leaving a balance of £360 due. The affair is compromised by the old man giving £250 now, and engaging himself to pay the allowance

regularly hereafter *from this date*. To swindle his own son!
Poor body, there is some hitch about his mortgages on the
O'Brien property, by which he is like to be a loser, and this
has distracted him. He insisted on my agreeing to this
bargain 'lest hereafter there should be any claim for the
arrears', so I punished the suspicious old creature by re-
capitulating all the above statement and advising James to be
satisfied with the loss! James gave his respectable parent well
for writing me such an ungentlemanly letter – and I believe
had to threaten to inform his mother of several particulars
her husband would rather that she did not hear. It is all over
now – we are to try and forget it, I have burned his letter.
James and Annie will leave town tomorrow, I shall go with
them being well enough and very much wanted at Baltiboys,
not only to receive rents, but to set some matters to rights
that have gone very wrong. Mrs. Bourne up early, well and
cheerful, the Colonel quite himself, weather better, markets
rising, priests put down and ministry firm.

SUNDAY, DECEMBER 5. I have been at home, went down on
Tuesday with the Kings by a late train. Wednesday arranged
my papers, walked with Annie – saw old Peggy – and
listened with amazement to the prices paid for the stock
on poor old General Saunders' farm – milch cows £20 to
£40 – young cattle, year olds £15 – James bought a cow for
£19, thought a bargain. They were prize cattle certainly, still
the prices were enormous. Thursday came the tenants,
paying generally well, about £40 owing on Baltiboys, some
of which will be paid by Xmas – £30 on Elverstown which
must be waited for. Poor Rutherfurd is doing his best, and is
promised help by his sons – the three and the two grandsons
and the two daughters and their husbands are all in America,
thriving.

Would any one guess who has been acting so badly as to
call forth extreme disapproval – Tom Darker. He has
neither servants nor implements nor stock, and has sublet
his farm for which he pays 25/- an acre, a low rent as the
land was hardly supposed to have recovered the exhaustion
of Pat Quin's mode of husbandry, tho' the Colonel had been
petting [indulging] it for years, sublet it for three years, four
acres to Garrett Doyle at £4 an acre, 15 acres to the brothers

Quin at Ballinahead at £3.10.0 an acre, permitting them to take two white crops out of it carrying off all the straw – and a third white crop the third year at a reduced rent, the ground to be then *laid down in grass*, no manure mentioned. The pasturage is let for £2.10.0 and the cattle are not *folded* [enclosed for the purpose of manuring] on it, they cross the river to sleep at home. I could not have believed it – I did not believe it when it was first told to me – but enquiries proved it, and Garett Doyle himself and Tom Darker could not deny it – did not – tried to justify himself, to ward off by pretending he was ill used, maligned, disliked, was ignorant of the Colonel's most stringent rule – he who had been his confidential servant eighteen years, had received the Colonel's permission! any thing, every thing, but he could not escape – I pinned him down to the facts, very calmly but very steadily, so was threatened with the loss of all the Darkers. They are thinking of Australia whither the nephew George has already gone, and whither I am sure I have not the least objection that they should all follow. I forbade Doyle to go on with his agreement, wrote to the Quins to the same effect – and to Tom Darker prohibiting him from future proceedings likewise – all steps taken by the advice of John Robinson whom I consulted before leaving town. Whether I am to be obeyed or whether we must proceed to distrain this jobbing rogue remains to be seen. A middle man! the curse of Ireland, a character we abominate and never have permitted – what nuts to crack at Xmas! I am quite grieved at the discovery of such confirmed trickery. I have always thought Tom very slippery – had good reason to think so – this whole conduct about that farm has been discreditable – double dealing – sly – but such undisguised jobbing as this I never expected. There are two tenants beside him who must be brought to their senses, Pat Farrell and Dempsey – their arrears are too heavy, and they don't seem inclined to make any exertion to clear them up – a plague they are some of them.

Well, I had another scene – I asked the Doctor to walk out on Friday to see me, I wanted to pay him the last Instalment of his loan, thank God that's done with, and his fee for attending the Colonel, and seeing him in good humour made one last trial to restore him to happiness – there is so much good in him – he was so unremittingly kind to the Colonel. I failed, made some impression, yet failed. I do not believe any one has yet got at the truth regarding this singular estrangement, quarrel we cannot call it, where one party is so perfectly quiescent. There is some feeling deep down in the bottom of that half-broken heart which has never yet been let to see the light, which perhaps it is best should never see the light. I come to this conclusion from his soreness, his unreasonableness, his lack of argument and his inconsistency. Every time that we have spoken of it he has named a different cause for his taking offence, a new string of accidents which increased his ill humour. On this occasion I had an entirely new version of the whole affair – a most extraordinary one – the most false of all – and did I not give it him, ay till he shook – and I would have said more in the same stern quiet way, did I not think him hardly responsible for all his actions. From the singular perversity of his ideas, his morbid feelings, his vindictive sort of temper and total misapprehension and misrepresentation of all that occurred, I am persuaded that the malady inherent in his family is incipient in him, and that unless some gentle influence be brought to bear on his present irritability, we shall by and bye have to mourn the overthrow of that capacious mind, now most surely shaken. He should have married years ago – 'It is not good for man to be alone' – a wife, a happy home and children would have saved him. He is only an Irishman softened under reproof, as I have experienced before, there is something very low in such natures, the early influences were bad, a poor and harsh and vulgar home both in childhood and in youth, and years of dependence. It must have worked for evil on such an imperious nature – pity! I cannot help remembering our pleasant intercourse in years, such happy years, gone by for ever – when we were full of enjoyment and he was so cleverly agreeable and so kind. I believe the man is bewitched.

9. A note from James last night tells me that on his return home he found all his new stiles so neatly made, destroyed – the stones of some scattered about it and the woodwork of others broken up. The night he and Annie dined at the

Manor, when they entered their avenue they found their labourer James Moore waiting near the gate – he had not gone home so early as usual having been detained by a job of work he was doing. He found in three or four places drawn along the road the trunk of a tree as would have done mischief to the carriage. They must have been taken from the plantation which they are thinning, by no means small trees, and carried *up* the bank. Moore removed them and remained to prevent them being replaced. Very disagreeable, so silly and so spiteful and annoying to have people at hand so wickedly inclined. James has been with Mr. Owen and is determined to use every endeavour to find out the offenders. I should think the hall door was set fire to by the same parties – *servants* of an irritable disappointed man – not the man himself, he is quite above it, but he is very violent and incautious with his tongue, detests James King and has a crew of attendants equally suffering with himself from his dismissal. Nicely they *did* him and cheated us, and most unjustly did he use others for their sake so that nobody now favours him. He is a good creature under bad influences the result must be bad. There surely will be some changes in this almost savage land. How annoying it is to have to deal with such tempers destitute of principles – can we wonder at Tom Darker and the Doctor when we have old Mr. King and young Mr. King beside them.

12. Our Quaker book is a most curious composition. We must bear in mind that the writer, Mrs. Grier, was turned out of the society for attending Church and in some ways departing from the very strict ceremonials of the Sect. She can never therefore have been a devoted disciple and her expulsion must have left a soreness. Still unless her details are one system of falsehood, she describes a set of cold, worldly-minded, purse-proud, selfish, sensual, indolent, stupid, ignorant, immoral human beings, deserving of every reprobation – religion they have none, virtue very little – and the studious care with which every gentle or civilising or refining influence is kept from them, is argument of itself in favour of the low estimate Mrs. Grier takes of Quaker character. Another work of hers is advertised promising further very curious revelations. She can give us none more

amusing than her account of that celebrated humbug Elizabeth Fry, with her puffed up obsequious brother – her vanity, her gluttony, her egotism and her pretension.*

Mary Barton [Elizabeth Gaskell's 1848 novel] an old tale of factory life new to me, interested me thoroughly – there is matter enough well worthy of the deep reflexion of those in power in these simply related details of artificial life – the ignorant, ill-used operative – the ill-educated and rich manufacturer. Well may Mr. Macaulay say we have at our doors, round our palace homes and near our hearths, hordes of barbarians more dangerous to the empire than the Goths and Vandals who overwhelmed Rome.

Jane so much wants me to sketch the Irish slave with the lash of the Priest over him – I fear it is beyond my powers – my information is not sufficient – neither could I be sure of getting it truthfully in this false country. Yet I have anecdotes enough were they all as authentick as Mrs. Bowler's report of the sermon at Ballymore which was one string of furious invectives against any one of the congregation daring to borrow a newspaper from a Protestant neighbour, or to read a newspaper on the Protestant side. The preacher had a man in his eye who had thus disobeyed his mandate – thus perilled his precious soul here and hereafter for to . . . &c., &c. all the elegant epithets used on such occasions, such reprobates were doomed. Now would the man laugh or be frightened, that's just the question.

21. Lord Derby out – House tax lost by nineteen, so ministers resigned next day. A grand dilemma – the general belief is that Lord Aberdeen will accept the office with the promise of a suite of a sort of omnium gatherem – all to be mixed up higgledy piggledy, heads where tails were and vice versa in an upside down topsy turvy style to be called by the name of the enlightened coalition. It may or may not do, perhaps in England better than those ousted – but not here – any change must be for the worse in Ireland. Where shall we find such a Chancellor as Blackburne – where two such Law Officers of the Crown as Whiteside and Napier – where any Lord Lieutenant within a thousand degrees of Lord Eglinton. Poor unhappy Ireland, just as she was raising her head, everything so prosperous, land selling higher than ever was

known, markets rising – not a house in Dublin to be had, all the trades people in such spirits. An universal gloom pervaded our whole town as if a nightmare had settled on it – to be given over to Messr.s Somerville, Brewster, Keogh and the Popish brigade. It will all come right in the end but we must go through some martyrdom first – how much! Who can say if we are to be again exasperated as heretofore. Lord Derby is much blamed for giving up power on such a minority which was in fact none, the brass band numbering above thirty, all voting against him and not worth reckoning as of any account.* Deducting that precious crew he had a majority – some say he must come in again – that this new compound of heterogeneous materials can never stick together. Others again have it that he is quite tired of office and gladly seized the first opportunity to be rid of it.

24. All busy at this moment ornamenting the house – sticking holly everywhere – a great tree in a tub to hang the presents on. Papa and I are not in this doings, we keep quiet till the New Year – New Year again, another stage in the journey of time. Such a rabble as that old tory Lord Aberdeen is collecting. Every hue or shade of politicks except the good old honest whig, that true John Bull will be unrepresented in the new Cabinet which is but very tardily forming.

26. Last night My Aunt got really a beautiful letter from poor William – expressing naturally and warmly and very touchingly how grateful he feels to her for this gift of hers to Uncle Ralph – this second gift. He is now none the worse for having thirty years ago assisted my father by lending his name, along with James Grant's and Corrimony's as security for £1,500. On the last two becoming bankrupt, my Uncle had the whole to bear – on my father's bankruptcy this money was called up by the creditors – my father always considering it as a private debt and reckoning interest on it from that hour. By the time he got his Calcutta judgeship, these arrears amounted to £500, making the debt £2,000, for which to the hour of his death he paid my Uncle four percent yearly. After his death my mother, my Aunt and my sister continued to pay the £80, till my Aunt paid off £1,000. They then paid him annually £40, till now that my Aunt has

presented him with the second £1,000 – so that he has never for even one half year suffered loss by my father from the hour that he had an income from which he could spare – and the £500 arrears my Uncle may look on as gain, for he would never have saved that little sum himself. I do feel so grateful to my Aunt for all she has done to save my poor father's memory from reproach. Dear good woman, she loved him faults and all – and she still loves the recollection of the bright young days he and she and her favourite sister spent together. She is much pleased with William's letter. It was very right in him to write it, so proper the feeling – it has thrown a warm gleam over Xmas for me.

1853

Janey and the Kings enjoy the usual frantic social whirl, in spite of the Highland Lady's reservations ('really I do believe Dublin to be a very dissipated town'), thoughts which echo her doubts about whether improvements are really taking place either in Blessington or society at large. Attempts are being made to rent the family house and land at Baltiboys in an attempt to prise her son-in-law out of his unsuccessful attempts at making a living here. There is great interest in Janey's suitors, particularly when one of the front runners turns out to be the heir to the Earl of Westmeath. Colonel and Mrs. Smith return the hospitality they have received and there are vivid descriptions of Dublin society in the months before war clouds gather over the Black Sea. James King's affairs go from bad to worse and it is clear that her apprehensions about developments in Church and State are matched by her unease at all that has to be done on a limited income, including searching for a solution to the Kings' difficulties.

Illustration: St Patrick's Cathedral

SUNDAY, JANUARY 2. Aunt Bourne at her serious reading in her room with her luncheon and her good glass of Madeira. Ogle Moore writes me word there is no truth in William Grindon's tale, at least Miss Macdonnell entirely denies her part in it, and is prepared to return to her duties forthwith, and do her very best. Such a *lying* country, no believing anybody.

We spent most of Thursday morning with Lady Milltown, who brought her girls to town and sent them on with Russy to Hillsborough for a happy fortnight, Pysie returning with her Aunt to act as maid and companion, the maid having gone with the young ladies. Poor Miladi, she is in wretched spirits – dull – depressed, and ill in health. She has some hope again about the loan, but her Lord is so mysterious, so false, so uncertain, no one can answer for his speaking the truth on any subject. She says how they get on *at all* is a marvel. The fact is, tradespeople bear much from the peerage, and in Ireland they are so used to bad pay, neither the one side nor the other seems very much to mind it – 'tis all on the credit system together. How long that will answer we may live to see. We had one warning in the famine times.

9. We sing at home now, daily, a morning practice and an evening concert, and twice a week just now a lesson from Dr. Frank Robinson. He is perfectly enchanted with Janey's voice, with Annie's too, but she is uncertain while Janey never tiring, never even getting husky, her clear sweet very high notes *welling* out, as this conceited body says – ' 'tis an ever flowing spring of melody' her strength of chest enabling her to hold a note to almost any length of time. She amazed Sir Philip Crampton with it the other day, he actually stood entranced beside her while she poured out without visible effort a beautiful serenade of Donizetti's. In a duett by the same graceful composer she and Annie are enchanting. Dr. F. Robinson really was astonished, and said so; he also said 'there was no such singing in Dublin'*, *and so I think*, and I am ill to please, and it is all kept for *home*, there is no display to crowds. It is love of the art, love of us all, real happiness, without an atom of vanity, except in my foolish old head – no – I do myself injustice, it is a far deeper feeling.

These good Eglintons are gone, so regretted, so sad themselves. She wept abundantly, poor little woman, as the steam boat moved away. Everyone was prejudiced against poor lowly Miss Newcomen, or the Indian Banker's wife, or the *parvenue* Countess, owing her position to her purse, her simple good-nature, her true heart, her kindness, her ease, gained her everybody's good-will. The household made her a present of a handsome bracelet as a keepsake, that household which ridiculed her at first, the only thing of its kind I ever heard of. I did not know her but all knew her worth. The Countess of Eglinton never forgot Miss Newcomen, nor anyone high or low who had ever shewn her a kindness. He is a shrewd, soundheaded man, no respecter of persons or parties, a great blessing while with us and a loss not easily replaced. Lord St. Germains [sic] is said to have good qualities and an obliging wife, and they are rich, but they belong to the wrong side in every sense.* These Comedians in Downing Street can't act together quite, even so early in the farce.

16. All the appointments in the new ministry not yet filled. We are learning to be thankful for small mercies, to accept of negative good. We are relieved from Sir Thomas Readington,* they have promoted him in England. Lord St. Germains too is a Peelite, but Mr. Keogh is a scandalous appointment. He is very young, of no reputation at the bar, not exactly respectable in private life and a violant agitator, one of the rebel *crew*, bigotted for party purposes, giving the Pope's health before the Queen's, publickly pledged to overthrow the established church etc., etc.* Mrs. O'Reilly tells me her respectable Roman Catholick friends are as indignant as we are, for good lawyers and good subjects have been passed over, men of standing, to throw a sop to this terrier cur – the old wretched whig policy, otherwise these queer changes are taking place very quietly, nobody affecting even to believe in their permanency.

James has been busy assisting to transport a gang of sheepstealers some of whom were caught last year and punished by so many months imprisonment which so infuriated them that on leaving jail they resolved on shooting Richard Hornidge, Tulfarris, James King, their respective herds and a farmer of the neighbourhood. James escaped the ambush prepared for him by riding past it uncommonly quick from being late, and Richard Hornidge by going another road. An accomplice, denied his fair share of the spoil, betrayed them, they are all Ballymore men.

23. Quite a remarkable week for we have actually seen company! a very minimus affair, but as Janey says, a beginning. Lady Stannus called and talked so sociably; Sam Finnemore and Edward Moore came in the evening. It was quite a pleasant evening and the Colonel and my Aunt none the worse of it, 'tis a change from that eternal whist.

Those two enchanting youths, Gerald and Michael Aylmer, are really going to be married immediately and to two very fine girls. Michael to Miss Hendrick, some years older than himself, Gerald to a very pretty Miss Dobbs, sister to the young Duchess of Manchester.* I hear that their conversation upon the subject of these 'hiefers' and the use to be made of them is actually disgusting, that at a man party the other guests cried 'shame'. This is indeed a very far behind country, the *polished* Irishman may be outwardly charming, the unpolished is odious, and I can't help feeling that at the bottom of the best appearance a fund of vulgarity lies thick from whence a good splash can rise occasionally. What mad people they are.

I have had three notes from Miss Macdonnell since her return to her duties. The first two were very petted, full of imaginary evils, praise of herself for enduring them, requests quite unreasonable, etc. I took no notice of her temper, acceding to what was right, gave her proper orders, sent the proper supplies, refused what was unnecessary, so there comes a third *letter* quite impertinent, so much so that I have enclosed it to Ogle Moore and told her I have done so, and given her a pretty smart bit of my mind besides. William Grindon probably made no mistake about this young lady's intentions. I am not able to put myself to any inconvenience about her. I shall keep her to her contract till it suits me to let her off, but I shall begin to look about for her successor.

Sir Philip Crampton, who came here last Monday again 'to catch a little singing' told me his daughter had taken charge of poor Miss Borrowes' Infant School from the time of her death, supported it by the sale of her drawings, teaches there daily, and trains teachers, so I go to visit her!

25. We are all of us perfectly enchanted with a book by Julia Kavanagh – *Nathalie*. The scene is in France, the characters, manners, habits, localities, all so truthful, the development of feeling interesting beyond idea. Conversations delightful. Men might not like so mere a history of the heart, to women it is actual enjoyment, and all so life-like, we live with the people described as if it were no fiction. Another charm is the beauty of the tale – agreeable people, agreeable scenery, agreeable scenes. I have not for ages been so captivated. How is the gifted authoress so little known. She goes a step too far with her very charming heroine and her irresistible hero, two volumes would have done it all and better maybe, but 'the trade', the arbitrary 'trade' requires the three.*

30. Mrs. Montgomery and Kitty Hawtayne dined on Friday with us. In the evening we had about a dozen more to tea and muffins and after three good hours of musick and dancing a table was laid out with refreshments. Of course we had disappointments. Some ladies requested to bring female friends, we not wanting such, and some gentlemen failed us which was a distress, but on the whole we were eighteen merry people all doing our best to pass the time agreeably.

We have got an Under Secretary, Captain Larcom, one of the Poor Law Commissioners, an able man.* All is therefore at last in working order here, it is wonderful how very little the publick seem interested now in politicks. We have all too much else to think of. Louis Napoleon has got a wife, no Princess to whom he would be a stranger, but a young gifted Spanish woman of high birth with whom he is madly in love. He has carried his Empress through all opposition, made a very clever speech so suited to the times, the advancing times, and again repudiating all worn out legitimacies, bases his power on the choice of the people and to them presents his Consort, chosen from his own rank, a second Josephine. It is admirably well done, and very wise, I think. He would have done as wisely to have remained President, a less irritating title to the Royalties of Europe, equally good for his purposes, and he might have had as much luxury as the vain people he governs like without restoring the Court fripperies everybody of sense is sick of.

SUNDAY, FEBRUARY 6. The new Lord Lieutenant has arrived, and though by way of entering privately he had a good big crowd around him. Old Sir Philip Crampton careering at his side on a splendid horse, not more spirited looking than the rider. Three leading ribbonmen have been arrested through an *approver* [informer] which may lead, it is hoped, to the eventual breaking up of this detestable confederacy into which none but Roman Catholicks are admitted.* The persecution of Protestants all over Italy continues, the conversions at home here in Ireland encrease, in the face of a very uproarious priesthood, they certainly fear the times are changing for them, and like other angry people help on their own ruin by their despotick conduct.

Louis Napoleon and his beautiful half Spanish, half Scotch Empress have begun their married life all sunshine. Her grandfather was a Kirkpatrick of Closeburn in regular descent from him who 'mak siccar' [made sure] the blow of the Bruce.* The Parisians seem quite satisfied so far.

13. The first gaiety of the week was the *Levée* on Monday, very crowded. On Tuesday the Drawing-room, and poor Janey could not go, for though the toe was better the swelling and the pain remained and might have been encreased had she used it. Annie's dress was very pretty – white lace petticoat, pink train, my pearls. She looked well and was much admired. It was an excellent Drawing-room, plenty of people, much less rubbish than usual. Wednesday the three went to a small party at Mrs. Montgomery's, Thursday to another at Lady Stannus',* singing at both. Friday James and Annie went to Castletown without poor Janey who could not have danced. Tom Connolly did it admirably well – engaged a special train to carry his company to Hazelhatch and back, had omnibuses there to bring them on, the one for the ladies, new lined with glazed cotton to save their dresses. About two hundred people, Hanlon's Band, the whole house thrown open, quantities of refreshments and a good supper. It was all very charming! but considering that they had to be dressed by nine, were to be an hour on the way, that it was a perfect storm of snow, and that they returned

home a little before seven in the morning, I can't but think that we who were all the while snug in bed were in a better place, Lady Milltown tells me Annie is quite the *Belle* this winter, admired by all, and the men mad about her. She is all right however, and quite safe, the young head won't turn.

Mr. Sheehan frequently pops in late in the afternoon and sits till the dinner bell rings, chattering so pleasantly. He knows everybody that ever lived and every thing that ever happened, and has such a happy knack of telling a story well.* Lady St. Germains he mentioned was a Cornwallis, one of the five plain well portioned daughters of the last Marquis, her mother of Gordon blood. At the first Castle dinner, Mrs. John Latouche was seated between Wyndham Goold [M.P. for Limerick] and the Archbishop of Dublin; the first she knew and was carrying on a lively conversation with him when he suggested that a few words to her right hand neighbour should be ventured. The ill-bred reply of these shy undereducated little great, that she was unacquainted with him produced the remark that a wish to pay a proper attention to an elderly man, evidently neglected, might act as an introduction. So, good naturedly, she turned and taking advantage of an offering of cutlets dressed with green pease and salsify, she said to the Archbishop, – 'pease at this season!' 'old ones', grunted out he – 'and this other vegetable' – 'salsify',* in the same tone. 'Dear me, how do you eat it', 'you put it in your mouth, you masticate it, you swallow it', and there it ended. He was driving out of town one very hot day in his *chariot*, leaning back, his hat off, a handkerchief over his face, his two legs stuck out in front, one from each window. Mad certainly, but such a good man, charitable in its widest sense, going on some errand of mercy probably, for it is his unceasing business.

We got upon Authors, editing, reviewing, puffing – it is humbug altogether, a trading all through on false pretences, till the voice of the publick breaks the bubble. The Editors of novels seldom see them, never read them, pocket their thirty to fifty guineas for the loan of their name on the title page. The reviewers have orders to do their cutting favourably or otherwise as suits the private views of the management. Mrs. John Latouche has written a novel and sold it to

Bentley for one hundred pounds; poor pay, they say 'tis good and he has bid her begin another, a romance of real life, he, Mr. Sheehan, told us, should be preserved.*

The old Marquis of Headfort, some years a widower, married last week for riches, Lady Macnaughton, the widow of him who was murdered in Cabool.* These gossippy tales are pleasant diversions from my domestick troubles. We have had to part with our new servant. He was quite lame, hip diseased, poor creature and ankles too. It was a great disappointment, for he seemed decent though very poor. We have taken Marianne's father for the present, he is out of place, and he may suit us for a permanence, he understands his business very well.

14. My poor dear children, they gave me such a lecture last night upon looking dull, upon looking ill, upon moving slow, seeming half dead in short. Little they know. Never out of pain, overworked, irritated, anxious, only just by dint of economy able to pay our way; how can I possess the lively spirits they remember. Were it not for them, for Janey still to protect, for Jack to be guided yet a while, I would not care how soon my wearied body freed the soul. Still, though quiet, I am happy in my own still way, not gay, but very grateful for many blessings, and quite disposed to resume a smile if ever I am in tolerable health again.

20. There has been no news worth mentioning, nor much gaiety for us, our private acquaintance being few and none of them in the Ball giving line. There was a Ball though at the Castle on Wednesday to which the young people went. Remarkably pleasant, no scrubs, eight hundred persons, a mere handful in that large St. Patrick's Hall. We have heard from several quarters that our two dear girls were exceedingly admired. Annie is considered quite the handsomest of the young married women and Janey one of the prettiest of the maidens, their manners, dress and dancing pre-eminent. I shall be getting too vain of these monkeys. So long as they do not get vain themselves, it don't much matter. They take admiration now as they have always taken it – as natural and suitable and all in the way of youth with its many advantages. There was a hitch about Janey getting to the Ball as she had not been to the Drawing-room. Kind Mr. Sheehan

explained the cause to his friend the Chamberlain and Mr. L'Estrange has therefore invited her again with the greatest civility to the next ball next Wednesday along with James and Annie.

James dined with the Lord Mayor [Robert Henry] Kinahan, on Thursday – five hundred people in the round room, Lord Lieutenant etc. The young men of fashion among whom he was seated at the table set apart for the Household appear to me to be very like schoolboys still in the peculiar style of their amusements – filling each other's pockets with fruit cake, breadcrumbs, *custard*, and decorating each other's persons with the cut carrots and turnips and other ornaments plucked off the dishes. The idle, useless lives these unfortunate young men lead is really a subject almost of sadness. Vacuity in all its hideous forms is the type of their frivolous existence. When their folly is innocent it is in its best phase. In the army vicious amusements are gaining ground. One regiment, the 57th, is in sad disgrace. Drinking, gaming, skying, are universal throughout all and have in many instances ended in individual disgrace, but this wretched set have added vulgar, cruel practical jokes to their catalogue of misdemeanours, and the result is that they are ruined, the Colonel ordered off to Head quarters, an end of him, the others some will have to sell out, some to exchange, all will lose any chance of promotion. How badly we do educate our boys. It makes one shudder to think of the misspent time of creatures who will have to give an account both of what they do and what they don't do. Really I do believe Dublin to be a very dissipated town.

We have had a good many visitors in the afternoons which is pleasant enough. Mr. Sheehan constantly, always with something amusing to say. Another well-written book, melancholy though, natural I dare say, but it is always so disagreeable to me to find people doing wrong while knowing the right, one can hardly understand it. The authouress, poor woman, does well. This *Stewart of Dunleath* is written by Mrs. Norton, and it certainly does her equal credit with her poetry. She is an accomplished creature and a talented one, and should have fallen into better hands. 'Imprisoned mind' it must have been with her during the years she lived with her most unsuitable husband, who is no goose, the contrary, but he was not fit for her. Maybe she was not fit for him either, too much lifted up above 'this working day world'.*

A dreadful misfortune has happened this week. During the height of the snow storm the Liverpool steamer went down off Howth, struck the rock and filled and sunk in sixteen minutes, fifty-three persons perished, fifty one were saved, the Captain and all the cabin passengers but two were drowned. The accident cast quite a gloom over our city. The telegraph carried the news to London and brought it back to us next day in my Aunt's English paper. Is it not fairy times. Between steam and gas and electricity life is quite charmed to us, a sort of magic.

27. This has been rather a gay week with the young set. Wednesday another Castle Ball, Tuesday the Garrison Play, Friday Subscription Ball, and Saturday Philharmonick Concert, very bad indeed. Subscription Ball had nobody at it, less than three hundred people, all scrubs save the one small party to which our trio belonged and which danced on merrily with one another till long after mid-night, very long. The Castle Ball they said, was delightful, the Garrison play amusing from its absurdity, such wretched acting with one or two exceptions was never seen. It is a very foolish life this led by the gay world. I wish to goodness it were all over and the town quiet, which, alas! it won't be these two months, for the late hours are disagreeable to me, and certainly detrimental to the health of the ball-goers. What must it be to those who really are in the full whirl of the round when my girls, who enter so very moderately into it, look paler already.

We have had a sad week of casualties. Lord Belfast died of measles at Naples. He was an admirable young man, clever and actively benevolent, devoted to the good of his fellow creatures, an able lecturer to the working classes. His cousin George Chichester steps into his place, one of the most disreputable of that disreputable race, so it is a publick calamity.* Mr. Kavanagh has been burned to death, his fine old name and large fortune fall to that poor object his brother, a poor cripple without either arms or legs only stumps. In this miserable condition he hunts! tied to his basket saddle, holding the reins between his mouth and shoulder, and he rides hard! He draws, writes, is really accomplished and intelligent. An old prophesy, it seems, foretold that the house of Boris would end with a cripple. Strange if true.*

MONDAY, MARCH 14. Pretty doings, what can have kept me a whole fortnight silent, I who am so fond of a good long soliloquy face to face with my journal; part business and part pleasure and part anxiety and part fatigue. But all occupation other than that I choose to give myself being over now, we will have a pleasant little *résumé* of past transactions, and begin with the famous party of course on Monday the last day of February.

It was musical, intended for about thirty people, but swelled to fifty three, all really very nice, none disagreeable, and some quite first rate. Stannus's, Layards, Mrs. Montgomery and Kitty, Owens, poor Mrs. O'Reilly and Pysie, so happy, and lots of *beaux*. Hamlet Thompson [sang] very well, Annie Fraser beautifully, Miss Stokes played brilliantly, and Janey and Annie and Doctor [Frank] Robinson were really charming. The musick began however with Mrs. Harper, the much praised *prima* of Hillsborough about whom Lady Downshire is really crazy, forcing her on the ears of we Dublin people trained to much sweeter strains. To oblige Miss Owen, I had her here, paid her a guinea for three songs and didn't repent it, for it gave us *éclat* and served a foil to better notes. Such whooping and hallowing never was heard out of the theatres, vicious style, tuneless voice and no taste. She went from us to the Castle and pleased as little there. About eleven they all set to dancing, performing orchestra in turns and seemed to be very happy, as they staid to one though there were other dances that evening.

The arrangements were very simple. The staircase was lighted with candles, the back drawing-room by a hired lustre [chandelier], leaving us all our own luminaries for the front room. The study received the gentlemen's hats etc., my dressing-room with fire and lights, toilette and work table and Marianne was prepared for the ladies. The refreshments were all laid on a long table at the end of the front drawing-room and were nothing particular. Tea with accompaniments, then wine, port and sherry, ginger and orange water of course, lemonade in large jugs, confectionery and four silver dishes full of sandwiches constantly replenished. One man hired to help Daly. The whole affair, Mrs. Harper included, only cost six pounds and I am sure it gave much more pleasure and much less trouble than a dinner would have done to a fourth only of the people. My Aunt was in great spirits, well dressed, very animated, very obliging and a regular rake for she sat out the whole and was none the worse for it, neither was the Colonel apparently.

16. Friday an admirable subscription Ball, never was a pleasanter; quiet since then mercifully, for my pets are beginning to look a little fagged. They are *quite* the fashion, both of them run after by ball givers and ball goers, Janey dancing with a higher class of b*eaux* than heretofore. They are in much happier spirits too from having got intimate with so many agreeable people – my favourite among the young men is Ambrose Hickey, out and out. Janey says I should like Walter Stannus better, the old Dean of Ross's second son. I can well believe it for the Dean himself is charming, one of the most amiable persons I ever met. Poor Hamlet Thompson is also very likeable, he comes here for ever, on all sorts of pretences, sends his bouquets, but it will not do, the little lady disapproves.

18. Wednesday my morning reading interested me so much that I went on with my book, Archbishop Whateley on *The Errours of Romanism* [*The Errors of Romanism traced to their Origin in Human Nature*, published in 1830 was, for the *D.N.B.*, a 'polemical treatise'] till the clock struck eleven, my hour for leaving my little chamber. This Wednesday I went out late and met Janey and Annie with Lord Russborough, as usual I may say, for he is always lounging about here, poor fellow, he knows we all love him and feel for him and he is at home amongst us.

Janey and Annie had been with the Layards by appointment where, of course, they found half Dublin – Dr. Todd, the Archbishop, and ever so many more. Colonel Layard is more crazy about his mesmerising powers than ever, quite got the charlatan style they say, he has found a third maiden to submit to his powerful will, and there he parades his unconscious victims, making them do the most extraordinary acts to the amazement of all lookers on. The Archbishop is a most devout believer in the whole art or arts, he called out every moment 'who can doubt this' – 'whoever doubts this, must doubt his own senses, his own feelings'. Huge, queer, shapeless monster of a man, with his giant's intellect, yet simple, credulous as a child. Did I ever set down a story of his wife that sent him chuckling all over Dublin to tell it in an extasy to everybody. Mrs. Whateley went to Todd and Burns to buy a ribbon, which, on comparing it with the silk it was to match, she found unsuited. So she took it back to have it changed. 'We canna do it, Madam,' said the sturdy Scot, 'we canna do it, 'tis against the rules of the house'. 'You must mistake me, Sir', said this very ugly, clumsy looking old woman, 'I do not want to give it back, I want to change it for a better match'. 'No, matter, Madam, what ye want, we canna do it, 'tis against the rules of the house'. 'Probably Sir, you are not aware of who I am. I am the Archbishop of Dublin's Lady'. 'If ye were his lawfu' wife we could na do it, mem, 'tis against the rules of the house'. Fancy the horrour, the indignation of a virtuous dame. Only to be equalled by the extravagant delight of her most singular husband.*

19. Thursday the seventeenth, the latest St Patrick's Ball ever known.* The Viceregal party remained till the clock struck four, so that before our set got home and got over their laughter in the Colonel's room and a second edition of it in mine, it was almost five. I never saw Janey so tired, she had not missed a dance. There were some scenes, amusing, disgusting, annoying as usual; all descriptions of company of course, but they liked their night. It is really an absurd habit we have got into of sitting up entertaining each other all the dark hours intended by nature for our rest, no doubt 'tis very hurtful to the health and I don't think this constant dissipation good for the character. How to change it or avoid it is the problem. Yesterday, as I never have them disturbed after these orgies, they had their breakfast about twelve, then between the snow showers got out to leave their

cards at the Castle. I did not stir, I was busy with some
needlework and I also had a book I found amusing, the
Memoirs of Madame d'Oberkirsch, an Alsatian noble, the
private friend of that Dorothea, Princes of Wirtemburg
[sic], who married the Grand Duke Paul and was the mother
of the Russian Emperours Alexander, Nicholas etc. The
Memoirs are not well written, the Lady not being clever,
though quick, not intellectual though intelligent, but they
amuse, or rather interest one from the notability of the
names mentioned, places visited, times lived in. Strasburg
and Paris in the early days of Marie Antoionette.

20. In the *Household Words* this week there is an interesting
account of the Foundling Hospital in London, written in
the lively manner peculiar to Dickens and very agreeable,
but which no other pen can try without degenerating into a
sort of halting buffoonery.* Excellent as are these institutions in design and good as may be their effects sometimes
(ills they relieve certainly), can they be rigidly allowed to
bring up these little Blanks in the most suitable way. That
Palace with its giant staircase, noble corridors, monster
halls, cathedral service, and space, grandeur, vastness in
all; will such rearing make humble apprentices, contented
servants, a happy workman and workman's wife. Depend
upon it we are all wrong in our charities as in most things
else, have the wrong end of the clew [ball of thread] in our
awkward fingers. Did we set rightly to work there would be
no need of such plasters, for there would be no sores. When
shall we see our wise people devoted to the study of Cause
and Effect, the simple problem on which hangs the well
being of our race.

Jane and Annie and I went out yesterday, cold as it was.
We knew it was the Milltowns' last day, so we went to take
our leave, when we found they had taken on their house for
another month, my Lord relenting when the snow fell. The
Nugents came in with their father, almost as young looking
a man as his son, and without the very flaming red hair of
that gallant officer, although a little sandy like the daughters. I was amused recollecting what James overhead between the son and Janey. They were talking of continental
tours, visits to Rome ending in conversations, ecclesiastical

matters in fact. 'There will be little fear of me' said Janey, 'Rome or no Rome they will never convert me'. 'I must tell you one thing 'said Mr. Nugent 'you will not like to hear it, and it has often made myself very uncomfortable, particularly in my Regiment, where I am the only one of that persuasion, but I am a R. Cath.k'. 'Oh! I am so sorry', said Janey!! The future Earl of Westmeath will nevertheless find his faith swallowed even by a puritan *Irishwoman*.*

Then came Lady Milltown, very happy, her girls however had rather have returned to Russborough, they had gone out walking with [her second son] Edward so she drove here alone and went back to fetch my Aunt a book! good-natured woman. Mr. Douglas, she told me she went to see the other day when he gave her a letter for Edward which he said she might read. It contained twenty pounds for books for his college course and a promise that if he lived till May the dose would be repeated. People are very kind to that anxious mother and her poor children. Last year Lord Cloncurry gave her fifty pounds to pay her lodgings, bought trains and dresses for the girls, pouched the boys heavily, etc., and Lord Milltown is content to let his children be thus indebted to charity, gambling still, gambling ever, with *her* money, not his own. Lord Cloncurry is ill we fear, his breathing affected, the wheezing painfully distinct. He has been cupped but is little better and eighty. He would be a dreadful loss to these children, who though no way related to him he looks on as his own, for their Godmother's sake. Miss Sçavoy too keeps this feeling alive in him and so has won her way in spite of scandal I never myself would believe in those evil tales, two such old people, a sickly septuagenarian and a *thin* fright of a woman, fifty five, could have never gone together *par amour*, and the arrangement of a female companion of mature years, as nurse, housekeeper, reader, Secretary, very clever and very agreeable, seems so reasonable [see note to 7 November].

Mr. Sheehan has been ever since we knew him intimately talking of his cousin Wyndham Goold, M.P. for Clare. On all occasions, at every opportunity there was reference made to Wyndham Goold, I got quite sick of Wyndham Goold. Who is he, what is he, where is he, am I never to see

Wyndham Goold. Mr. Sheehan asked us to dinner to meet him, he did not come. We were to find him at a luncheon at Mespile [his suburban retreat], he had gone to England, he was to come here to call, he was off to Clare. Still we were deafened with his name, his looks, his talents, his puns, his acres, his houses and his thousands of pounds. I gave the matter up, considered the man a myth, a shadow. So the fun gathered and yesterday this shadow was really met in the substance, a very agreeable, gentlemanly man about half aware of the joke and perfectly easy under it. One of his sisters, Lady Gore Booth, a most amiable person, came with him.*

21. The Dean and Walter Stannus walked home from Christ Church with my trio and arranged a further promenade at four o'clock, but the heavy showers of sleet prevented this. My mind begins to misgive me. Pray heaven another nine months courtship be not impending over my devoted head, here where there are no shrubbery walks, nor seats under trees. Mothers with a dozen daughters surely die. The dirty linen departed, all orders were rapidly given, an interview with the butcher confounded my senses, for he announced one penny a pound of rise upon all meat, prime pieces sixpence halfpenny, mediums sixpence, coarse fivepence halfpenny. Every description of goods is advancing in price, more particularly eatables, butter is up to fifteenpence, some say the bad weather is the cause, others that there is a scarcity, others again that the higher rate of wages allows of meat to the labourer and so has encreased the demand. If so, we must not grudge our higher market bills. My fingers are perished at this table close to the fire. Such a month of March, all lion so far.

22. We have had letters from all parts with good news. One from Jane enquires the character, etc., of John Latouche, who had offered for the Doune, for the poor Duchess of Bedford is gone. She died at Nice of bronchitis about three weeks ago. Lord Abercorn wishes for the Doune, the sons amongst them propose to take it on, I would myself rather any of them than these strangers, they have lived among our beauties all their lives, love the scenes, the people, the old family now dispersed, not as the warm hearted Duchess did,

that can't be looked for, but they are more interested in our dear old Duchus* than any mere shooters of the season. The poor Duchess, all our life our connexion has been kept up, in my childhood I so well remember her, in the highlands, in London, even travelling in Flanders.* My drop of Gordon blood warms to hers, they were all, all her family so much a part of my early days that this loss of the last of them is another blank in all the Grant part of my old heart. Such another Tenant we shall never get, with all her highland heart in action there. I felt her death very sorrowfully, though I omitted to note it here. We heard it during the fortnight of the Colonel's illness when my journal was not thought of. The Castle doings here were stopped for ten days in consequence, Lady St. Germains being her niece, one of the plain Cornwallis's, all good and amiable and rich, having no brother. The last Marquis therefore left them all he could, and as little as he could to his far away cousin who succeeded only to the Viscountcy, the Marquisate being extinct. Now to sew on buttons!

23. All did well. Our rubber was very gay. James and Annie returned well pleased and we lost enough, Janey and I, to put the Colonel in capital humour and to pay Mrs. O'Reilly's car home. Poor woman she repaid me one pound she had borrowed and I really don't believe she had more than another in her lean-looking purse, but I thought it more delicate to take it, it can be re-lent. James is off this snow-covered! morning to the hills, Annie will remain till Saturday, when if the weather change for the better she and Janey and Pysey will set out for Baltiboys that they may attend the Kildare Hunt races at Punchestown on Monday and Tuesday. Should this wretched cold and snow and sleet continue, they will not think of such a move, especially as they must be back for the Castle Ball on Wednesday.

I had a very little morsel of a conversation with James yesterday, begun by himself, which has given me much comfort. He is at length aware of the folly of living beyond his means, the irksomeness of debt has done its work, there is nothing like experience. Man, proud man, will not listen to advice. He says when once freed from the remainder of the chain he has felt so galling he never again will run an account. What he cannot pay for he will do without, live within his income determinedly.

This is an excellent beginning, but there is more to do, there must be self sacrifices. The stud must be touched, there are too many horses for so small an income, and some of them are of an useless sort. There should be none for the carriage but those borrowed for the occasion from the plough. The car horse should be the hack for fairs when my Lady wife should *walk* like her mother! One hunter should do, and the meets near at hand be sufficient, and a John Fitzpatrick who suited *us* should do for them, no fine head groom, requiring as much *meat* as helped to swell their butcher's bill last year to upward of one hundred pounds. Ours was never fifty, with our open house ways and people on long visits to us. Their expensive gardener, who kept the grounds neat certainly but gave them no vegetables, is gone, and the steward very properly undertakes his work. Also they have got rid of their butler and I hope he will not be replaced. I have taken away my washing, so Mary is gone and Annie makes her cook and housemaid do her washing. If they will be wise enough, she and James, to hire a parlour maid who can use her needle they would find themselves much more comfortable and their expenses about half.

Both of them required a lesson. I hope and trust they are the wiser of it. I was sure from James' cranky temper that he was in difficulties again. It shews such a foolish childish vanity to distress oneself this way for the mere *shew* of the thing. There is so much good in him, a warm kind generous heart, sweet temper, activity, fun etc., that it grieved me really to see him so improvident. 'Tis a mercy they have had no children yet. Annie is wrong too, too fond of gaiety, of admiration, of ease and so forth. She don't remember she is the wife of a poor man, *would* marry him, and is therefore doubly bound to make his means go as far as careful house-wifery can manage. This will be their last gay year. Even should Janey not be married I cannot another season have this racket here. My Aunt will be more infirm, my husband ditto, we must have a quiet house for both their sakes. Also I must save some money for our boy's start in life. All this I mean to take an opportunity to tell my daughters.

25. Good Friday, bright, dry, cold. The Colonel went off early yesterday about his photograph which he brought back with him, really very like, more agreeably so than these sun portraits usually are. Mrs. O'Reilly was our only visitor, she dragged me out to walk, bitter cold as it was, and to call with her on Lady Milltown. We met only Lord Russborough and Edward that we knew. Lady Milltown was alone and delighted to see us, she was in good humour, in a gossipping vein, full of Wyndham Goold! who really much admires Lady Barbara, so we could not get away till after six.

I don't like *Queechy* so well as the *Wide Wide World.* 'Tis the same little girl of nervous temperament in circumstances not very different, no longer new to the reader, so that the charm of novelty, nay of originality, is wanting. The poverty stricken family, the useless husband, the subdued wife, the careworn overworked children, carried my thoughts back many a long year to those anxious Highland days when raiment was as scant with me, food uncertain, servants few and those unpaid, the fuel forgotten, the house a wreck, hope wanting and only troubles present. Well, it worked together for good with me at any rate. How proud, how vain, how thoughtless I was before. How ill I bore my poor mother's much vexed temper. The temper was weighty enough but it steadied giddy me. How have I watched, like Fleda, for a present of some dainty for my mother's dinner, stored the eggs to sell at Robbie Cumming's shop for tea, for thread, for pepper, kept all locked at house and farm and served all rations with such nicety, cooked little dishes, learned from books, stored the wool, the feathers as a farmer's dame, patched! darned, knit, and was not unhappy, catching half an hour to read and hailing Sunday, feeling the full value of that day of rest. But it wore me out, was too much for me, not the physical labour, but the fevered mind, the strain was great and too long continued. I can feel for Hugh and Fleda and I had no Hugh, but the dear good Mrs. McPherson was my Aunt Miriam.*

Just as we were setting off for St. Patrick's, Mrs. O'Reilly came up in such a fuss to carry me away with her back to Lady Milltown who has so overexcited herself about all this affair of Barby's that she must see me again, so I promised to call in after service. We had no difficulty in getting seats we went so early. We did not like taking possession of Wyndham Goold's as his sisters are all in town and very musical. So we had to content ourselves with a pew further back. The preliminary chantings were not so fine, as usual, but the anthem was one of Mendelsohn's, the 22nd Psalm was extremely beautiful, well worth getting chilled to the bone to listen to, for the choir was as cold as a well. There never was weather so harsh at this season within my memory. My girls went home and I went to Molesworth Street where I calmed matters down as well as I could. My Lady *and my Lord*, would give Barbara to Mr. Goold with pleasure, and would go any lengths to promote an intimacy, too great lengths I fear, and finding Mr. Sheehan is a cousin and that through him we have become acquainted with this prize, *she* is wild to get introduced to Mespile. 'How did you manage it?' said she. 'I did not manage it at all' said I. 'How happened it then' said she. 'It happened naturally' said I. 'We made his acquaintance in the country and he followed it up when we came to town'. 'How did you get to know him in the country? 'Colonel Smith went to call upon him as soon as he bought that Lodge and became our neighbour, and he never forgot that piece of attention.' 'Milltown calls on no one' – silence – 'I often longed to know him when I heard of his pleasant parties, you and the Downshires and every-body, I wish I knew him now, you must manage this for me, my dear Mrs. Smith, and then he has heard the most dreadful lies of me, that I begged not to be introduced to him, undervalued him, called him I don't know what, etc., etc.' There is just the hitch, Lord Milltown with his absurd pride declined noticing that '*Mail* man' or 'man of the *Mail*' and she did say all sorts of outrageous absurdities and he was told of them. Now that she finds he is cousin to Wyndham Goold, that they are intimate and that they value one another, she wants to get at the one through the other, and I know she will make a mess of it.

She declared she would undeceive Mr. Sheehan and so on; but she can't, for the tale is too true. Her only way is to let bygones be bygones, get herself introduced to Mr. Sheehan by her son, who knows him well, make herself agreeable to him, carefully avoiding any allusion to her folly, and let matters take their chance. So with Mr. Goold; let Barbara introduce him to her mother, then she may invite him to the house. If he incline he will follow up this opening; if he do not no harm is done. I must see her again to beseech her to be quiescent or she will make such a mess of the matter as will redound to their discredit. I wish she had never heard of Mr. Goold's admiration. It was all our fault speaking of it before Mrs. O'Reilly. I hate meddling in matrimonials. This would be an admirable match for both parties, she deserves him and he is mark enough for her, but were it Janey, I would not stir in the business, no maneuvring for husbands, it is hateful. The only excuse for my Lady's over anxiety is her position, so well nigh desperate and my Lord's selfish vanity in secluding them from any intimacies because his gambling prevents his living in the style suited to his rank, he don't choose this to be *seen*, but it is well known and commented on. We had no whist, the 'man of the *Mail*' having filled his paper with sufficient news to interest the Colonel all the evening.

26. Janey and I went out early to call on my Lady and reiterate our entreaties that she would take no notice to Mr. Sheehan of it having been told to him of what she I am afraid said. We could not get away again, she had so much to say, and her girls had so much to say, and Russy came in and Edward, with a frightful account of a tragedy at St. Columba's – ten boys flogged and two expelled, privately, that is their friends informed they must be removed. That unfortunate school is always in hot water. Harry Leeson is not in the row, nor Smith O'Brien and Edward is sure not Jack. Poor little Charlie Crichton is, I shall be in a fidget till Monday morning which will bring us Jack, if all be right, for his two days of Easter holidays. I don't think he would be in anything wrong because he is so prudent and so right judging and because he has more than once helped to keep unquiet spirits right. I shall be very much relieved to see him though.

27. Easter Sunday and Janey and I intended to give ourselves the Cathedral service but every part of Christ Church was so crowded that we went to St. Anne's, where I can never hear

and nobody with those high backed pews can see. We found Mrs. O'Reilly at home with my Aunt. She carried off Janey to meet Lady Milltown and her party, who had been seen from the windows. They further met Mr. Nugent and his sisters, so paraded in great force among the *élite*. We don't think Mr. Nugent's hair near so red since we found he really will be the Earl of Westmeath!

28. Jack arrived an hour later than usual which made me very uneasy, his bright face when he did arrive cheered me up in a moment. The tale was true, and all the school think the Warden and Subwarden wrong to have acted with such severity. Expulsion is such a blow. The two boys expelled were of course to blame, but there might have been a less crushing punishment. They were the heads of the offence, which was an immorality and is not to be divulged, and all ten were flogged, pitilessly, a shocking sight, revolting to a good nature and of no use, or rather harmful to a bad one. It is less the victim than the spectator who is hurt by such savage proceedings. With such training we wonder men grow up vicious.

30. Ogle Moore has completed the preliminaries of his sale. A few weeks now will see him an independant man. *All* debts paid, his little income clear, and twenty thousand pounds to leave among his six daughters. He will educate and start his sons and they must make their own way. This has made me very happy. He fudged it a bit of course. 'The lesson was hard but is not thrown away, has taught them much etc.' He believes all this pretty talk at the time, living in an imaginary world of his own always which of course deludes him, the fancied feeling is right however, the only pity is that it is only fancy.

Annie and James amused Papa first by singing so prettily, next by their mesmerick experiences and last by the never palling rubber. Colonel Layard and his three victims go about now in a car to exhibit, went to the Palace to perform at ease to the Whateleys. One of the maids is beginning to feel her head weary she says, and it aches a little when the trance is over. He will kill the poor girl. Mr. Nugent says he expects to see his commanding Officer tried for manslaughter some day. This flaming admirer of Janey's walked home with her and Annie and announced his intention of calling on me to-day. Not to lay his coronet at our feet I hope.

SUNDAY, APRIL 3. Mild, charming Spring weather with a bright sun this summer morning that is quite reviving. Thursday the thirty-first was the last Cattle Show day, so the streets were fuller even than usual. It often surprises me to find them always so crowded. Strangers fancy something unusual to be going on, but it is merely the peripatetick habits of the population. All persons of all ranks pass most of their time in wandering about the town. Fifty errands are made out of what might all have been done at once: the servants really live in the streets, what between their own business real and fancied, their gossipping propensities and the thousand and one messages they are running the whole day for their masters, there is a mob of busy idlers in perpetual motion. It is not wonderful that so little is done within doors, it is good work for an able frame merely to answer the never ending ring.

Friday James and Annie dined in Merrion Square to meet Lord Erne whom Annie very much likes. Mr. Nugent! and one of his sisters called also, sister said she came to see Mrs. King, the brother was silent as to the object of his visit. James has laid a bet with Janey that red hair and all she will be Countess of Westmeath some day. It looks as if she might be, certainly, and yet 'I have my doubts'. The future Earl goes off on Tuesday to join his regiment but is to get a fortnight's leave by and bye for the Exhibition and Colonel Layard says he would not be inaccessible to the plea of 'urgent private affairs'. We have begun to ignore the complexion, talk of gentlemanly manners, pleasant expression etc.

8. I went on Wednesday evening to see poor Pysie. It really was a miserable scene. She lay on a pallet bed, one mattress, no under sheet, an old cloke for a coverlet, no chair in the little room, a stool on which stood her jug of barley water, a trunk on which I sat, a cupboard half open containing all the quantity of dresses the poor little body's head is filled with. Her mother had run home just to see her. She is staying with Lady Milltown who is ill and in low spirits etc., 'but' said Pysie, 'my brother Eyre is my nurse, he leeched me, dressed

my blister, carries me up and down', for she can't walk 'takes motherly care of me' added the poor little thing, her large eyes filling with tears, 'he will be home now directly and then he will bring me downstairs'. The only maid was in the kitchen with the poor baby, nursed up into a fine child. How strange it is to my Scotch nature. With such a distressed home, Mrs. O'Reilly gadding about from morning to night, dining anywhere, accepting anything, dress, money, food, reading and cooking her only other pursuits. Pysie, whose ill behaviour encreased all the evils, and now separated from her husband and penniless, gadding too, dress and dancing her delight. Surely home, the strictest most private home, home with a curtain round it and every energy directed to the management of such small funds, the payment of such pressing debts, the education of those unfortunate children should be the thought by day and dream by night of those two women. Well, it would not be Irish, *or* Roman Cath.

James and Annie went to the Play too, a command night, house crowded and the performance excellent. Janey had a slight touch of English cholera which had kept her and me awake half the night. I had to go down for wine, spices, a saucepan, laudanum etc., and cured the little lady though she still looks 'pale and wan' like Suckling's lover, quite unfitted for the Play.* She bears disappointment so well, so do the poor Leesons, and they have more than disappointments to bear – daily, hourly mortifications. Their parents are so unpopular that the children are neglected. Here have they been two months in town, dined but once at the Castle, not half a dozen private parties have they been asked to, nor does a mortal ever call on them with scarce half a dozen exceptions. The long mornings and longer evenings are mostly spent in silence and solitude. My Lord is mostly at the Club gambling, when at home he never speaks. My Lady is equally mum when her Lord is by, and in his absence her conversation is one never ending finding fault – with him, with the world, with their life, with her poor daughters' dress and carriage and manners and wishes – till Mrs. O'Reilly, who is my informant, actually weeps for them. Poor things. There is no help, their mother's *tongue* so often used so ill-advisedly keeps a bar up between them and any comfort. It is even more against them than the discreditable conduct of the father and the brother, a brother who deserves as much pity as his sisters. Lady Milltown seems to me not very unlikely to go mad. Sometimes when my few vexations encrease enough to worry me, more than they would do were my health stronger, I think of that devoted house and thank God from my heart for my better fortunes.

9. That restless pair off for good. Son-in-law and I had a little storm at parting. There has been an offer for the house of Baltiboys which of course I shall enquire into. Poor James, he vapours and he splutters and he fumes, shewing selfishness and ostentatious vanity with every angry word. He don't feel grateful either, not the least for all we have done for him, on the contrary seems to consider us as the obliged party; d——d nonsense as the Colonel would say, but for their own sakes, poor children, this must be put an end to.

I must buckle to and set in earnest about a deal of business that must be got through without further delay. This determination of Jack's to seek his fortunes in India alters all previous arrangements. Why should I grieve, my Colonel's life hangs on a thread, my own on a few strands, the knowledge of their happiness should be sufficient for the right thinking mother of children, but to lose my boy, my dreams over, the sun of my few remaining years obscured. To other young men, born without position, Jack's little inheritance, the work to do in it, the money to be made of it, the happy useful healthy life to be led in it, old associations all around, loving hearts all near – to such young men such a stay would be the heaven to which their weary years would tend. My boy throws all away. Change, movement, new faces, new habits, excitement in short his still nature requires. Will Janey disappoint me too? Yes, when her turn comes. I try to bear it all, I try to be content, submissive at any rate, but the spring of my mind is gone.

17. Friday was a wonderful day for I went to a concert [at] the College Choral; the crowd was so great we had difficulty in keeping our stand and then the pressure sent us forward in such a squeeze we were glad to take refuge in any vacant

seat. Mr. Hickey, 'Martin Doyle',* and I got next to Kitty Hawtayne and Mrs. Montgomery. The old man was so delighted to talk of Avranches days and Avranches friends and of his own family affairs, that I am quite sure he passed a pleasant evening. *The Last Judgement* by Spohr, a short Oratorio, on the whole disappointed me, it is more graceful than grand, wanting in sublimity suited to the subject, the chorusses poor. It is good musick, the quartettes very satisfying, harmonies, beautiful. A miscellaneous addition filled up the time, Mendelsohn, Beethoven, Schubert and last and best, Mozart, so full, so rich after the more *meagre* compositions.

A deputation with long rods, Lord Gough and the Chancellor, a little sturdy bulletheaded vulgar man with a grand forehead, marshalled in my Lord and my Lady Lieutenant, who seemed attentive to the *treat*; their suite however chattered. Lord Gough, quite gray, is veteran looking altogether but he has not much countenance, my Lady very large and fat, was a mass of gold tissue, Delhi scarf, Persian silk dress with gold embroideries and tassels and fringes and a cap to suit with two gold tails hanging chowrie fashion from each side of her head.* I am none the worse of my raking now, but I could not sleep a wink that night, fancying all the musick over again.

24. We have had such a business with our most tiresome son-in-law. Mr. Gledstanes came to me and asked whether we would let Baltiboys. I told him we would willingly, the house, for more reasons than one. Several times during this past year I have mentioned to James that I should like to let it, the loss of a rent for it was a considerable inconvenience. I repeated to him that we never had even contemplated letting him the house. I am sure I have told him this a hundred times and it seems I might as well have held my tongue for any impression I made on a man who, like his father, can comprehend just only what he chooses and who imagines that what he announces is law, his view of matters the only right one. So when I told him of this offer did he not fume up like a burst bottle of pop and there I left him.

In the meantime Mr. Gledstanes, having reported progress, came to say that the proposed tenant was the wealthy

Mr. Tyrrell but that he wanted land; *that* I said we could not give him without consulting Mr. King, [to whom] I wrote my tale. Such an answer as came, five sheets of abuse, complaint, misstatements, misrepresentations, impertinence, insolence, I was so shocked, so much ashamed, for unluckily this ungrateful production arrived at tea time and the Colonel took one of his inquisitive fits and have it read aloud he would.

Oh, how angry they all were, poor Janey so shocked. The Colonel ordered me to write to forbid this little piece of arrogance the house for the present. I am so sorry. I thought James had improved. I fear now he will never improve and alas! I fear he may spoil my Annie. That marriage was half a dozen nails in my coffin.

I had written to him at first so kindly and then to have such a spitfire of an answer. All thought my reply very moderate, for I read it here, yet Annie wrote that its 'bitter words' had so distressed her, so exasperated her husband! whose letter to me she had read and approved and could not fancy how I could feel offended with it!

On Thursday he came up to talk the matter over. He vapoured on with very little sense. He had all along been the benefactor, we the obliged! We had injured him! were going to ruin him, in short he seemed crazed. Alas! I have found out why, and that determined me on getting him back to the small farm, for which he will have capital, *coute qui coute*. It is plain he has not taken in the meaning of any one thing said to him or written to him. All the pains I had taken to show him how carefully we should study his interests in new arrangements, repaying him for improvements, disposing well of his stock and crop, all that he had overlooked. To leave the fine house for a small one, to give place to 'Attorney Tyrrell' – 'a snob' – 'unvisitable' – 'on whom the whole neighbourhood would turn their backs' – with his handsome, well born wife and her five well portioned daughters!

Really for his own sake we must be firm. What has become of the three hundred pounds our auction brought him, who can say. He is now purchasing stock by bills, running here and there to borrow money when they become due, of course at high interest, or renewing them at equal cost. As my information is quite correct, I have written it to Annie very delicately, as a reason for getting him out of a position which most surely would be his ruin; his involvements are the town's talk, exaggerated of course, but I know they are there, he could not deny it, for he perpetually tries to borrow from me and he has borrowed from Mrs. Bourne, repaid her nearly it is true, but who can get on ever scrambling for means thus. He behaved very badly Thursday, spoke so rudely, like a rude vulgar angry schoolboy, not like a man seriously arguing.

I am sure it is these money difficulties that distract him. He was much in the same style all last summer, when his behaviour was unbearable. Then after we forced the horrid father to pay up his arrears, James, rid for the moment of debt, got as good humoured as possible, now just before the term his rent is coming on, God knows how many bills he has flying over the country, with very little funds to meet them. He has had the grace to write to say he will offer no further obstructions, give up all, now, if wanted, and I hope we may bring him round by degrees to better sense in all ways, he vexes me sadly. We that lived in harmony with all the world till he came amongst us, he sets everyone by the ears, one special reason why I wish him out away from our place and people.

25. Having no particular business to keep me in my little cold dressing-room this morning, I am in the warm drawing-room early enough to read these my strictures on poor James King again and see whether aught has been set down in malice [*Othello* V ii 345]. No, he is very troublesome to deal with, very slippery, saying what suits him, unsaying as it suits him, he is wanting in steady principles, of course his conduct is unsteady too. And this is Annie's husband, that pure and bright and lovely one, whom we nurtured with such care and gave out of our safekeeping far too soon. What remains to do is to make the best of it. He is a kind affectionate husband, adores her, loves us all I believe, after his fashion, but between his temper and his gambling manner of management his business would ruin everyone whom he could win over to trust him. I shall disconnect him

with our affairs at any cost. He shall never have the power of a *smile* over Jack. At a safe distance after all this storm has blown over we shall get on very harmoniously, and being our Annie's husband I will still lend the helping hand to set him right.

He consents to leave Baltiboys; back at Humfreystown in that small farm and house suited to his means, with his little money income paid him in cash, active and clever as he really is, he will get on well. The ready money for all he gives up at Baltiboys will, I hope, suffice to redeem those mischievous bills, and Annie must be brought to her Smith senses. All the ridiculous *King* vanity, for it is not pride, must go. Poor they are and poor they are ever likely to be, for my persuasion is that the old people are not really rich, merely pretend to be and have hard enough work to get along in the absurd airified style they affect and which is trebly absurd in them who have hardly an acquaintance. So now I begin in earnest to disentangle the skein, for I have grand schemes hatching, resolved, well considered, determined on, in my bed during many a long sleepless hour.

26. Yesterday was bitter cold, the raw rainy air was warmed by a little note from Annie in a much more proper tone than her former but still under the delusion that she and her husband have been ill used, have done nothing wrong, that he is in no difficulties, thriving and open to her, telling her candidly how he stands when she asks, which she seldom does, having such confidence in his principles, his courage, his shrewdness.

Mr. Tyrrell seems in no hurry even to look at the place, which I had cautioned them from the first might or might not suit him. I called on Mr. Gledstanes to try and hurry the 'Attorney', but did not find him in. I want matters settled much.

28. Mr. West called on John Robinson to say he heard Baltiboys was to be let, that he wished to have it, but could only afford to give one hundred pounds, it was certainly worth more but he was not able to give more. John was a little amazed to find he and I had had two interviews, and that I had mentioned the rent from which there would be no abatement. I fancy he will come to terms, this is a dodge – cuteness.

29. Louise Hornidge and Cilla were here to engage Janey to join in a grown up dancing class, for the purpose of learning these new quadrille figures etc. It will be nice amusement for her. My Janey is a dear little thing, affectionate and sensible and very agreeable, but not useful. She is no help to me or anyone in any way. Why, I can't make out, but so it is, on she goes in her quiet walk through life, all along the straight road, carefully gathering up her skirts so that not a fold nor a hem should touch another traveller. Maybe in *Irish* company she is wise, yet it seems a strange unnatural character to *me*. Jack is much the same, they take after their dear good father who always was not only unhelping but helpless; Janey is not the last, I fear, Jack is.

30. Janey and I walked to Pim's to buy some household requisites, Mr. Sheehan our escort the whole way and back. We then all went on to Mespile, walked to the flower garden, back to the gate, still could not part! for there were letters waiting, one from Wyndham Goold, one from a Mr. Johnson, both M.P.s, giving the news of London. Whisper goes that Lord Derby will give up politicks in disgust, extremely dissatisfied with the usage he has met with from his so called adherents. Many have been coquetting with the Government, many have deserted, and Dizzy and Walpole left the House the other night arm in arm before the division on some motion of consequence.* To me it seems to be little matter who is in or who is out, the welfare of the country is the last thing any of them think of, they never look after our true interests any of them. Not one human being seems to set to work in earnest to 'red [tidy] up the house' in good housewifely fashion, except Charles Dickens in his wonderful writings.

James was in town, another scramble I suppose. He is sore still, not exactly amiable but amenable. I feel pretty sure now that if we could save his vanity and get him in a little ready money he would put up with the change very philosophically. He denied being much pressed but confessed to having some bills out, and to owing his cousin David Charles Latouche a sum of money. It is a frightful way of living, this gambling style. He was such a goose too with ever so many fine servants at high wages. I am sure he

wasted more than one hundred pounds last year in ostentatious folly. I hope to get him and *her* back to their senses,
to a style of living suited to their means, a size of farm within
their capital, poor dear children, their heads were turned.
SUNDAY 8 MAY. Pleasant news from Jane, happy at Riccarton and
not without hopes for Jack, William G. Craig* being en-
listed in his favour. Poor Jack, so long as he is happy, is
doing well, what should it matter seeing the end of me, the
health I had fancied bolstered up has been again completely
broken and unless I were saved and comforted and nursed
instead of having to save and comfort and nurse others, I do
not at present feel as if I should be very long here. To
lighten my burthen, I have determined on searching out an
Agent for Baltiboys. While living there on the spot with
John Robinson to appeal to and do the Dublin business, I
could get on very well, at this distance I cannot manage the
tenantry, cannot look after the property, besides that, it is an
over anxious charge. It would be a great relief to have an
active, responsible Agent, to receive so much without accounting for it, sure, no deductions however small the sum,
and to have my head clear for the proper business of a
woman.

We are reading such a book – *My Novel* by Bulwer, full of
faults of story, exaggeration of character and so forth, but
full of beauty, full of wisdom, full of truth, there is such a
strength in the manly mind, depth of thought, of reading, of
judgement. We women do the feeling better, perhaps, but
we sadly want the vigour, the knowledge, the 'Attick salt'.*
Also in a work by D'Israeli there is much good – *Sybil*. Mrs.
Beecher Stowe did not do her slaves better. Our Goths and
Vandals are indeed a perilous horde.

15. Sunday. I *will* set down James' improprieties that Jack may
see I do not wrongfully condemn. He asked leave to buy one
hundred pounds worth of stock at our sale, he bought two
hundred and sixty, left me to pay the auction fee, took the
coals at a valuation on credit, without consulting me,
borrowed fifteen pounds, my brain's money, saved to give
Janey her dance which I told him, etc. This fifteen pounds
was to be repaid in a week, the coals in a month, the stock in
May when the father's one hundred pounds was due, that

failing he promised it at Christmas when the allowance *I fought* for was paid up, and to this hour never a penny has come to me of anything. He sold the Colonel's two young horses, his darlings, pocketted the price. He grumbled at the board we paid him during our stay at home. I gave him in our own house, with our own furniture, coals, wine, plate, linen, for our diminished party, the Colonel, my Aunt, Janey, Jack, one maid and me more than it had cost me to keep us all, himself his wife and our other three servants! I had to add a ten pound more, and allow this, that and the other to make out his rent! The more I did the more he wanted, just lived the more expensively on our money, trusting to be helped again. I am very credulous.

A thought of false dealing never entered my unsuspicious head, but when once it is shewn to me, once I am undeceived, all confidence in the deceiver vanishes for ever, and after the first sting of disappointment all affection too. As I have forgotten that I can no longer esteem the poor Doctor, so shall I forget from the same cause James King. The presence of neither ever will affect me in any way, it is not even disagreeable. I have the happy faculty of considering such persons as mere chairs and tables unsuited to me, quite indifferent to me. It will be no effort to me to be civil to James King. He is my daughter's husband and a very kind one, makes her, in as far as in him lies, very happy, the less she can discover of his being but zero with me the better. He will take care to be very agreeable in company; we shall have no private intercourse, and as I am quite willing to let him have the best of the bargain that is to end in getting rid of him we shall have no more scenes. I will uphold him all I can, help him all I can, but 'never more [can he] be friend of mine'.

I had a satisfactory interview with Mr. West whom I must now write to, to put an end for present to all negotiation between us. We must lose the half year's better rent, some fifty pounds and all I can reckon on for the winter is the furniture, a gain of fifty pounds. How horrid it is to have to look after the pounds this way. I live in hopes, delusive hopes, of each succeeding year turning out better in the income way, but it don't a bit, something or another always comes as a check. Now we have high markets, unprecedently high markets, prices to which we have been hitherto quite unaccustomed in this country.

22. And Sunday again. A whole week too of fine weather, not one rainy day. The Colonel goes every morning to the Exhibition by himself and every afternoon from four to six, the crowded time, he goes with Janey. She has also been to a concert of Sims Reeves [Drury Lane, La Scala and Paris English tenor] with the Gledstanes party, dining with them first, and to the famous Fancy Ball in the dress of a Greek lady – two petticoats of soft muslin edged with silver, one shorter than the other, a low cut jacket of blue silk edged with silver over a vest of white satin, half long sleeves with very full muslin undersleeves, looped with pearls, plenty of rows of pearls on the neck – *beads* of course. The head was the prettiest part – two long curls at each ear, three plaits hanging down behind, a little blue velvet cap called a *Calotte*, beautifully embroidered by kind Madame in pearls and silver, very coquettishly stuck to one side at the back of the head with a tassal to it and to fill up the other side a camilia from which jasmine drooped. Almost half the room wore veils, which did not look well in dancing, though very pretty in the single figure. Kitty Hawtayne as the White Lady of Avenal, with Mary Finnemore as the Princess called here on their way.

They came for Janey at eleven, at twelve they had reached the railway station! after another half hour in the file, they got out and walked the rest! Sixteen hundred people at the least, dresses superb, ladies and gentlemen of the olden time abounded. Janey said it put her mind of the *Vignettes* and prints and pictures of that day, to see ladies in powder, rolled hair, high heads, fardingales, hoops, rouge, patches etc., seated simpering behind large fans, with smiling gentlemen hanging over them dressed in wigs, curls, bags, swords, ruffles, buckles and coats stiff with embroidery.* Costumes of all nations well got up – peasants, sailors, remarkable characters etc., etc., all fresh and all faithful were crowded there. Captain Scott's Albanian dress coat cost him eighty pounds, for no expense seemed to be spared by anyone. There was the utmost good humour, a great deal of dancing, everybody looked well, and Janey got back at six in the morning. Were I in the mood I could make quite a history of this Fancy Ball, but I am far from well, and feel equal to neither thought nor penwork. We have passed a pleasant week but for my private sufferings.

Dublin is so full, streets crowded, carriages for ever rolling, all the shops so fine, gay goods within, fresh paint without; better than all an universal cheerfulness pervades the *air* – reaching to St. Columba's, where Janey and her Papa went on Tuesday last, the Examination day. Jack looking so well they said.

24. Thank God I am better, freer from pain than for some weeks past, free I may say, merely a tenderness remaining. The medicine resumed, wine given up, have atchieved this most blessed effect. I would have been content to die the other night, to cease to be, so as I ceased to feel, and Doctors can do me no more good. My own prudence, time and as little exertion of any sort as is possible. There's the rub. No one else but little Marianne appears to have the power of going out of self, and for self they require help. They call me dull, idle, cross, odd, everything that I am not, because I am no longer physically able to do my overwork with alacrity.

27. Summer weather all the week I have paid a second visit to the Exhibition* which has made great progress, an infinity of vacant spaces filled since my first, yet any description seems impossible. There are five large halls lying side by side, the centre one much the largest; each is surrounded by a gallery approached by handsome double staircases. All this space being insufficient, the largest yard of the society to the south has been roofed in and two semicircular corridors have been constructed round the sides of the Court in front of Kildare House. These extra buildings which I understand are for large specimens of machinery, implements, carriages, carts, etc., have not yet been opened. The three centre halls are filled with the most costly objects of art, – the outer one to the south is the picture gallery, the outer one to the north is a steam factory. Here we have an idea given of the wonderful power man has made unto himself out of the simplest most abounding element provided for us. A model of every one of these beautiful helps to labour, these creators

of wealth, and alas! to say, these corruptors of our purer natures, are here at full work. From the chopping asunder of iron bars, to the ribbon loom weaving, and the pottery wheel, we have a sample of each steam driven manufacture throughout our toiling country.

Interesting beyond idea, melancholy to reflect on, for what does this over labour do? – Enriches the few, enslaves the many, loosens principles, and let them boast as they will, does not raise the country either in position or in character. I am quite convinced of this that the moment it becomes necessary for women to go out of their proper sphere, their *home*, there is something wrong in social politicks. Man is to provide, woman to preserve. When he cannot provide sufficient, and she has to *aid* his work and neglect her own begins the course of evil. Factory life, a life of sin, unnatural, deleterious, revolting. Through all the grandeur of these wonderful machines, wonderful in their construction, wonderful in their produce, wonderful from the long chain of human skill and human toil attending the dispersion of their wonderful creations, I see in my sad mind's eye, the workman's home – cold, bare, dirty, unregulated; low sensuality its pleasure, discontent the spirit pervading it. Our Agricultural labourer is poorer certainly in wages, yet richer far in comforts. But we are wrong altogether in our system with the labourer. He was hardly used in the olden time, the collar, the whip, the dungeon, the despotism of the feudal times remain to these, modified by the era, equally tyrannick, equally debasing.

Will our children live to see labour dignified, the labourer exalted, intelligence and with it wealth more equally diffused. No, nor our grandchildren. But the day *will* come unless we fall to pieces all together. Great strides have been made of late years, and here I am on my hobby, as my brother John says: – 'Let Eli begin where she will, by Jove! she gets on to her infant schools'. But I repudiate the 'infant', the best 'infant school' is the mother's knee, only in this age that knee is either so out of the way or so unfit for its burden, that we must fosternurse the deserted child to have it live to be in its turn a mother.

31. Janey and I went on Saturday to St. Columba's, saw Jack looking well and happy. All sunny within, without. Faults

the institution has, what of human invention has not, tempers the masters undoubtedly have, which of us has them not, but take it for all in all where is a better place of education to be found. It always falls on my heart like healing balm to see my boy there, thriving in so pure an atmosphere. Sunday I went to St. Peter's to Mr. Wolseley's sermon for the protestant Orphans. At the close of the Communion Service the vestry door beside the altar opened and two by two came out in one long file the hundred little orphan girls in their snow white, curious high crowned caps, chaunting without musick part of the hundred and nineteenth Psalm as they moved noiselessly on through the middle aisle to the gallery stairs to seat themselves high up on either side of the organ, where they looked like a set of cherubim watching over us. It was an excellent practical sermon, full of lessons to us all and most satisfactory as to the morale of this excellent institution to which the gray haired preacher had been chaplain for twenty years. We might all do more good, the least of us, were we more active. Lay this to heart, E.S. Yesterday my Aunt and I finished our airing by a drive to the national schools where I had business. She was charmed. Today at four I am off to Baltiboys.

SUNDAY, JUNE 5. An idle week for the Journal but a very busy one for me. I went down by train to Sallins on Tuesday the last day of May. Annie met me and drove me home. Next day only some of the tenants came so I finished the morning in the school and, as recreation, Annie picked me up and took me a round of calls but nobody was at home. That kind, poor, desolate Lady Milltown actually returned our visit at tea time, fearing my stay would be so short that otherwise she might miss me. Friday I made up the books, a good three hours' work and then set out to pay humble visits, look in at the Repository and the school again, but poor Lady Milltown came driving along the road with Edward and *Annie* and she caught me at the gate of the school so there was no help for it, I had to give up the children and give two hours to her.

Not so tidy, our people as when we lived among them; nor, spite of the rising markets, altogether as cheerful, as hopeful as in our day. The priests are very busy making mischief. Good Father Germaine is ridden over by a fire-brand of a cleric sent down on purpose to breed evil. They have set up a hedge school, taken away some of my children, others have been very impudent to the mistress. She has come to her senses but she wants the overseer a little, or rather she is falling off for want of encouragement from some one; she will do better now for a while at any rate.

6. It makes me sad to be at Baltiboys. I was on the whole very happy there, happier than most married women, very happy when my children were young enough to occupy me, and we had kind cheerful friends – now gone. It seems like deserted by the dead somehow. Very neatly kept, neater than in our time; trees grown, many improvements, but not one well remembered face. All the old servants dismissed, except old Peggy who can't be moved; none of the old neighbours to be seen save the Milltowns. I felt so utterly alone I was quite glad to come away, and almost wish never to set my foot there again. Mr. Hornidge values that fine house, unfurn-ished, at forty pounds a year! At present James King is determined to pay this, not having as yet paid his rent – his present rent, and there are the hunters, the carriage horses, the coachman, the helper, and McMahon for butler, all very nicely appointed, suitable quite to a man with eight hundred a year. The gardener and the herd are gone, which is some small reduction, but it is impossible this sort of ostentatious folly can last so that a little patience will bring us clear of the difficulty we so very unwisely let ourselves be entrapped into. Well, that dream is over.

13. *Villette*, such a pretty book by Currer Bell. Nothing in it, hardly any incident, no purpose even that I can discover, no moral worked out, just a set of people described so naturally. It is principally French life in a school; the heroine is the *plain* English teacher, the heroes, for there are two, an English Doctor, very handsome, though with reddish hair, and the French elocution teacher, a very little, very ugly man, extremely eccentrick, poor and not over clean. All the characters are perfect in their way, no exaggeration. The life in the French school exact, the mistress of it so very true to nature; – and Villette is Brussels; I am convinced that Currer

Bell must have lived here and in the capacity she describes so well. At present she lives with Charles Dickens, I understand, who has a wife! be it observed, for she was left homeless by the death of her two sisters, who also wrote but not as well as this gifted creature.*

Mr. D'Israeli, in his *Contarini Fleming*, which I don't like [Dizzy's favourite; he called it a 'Psychological Auto-Biography'], it seems to me to be the memoirs of a madman solely concerned for self, says nature intended man to marry at eighteen and till that becomes a custom, there will be no virtue anywhere, consequently little happiness. I wonder what sort of wives such men would get, either women older than themselves, who would age by comparison so soon that immorality would just begin at the other end, or girls so inexperienced that the want of home comforts would drive the boys abroad. There is a *juste milieu* in all things. Moralists can't advocate late marriage, nor mercenary ones, but a few years of folly should be permitted to weary the very young of both sexes, before they settled steadily down to the duties of wedded life.

28. I have fallen on the queerest [of] books. I have taken up Humboldt's *Letters to Charlotte*,* the elder brother, not the Naturalist, the Statesman. Charlotte is a Lady he once spent three days with at a quiet watering place in the early youth of both. Three sunny days to him as her cultivated mind, simple manners and agreeable appearance and habits all united to make her a charming companion, the more so as the meeting with its pleasures was an accident. To her it was her life, for the recollection, the fond recollection, of this remarkable man never left the *woman's* heart which seemed to have been thrown away upon some respectable person in her own sphere to whom she was married. Five years released her and she would probably have enjoyed her long widowhood in peace at any rate had not the continental troubles broken out [French Revolutionary and Napoleonic Wars] and ruined her amongst a crowd of sufferers. In her destitution she thought of her Pyrmont friend now high in office in Berlin, and enclosing him some sentimental lines he had written in her Album on their parting, she recalled those three heavenly days as an excuse

for her application. The result was immediate relief and this correspondence, the most intimate, familiar, unreserved, tender, that it was possible for man and woman to carry on, he all the time most happily married to a charming wife whom he had loved for herself, although she had brought him great possessions. They had children, a quiver full of blessings, and he prospered in every way. His letters are beautiful, full of wisdom too, yet I question whether his wife would have been gratified by reading such affectionate effusions addressed at such short intervals to his Charlotte. He writes several times in a month frequently, however busy he may be, and it is plain that the childless widow, saddened by ill-fortune and ill-health, has less place in his fancy than the lively, artless, intelligent, handsome girl who was the heroine of his short romance; twenty odd years have only brought him back to that bright day dream often recurred to, yet on the whole forgotten, while she, faithful to her first impression, preserved his image in her inmost heart, cherishing every recollection, feeding memory as it were, making it the only companion of her solitude – a plan he highly approves. He has no wish she should set him aside, on the contrary he delights in the consciousness of her faithful attachment, is jealous of it, counsels her continued seclusion with one engrossing occupation! to think of and to write to him. There never was such a romance imagined out of Germany. They should never meet, but I am afraid they do. Will the correspondence afterwards be equally tender?

FRIDAY, JULY 1. My son-in-law tapped at my door yesterday looking a little sullen, but civil enough; he begged of me to accompany him to the Colonel's room where he had a few words to say. They were not many. He had had an interview with John Robinson and had agreed to give up his tenancy on the 1st of November, etc., and he merely wished to know whether we should be satisfied with such pecuniary arrangements as Mr. Robinson would agree to. The answer was 'of course'. What a weight off my mind, all will go right now. We shall save Jack and ourselves from further loss and those foolish young things themselves perhaps; but a vile headache prevents details at present.

3. Sunday. John Robinson called yesterday to say our 'good son' must be well held in hand, for he considers him a most slippery gentleman, he intends to serve him with a notice to quit – amicably – as a piece of business – the routine – but he considers it necessary as he cannot trust him. He is talking very extravagantly of his 'meliorations', they are magical, priceless, etc., to which the answer was that they would be *discussed* and *fairly* paid for. In short, swindling is a mild term, imposing on honesty and kindness is the true one. Irish cuteness, God forgive me, they are my fellow creatures, but how I do despise the race, not one noble quality.

We take our warm baths, Janey and I at Salt hill, to save a little time we had hoped. The ladies' bathing place is a large basin, an oblong, protected on the land side by high walls against which is built a set of dressing rooms, a neatly bricked quay stretched round half way in front of them with steps at intervals descending to the water; a wide barrier of stone divides this basin from the sea, a sluice gate serving to change the water. At one end of this circular row! are the warm baths, two in number, a boiler, a cistern, the sea, and we never find them ready. Either the fire is low, though there are coals at hand, or the cistern is empty, with the pump handle in sight, or the attendant is 'just over-powered, Ladies', – with what we are not told, nor how we cannot fancy. She a great tall strapping wench, beaming with health, obliging too, but such a slattern, a sort of randy – clothes in tatters, hair uncombed, such a dirty, a very dirty half of a cap, that was once covered with white! satin ribbons, no method, no management could be expected from so wild a creature at her poor wage of two shillings a week! and to keep herself. There is a boy to help her but he is always 'mitchen', so well scolded on a chance appearance that he takes to 'mitch' [to steal, skulk or loiter with intent].

There is a superintendent, a young woman of very neat appearance with quiet, civil manners, who regrets all these annoyances so much and cannot fancy why such mistakes are made. It is the proprietor's wish to have everything satisfactory; while she thus apologises in her little bare room, the most uncomfortable and very nearly the dirtiest, and quite certainly the most untidy place any decent person ever made a home of, as she does, for she sleeps there, some filthy beggar women, all rags, with such *threatening* tangled heads of staring hair, are lounging, half naked as they are, about the steps with long straw ropes in their hands. These are the bathing women, how unlike to Ramsgate, Margate, Weymouth, etc. Visions of a neat made petticoat of blue flannel, a tidy cotton jacket and a coarse cottage bonnet rose on memory's eye, as these horrid shapes filled the eye of reality. No wonder that so few ladies ask their aid – some one or two descending timidly into the bath hold one end of the rope this beldam clutches at the other, standing on the stairs out of the water, tucking her tatters between her knees. I saw most of the bathers walk boldly down and then throw themselves backwards off a proper height into the deep water where they ducked and dived and floated and floundered like the oldest inhabitants of the sea. I had leisure enough for I never got my bath, no ingenuity could raise the heat to 92 while my limited time ran out. I thought of speaking to the proprietor! but he is Legion! the railway company in fact. As too many cooks spoil the broth, and as Irish meanness will meet in return Irish slovenliness, there don't seem to be much hope of improvement at Salt hill at all.

4. The priests again have won the County Clare. This time without bloodshed for they did not prominently interfere with the election. All their work was done in the chapels or by private visits, their majority is large – seventy one. A strong body of police kept order, plenty of military too were at hand and all knew that the authorities were in earnest, no more Sixmile bridge massacres, which affair the soldiery are not like to forget in a hurry. Rome is making wonderful exertions but she will fail, even though she may appear to triumph in the meanwhile. Dr. Cullen may prohibit our best books, he may pervert the morale of our national schools, he may keep the spirit of enquiry back, but he can't entirely paralise the awakening mind. The fruits of the more reflective training will shew in time, we must be patient.

My Baron writes very beautifully to his Charlotte. It is plain he required an intelligent recipient of his outpourings and did not dislike the tender homage of his correspondent, also he wished to study her character, he had a turn that way naturally, and here a pure page unfolded its treasures to him alone, so confidingly, it touched the sentimental chord as well as interested the scientifick research of this amiable philosopher.

What Charlotte was to Humboldt, this odd journal is to me. There are natures not all sufficient to themselves, they must have a *confidante*, contemplative natures too, unsocial rather, yet they must speak their thoughts. Lord Jeffrey used to utter his to Jane and me, the trees on Corstorphine hill might perhaps have done for him, he had his *Review* too. We poets must *utter*, publish is another affair, but write we must if we have none to speak to. It is not in a spirit of arrogance that I say *we*, all are poets who think and feel and compare and *remember*; there are degrees in all ranks, the rank itself is an honour, a blessing, those on the lower lines have still a place and they rise, rise by their own improvement, and they feel it and it rewards them; and if they are more easily offended by contact with less intellectual natures, they have higher pleasure in an intercourse with superiours, whether in books, or by letter or in conversation, or reflexion.

Dear little journal, what a blessing you have been to me, mine would have been a dreary life but for the companionship of pen, ink and paper; to sit and think is not sufficient, we must express our thoughts. There is just one disadvantage attending this indulgence, – I have to watch lest it become too engrossing, almost selfish and hinder the necessary activity in the discharge of duties.

10. Sunday, sunny, warm at this hour of the evening, seven o'clock, still. Not a sound beyond the chirping of the sparrows from this back room. It has been a busy week, we are receiving a visit from [brother] William. I can't account for this apathy. He came on Tuesday and has been very happy at the Exhibition and visiting a good many acquaintances he happens to have here, and playing whist of an evening with Madame Giordano for a partner in whose lively companionship he delights. They have arranged a trip to Killarney with Janey and Jack, and go the whole set of them next Saturday.

He is not looking as I like to see elderly people look. He

has grown immensely large, must weigh near eighteen stone and the fat hangs on him so that the countenance is heavy and the eyes which were never fine are never seen. Of course, so much to carry makes his movements slow, he is not so noisy either as heretofore, just a pleasant vein of cheerfulness pervades his manners, there is not one tinge of regret or disappointment or annoyance, no sour feeling nor sore spot. It is an exemplification of 'how to make the best of it', without an effort either, it comes naturally. His personal requirements are so few that the loss of income he hardly feels, and, if below this calm surface any under currents agitate, no one, not his wife even, is ever aware of such secret grief. A principal fault in his strange character is that complete reserve which shrouded him from all eyes since I can remember. We knew nothing of him ever, neither in our childish days, nor in our youth, nor afterwards. He was impenetrable ever, his existence as it were distinct from ours, no sympathy between us. His *manner* was, and is, charming, irresistibly so, his talents great, his heart affectionate. The Clan spoiled him, Eton ruined him and the world completed the perversion of a noble creature. Well! he will be judged by his opportunities.

The world has been more than wagging with us of late; all in a whirl will best describe its perplexities. The Emperor of Russia is supposed to have gone mad or what is much the same, allowed his bad temper to get the better of his good sense. He rejects all mediation, listens to no remonstrances, Turkey he will over-run if he cannot conquer it. Masses of troops are moving down to overwhelm the Porte, a peaceable invasion he calls it, and as yet he shews no sign of yielding. The French and English fleets have therefore joined, they have entered the Bosphorus, and our navy is all astir at home, ready to join Denmark and Sweden in the Baltic – and our army! the evolutions at Chobham are rivalling the Dublin Exhibition.

Poor Madame [Giordano] has at last had an invitation to Russborough which she has declined. It is most unkindly illbred in them to neglect so near a relation. It is *him*, he says he cannot 'stand her silly clack'. It is tiresome, the tone of the voice very shrill and disagreeable, the gabble incessant, a foolish childish manner. All I dare say unpleasant. I often wish she would be silent for a little while. But she is so good, so kind, so desolate, who could add to her loneliness by failing in civility to one so easily satisfied. Lord Milltown is a vile selfish man now, whatever he once was. My Lady as bad in her own way, and then all the little that was sweet is turned to gall by their unfortunate circumstances. He has gone to London. She had taken lodgings for the week of the Queen's visit, as I found on going to pay a little balance due to her landlady out of money I owed her for butter. A Countess watching her dairy to make a few shillings of its over produce! she is both just and generous, virtues certainly.

17. William went off to Baltiboys on Wednesday, he sat writing beside us most of the morning, chatting so cheerfully and amongst other matters told us quite naturally to congratulate him upon being now a rich man, his income raised forty pounds by a lucky investment. He now has three hundred pounds a year fully! – riches! to him and Sally, for their excellent lodgings cost but one hundred pounds a year, servants and many etc.s included. They always have a good dinner, meat every day, sometimes cold certainly, but then a bit of fish or a pudding or a Stilton cheese is added, they drink no wine, but they have the best London porter, and they bought a whole dozen of wine once last winter, to have a little in the house, and because they gave a dinner party, – salmon, tarts and so on, to six people. He seemed to enjoy this description, shewing a fine waistcoat too, bought for his Irish trip. This is William Grant, who as a young man had his horses and his valet, groom and his private sitting room, and such tailors' bills, and was more particular about the dinner and the wines and the dress of his sisters than my father himself. My Aunt was thoughtful and I wept.

Granny Ryan, who came up newly dressed to see the Queen and the Exhibition, and Miss Macdonnell brought us the news. My school is up again, forty children and more in attendance, the Priests at peace. Not here in Dublin though. A little book of our Archbishop's [possibly *Introductory Lectures on the History of Religious Worship*, 1849] has been proscribed by Dr. Cullen, who brought his objections before the National Board and carried its expulsion from the schools. I never used the book, it not suiting my plan of education to put arguments for or against their religion into the heads of children. I prefer simply to teach them the creed of the parents, they can examine it when they grow up if they choose, and by training their minds to reason on all secular subjects they can apply the clear judgement thus promoted, in any way required by their maturer reflexions. The book is clever, lucid, candid and may be useful to grown up intellects, not the least sectarian.

24. The Killarney party arrived Friday evening. They were out all day, in boats or on the lakes, on pony back over the mountains, in a car for good long drives. Only one day of rain. Beautiful scenery, rich and bold and picturesque, but not wild, not the sublimity of our highlands. A happy party they seem to have been. The hotel was not very well kept, a great many deficiencies and extravagant charges. They have been imposed upon grossly for want of an Irish friend with them. The six days' Bill for the four including boats, guides, ponies, cars, was twenty pounds, then the various assistants all expected private additions to the charges made for them.

TUESDAY, AUGUST 9. Parliament will be prorogued before the twentieth having done but little and, in that little, little good. A Tenant Compensation Bill, with a retrospective clause in it, will complete not the ruin only but the annihilation of the Irish aristocracy. Any tenant who chooses to swear to any improvements up to any amount that have been made on the farm by himself or his predecessors, being relations, within fifty years, is entitled to have them paid for unless disproved or else to remain on his land at the same rent. It will be very hard to disprove back for fifty years any *gate, fence, drain, path*, all classed under improvements which a man may have made for his own convenience and has fully enjoyed the benefit of, and in this unscrupulous country what does an oath or a string of oaths cost a man who will gain a fortune by false swearing and be absolved of the sin for a few shillings. Besides it is the custom of the country to give farms at low rents on the understanding that the landlord not having the cash to make all such improvements himself, he takes the only way in his power to have them made, viz. by the tenant who can do them cheapest, and is remunerated by his low rent. A bad system, maybe, let it then be avoided in future, but that retrospective clause is unjust to robbery.

It has been a dull profitless session [of Parliament], very unsatisfactory in every way, no talent, no principle, no industry, no right intention to be seen among that crowd of incessant talkers. A poor display indeed, not one head rising above the rest. Papal aggression becomes daily more insolent, war with Russia seems inevitable. The wily Czar temporised till all his formidable preparations were complete and now comes out the great bear in earnest. He has seized on Moldavia and Wallachia, issued his orders there, appropriated their revenues, bearded us in all fact, and so, we have sent another courier to St. Petersburgh!!

Dear John Peter Grant [nephew] has passed for Haylebury with credit – first in classicks. Jack is all anxiety now, and some thing must be wrong at St. Columba's, for the boy quite dislikes the place, his spirits seem crushed, not the merry laugh and light ways of his age, it is as if the oppressive discipline of the Jesuits were in force there, fetters on the mind. There is certainly too much study and far too little play, and too much methodical supervision, no free agency. Still it is a good school; the boys are well mannered and healthy and 'get on' as the saying is. However I must turn in my mind removing Jack at Christmas, a year or two of England would do him good whether he be for India or for home. Dear little fellow, he leaves us tomorrow after very quiet, hardly happy holidays, his time here having been dull enough. What could be expected in this Hospital, and myself laid up so entirely. I have been employing my fingers in needlework and *writing*, making a paper for *Chambers'* out of Madame's notes of Killarney, which was sent off yesterday to Mr. Ritchie.

11. Our fine Landlord and Tenant Bill has not passed the Lords. Lord Clanricarde [a notorious evicting absentee landlord] moved that it be referred to a Committee, which amendment was carried nearly unanimously, so there's an end to that. What a strange state of things, party gone, the Conservatives quite gone, extinct we may call them. These

waifs and strays who have coalesced to manage the nation are really fools, suggesting all sorts of ill-considered measures and then, after a flogging from the press, abandoning them. The Editors of the newspapers are the *de facto* ministers of Great Britain.

14. Another letter from Mr. Ritchie, he accepts *Killarney*, it has gone indeed to the printer. So Madame's amusing notes and my week's work with them have not been thrown away. Mr. Ritchie gives more than a hint that the sight of my handwriting would be more frequently agreeable. I dare say he is put to his wits' ends to keep up the journal against Dickens, Lever, Miss Cooke and a thousand more.*

26. Annie writes me a very stiff answer declining my invitation for the Queen's week. They mean to take lodgings if they come, but she rather inclines to a trip to Killarney! She must be very wilful, or a little mad, or entirely deceived by her husband. And all this time not one enquiry after my health, but total silence. Unkind Annie. How much we have to bear some of us. The carriage *if* she comes will be at our service, that is seats in it. Poor Annie, storing up bitter reflexions for a future day when her own sad lot will break upon her and there will be no mother to receive and comfort her.

31. And the end of August. All the house and all the town in such a bustle with the Queen that any private occupation is almost entirely out of the question, especially for me. Janey is completely engaged out of doors running after Her Majesty. We have dinners here at all hours, luncheons, breakfasts ditto. Mrs. O'Reilly and Pysie here for ever. Lady Milltown and all her family in town; and here of course. The priests had issued orders to receive the 'English' Queen with decent quiet, no joyful demonstrations, being undeserving of any. So there was little enthusiasm on her first appearing, but it rose as she proceeded, her sweet, very sweet smiles, her boys, her care of them and the mob love of noise, etc., prevailed and she was most heartily cheered in Westland Row. Our party saw the procession well from the Aylmers' Balcony. The town very full yet the streets very orderly, which considering that Donnibrook fair is just over is creditable to the Police. Very few of our nobility have come up to receive her Majesty, and not many of the gentry,

it is more travelling strangers who form the crowds. My Aunt and I remain at home, much appreciated as listeners, I at least, very glad to be out of the clamour.

SUNDAY, SEPTEMBER 4. Another interval, surely the journal is getting out of favour, or I am so occupied with all sorts of things, a moment for private reflection can hardly be stolen from a short day. These four last days have been very full of events, the Queen absorbing the time of the gay set who followed her all about the town among the crowds collected at every point where a chance view of her was possible. As I had never called on this dynasty, they [the girls] of course got no invitations to any of the parties at the Park. We were content with the descriptions of the Ladies Leesons. The dinner parties were small, the attendance of the Peerage not large. A selection of the officials and a few prominent persons in the evenings, two dancing evenings, one concert. She was very affable but extremely strict as to matters of etiquette, generally gracious, yet cross enough sometimes timid the first day, but as soon as she was reassured by the heartiness of her reception she got into good humour. She was always beautifully dressed, and both she and her Prince managed all through, to say always the right words at the right times. Mr. Dargan she very properly made the great man, the others she noticed had all good claim to such distinction.

We have heard no word of dissatisfaction from anywhere, but *I* am dissatisfied. Lord Cardigan dined at her table and she went to visit Lord Howth. These were two mistakes she should have avoided.* She might have staid longer among us, as there was still much to see, but she could not stand the stupidity of Lord and Lady St. Germains, who really are the most humdrum people such as she detests. *He* always kept her waiting too, and *she* is so dull, so plain, so badly dressed, she is an affliction, at least so goes Castle gossip. Well, Her Majesty departed late on Saturday afternoon and we are all quiet again for the mob of strangers which fills the streets, don't in any way interfere with the regular inhabitants.

6. Mr. Greene, the subwarden of St. Columba's, is a clever classick scholar and nothing else; he therefore undervalues all the knowledge he is incompetent to teach; he is quick,

irritable, spiteful, a slow pupil has no chance with him, he sneers and he *naggs* and he deprives the deficient scholar of his hours of exercise, even boxing the ears of an aching head etc. Jack has been removed to this odious man's form, and his spirits which always required encouragement are totally depressed. The creature is changed, no cheerfulness left, he is like the poor crushed victim of the Jesuits' schools.

This could not be so I wrote to the Warden who most kindly came to see me the same day. I tried to impress on the Warden the futility of fighting against inborn dispositions and though allowing that a certain proficiency in ancient lore is essential, a scholar of repute can never be elaborated from brains decidedly averse to the study of languages. I mentioned Jack's really plain turn for science of all kinds, his love for mathematicks, mechanicks, chemistry, etc., etc., and told him his father's wish was to send him in the Civil service to India, where a more general style of education would be of greater use to him than the mere scholastick one, and that above all good health was the first requisite.

7. The Doctor came on Saturday, like his old self, and very kind he shewed himself to Annie. He and I got on as old friends, and we together shall put this very foolish pair on their legs once more. We had a very confidential interview, then a long conversation with James by no means satisfactory, however, as I expect nothing good from him, this was no disappointment. I am quite content if we can get him to conduct himself a little more rationally. Next we took Annie and it did grieve me to find her all wrong. That she should stand by her husband is natural and right, but that she should outrage all others for his sake is wrong; her feelings at present are quite of the wrong kind. She neither understands her duty to her husband nor to her parents. She shews a perverse temper, unyielding to the Doctor's representations even. In short the cat's back is up when the head should be laid humbly down, a mock heroick injured innocence manner assumed when she ought to be gentle and grateful.

She flinched at hearing we, her best friends, considered her and James incompetent to manage their own affairs, neither did she relish the Doctor's severe arithmetical calculations by means of which he made it too plain that ever since their marriage they had been living at double their income, at three times their income since they came to Baltiboys. The present plan of borrowing from five to one hundred pounds from any one silly enough to lend it, and never dreaming of repayment, spending these extorted loans on luxurious, I may say ostentatious living, is so disgusting that I am sure if Annie have not totally lost her Smith principles and were aware of such meanness, it would go nigh either to break her heart or render her desperate.

The Doctor is going to advance the money for the purchase of Rathbally, the fine is four hundred pounds; one hundred he adds to his loan for the law expenses and some furniture; the interest is twenty pounds a year. James is to prevail on his father to give a Bond for the repayment of this money at his death, and I am going to try whether he will consent to pay half the yearly interest and I will pay the other half. So, with their little income clear, their small house in perfect order and furnished, they can begin the world again. They will have a rent of fifty pounds to pay, but as there are twenty Irish acres of prime land requiring hardly any costs of labour, they can easily manage that and have a profit besides. We must hope that Humfreystown pays itself; at all events he is quit of it in a twelvemonth. If there were no debts, all would be plain sailing. What the debts are we can only guess, James is very untruthful about them; of my own knowledge, I am only aware of these items – three hundred pounds to David C. Latouche, three hundred to the Colonel, the year's rent of Baltiboys – fifty pounds; and to the Doctor for Carpenter, the butcher's bill seventy pounds. The crops will pay some of these, the Stock will pay more some day – all I never expect will be liquidated, neither can I be certain that there are no more.

His establishment has consisted of six horses, three stablemen, three carriages, a butler, two maids, steward, herd, yardman, two labourers, ploughman; at Baltiboys steward, yardman, herd, labourer, pigman, boy, two dairymaids at Humfreystown. All at good wages, the head ones very highly paid. The Humfreystown farm, rent and taxes stands him in three hundred and sixty pounds a year – about a hundred and fifty acres. The servants' wages alone we calculate to three hundred and nineteen pounds, the feeding of two men and three maids seventy seven pounds, with a Livery and stabledress for the coachman. There is also seedtime and harvest when additional labour is necessary, and there are their own expenses, eating, dressing, journeys, medicine, fire, candle, washing, wine, company – one hundred pounds would be little enough for that. Let us state the items:–

One rent	£360
The other	50
Wages	319
Servants' eating etc.	77
Additional labour	35
Farm horses	50
Private ditto	120
James and Annie extra	——
	£911

Nine hundred pounds say in round figures, and to provide for this expenditure there is the annuity of three hundred pounds and the profits of the two farms; add the hundred pounds for themselves, and considering all they spend on themselves, I really might say two hundred, and there is no room to wonder at their having spent Miss King's legacy of one thousand pounds, and begged and borrowed from everyone, and owing another thousand pounds now. The Doctor has undertaken to shew Annie these figures, and James too, he *must be made to feel* that everybody else knows his circumstances, that all right thinking persons despise his dishonesty, but on his wife's account will forgive him *if he* mend his ways. Shall we succeed – Alas.

18. On Friday I had a long conference with John Hornidge, who has offered to take the Colonel's Agency for Jack's sake. With what glad gratitude we accept this most kind friend's assistance. He is so honest, so honourable, conscientious, firm, good, that both Landlord and Tenants will be benefitted by his management. He entered at once on all matters. I am to go down to Baltiboys to meet him this very week, which will indeed be a busy one. Day by day I must note the doings, dear Jack, that by and bye when I am

gone you may be reminded of your poor mother's anxiety for all of you.

Janey has written some very fair lines on the Russborough Ball which by the way turned out first rate, about one hundred people, all the seven rooms open, well lighted, plenty of refreshments, beautiful supper, everything, wines and all, so good, and host and hostess attentive to all. Every neighbourhood invited, Annie acknowledged to be by far the most distinguished looking woman in the rooms. Janey danced the whole night and with the best partners.

Poor Mrs. O'Reilly who slept here these two nights is bitterly hurt by Pysie not being invited, she has no idea of herself and her daughter slaving in attendance, doing my lady's bidding, and my young ladies' commissions, serving in fact as props and errand goers, and then to be passed over when not wanted. The omission will never be forgiven and seems even to have affected the mother more than the systematick neglect of her really fine sons. They are none of them right or safe. Madame Giordano, incensed by their most impertinent usage, yet fell at their feet at the first beckon of a noble finger, and to ensure further civility entertained malicious ears with all my family troubles, thus making very publick what need never have been known, and most surely never should have been told by one so perfectly domesticated with us and from whom we no more thought of concealing these affairs than from one of ourselves, little dreaming such confidence would be abused. I don't think the poor woman dreamed of doing mischief, she was very indignant with James and Annie for being ungrateful to me, and she must talk, and has little to talk of but the concerns of her neighbours.

SUNDAY, OCTOBER 9. Jack writes a little more cheerfully; he is however much dispirited; cannot I think be well. I wrote to him to bear up better, not to give up all because something went wrong, to fight a good battle with himself now, he will all through life meet with these crosses, that they are required in the formation of his character or he would not have met with them. Just to make the best of it – 'twould be but for a short time – not to allow himself to be depressed, to rise above these difficulties. Call up the

Saxon half of his mother's blood and shew himself manly
and courageous, not boyishly petulant etc., etc. This *dram*
and the pills may do for the present. The poor boy inherits
his father's easily depressed irritable temperament and my
bilious one. Air and exercise and happiness are therefore
indispensable to his well-being. If I find a proper amount of
recreation still denied him, he must be removed even before
Christmas, though at the risk of injuring the school, and the
poor Warden's feelings, – an excellent man whom I like
much, though he is hardly sufficiently intelligent to manage
in his very difficult situation.

John Robinson has called twice to see me; he is winding
up our accounts and will have a balance of a few pounds to
make over to me as a finish. Different rather from what it
used to be when I used to look grave over three figures, as
the Americans say, the other way. I may therefore be
content. On giving up my Agency, far from running my
husband into debt, I have got him out of it, a large balance to
John and a good round sum to the Doctor have been paid
off, and now I hope, small though our income be, it will
suffice for our reduced expenditure, at any rate the worry of
much business will be taken from me, confided to honest,
able hands, off my wearied mind for ever. Perhaps I made
too much of the very little after all there was to do; some of it
was vexatious, most of it unsuitable to a woman, and then I
was so ill, so worried with home matters, I did it ill, and
overworked myself into the bargain. Life will be mere play
after these last harrassing years.

12. James King was in town yesterday in the height of good
humour with himself, the world and me, one could hardly
suppose that smiling countenance and civil tongue could
ever be as we have known them. How fortunate this is, it
makes my resolution to avoid a quarrel so easy. He came in
with Mr. Corbett [previous tenant] to sign the papers, got
his four hundred pounds from me and departed all smiles.
The manners of his wife are by no means so amiable. I shall
leave her to time and the after reflexions of a good judgement. I am afraid she has not as much heart as I thought she
had, but her extreme reserve with us prevents us from
knowing her impressions, we can only judge of her actions

and they are wrong. But I shall dismiss the very painful subject – I have lost her from over indulgence and over care. When they have gone alone for a little while, they will the better comprehend the value of the support they leaned too much on. Most certainly James King has done the Colonel out of a couple of hundred pounds, and he still owes him two more, besides having half lived on us and by us, and received presents innumerable both himself and Annie. We shall leave them now to St. Fintan's.

14. Dr. Robinson came for a long two hours gossip with Janey and me. King affairs of course the engrossing topick. He is wonderfully kind, managing all things well with a high hand as of old and talking of it all more than pleases me. Much as I owe him and grateful as I feel to him, and forgiving, still it annoys me to find our private affairs the common gossip of his parlour. The whole of the arrangements conned over by Messrs. Owen, Hornidges etc. There is such an exceeding want of delicacy in he the arbiter of the dispute, informing all the country of all the particulars, involving as they do the character for probity of the husband of that Annie so dear to him, and laughing over the liberality or the prodigality of my concessions, after hearing from me that it was my intention to pay well for peace and counselling this myself. I am wise enough now to keep my opinions to myself, and have been well punished for trusting to the honour of acquaintance, allowing myself to make remarks harmless enough and truthful, yet capable of amplifications most mischievously added to them – So – thankful that to all appearance our ancient cordiality is restored, I mourn in secret over the disappointment: well, we are but human. Janey and I called on Mr. Cathcart and desired a proper Bond to be drawn up to secure the generous Doctor his four hundred pounds – he will keep his eye over those foolish young people and as they owe him much and respect him more, he may keep them in some degree of order.

19. A letter from Mrs. James Grant, introducing her granddaughter Louis Macdonald. Lame James Grant was my father's first cousin, brother to the Glenmoriston of the day, Uncle to the present Laird. He married a very nice looking woman with a little money, but no blood! and she

made him a good wife. Mrs. James in her note tells me she lives happily near Inverness with her daughter Helen's orphan children. Poor Helen! what an odious little creature it was, clever enough, and for so short a stature not bad looking in spite of enormous feet, but such a prying, gossiping, tiresome girl, we none of us could bear her, and May Anne Cumming with her majestick height, whom Helen particularly attached herself to, could not bear marching about with such a companion in her beauty days, like the giant and the dwarf. All at once Helen married, such a grand affair, Mr. Macdonald from the West Indies with £100,000, a house in the Regent's Park! carriages, flunkeys etc. This lasted but a twelvemonth when the pair vanished, returned to the West Indies to look after their estates, from whence after another year came the cleverest possible letter from Mrs. Macdonald to Lord Glenelg, then President of the Board of Trade applying for some government situation for her ruined husband. She got it, something in the Customs, I think, and we never heard any more of the poor thing till she came home a widow with these four children and died.

Her brothers, John and James, who were very much with my brother John in their School days, turned out remarkably well. John Peter went in the Civil service to India and gained a high character. James travelling to Liverpool to visit a College friend met in the coach a little short fat oldish man, a James Grant likewise, who took such a fancy to his namesake that he adopted first into his house, he and his twin brother and perfect ditto, were heads of a good mercantile firm in Liverpool, and next into his home and heart; it was quite a romance and Dickens seized on it, for these two little old oddities were the originals of the Cheeryble brothers, who made the fortune of Nicholas Nickleby.*

21. Our Doctor here for three hours, regular old gossip, taking charge too of us all, ordering and dictating and announcing as in long past days. Full to overflowing about King affairs; very busy, very kind, very generous, very prejudiced and very queer. However, he will not alter me; I will do no more for them than I have done, it would be unjust towards the

others, and I shall keep an account of what they have got already and deduct it from the small legacy I shall have it in my power to leave Annie, so that though Jack may have to wait for his own, it will come to him in the end. As for the Colonel wanting it in the meanwhile, that can't be helped; he made this odious marriage and must suffer for it; I don't feel the least bound to go on supporting the follies of Mr. King's son. Any money he gets he spends it in ostentatious display instead of in paying his debts and I don't think it right to encourage this. So I told the Doctor also that all we can spare is little enough for Jack's education which must not be neglected and there must be some prudent care and some personal sacrifices even to do that. Our sick house is necessarily so expensive and our income very small.

22. Our Doctor! having prohibited me from any attempt so mad! as a return to Baltiboys to pack, Janey, according to his arrangements went off this day by herself for this purpose, that is she had only Susan with her who came back from Blesington. We had all the plague in the world to find a covered car to take them. None of the jobbers would send a single horse up those hills, none of the post houses had covered cars, none of the street cars would go for the regulation price. At last after running about for a couple of hours, John bribed a man with an extra three shillings to convey the young lady and her maid these eighteen miles, English measure. The lower classes everywhere seem to be run mad, twenty thousand people struck work at Manchester and in most other places the operatives are doing the same; higher wages the demand. Perhaps they are right, maybe they get too little of the profits of their earnings, but most assuredly with their present habits they don't deserve more. It would only be ill spent like the wages they now get. Tradesmen of all ranks being the most dissipated creatures going. It is God's will that I should be weak in health, unable to do as much active work as it is my nature to wish, but I may bear, submit, that is plainly my part, and of course for some good reason. I long to do more for them, for all, but none of them miss what I feel is wanting, therefore why should I vex myself. I will try to be wiser, more patient.

23. Sunday. I have great pleasure in walking along under the row of elms by the banks of the canal, the gravel instead of the pavement, the fields beyond the water, the glimpse of the hills, and the fresh air, always blowing free from the open space around, give me a little feel of 'country' which seems somehow to be invigorating. Today I wandered on for three quarters of an hour, a long saunter now for me, the wind being southerly, the sun shining and many a meek tired worker taking advantage of our day of rest. Sunday in a town, a quiet town, is very interesting.

Certainly, of late years the dress, the demeanour, the whole appearance of the lower orders of the population have wonderfully improved. There is more neatness and less shew, in the attire of the tradespeople, and rags are seldom seen on the class below them. The servants shew the worst, the maids tawdry and the men seem to be rather from the publick house than the church, but in the streets in this part of the city throughout the day there is perfect decorum. The protestantism of the country is quite in the puritan style and in a great style influences the habits of the R. Cath.ks, who do not generally make a gay day of our holyday.

24. In my half country walk this day I fell in with a scene for Dickens, – a wretched one. Four children from six to ten years of age were grouped upon the pavement before a dead wall. They all looked well fed, sturdy firm brats, but very dirty, faces begrimed, and the eldest of the set a girl, had bare feet. She was extremely excited, gesticulating violently, and she was thus addressing a boy of seven or so who was looking defiance at her – 'Me care! the divil a bit – me cry! the divil a tear; I'll keep up my heart an' go an' an' my way an' never let an' nor consort wid the likes of you. Do I lave my home of a night an' stay widout to all hours!, may be till cock crow, do I?' . . . Here a gentleman passing stept up to the young vagabonds and I went on really bewildered.

What home could that child girl have, and what home could that baby of a boy prefer to leave. This the rising generation, I have a mind to send the bit to Dickens. We have ragged schools,* not enough or not efficient evidently, and on we go singing and dancing like the butterflies over a volcano like this. And that was a fine creature too, with her devil me care and courageous heart. The evening concluded by John's *punchifying*, ascending to the drawing-room and influencing his demeanour too much to be overlooked. This going to market puts temptation in his way, drams being offered as a rule and as a bribe, and then a little more at home completes the business. I told him last time this happened, that the next exhibition would be his dismissal without more ado. In a house full of invalids, a sober head servant is indispensable. More volcanoes. It makes one fancy all the whole *state* worthy of Hamlet's soliloquy. No letters to-day, nor war declared as yet.

29. Last day of the Exhibition, for it closes on Monday. Janey and I had a little business over the water so on our way she and her Papa stept into that beehive while I waited for them outside. Eighteen thousand were there yesterday, sixteen the day before. There must have been above twenty thousand to-day; the outside balconies were full, the street in front was a mob, the doors besieged. I just peeped in and saw only a moving mass of heads – up in the galleries, down in the aisles. The close is to be musical, a swan-like end, five hundred in the orchestra, organs, bands of regiments, marches, choruses, the hundredth Psalm and the Lord Lieutenant.

30. Sunday, very fine, very near the end of the month, they fly past so swiftly now. My Aunt is quite looking like herself again, able to be abundantly amused, yesterday with a renewed attempt of Augustus West to save a second five pounds. He called to talk over our joint affairs and amongst other little dodges proposed to pay his rent to me direct, and not through John Hornidge and as in that case we should have no Agency percentage to pay we might allow him to deduct that small sum from his rent which would be of importance to him, and no loss to us! I told him it would be utterly unfair to John Hornidge, who having taken upon himself the trouble of managing the Colonel's affairs, was entitled to an Agent's profit on them, that besides, I meant to give myself no further trouble about them, nor could I say that I should be always here etc. Next he regretted not having seen me when I called on Mrs. West and she declined

the cornices, blinds and such things as fitted the house, he evidently had hoped we would have left them there, so he went off to Crook's to buy them now. Such bargain makers, really the Irish are very queer.

MONDAY, NOVEMBER 7. Lord Cloncurry was buried on Saturday week last, and his son Cecil was buried last Saturday. He came up for his father's funeral, went home to some place near Cork, took inflammation of the brain and died in three days. I am pretty sure the contents of the father's will brought on the attack. He has been keeping his creditors quiet by the hope of a large inheritance from his rich father. He only got £12,000, a mere nothing against his debts. A warning, J.K.*

8. Janey and I went to the Royal Hospital in a brougham to see Sir Edward [Blakeney] himself for a few minutes – dreadfully altered, that fall has told. They should get him away from here if possible but I fear there is little chance of his giving up unless the Brevet forces him and now they say the Exchequer is so empty it will not bear the expense, although there is really not a Major General in the service. Had the war gone on they must have made some, but the Czar seeming more pacifick since his checks on the Danube, Mr. Gladstone resumes his economical tactics.

13. Two trials lately concluded here prove the necessity of some change in our jury laws – twelve good men and true are not to be had among the R. Cath. citizens in these times, nor even one, in the rank of life from which jurors are taken in common cases. The first trial was about a child which was abducted from the Guardian appointed by its parent. The other case is worse because the influence of the priests was more paraded. The defence was an impeachment of the credibility of the witnesses, quite unsupported by evidence. The judge charged against the prisoner and the jury acquitted her. She is niece to Dr. Cantwell, one of their Bishops, it would have been a scandal to have convicted his relation. A mob of priests filled the court, a strong band of Reverends surrounded the Dock, it was made a religious question. Everybody believes the woman guilty and everybody said she would get off. Luckily for her accuser he is of her persuasion or the populace would have murdered him,

and luckily for the windows of the warehouse half the firm are ditto – as to his honour, be it recorded, is the judge – Pigott. He was so angry he rose abruptly and left the court, ordering silence which could not be enforced, the cheering was so general. The 'Romans' are 'going it' – how long will the race last? that is just the question. Till *we* behave ourselves better, more according to the tenets we pretend to be guided by and which they are for the most part ignorant of.

15. James Ryan arrived with some stray bits of furniture and to do a number of odd jobs still required here and there about the house. He could not get on for my poor Aunt being too nervous to bear the noise, except in her own room! where she had some knocking of nails, etc. Been all the evening preparing the Agency accounts to make over the books to John Hornidge. A nice little property it would be, were it unincumbered and untenanted.

21. What are we to think of Mr. West . . . I sometimes think him flighty, or anxious to get out of the bargain, he is constantly raising up so many new provisoes. Now he wants us to keep the roof in repair, a thing never done by the landlord when the tenant has a lease. He has acted more shabbily, more meanly than anyone would believe who had not our proof of it, and I should be very glad to be able to decline further dealings with him.

26. John Hornidge yesterday at last relieved me of the Agency accounts. We were a couple of hours going through them. He made very short work with Mr. West, took him a proper agreement drawn up by Mr. Cathcart which this singular man signed without another word and so ends the pantomime.

MONDAY, DECEMBER 4. The last month of a troubled year. My Colonel very well; he has resumed his Billiard playing at the Club since the return of so many friendly members to town, he goes after his dinner about five o'clock and stays till seven, returning always in a car. Sometimes he is dressed time enough of a fine day to take a short walk before dinner. His evenings are spent very comfortably without whist! which is a wonderful relief to Janey and me, thrice a week he has the *Mail* which occupies him completely, the other three nights he takes up one of Walter Scott's novels, the same one does for a long time and always pleases; then we have generally letters to read to him or some little bit of news to tell; he can't converse now, but chatter amuses him, tea too is a long affair, and bedtime early. He is really well, in no pain whatever, nor is there any remaining annoyance worth speaking of. He is in great delight with a new dressing gown of the small set Stewart tartan and fur lined slippers. His room has every comfort in it, he himself taking good care that the first of all, a good fire, shall never fail there. He is really happy, and so patient. Mrs. Bourne has been this whole week very much better, she still keeps her room as ever amazingly careful of herself. She eats well, reads, talks like a cataract and is no longer afraid of dying. Still she must be watched, cannot give up her medicines or all might return as at first. Thank heaven! most of *my* cares are over. Done with James King, with the Agency, with Mr. West, and now as Janey says, let us see what next I can make out to fret about . . .

11. Our first business this last week was to find a man servant; poor John, with a thousand good qualities springing from a kind and honest nature, having three faults he will not cure, and so rather than reform, he goes. He is dirty, he drinks and he smokes. He don't get drunk or even tipsy, but he gets stupid, smells of punch at night, and raw whiskey in the morning and tobacco all day. We hope we have succeeded in finding a very respectable looking man, very highly *spoken* of by his last two masters, for discharges are not to be trusted (I must call John sober!) but he, the new man, has a delicate look; our quiet place may not be too much for him, if it prove so we must only hunt for another. I have only hired Aiken for a month.

The next affair was my departure in a covered car all the way by myself to Russellstown on Thursday. John Hornidge wished me to be present at the first meeting of him and the tenants. We were to have prepared our rent sheets, etc. that evening but the Doctor coming to dinner, we chattered instead, and were very snug in the little parlour with our good dinner and good fire and good glass of punch. I do like that old house and I like the memory of poor (old) John

Hornidge, who was so hospitable and so clever and so kindly. The nephew puts me very much in mind of the Uncle, the same habits, the same ways, even to the sigh when writing – a slow, methodical, business-like manner. Perhaps he copies him, the figure is like too, but the very handsome face with the dark hair and wonderful eyes is an improvement. My bed was in the drawing-room, which enacts state bedchamber now. Everything possible was done to make me comfortable. It was so odd to me to be made of once more, as in days when the Doctor mounted guard over me.

Soon after our rather late breakfast on Thursday, the tenants arrived, all decently dressed, all looking well fed and cheerful; they spoke hopefully, had no griefs, were kind and cordial, and everyone without exception paid his full half year's rent. Some brought a few odd pounds towards arrears. These last are not heavy but they need not be at all, nor will they be in future with so very strict an agent, kind though he be; more considerately liberal than I expected, but firm, as is best even for the tenants themselves. The Doctor dined again and helped to count over the money in the evening. Next day old Peggy came to see me wearing the new duffle cloke Aunt Bourne had sent her and Lady Milltown and her daughters walked down too, to beg we would dine at Russborough, but we could not as we had arranged to be in town before the Bank closed. Well packed upon an *easy* car my host and I departed, stopping at the Doctor's to get the horse frosted and my hot water footstool refilled. It was a fine frosty winter's day; I enjoyed the drive much and felt pleased too to be so cared for, my comfort studied! It seemed so odd, quite warmed the feelings. We found all well in this little cheerful house; the Colonel quite himself and so good; he had not attempted to go out. Mrs Bourne still in her room but very comfortable. Little Janey in great glee; all sunshine around us.

25. Sunday – Christmas day, bitterly cold but fine and dry. The Colonel and I all alone over good fires; dining off crammed fowl and sausages, the regular fare of the day, roast beef and plum pudding being on the kitchen table for the four servants. The first Christmas we have spent on our own

for many a long day. I rather like it, prefer it to the loss of any – all – that used to make this season gay in the 'olden time'.

We have seen no one from our mountains but Dick, looking very bright as he may well do for he is making a fortune. He has taken in earnest to manage his acres, bought up all he could from bad tenants and settled down in one of his Cottages made sufficiently tidy for a bachelour, and there he is having already more than doubled the rent of his farms.

It makes them all in that country furious to hear of Jack throwing away the happy life of a country gentleman and persist in roaming the world in pursuit of what is waiting on him at home, risking health and weakening family ties. It is not for fame and money that my boy leaves us all, it is a restless inquisitive excitable temperament which can only be satisfied by a few years' roaming. A few years of the East, will I think, content him and then, as John Hornidge will have done well for him and I, dead or alive, will have more to leave him, he may still return, a young man, glad of such a refuge from a disappointing world as his pretty little inheritance will prove. I have written to Mr. Day and Mr. Gardiner and have heard from both. Mr. Day writes sensibly, he has a vacancy, encloses his terms, not by any means immoderate, and a note of the plan of study – good. Mr. Gardiner highly approves of the plan, thinks whatever his future may be, a couple of years of an English school will be invaluable to Jack. He promises to watch over him as a father, to go to London to meet him, to carry him for a few days to Twickenham, and then escort him to Brixton. Was there ever any body in this world kinder.

The poor Warden will regret this change; he was truly interested in Sprat, kind to him, judicious with him and most certainly wherever the want of orthodoxy may be, it did not enter into the instruction he gave the boys. Jack's scriptural knowledge is great and right, his piety earnest without being obtrusive; his intellect has made a spring this last half which has surprised me, he has improved in every respect extremely. He and we owe Mr. Williams much.

But he is a foolish man; he has put himself very much in the wrong and indeed done up the school. A long correspondence between him and others, principally the Primate, has been published and privately circulated and at last got into the newspapers; the Primate sent the Colonel a copy, and here is the cream. The late Bishop of Jerusalem, who was also the first, and the present, hold different opinions upon certain ecclesiastical matters and act in different manners. The party in our church known as the Tractarians, Pusey, Newnham [sic], Wilberforce, Grierson, the Bishop of Exeter etc. have drawn up a protest against the present Bishop's mode of proceeding and appointed a committee for some purposes connected with this demonstration. To both these papers the Warden's name was appended. On this the Primate, who is patron and visitor of St. Columba's, founded it indeed, and supported it, wrote to enquire how this was. The Warden replied that it had been done without his sanction but that he approved of the proceedings and having been chaplain to the first bishop considered himself entitled to pass a judgement on the second. The Primate writes again to say he considers such demonstrations inconsistent with the duties of a schoolmaster, and such a publick connexion with that extreme party which was doing so much mischief in our church, so questionable a proceeding in one who had the charge of the principles of the young, as to force him reluctantly to withdraw his confidence from the Warden, as he knew many parents would also do, and therefore it would be for the advantage of the interests of the College were he to resign the headship, say at the approaching Christmas vacation.

The Warden is stunned! asks time to consider, goes to England to consult his friends, then writes a specious but shuffling answer, perhaps as good a one as his case admits of, but refuses to resign as having done nothing which by the statutes of the college is illegal. The Primate gives him a short time for consideration, the Warden is obstinate, and the Primate resigns his office of visitor, throws up all connexion with the school, which has hitherto cost him near £1,000 a year, and closes the correspondence with expressions of regret for the time and money wasted and of disappointment in the character of Mr. Williams, whose want of judgement, etc., have kept him and his school in hot water ever since he entered upon his duties there. These are not the exact words but quite the sense. There are other letters to and from other clergymen on the same subject, all having a proper bearing on the case but unnecessary to repeat here. Now that the school can get along without the Primate's purse, now that at least half the boys will leave it, when it but hobbled on before, is not to be expected. Probably a little time and better advice may induce the Warden to yield, and then an entire remodelling may satisfy the Low Church of Ireland. If he do not, he and a dozen boys may battle on awhile, and then St. Columba's will be bankrupt. How glad I am that we have had our good three years of it and now want it no more.*

The next dish of walnuts has been Lord Palmerston's resignation, some say on the Eastern question where truth to say our snoring lion looks but small – some, a decisive opposition to a new reform bill of little Lord John's of a very democratick tendency, or Cotton sop rather – some, on account of Prince Albert's interference, a new habit, disagreeable to our national jealousy. He has begun to attend the Cabinet Councils, though without the right, having no seat in the Cabinet, and to advise and remonstrate and even it is whispered to send news abroad never meant to travel from home. At all events there is a stir about this. John Bull angry. We hear too that Lord Lansdowne, the Duke of Devonshire, Mr. Gladstones and others will all secede likewise if that new reform Bill be persisted in, and that we don't rouse up in earnest to help our old allies the Turks. Nobody will take the vacant Secretaryship, and nobody knows what to do. The poor Turks have been beat at sea though hitherto successful by land. It was quite a piratical affair, the Russians mounting English colours and following a convoy with troops and provisions into the harbour of Sinope where being about double in number, size of ships, etc., they murdered four thousand men and blew up or sunk most of the vessels. The Turks fought gallantly, crippled their attackers and landed their freight, but at what cost. We had better keep up the skreen between civilised Europe and these barbarians, otherwise there will be another irruption of worse than Goths and Vandals.

1854

'War, nothing but war' as hostilities commence in the Crimea and she takes Jack from a languishing St. Columba's to send him with some reluctance to prepare for a career in the Army at Mr. Day's London crammer. King finances continue to deteriorate and the Highland Lady is saddened as Annie loyally takes her husband's side. There are further calls on her energies with the demands made by her two elderly, intractable invalids, unreliable servants, Jack's serious illness and the appeals for help from Lady Milltown's poverty-stricken and unfortunate sister, Mrs. O'Reilly. A Baltiboys holiday in August provides a welcome break and she is enchanted by the safe birth of her first grandchild but the year is increasingly dominated by the way in which she traces with critical interest the involvement of Florence Nightingale, an old family friend, and accurately records the Charge of the Light Brigade.

Illustration: Trinity College Quadrangle

THURSDAY, JANUARY 12. No journal since before Christmas. What a deal of leeway to make up. First we sent Janey and Jack to keep this festive season in the country, this invalid house being no place for young merry people and we invalids not able to bear any gaiety, or late hours, noise overhead, etc. However, there was little fun for them anywhere; the snow lay thick on the ground for above a week so that the two sisters never got out; Jack and James skated on the ponds and had a frosty frolick after boy fashion; but it was dull and in the house little comfort. We have books, I have my work, my chairs, doing a very handsome one just now, and a few letters received and answered, with the newspapers which are engrossing enough just now.

We get on very happily we three. The new Butler is a very agreeable servant; Susan a perfect plague; the old Cook requires looking after as indeed they all do. She would be dirty, and she is unpunctual and Susan bullies her. The strong hand of the mistress can't be slacked. Susan I fancy is a fool. She is forty or thereabouts – dark-skinned, *very* thin, scraggy, and fancies herself a beauty! and always in love. Having lived on salt beef at Ballyward, very little at Mrs. Hornidge's and on rabbits at Mr. Wills, there is almost nothing she can eat here – neither hash, nor stew nor broth nor soup. She came to me as a housemaid, had lived with Mr. Wills as a cook and had been the only servant with Mrs. Hornidge and Miss Finnemore; first she could not iron in the kitchen, next she could not sew in it, and rather than sully her newly atchieved dignity she staid up in her bedroom without a fire during the snow storm. I never let on. She got a bad cough and I told her she wanted medicine; to all else I was deaf and blind so she is conforming by degrees to her unfortunate circumstances; her last attempt was to have her wages raised. I said it would not be here. She would be very sorry to leave. I was sure she would. Such another place she would hardly get again; her tea cost so much – because she used an extravagant quantity; her dress – that I was going to speak about; she was beginning to dress far too fine; we wanted no smart lady's maid but a good decent working servant, which was all she could pretend to be. So the poor creature made very little of me. She really is a good

servant, suits my Aunt in every respect and is thoroughly
attentive to her; only regularly Irish dying to get up on
horseback.

Kitty Hawtayne has come over looking brilliant. She left
her brother very ill in Cheltenham, feeble in body, depressed in mind, nervous; with the father's fate* before him
one can't but dread the event. Colonel Layard too: he cut his
throat a fortnight ago, raving mad; he had not been well,
bilious, low-spirited etc.; the country life not so cheering as
he expected. An idle man must have felt it dull after his
regiment and Dublin. The country doctor sent him back to
town to consult physicians, here. She came in with him to
lodgings where he did the deed. It was all that mesmerism
without a doubt; over-excited, a naturally irritable temperament. Poor little woman, she was examined on the coroner's
inquest and gave her evidence so well. I remember her
telling us with her sad, anxious face that she must do just
as she was bid, that she was well drilled! The shock over she
will not be inconsolable for certainly he worried her greatly.
The boy is called half-mad at St. Columba's. The Warden
has *advertised* the resumption of the School after the holidays. I wonder how many boys will return. Dr. Todd and
several of the Fellows stand by him.

15. Sunday. All the world is full of Lord Palmerston: his
resignation, his subsequent return to the ministry, the
causes whereof, etc. It is all Prince Albert – foolish Prince
Albert, with all his natural talents but a tool in the hands of
his Mephistopheles of an uncle, ignorant of the peculiar
jealousy of our constitution with regard to the interference
of foreigners in our policy, he has been meddling in every
department till he has everybody in a ferment. But this sort
of Russian despotism can't be tolerated in this country; the
whole nation is roused as one man; the meeting of Parliament will see the entire business enquired into, and put an
end to. And what is it all for? The aggrandisement of the
Saxe-Coburg family.

That the kingdom of Belgium be acknowledged by the
Czar we have played false and loose with our old ally the
Turk, and bulwark against barbarism. There is plot within
plot, intrigue beyond intrigue, to raise the different

members of the Saxe-Coburg connexion; and we [are] inundated with visits from the wily uncle and the papist nephews and nieces and cousins who plot all their follies beneath the roof of old Windsor Castle. Everyone thought the Prince so prudent too, occupied with the education of his children, the good of the country, the advancement of science, solely, – while all the time he was betraying our interests and hastening on the revolution which will reduce his royal offspring to simple citizens of a republick fatigued with the futile expenses of a Court.*

The weather continues very severe. I never passed such a winter since I lived in Ireland. Our poor school children are taken care of mercifully; my good Aunt helped me to send clothing, meal and broth to the poorest of them, Miss Macdonnell the Agent.

22. War seemingly inevitable. We have so shilly shallied about that eastern question the Czar has had time to make great preparations and to overexcite his half crazy brain with religious fanaticism, till he imagines himself a sort of prophet commissioned to extirpate Mahometanism. It is curious how all that family become deranged at forty. Clever sovereigns till towards that age, either the habit of despotick power or irrepressible natural infirmity, or more likely the union of the two unfortunate elements, always end in over-throwing reason. On this occasion, his subjects are said fully to share the enthusiasm of their ruler, so Nicholas may be safe till the Turkish Successes become more frequent and more imposing.

The massacre at Sinope has been followed by another on land at or near Kalafat, the Turks victorious. Our united fleets are in the Black Sea at last. A protocol from the four powers of a peremptory nature sent to St. Petersburgh as the ultimatum. The Answer will decide the fate of Europe. We are fortifying our coasts, organising the coast guard, re-cruiting for the Navy, and Army, putting all in readiness for war while talking still of peace. The French are equally busy, but say less, and what they do say is more to the purpose. People begin to look serious about this, which under a more honest ministry might have been an easily settled question.

Our first Drawing-room is fixed for Thursday next after

which all the gaiety will rattle on ball after ball till people are exhausted. I am quite unequal to any of it. I do not mean to invite Annie up to town. Janey therefore will lose the Castle gaieties, and more perhaps, and little matter. She has had a good deal of amusement, so may lay by now with the reflexion that she has had her day! She seems perfectly content. We have plenty of books; she is fond of musick; we have some intimate friends, and she and I are very happy together. She does a great deal for me one way or another and though she will never be a good active managing mistress of a household or indeed take much trouble anyhow, she is admirable as a companion, useful in many respects. Her father dotes on her, ditto our Aunt.

Jack too is in favour. I am sure that the *rousing* of this change to England will be of infinite advantage to the indolent habit of that dear Boy; he hates exertion of any kind; therefore learning is a bore, company is a bore, civility is a bore etc. When driven by circumstances, or excitement sufficient, on he goes swimmingly, on over through everything. Perhaps the impelling motive has never yet been properly powerful, or the way made so agreeable as it might be. He had no companion to his mind at his late school, nor any sufficient relaxation for a character of his temperament. I do hope for a complete revival of vigour from our present plan.

Annie is not all right yet. She has taken up a wrong idea that a wife's duties are to supersede all others, swamp all others, a husband's love monopolises all affection; in that inflated style she has got her young head entangled, but she will right yet. I shall continue to take her very quietly; do all that can improve here, by sending books, messages, a note sometimes, attentions always, and trust to time and her own heart. If I could enlighten her on events, she would be ours again, but we dare not so peril her happiness.

24. It was a dreadful night – a hurricane, rain and wind that beat against the windows threatening to blow the house down. My poor Jack; he was to start before eight, reach Kingstown in time to sail at nine [for London and Mr. Hall's military crammer]. Fairly launched upon the wide wide world is that dear Boy – no home for him but of his own winning –

nothing here save a chance visitor – it is very wretched this breaking up of a childhood's tie. All night long I lay listening to the storm.

25. How fortunate was my boy in starting yesterday. His beginning of independance – my darling child. I do not love him better than the others but I am more filled with anxiety about him. Women are comparatively shielded from evil. Evil meets men, surrounds them, almost seizes them. My fear for you, dear Jack, is this – you are Irish, and your father's son, and so inherit a sort of desponding *give-up* disposition, the reverse of Bruce and the spider, which with some indolence prevented your father from rising to where his abilities and his integrity would have placed him. In a degree this failing has kept back his family – prevented his own usefulness. To educate you out of this *weakness*, to give you the raven's never say die! must be my unremitting care. Ask yourself when you read these words whether the poor old mammy has succeeded; if not, let her succeed *now* – it is never too late. Mammy seldom lectured. Mind her when she does.

29. Janey and I have got out only twice this week. We called one day on Lady Milltown who seemed much out of sorts; no invitations had come from the Castle; they were to remain another day in hopes it would. We have some amusing books in the house worth noticing – Moore, who really is a little mean body when seen in the way Lord John [Russell] shows him.* Vain, fond of pleasure, fond of flattery, self-indulgent, depending on patronage, worshipping the great, prodigal, shuffling, ill-managing, throwing away a perfect fortune without being one bit the better for it. But he sprung from the low, was indifferently educated, and fell into very questionable company. His beautiful poetry disarms our censure. Still one cannot admire these tender sort of men. Goethe promises better, more nerve about the style, but very tedious.

SUNDAY, FEBRUARY 5. Annie has made quite a clever set of *vignettes* of the Tulfarris burglary – the house was broke into and robbed but the thieves did not get off with their booty. A maid heard them – followed them to the kitchen, called the men quietly, locked the thieves in, and the Police secured them. As their faces were blackened they will be transported. She begins with the men creeping along the passage, the maid in her night-cap peering at them; then the maid calls the melancholy footman, the long man with the heart complaint; then the footman and Barney are bolting the kitchen door; then the thieves in the kitchen are trying to escape by the chimney and the window; then Edward is mounting guard outside patting back a thief's head with the flat of his 'father's sword'. Burglary is quite a new crime in Ireland. These high markets and no work.

12. Very happy letters from Jack. After the severe studies of St. Columba's he will find the plan of Brixton easy. We have had the third volume of Moore – wretched literary trifler. His Paris life one round of dissipation; dinners, very expensive ones, at restaurants, the same at home with dozens of wines consumed; champaign suppers; dances with brandy punch; plays or operas when nothing else offered; Bessy sick or well left mostly at home with the babies, all darlings as they were. The diary a mere statement of these disgraceful facts. A few witticisms recorded here and there but no creditable observations, no reflections, no good sense anywhere. It was a profligate life in a low way – his dearly prized Lords and Ladies being none of the most respectable. It is very unfair in Lord John to unveil such a picture. A selection might have been managed that would have left a pleasanter picture of the *genius*, – the man we must give up; he had kind impulses, no principles. All his profuse expenditure on mere sensual gratification was run into part on credit with tradespeople, part on engagement with his bookseller for whom he should have been continuing works begun and partly paid for and which his idleness prevented his going on with. One has no patience with such dishonesty.

We are proving much of what this bigotted ignorance will lead to in this town at the present. Miss Cantwell has brought her action against Cannock and White for 'malignant charges etc.', the trial has already occupied four days. On the first trial the jury found a verdict for her against the evidence and the Judge's summing up, because there was a link wanting in the chain of circumstantial evidence. That link is now supplied. A lad of sixteen saw her drop the velvet ribbon behind the oilcloths and dared not come forward because he was the only support of a widowed mother and his family, and his master a R. Cath. threatened him with dismissal if he breathed a syllable that would make against the Bishop's niece. His friends have found him another situation and he now feels at liberty to tell the truth. Was there ever such a system of slavery. The whole evidence of this woman's guilt is now complete; no one can by any casuistry make themselves doubt it, though they may not say so.

My private reading in my quiet hour at night is still Goethe, his *Autobiography*. That he was crazy I have no doubt; he is impulsive, unsteady, excitable, irrational; his conduct to women indefensible, his studies unregulated, his fancies changeable, his ideas flighty, his style diffuse, unconnected. One can neither follow his course of life nor his course of thought. If this be a great man I shall content myself with lesser ones.

As far as I have yet got he has published only his Play *Gotz von Berlichingen* and *Werther*. Poets whether in Prose or Verse, that is thinkers and feelers, cannot help writing; the tiresome verses of one age and the Sevigné letters of another were alike the outpourings of full minds, irrespective of the addressed objects; Goethe's Gretchens, Annettes, Fredericas, Charlottes, etc.,* that disagreeable Madame de Grignan, were all nothing more than what the journals of this later age are to the Authors and gossips existing. Perhaps congenial conversers might supersede the necessity of so much pen work though I don't know. I used to long to write down all I heard, *with comments*, in those days when what I heard was worth remembering.

14. Out of doors there is great bustle – twelve thousand troops, all infantry, are off for Constantinople. All to encamp within six miles of Constantinople, Sir John Burgoyne* and his Engineers being there already marking out the Lines. Forty thousand men, the pick of the French Army, are to sail at the same time for Varna; the united fleet in the Black Sea has been considerably strengthened. And now we are preparing for the Baltick, both nations. We have thirty three vessels commissioned already. The Czar had better keep awake.

Miss Cantwell has got her damages – three hundred pounds and sixpence costs – not against the firm – that has been exonerated, but against poor Mr. Dudley, the malicious count in the prosecution was abandoned, but having been acquitted by the former Jury, the Law must consider her innocent and therefore aggrieved, despite the additional evidence and the unwavering assertions of the whole chain of witnesses. Mr. Dudley was hasty, which saved the Lady. Every one believes her to be guilty but the clique of bigots.*

15. Twenty thousand men for Turkey, Lord Raglan Commander in Chief; Prince George second in command. It is well we have the papers and Goethe to divert us, for little is doing in our quiet home life. Arabella King was here yesterday about her brother. The father is going to write to his two noble cousins to see if anything can be done for him in the way of some small office the duties of which he would perform well for he is clever, active and fond of business. I have completely cast him out of my thoughts, really believing him to be mad, and so hardly responsible for the incredible absurdity of his conduct; it is only on my poor Annie's account that I recognise him at all. Poor deceived Annie. May she never waken from the dream during which she is lost to me.

17. The fourth volume of Moore more interesting in as much as he quits France, returns to Sloperton Cottage as his home, wandering to Bath, London, Killarney and Abbotsford. The people he lives with being less frivolous than his Paris society, his own turn of *thought* rises higher; his habits however remain irregular. Dissipation of any kind is welcome. It is pleasant to me to meet with so many names familiar to my childhood. There are the dinners at Holland House described to us so often by my father and Fanny Mackintosh [daughter of Sir James the writer and politician] – the whole political party to which we were attached all known by name, many of them personal acquaintance.

SUNDAY, MARCH 12. It is most curious that with regard to my children the very things the most distasteful to me they do – not intentionally, poor pets. It is fate. An early marriage for a daughter – India or the army for a son – these were my aversions and if in the son's case his choice is to turn out as unfortunate as his sister's, may God help those who will have to bear another blow. We must hope the best, believe that the climate may suit him, that his principles may stand firm against the dangerous habits of military life, and that he may be restored to the rational existence of a country gentleman none the worse for some years' experience of a more restless career. War! and all pertaining to it is so hateful to me, the mummery, the frivolity, the idleness, the cruelty, the carelessness, the inutility, of such a life all so shock my every feeling that the idea of my only son voluntarily fixing on the profession of arms is really a grief that will be abiding. A cadetship! I to ask for one! for Jack! A year ago I would not have believed it!

One comfort in this sea of discomfort I hail as the plank among the wreck to cling to. This change to England has already roused my dear boy's mind; his letters are happy; his energies seem all alive; he sees and hears and feels and acts like other rational creatures to whom God has given the charge of themselves; he says he likes all he learns, likes his masters, his companions, and they apparently like him for a great deal of kindness is shewn him. It was a good move from what he calls that 'dead alive place' St. Columba's and for the rest, may be I am foolish to expect his father's son to be studious, an Irish boy to think of much beyond himself and the present, or a young spirit to believe repose to be happiness. We must weary the spirit, and age it, first.

I can't muster up spirits to journalise, dear Boy. All I do seems an effort; I suppose I am not well. I dawdle in the morning, I dawdle in the day. We have no evening – always whist. Janey has to call me for this, and set me to that, and try to bustle me up a bit. So unlike am I to the 'Busy Bee' who once hummed cheerfully through such loads of work. I begin to understand being weary of the world and longing for the night of rest; but I will try and rouse up for your dear sakes. All three may have need of help yet.

19. I have made up my mind to behave well. For a few days I was sadly unhappy – quite unable to think, except at night when like a fool I cried. So I just gave 'nature way' and now I'm all right again. I will never dwell more on the dark side. So, I

have written to Mr. Day to tell him of my son's determination and I have written to my brother John to ask him to ask
for a cavalry cadetship for his nephew, as a man decidedly A.
No. 1 with the Directors is not at all likely to be refused so
trifling a favour.* I the more readily yield to this desire of
Jack's from a foreknowledge that it is from the more usefully
educated military of *this* day that the Indian Governments
will have to select their more efficient servants for civil
appointments, as this Horace and Virgil whim with the
overstudy now necessary must send forth a batch of sickly
students instead of young energetick spirits. And in this
hope I prefer the Indian to the home service where there is
no employment during peace and mere fighting while at
war.

Mary Anne *Bauman* and Antoine have taken a house and
shop in Park Street; twenty pounds fine, and fifty pounds
rent, and intend to sell French lamps, seventy of which they
have brought over with them like two mad idiots. Lamps
amongst other things may bring a fair profit on the few that
will be sold, but lamps alone will never pay that rent and
feed the tradesman too.

Janey sent for her to put her feathers in for the Ball. A
Congreve rocket* could not have caused more commotion.
The head done and very nicely, really beautifully, Janey not
seeing Susan, rang for her to finish dressing. Susan 'not
supposing herself wanting' had stept out. Her next morning's
salutation to my poor old Aunt was 'It's a fine thing to have a
tongue! them as has tongues can push *theirselves* on a deal
better than *them* that has only hands! *I* can put in feathers' etc.,
etc. Janey's mild enquiry of how Susan came to go out when
she knew she, Janey, was dressing for a Ball, was met by
'Indeed, Miss after the affront put on me it was no wonder for
me to *lave* the place to them that insulted me. Who began
could finish. It's not the first head I've dressed. Mary Anne
may *plase* some but others could find her out. Madame was not
to be *desaved* by a good tongue. She knew better than to be
satisfied with Mary Anne. Little would cause me to quit after
such a girl as that brought in to' etc., etc.

My Aunt and Janey met this torrent very unwisely by
gentle expostulatings, calm reasonings, kind expressions;

the storm grew to a whirlwind which reaching *me* encountered a tornado! that soon lulled the lesser force. I gave it her right well, told her she was madly jealous of a superiour! had exposed herself to the mockery of all the house, that without consulting her, my daughter would have her head dressed by any person she pleased, and if she, Susan, annoyed us by any further exhibition of impertinence, I would get quit of such a fool in no time. So we had her all in smiles in no time.

Aiken the butler then thought he would begin. So he went to his tailor's at ten o'clock, came back at three very much bewildered, went to the chemist's for the Colonel's cough mixture and returned *in a car* too drunk to stand steady. I will get no more servants from those offices. Aiken was quite sober while he was penniless, a most excellent servant, really a great comfort to us, till within the last fortnight. I first noticed that he got to stay long out when sent an errand, and then that he smelt of spirits; but he was always steady at dinner till yesterday. What can bewitch the people so with drink. Clothes, food, fire, shelter, all bartered for Whiskey punch. What a worry to have to go butler hunting again. Lists, directions, tidyings, two whole day's work. The Irish are a nation of lunaticks, that I have made up my mind about – with some method in their madness – I, dear I, *dearest I*, figuring in chief through their paroxysms.

20. Great distress in the household about Aiken; he is such a quiet poor man, been in tears himself and miserable – of course for his character is gone. I pity him sincerely, and were this an accident would overlook it, but I feel sure it is a habit; his bad clothes, his hacking cough, all tell the tale of confirmed drunkenness which in my peculiar position, let lone the immorality of such a vice, and the impossibility of countenancing it, is out of the question to put up with. There is no gentleman in the family to keep order, to go out with Janey, watch the invalid etc. who might at any moment require all the senses of everybody.

21. We have the sixth volume of Moore at last – the best – he is wiser, less frivolous, having felt the poor little daughter's death. Age also approaches; he thinks more and to better purpose, but bless me, what folly is set down in journals! Jack, my dear, I've a mind to burn mine lest instead of being

interested in it you should throw the sheets away in a pet with the absurdity of your mother. I don't care for it as I used to. I care for nothing, just get through the day the best way I can.

22. A letter from Mr. Day, approving of Jack's resolve to be a cavalry cadet; he could not now overtake the work for the Writership, neither is he sufficiently advanced in mathematicks to try for the Engineers; he evidently considers my boy to be dull at his book – slow, though *very* sure, and his turn to be for active life. As to morals, he gives him a high moral character – 'honest, conscientious, trust-worthy – well-thought of by the best of the boys his companions;' he has found out the little crank in the temper – 'finds it necessary to keep him in good humour with his work.' So I must be content – thankful to have him *good* and happy, though far from me. I shall try and make up my mind to it all.

28. Well, war is declared to both Houses by a message from the Queen. The Czar returned no answer! to our last communication! Our messenger came back with this report! The Czar had gone off somewhere but Count Somebody informed the Honble. Captain Something who carried the united missive of the Western powers that 'there was no answer'. Civil in the great Bear; he is crazed with religious enthusiasm and self-conceit; fancies himself a God whom all the world must worship, and he is as unscrupulous as an Irishman. We have to fight this savage or be overrun by his hosts of barbarians. It will be tough work, they say; the Russians are very indomitable, well-disciplined, and their country and climate impracticable, We are on the verge of cruel times – there is no doubt of it.

29. My dear husband's birthday – seventy four. May God grant us a few more years together. If we could see our Janey settled and Jack fairly afloat, our work would be done. But two such invalids must be thankful to have been spared over our children so long and wait with submission for whatever chances. Jack has again written a very happy letter; the boy is still alive; he is learning fortification and engineering which he likes much; fencing etc. And he has given up Greek.

SUNDAY, APRIL 2. There's quite a revolution taking place at home here – the moustache movement – every man one meets is 'bearded like the pard' [*As You Like It*, II vii 150]. It is quite amusing. All ranks alike: nothing to be seen but hair. Ogle Moore is quite an object, and he a clergyman. As for the railway porters and the gentlemen of Pims, Cannock and White, Todd and Burns, and other linen draperies, they are fearfully martialised. Turks and Persians are nothing to them. It is a regular mania – the town has a foreign air already. Individuals are improved by this fashion but the aggregate have a dirty look.

9. Annie has had so little amusement lately, I see no harm in the pound note it costs her husband to bring her up to town so rarely; if that were all; but John Hornidge who came here on other business told Janey and me that James is again just as much embarrassed as ever. He is not living extravagantly as far as anyone knows, but the bill system goes on as before, and had it not been for the Doctor the other day a crash must have come. A bill for £200 was due and not a penny to pay it with. The Doctor wrote to the father who advanced the May allowance, £112.10.0, and the Doctor made up the difference; and there's the Humfreystown rent in July, all the Dublin and Blesington accounts and nothing that anybody can see to meet them with. They say it is his reckless farming – speculating instead of careful saving; goodness knows whatever brings it, it seems to be ruin coming. I must see the Doctor, make him, who has now the right, insist on Humfreystown being given up when the lease is out in December and then old Mr. King must meet us in encreasing the allowance made to this half idiot of a boy. He *will* manage himself – buy and sell and order and arrange. Clever thrifty Annie is a mere cypher – this certainly saves her the knowledge of his embarrassments, and if we can keep him swimming until his father's death he will then be able to repay the Doctor though little may be left besides. I see no way made towards the office the father hoped to get for him. However, I don't mean to vex myself about them. It is of no use; he will take no advice; she thinks him never wrong; and his total want of principle and her arrogant temper must both be punished.

Annie will come right for she has both heart and head and will by and bye open her eyes to the truth which he has taken very good care she should never have heard yet. She seems happy, is merry, fat, bright looking, and in all but her conduct to her parents irreproachable. Poor child! I am sure I forgive her – feel with and for her – and for her sake would endure him. The Colonel is not so placable. Janey and I together can hardly keep him within the bounds of civility to either; beyond this freezing point at present we dare not adventure to go.

Now for the War. Our infantry is on the way, our cavalry *preparing*! French preparing too! Our Generals are dining with one another and making congratulatory speeches to publick bodies in *London* and Lord Raglan has sent out a camp equipment for himself that would have suited Xerxes. Very different from old Napier's shirt, towel, razor and bit of soap are the prepared tent *flooring*, carpets, couches, portable furniture, plate, etc., etc. which have half freighted a steamer; the season is advancing rapidly; why we don't take advantage of it in the South East who can tell.*

10. Mr Sheehan told them yesterday that Charles Dickens began life as a reporter, the best he ever knew; he liked him personally, often employed him, thought him so clever, so absorbing, that he took him into Bellamy's* where all the M.P.s were eating their chops to show him 'the House' in *negligée*; the result was a paper signed *Boz* – the first of a series, some bad, some better which in time developed to what we see. *Copperfield* was his own career dramatised.

16. I have been all this day entranced with Macaulay's review of Hallam's *Middle Ages** and was so fatigued at the end of it I actually had to lay back in my chair quite still and idle for half an hour afterwards. It is plain the idea of his own future history was then running in his head; it is an essay every young enquirer should read, though I don't exactly agree with him all through, but it is the right end of the skein he has got; his style is improving, less tinsel in it, still a little claptrap, but it is going; these are wonderful writings for so young a man.

18. Three unhappy men have been executed at Belfast for the murder of Mr. Bateson – a ribbon business; he was merely

one on the black list and they drew lots to shoot him. Their 'clergy' had, of course, access to them in their cells and prepared them for their awful fate in a style of peculiar Roman impropriety. Instead of humble penitent sinners, these men died exulting martyrs, sure of heaven, so filled with the joys awaiting them in the next world that they would have disdained the pardon which would have restored them to this. Their ejaculations were really blasphemous, and their reverend attendants' reiterated assurances of blessed interviews with 'Jesus and holy Mary' were frightful. All was sunshine on that hideous scaffold and satisfactory approval throughout a crowd of thousands. The wives took leave of the condemned husbands without sorrow and probably the friends will bestir themselves to merit by similar crimes the certainty of rejoining in the abodes of the happy, these reputable associates. It is time to put an end to hanging.

30. Sunday. A busy time all this long fortnight or more notice would have been taken of it. And now has come a calm and life goes on with just another cloud over our limited horizon. We have lost . . . Lord Cockburn; he took ill at Ayr, while on the Circuit, got home, but did not rally, and died at his beautiful Bonally, regretted and respected by all – the last of that band of bright spirits who raised Edinburgh to a height she has now fallen from. Professor Wilson was buried the week before. Whig and Tory all are gone, and dull is the gloom they leave behind.* Jane feels this as much nearly as she felt Lord Jeffrey's loss, for latterly they had been very intimate, estimating each other thoroughly. I knew him little: better since I read his *Life* of his friend, which introduced me more completely into his character; he was the greater man of the two, I almost think the pleasanter; there was a manliness about him the other wanted, an honest candour, fearless yet gentle, which endeared him to all who knew him well. I saw him last at Bonally, walking on the terrace, looking at the prospect from among the flowers and talking over Lord Jeffrey's letters. He was seventy-six but did not look his age.

Our Doctor has been up with me two or three times about much more serious perplexities. [James'] debts are still great, his style of living much moderated, but though all economy is practised now the pressure of former extravagance remains. I have had to help to raise the two hundred pounds for the spring fairs without which he would have failed altogether, and rent day coming on; a step explained to me as quite necessary and yet more repugnant to my feelings than any one I almost ever took; I felt like a culprit myself when asking for the accommodation, though it was of John Robinson, my friend of more than twenty years; it was granted at once. I have only the honour of my son-in-law to rely on for the repayment.

Another bit of business has been the getting Jos. O'Reilly off to England to keep his [legal] terms; he goes immediately. I carried him the means yesterday; it was a good sum as he had fallen into arrears which must be paid up before he could be re-admitted. My Aunt *gives* him twenty pounds and twenty two I *lend* him, ten pounds of which I had to borrow from my Aunt. She had promised to lend me the whole twenty-two but her heart failed her to my sorrow, for the parting with such a sum at present, and all at once, is a serious inconvenience; trusting to her I had promised it so had to make it up myself, as his whole *future* depends on his pursuing his profession. Poor fellow, he has recovered his health from the moment the hope was held out to him and to hear him sing and whistle about the house after the sight of the [bank] notes was quite cheering. Poor Mrs. O'Reilly, her son saved, she says. Altogether it was very happy and my good Aunt may believe she never did a much kinder action or one more fully appreciated. A young spirit crushed. A young career blighted! How dreadful. To save both how holy! The power of being thus useful reconciles one to old age which has indeed few other pleasures.

SUNDAY, MAY 14. The Colonel and I went to Church today to St. Peter's to hear the Archbishop preach for the Protestant orphans. An excellent sermon, rivetting the attention after the ear became accustomed to the very familiar conversational tone in which it pleases him to read. The commandments did not sound well, just chattered out as one would tell some ordinary piece of news; the sermon was not so offensive; his voice is clear, enunciation distinct but there is vulgarism in the sort of county or cockney pronunciation – 'hearen, havin, childern, dooty'.

I forget when I last wrote in this journal. I am not happy enough to care for it. A cloud hangs over me somehow through which I see all things and nothing brightly; neither can I find an occupation that is interesting. I turn to many things, do all that should be done but nothing more, and above all things, writing which used to be my chief pleasure, is a task. Last Sunday I completed my fifty-seventh year. That I shall see many more is unlikely. I will do my best to *last* while I am wanted and then 'lay down in peace I hope, to take my rest' as they taught me to say in my childhood.

22. In the afternoon came our Doctor from Blesington with a very good report of his charges at Rathbally; the man-servant is gone and will not be replaced. Cattle really are bought, no extravagance is visible, and there is a very great improvement in the manners of the great little man; he acts now as if his neighbours were quite his equals although the Marquis of This and the Earl of That are not their cousins. But I was grieved on another point – Annie's strange infatuation about me – that I ill-used her husband, deceived him, broke my word with him, in fact caused all his difficulties, and then threw him off being tired of him. Of course he has told her all this *rhodomontae,* * but should she have believed him, or even believing him should she have acted towards a mother whom she or herself had never known to inflict an injury, however many she had helped to redress, with the childish petulance, unkindness, cruelty, tragedy queen airs that would have simply made her ridiculous had I been a looker on.

She wrote a letter to Janey the other day on the subject of her husband's griefs in which I figured so prominently and disadvantageously that Janey did not shew it, nor indeed read me any part of it, nor answer it. She never mentioned it till the Doctor introduced the subject by blaming me for not having yet overcome the Colonel's disinclination to receive the pair here; then Janey spoke; then she shewed him the letter, on which his observation was: 'My, my, I wish to God people did not know how to write'. 'I was determined,' said Janey, 'that you should see it because you could not rightly

understand matters without such an evidence of how Annie's mind has been perverted'. 'She should not have let it be
perverted' said he. 'She is very young,' said I, 'her principles
are rigid, her disposition proud, and yet she is easily influ-
enced. In this case unhappily we must leave it to time to
enlighten her, and then it had best be partially; but I must
own that her character has bitterly disappointed me.' The
Doctor first tore, then burned the letter which I am glad I
never read and we agreed to speak no more of it. The
Doctor staid till late and left me with such a headache! just
on the very night I could least afford to have it for I had
promised Hamlet to go with Janey to his musical party and a
pretty evening of suffering I passed, though the treat was
great. To our amazement the clock in the hall when we got
home pointed to past *two*.

23. My head very bad in the morning; medicines and starving
brought it round a bit, and a walk in the afternoon refreshed
me nicely. Who should call besides but Mrs. Haughton [the
Colonel's cousin]! Poor old woman, very feeble she is, quite
bent double, and very stupid. She flew out about the Queen
though in a most wonderful manner, called her Papist,
renegade, every bad name she could hit upon. Of course
there must be a party with these principles, ignorant bigots
who believe Prince Albert's family all to be R. Caths. Poor
Ireland! It is the middle ranks who most want education. I
have been busy trying to find a teacher for my school; there
are plenty of them and a nice clever active little widow quite
took my fancy until we came to particulars, then out came
such a string of the cant: 'Christ this, Christ that, Christ the
other, the type, the promise, the fulfilment, the one sin, the
curse, the heaven knows what', that I would as soon send a
firebrand down among our poor R. C. children as this
orthodox champion of the faith.

27. War! Hateful War! Every morning past my window files a
detachment of troops gaily marching to inspiring band
musick to Kingstown for their embarkation. 'Tis all the
Cavalry that pass this way; to me a melancholy sight. The
soldier's trade is hateful to me, and in this case we have the
misery of feeling all this waste of life and sacrifice of comfort
and wear of heart would have been saved had we had wiser

rulers. The want of vigour in our Councils has plunged Europe into a war no one can predict the duration of and by all accounts they are entering on it very ill prepared, our Commissariat being scandalously defective. With bodies weakened, spirits depressed and tempers chafed from excessive discomfort, our fine soldiery seeks in drunkenness to drown their cares – good preparation this for such a campaign as is expected. The French beside them have not a want. Light baggage, hot coffee, the gay *vivandières* and their natural happy adaptation to circumstances make the French camp a mere change of life rather pleasant than otherwise; while our long train of heavy baggage wagons, crowds of quarrelsome women, lumps of hard beef, and ill-contrived dress and want of arrangement all through the details, would annihilate the courage of any but the indomitable Saxon.* That barbarian Czar could have been resisted by the pen and this all spared us.

29. No comments for journal, no events taking place anywhere. The Brevet to come out immediately. All the colonels of '46 to be Major Generals. Poor dear Papa as the children call him, he will surely be promoted now as he was then, but for fear – we will not talk of it.

MONDAY, JUNE 5. John is to be with me today with his accounts. He came and we got through our business gallantly; he is slow but very exact. After all claims paid, he has one hundred pounds and odd over this half which I have desired him to invest in Bank Stock. Dear Jack, 'tis the beginning of the sinking fund that will I trust in time redeem all the charges on your pretty little property. A very small beginning truly.

8. We begin to notice the days now that Hamlet does *not* call; his attentions are all to *me*; he makes no secret of this admiration!

26. Here has been old Mr. King, about the Bill for two hundred pounds due last Saturday. James' part was £87.10.0, which if he had it not himself he was to get from the Doctor; he sent up five pounds short. Now if he made the sum himself by selling cattle he could as easily have made the whole as so very near the whole. That he might not think us in fault, and to keep my word with him of always acting openly, I told him I had paid all the expenses of the late visit to Dublin,

given his son five pounds for what could have only cost him but the half; and I also took advantage of the opportunity to tell him, according to my promise to the Doctor, that he and I had borrowed for James the two hundred pounds wanted to complete the stocking of the farm.

He opened his eyes a little. I wish he would open them a little wider and see that unless he adds fifty pounds a year to the son's allowance along with the twenty five pounds we will then give on our part, these distresses and scrambles and dirty tricks will continue to plague us. There are grave faults on both sides; the result is very unfortunate. As the Bill must be taken up today, I lent the five pounds, which the father will pay back if the son does not; the old man prefers thus borrowing it for some reason which is to act as a lesson to the son – even the good money he forfeits his good name to seize on. Poor Annie! with her spirit and her pride. Ignorance is indeed bliss to her. I am sure I will never try to make her wise.

27. A downpour of rain in the morning. In the evening the Colonel and I went to the Play. *Midsummer night's dream* and *The Corsican Brothers*. The first disappointed me; we had heard so much of it; the fairies were all too big. Puck like a beer barrel, a pretty girl with thick legs; the scenery was nothing particular, singing pretty, orchestra good. Bottom etc. not bad. But the lovers and Theseus were really afflictions. However it was fair enough; only Shakespeare depends so little on the getting up compared with the acting, the declaiming indeed of his poetry, that these rubbishy actors only make a burlesque of him. *The Corsican Brothers* suited the strength of the Company much better; it was very well done. Provincial theatres should keep to the melodrama and vaudeville style. The story is one of second sight where this faculty running in a family produces almost all the situation of the piece. The moral is frightful, vengeance gratified – ratified too, the spirit avenged assuring the murderer of his murderer that they should meet in heaven; the vindictive feelings are in the Corsican style, intense and undying and they are held up to admiration. My nerves are in such a curious state, that though I did not feel much excited at the time by the apparitions, no sooner was I alone

in my room than *there* stood the principal one beside me and after getting into bed, the head entered leisurely at the door, rising as it glided on till it stopt at my feet as I had seen it on the stage. I did not dare put out the candle though I was not afraid, only awestruck, and required the proof of light that this was mere fancy. So differently are we constituted that all the Colonel felt was tedium – 'damned nonsense and an hour too long'. I was quite disordered by it.

28. A few scraps from Jane tells that she [was] to be this day at Aviemore! What visions of the past does this name wake up – pony rides in tartan skirts, salmon fishing, enchanting loiterings among the birch woods on Speyside with those who never more on earth will meet again; and so as my spectre is hanging about the door again, I'll take a pill! as the best sedative in such cases.

29. Old Mr. King having given me the opening I have written him a note acknowledging the receipt of the five pounds, and then venturing on the son – excusing, palliating, accounting for the evil, and assuring him of my belief that the reformation was much more than begun. *Dexterously*! and delicately I got upon the encrease to the allowance, a second attempt which may have some effect, my promise to assist being now on paper; they are a queer set – poor foolish Annie.

30. The end of June. The town is very empty, the weather is very variable. There used to be summers long ago. I remember sunshine as a child – light clothing, open windows, etc. Now we wrap up warm – often have a fire – and sometimes shiver. It may be our years! No lines from old Mr. King. There is so little truth in this country I have begun to look on every person and all their acts suspiciously.

FRIDAY, 7 JULY. Nobody will stay at home above a week at a time by and bye when all these railroads are open. Bray being nearly ready, Wexford is to be done directly. Mrs. Montgomery and Kitty were here yesterday. Kitty has not given up hope yet. She will be patient, try the summer, even the winter if necessary. She is pale, thin, quiet: he in rude health and high spirits. 'Men die from time to time and worms have eaten them, but *not* for love', and though Kitty certainly does not let 'concealment' injure her, the more's the pity, 'the worm i' the bud' is there, poor soul, and keeps her very unhappy.*

27. A wide gap. More than a fortnight at the beginning of which time it was an even chance whether I ever should have heart to journalise again, the dear child for whom I keeping these memoranda of the past having frightened me almost out of my senses. His cough returned and violently, and he looked so wretchedly ill that I brought him down to Mr. Porter, who was attending the Colonel for a slight derangement. He was evidently staggered by the boy's appearance and examined him carefully, using the stethoscope: the result seems to sound in my ears yet – the right lung affected.

Even to my ears the dullness was perceptible; it was a too long neglected case – vigorous measures must be taken immediately, and he hoped to God we were in time. I was stunned. My darling Jack, the object of so much care – so much hope to so many. Every cough my treasure gave, and oh how frequent they were and how severe during the two days and longer nights that succeeded, every cough pierced right through me, made me shudder, made me feel dying myself, for what an existence was before him, even supposing we checked the evil. It was a waking nightmare.

Well, he was moved to Janey's airy room, she was at Rathbally; strictly dieted on fruit, milk, eggs, bread and vegetables – nothing that had had life, and no fermented liquors; fed every four hours, small quantities at a time, and clothed in flannel from the neck to wrists and ankles; hippo three times a day, and a blister on the offending lung; he suffered much, passed sleepless nights, I lying watching for every sound in his room just overhead; the quantity of phlegm he got rid of was really a marvel; it must have encumbered the lungs to a certainty – and so, the days wore away; he was relieved yet still the paroxysms of cough were frightful, his eyes were quite blood-shot and this attracted me: he had never had the whooping-cough – could it possibly be that.

He is soon to go to the country and he already goes out to walk and drive but we must be extremely careful of him till the spring is over and look well after him for a couple of years. His returning to Mr. Day is out of the question, to my joy, for I neither like the style of the school nor the style of the pupils there, though the boys are happy, and without doubt they get on well in their studies. We must first get him well and then bring him up in parts of education utterly and shamefully neglected: history, especially modern, geography, etc., common arithmetick, French, and the reading and writing of his own language. A couple of months or more will then fit him with as much military knowledge as will enable him to pass his first examination at Sandhurst. As I prefer keeping him back to pushing him on in his career, I should like to enter him for a course at Captain Orr's; he needs the excitement of emulation, and would be the better of living in a busier home than our invalid establishment – up early, all at work, all alive, plenty to do, and some fun, with an intelligent mind directing, dealing out bits of sense and bits of information seasonably, teaching the young idea what to shoot for. Here we vegetate. As soon as I am well again, I will turn this over in my failing mind, and write to Jane about it.

India is not thought good for Jack's constitution at present, so that our small chance of a cavalry cadetship is no grief. Dr. Robinson has written to William Cogan, the Roman Catholick M.P. for Kildare,* to put our boy's name down at the Horse Guards, and then when he is ready for his Commission we will apply through Lord Downshire, who volunteered his aid, to Lord Combermere [his father-in-law].

Poor me! My hope is that a few years of this kind of life will weary my son and that he will settle down on his pretty inheritance a wiser man for this experience; the schooling is rough and the ordeal frightful; it must be gone through in one shape or other by all young men in these our times; their mothers can only pray that they may cast off the slough thoroughly at last – never indeed to be what they in their womanly purity tried to make them and sent them forth to aim at, yet with an undying germ of good at heart, that will bring them back to virtue and happiness.

30. Sunday and Rathbally. I was called down on Friday to see Mr. Owen from Blesington. He had called thus early to say that, having come up to town in his wife's pony phaeton, he

and the Doctor, he would give a seat back to anyone who might fancy so easy a conveyance and a bed, without proceeding further should the traveller be weary at the end of the drive. I was quite taken aback having no way made up my mind for such a sudden start, but the kindness of the offer there was no need to debate about – neither was I allowed much voice in the matter. My Colonel said it would be madness to refuse it; and the Doctor calling concluded the business. Indeed I felt ill enough to let them arrange what they pleased, so at six o'clock my two friends called for me. Mrs. Bourne was at her window above to nod me off, Janey and Tom Gardiner at the door. Jack was up in his room out of the way of Tom who has never had the whooping-cough and the Colonel at his Club; they were therefore spared the pain of parting!

We had a pleasant drive in the cool of the fine summer's evening and I enjoyed it, yet was glad to find my journey end in Mrs. Owen's hospitable house. She had a truly kind welcome for me – excellent tea ready, and the bedroom all prepared so it had been all a scheme to entrap the irresolute. After breakfast yesterday morning, the Doctor came for his victim, carrying me off round the hill to shew his prize, stopping indeed at Peggy's that there might be no mistake about it. Janey had written to Annie, so all was ready for the old lady at Rathbally, James on the lawn superintending the making of as fine a crop of hay as ever was cut – fully sufficient to cover the rent, fifty six pounds. Annie has all as neat as a shew within, the most made of her scanty furniture, dear child, but the little house itself is so clean, so dry, so cheerful, so comfortable, and its situation is so extremely beautiful that it requires no extras to make it a most pleasant home. They seem quite satisfied with it, fond of it, and they are acting so much more wisely than heretofore, and in consequence their prospects are so every way brighter, that the aspect of all things is more hopeful than it has been since his first explosion of folly. His manner is extremely softened; no assumption, no bullying, no dictating, properly civil to me, and I hear from all sides, generally agreeable. A most happy change.

While all extravagance seems over: there is no stud, no

groom, no carriage coachman nor carriage horses, no Butler, no Dublin cook with assistants. There's a car and horse, a man to mind them, keep the yard, clean the avenue, etc. A lad in the garden directed by Annie. In the house Pressy, Dick Hornidge's *protegé*, who waits, drives, gardens, does anything he is put to. Good Mrs. Mack, with a stout girl under her, who between them do all the work and all the washing. The poor attempt at shew is all gone, comfort and peace remain, and Annie much now enlightened has forgiven me; her better knowledge has not altered her very pretty, very gracious manner to her husband, it has only restored my child to me. We do not go back upon the past, quite content as I am with the present. She knows I have excused her. My own private griefs remain with myself. We have all our cross to bear. As for him he has too little feeling to remember any incidents, he don't care to bring to mind; he forgets his ill humours, his hard words, his questionable deeds when it would not be for his interest to recall them; he fancies others think as lightly of these outbreaks as himself, having been used in his own family to considerable ill-breeding in this way, so though his character does not rise by this view of it, our relations with him now are rendered easier, and as he is under great obligations to me, is in my power, and has but me between him and his father's anger, I get on very well with him. He is a kind husband and will be kinder for a great event is at hand.

Sunday night after such a rainy afternoon as must entirely have soaked through all the hay in swathes. The morning was fine and I had an hour's stroll about the fields while they were all in church; the air very pleasant as my irritable chest feels, for I have coughed very little since the first night here. Mrs. Mack took the opportunity of stepping in to see me and tell me her news, which indeed I had discovered for myself. If all go well about Christmas Day we shall be presented with a gift which I hope and trust will be a source of much encreased happiness to all concerned. A grandchild may open Papa King's heart and purse, rouse Mrs. King to more active kindness, soften the Aunts elect and as for the Colonel he will be enchanted. Jack was the first to give a hint of this, the monkey herself keeping her secret close. I then questioned Janey and then the Doctor confided his hopes to me. My opinion is that the event is a certainty. It will make my Annie's home a different place; there will always be occupation for her in it, and interest, and her husband is so pleased and so *proud*, he is kinder to her than ever, his temper quite mollified. If he were but free of debt they would be all right; but he owes too much money yet, and then having had to apply the half yearly allowance from his father to the redemption of Latouche's Bond, it leaves him without a penny for his current expenses. It will be a hard struggle for a year or two unless this baby brings its parents help. Annie is remarkably well, has a fine appetite, good spirits, sleeps well, and has been as sick as her nurse could wish till within the last week.

TUESDAY, AUGUST 1. My Lady called yesterday of course and made me promise to spend the greater part of this day with her. My Lord much aged. She gave me a bad report of Jos. O'Reilly on whom I am afraid our help has been thrown away; he is still in London and though he has not written to his mother, he has written to his aunt to ask her to lend him money – in fact to endorse a Bill for him for twenty five pounds, which bill he enclosed ready filled up, all but her signature, and to induce her to oblige him he entered into a history of all the pleasures of the metropolis, the phalanx of beauty he admired at the Opera and his wish that her charming daughters could take their proper place among the aristocracy of the land etc.

As if she were a fool which she is not, nor the very least like one, nor the better inclined to assist him for all this blarney which she values at its just worth. She answered the 'meanly pitiful fellow' that she had no money to spare from the wants of her own family, not a penny, that considering the sum he got to take him over to London he ought not to have required even an additional five pounds to bring him back, begged and borrowed as it was from strangers who lent it out of pity for his mother, who would have a struggle to pay the borrowed back; a well principled young man would not have expended a sixpence beyond the merest necessaries, and a squandering under the circumstances of such a sum to him and her as twenty five pounds, proved that the charity which had sent him there had been most grievously misapplied.

As for his idea of hawking her name about on a bit of dirty paper among the lowest money lenders, it was only to be equalled by the act of applying to her at all after what she had already done for every one of them. He enclosed his letter under cover to the Doctor. She put it in the fire lest it should ever start up in judgement against him. I was extremely shocked at the meanness of the transaction – that part was a great deal worse than the dissipated folly in which he spent our money. I hope he may have paid his terms; only one cannot trust such a character. I know my loan was a pull on me I could ill enough bear. Mrs. Bourne having promised it and then drawn back, I did not like disappointing poor Mrs. O'Reilly. What would she feel, poor woman, if she knew all this?

2. I have been all this morning in the school. Thirty five children in pretty good order. She is a painstaking woman and will I think bring her pupils on well. The parents with their usual dishonesty have very few of them paid their quarter and no child has paid me for requisites, not one; they were tidy enough; the house is in bad order, the roof, the shores, sewers, and the sur-bases. I am sure I have spent a fortune on repairs too.

3. John Hornidge called according to promise to take me to dear old Baltiboys; the Doctor came with him and after a long gossip remained with Annie while John Hornidge and I drove off round the hill. We met Tom Kelly and the widow Ryan and called at Peggy's. She looks much aged, is pale and thin and bent; not so neat either in house or person as formerly, nor indeed is there much tidiness anywhere. The master's eye no other eye can supply – that's 'a fact' there is no contradicting. The avenue is in good order, a fine crop of hay on the lawn; but the house! there's not a single corner in it where anyone could sit comfortably to read or write or work. Quantities of handsome new furniture are lying about – no one room is yet finished. The drawing-rooms are spoiled by being thrown into one, the pretty little book room is gone, the fireplace walled up, chimney piece removed. A new very ugly bright steel grate is in the larger

division of this big apartment; the handsome embossed papers are torn off the walls, new rolls from Paris are waiting the hands of the painters.

5. These ten days of repose in the mountain air have been of incredible use to me. Besides the fright about Jack, a little worry, and the influenza, a small abscess had formed internally in a very delicate and very incommodious situation; it was very painful till it broke; the breaking was a mercy, but the discharge weakened me; now all is right. I feel not even uneasiness, so I dare say a little prudent care may set me up again for a while. I don't mean to deceive myself – these are all warnings. I was not strong naturally. I was not properly tended either in infancy or in youth and I have gone through a great deal. Mine has been a life full of severe trials – continued anxiety of mind, fatigue of body, some shocks, many disappointments; they were borne, I trust, patiently; but they tell in the end. The mind is fully more worn out than the body which is the hardest part to bear.

12. Here I am poor 'burd alane', dull enough but so thankful to feel well and to know that all else are happy, the young ones especially: Janey and Jack charmed with their change to Edinburgh, William and Sally delighted to have the young people with them. I never knew my Colonel so happy with any visitors as with my brother and his most amiable wife. Indeed adversity has much improved poor William. All that offensive superciliousness is gone; he harangues, dictates, finds fault, no longer; those odious high spirits affected by mistake in the hope of concealing his wounded feelings, are no more. Simple, natural, kindly, he passes along quietly, bearing his great reverses with an equanimity worthy of all respect; he is never idle, nor are the occupations he makes for himself frivolous: his mind is too well stored. Very clever, full of information, with a charming temper and the most engaging of manners, he wins his way to every heart, and keeps firm hold of mine though I so well know his frailties. Sally is almost faultless – admirably suited to him, being firm in the right, gentle in her firmness, never obtrusive and always ladylike. They went off rather sadly – Aunt Bourne presented a pretty Kilkenny box of *mine*! with twenty sovereigns in it to defray the extra expenses.

13. Sunday. No letters nor is there any news. The Queen is
going to Balmoral for three weeks so it is plain nothing very
material is expected to happen with regard to negotiations
for peace; the war is to be prosecuted with more vigour than
hitherto; truth to say, hitherto, we the allies have just done
nothing. In the Black Sea we are in full sail for Sebastopol
and the Crimea. The siege will be successful with the
sacrifice of very many lives.

Margaret Cameron has died at the Croft a few weeks after
the death of her mother. Lady Rachel [Russell] has asked for
that little loveliest spot on earth for her married brother
Alexander with whom she lives. The estate being in trust for
the payment of the heavy debt upon it, some nine thousand
pounds, and Jane being the Creditor and her husband the
Trustee, they manage it all their own way. They would sell
their charge for two thousand pounds which would pay off
Cameron's bond now held by Jane. William has written to
John to ask him to help to raise that sum. John might
himself give it, and then William could resume the possession of his beautiful property; the rents being now a thousand a year he could easily pay Jane the interest of her seven
thousand and he would have the wood besides, which now,
with a war, might again be valuable; he would have occupation too, an object of interest, hope before him, and if he
could prevail on his wife to give up her love for town and go
to live with him in the small house on the small farm of
Inverdruie, there might yet be many years of happiness in
store for him, if he would refrain from expensive improvements.

This way of living is merely vegetating, for he has no
employment and no society; they hardly know a creature in
Edinburgh, none but a few family connexions on either side;
the day must sometimes be very long to him, the evenings
duller. She sees this, but her dread of his speculating turn
makes her think idleness to him a lesser evil than activity.
But could we restrain that, with her three hundred a year
well paid, and a house and its few acres sufficient for their
supply, free, how comfortable they would be in his own
Duchus. When I think on his life's young promise and see
him now, what a lesson is read to me. The petted heir of

such a fortune, such an inheritance, reduced to the mere necessaries procurable by a small dowry of his wife. When I think of us all – how beginning – how ending – no sermon beyond this experience is needed to shew the emptiness of all the glories of this perishing world. Poor Rothiemurchus!

14. Quite a shower of letters this morning. Major Mair gives an excellent account of the Edinburgh Military College of which he is one of the working Directors and he sends the prospectus. The classes occupy seven hours a day, the studies varied every hour. A tutor for an hour in the evenings. The fees are twenty five pounds for the Session of ten months in which there are three short breaks. Respectable, well ordered boarding houses a guinea a week. It would be about a hundred pounds a year. I shall write to Jane on the subject. Anything is better for my boy than home.

20. My aunt and I amused ourselves watching the folk bound for Donnybrook fair; hundreds and hundreds of cars, three on a side besides children rattling off in a long string for hours. One wondered where all the crowds of people could have come from – more than anyone would have believed Dublin could hold of that peculiar class – humble artisans, labourers, servants and such like. An equal number of empty cars returning for fresh loads flew along the reverse way, and the pavements were crowded – families, father, mother and child or children, groups of young men, girls in parties of three, elderly women, all decently dressed, hurrying in the one direction till towards six o'clock when the tide turned t'other way; the empty cars then proceeded to Donnybrook and the full ones were coming back as was the mob upon the street. All steady, no noise, nor has there been a sound beyond a laugh till now, quite ten o'clock; all indeed seems to be over for this evening; the whirr of wheels has ceased; perhaps being Sunday the fun has broken up early, though of course there will be choice spirits preferring to spend the night out round the punch bowl. One fact struck me very much today – the dress of the greater part of what used to be a ragged company: there was hardly a tatter to be seen, except on some wretched boys, nor any very shabby clothing though many of the men were in their working dress. There

have been no murders owing to the efficiency of the police, I fear, more than to any improved habits of temperance – that movement seems to be over. It was like the house founded on sand.

21. Donnybrook still flourishing, not such crowds as went yesterday, but a steady flow of decent people all returning in steady condition none later than ten o'clock, the regulation to close all tents, etc. prevents those dreadful nights of vice once customary, and still leaves a good long day for all the sights and shews, so amusing to the class that visits them.

I have at last got Dr. Combe's *Memoirs* from the Library. They are done by George Combe and Mr. Cox and are very interesting to *me* with my peculiar turn. It is a history worth studying; although the melancholy mistakes of former days with regard to family morals are very much mended in these times; still in our publick education whether in girls' schools or boys' no proper principles are acted on, or even recognised. We should have neither so much ill temper nor so much vice nor so much ill health nor so much insanity did those in charge of the young fully understand how to deal with them; that iron bed of Procrustes, was it not, is the measure for all, however different may be the qualities of the unfortunate subjects of torture.*

My own childhood for ever recurs to me when these new lights are brought to view. Mary neglected, Jane misunderstood, William perverted, even John carelessly looked after, and I very nearly forced into utter heartlessness, artificial seeming, all that is hateful from the horrid system of tyranny pursued with a gentle nature that has always yielded to the tone of kindness. They who so used us knew no better, and in many respects they did well for us. It was not the custom to look on children as holy deposits to be given up again 'encreased in wisdom and knowledge' and 'in every good thing', an end only to be attained through the teaching of *Love*.

24. A giddy fit, rather a serious one with my Colonel. Indigestion, I think, as he has taken his dietary into his own hands of late: curry, corned beef, cold and hot, veal, etc. I have given up contending the point, he gets too irritable; orders home these things himself and *will* eat them; he was in a little bit of

a fright this evening, did all that was right and promises to behave better but with his memory so defective he can't be relied on.

That Donnybrook really should be put an end to. If necessary an act of Parliament could be got for the purpose. A day would do no harm but a week! is really making the people mad. This was a great day: the horse fair; thousands after thousands rushing along the road; long strings of crowded cars, and a mob of foot passengers. All returning early were quiet enough; but the later parties yelled, shouted, screamed, in a very riotous manner. The racket continuous from noon nearly distracted my poor head although I was as little in the front rooms of the house as I could be; James King dined with us and John Hornidge called with a brace of grouse of his own shooting; the Doctor was also in town but he did not come here.

27. The Colonel has quite startled me this Sunday morning by bringing me in the *Gazette*, and J. G. Smyth, appointed to the 39th Regiment. Upon reflexion, it can't be our boy; for we have not yet asked for his commission, only got his name put down, and the *y* is also against it, spite of the two initials. I hope it will be a full year before this sight afflicts my eye. Jane writes a very pleasant account of the impression he has made on them, and she gives wise advice concerning his college studies which coinciding with my own ideas, I approve! A year at Edinburgh, a session at least, eight or nine months will do him a great deal of good and even should he not quite be ready at the end of it, a few months then of a private tutor will be amply sufficient to fit him for the examination – no very searching affair. Jane and her husband had returned from Blair Adam much pleased with their visit.

The quiet has been very pleasant after this odious week of Donnybrook. A day for the poor to enjoy themselves after their fashion would be all quite right, but a week of such demoralising influence is deplorable; no one earns a penny either during this Saturnalia so that next week between hunger and weariness the labouring classes will have but a desolate time of it. The ragged department are no worse off than at other periods; but the rest with their families must be in distress, none of them ever being so provident as to save for need.

28. A grand falling out amongst all the servants to be set to rights. Susan as usual so dictatorial and unaccommodating besides being so idle. It is in fact her having so little to do that gives her leisure to torment everyone else. Aiken is very ill, poor creature; frightful colicks, looks like a corpse. No symptom of cholera mercifully. I have had a slight hint of this nature and feel the better for it; the heat too suits me. My Colonel was rather unwell for a day or two, a fit of indigestion, which however he got the better of without the help of Mr. Porter. Mrs. Bourne all alive. She has at last consented to have comfortable stays, having hitherto been wearing some made ten years ago when she was thin and before the present easy style of fit was common. I have put her into the hands of Mrs. Oldham who will place her in heaven! and make her pay for it!

It has been so hot we took our drive after dinner; the sun being so low was less powerful but there was very little air stirring though we went up near the mountains to look for it. On coming home we found Susan out, nor did she return until near nine o'clock; I having spoken to her in the morning about her having been out the greater part of yesterday without leave, also for having neglected her work; a nightgown of my aunt's having been nine days in hands and not a quarter done of it yet. She was really so saucy as to make us suppose she had been refreshing herself, and when she went downstairs she made such an uproar scolding the other servants, the Colonel had to go out and order her to her room. She is a very intolerable person. I do not think I can put up with her much longer; my Aunt is beginning to be annoyed by her idleness, so it won't be a very difficult matter to get rid of her.

29. Aiken has given up his place this morning; he feels himself too weak for work and thinks if his health is to be restored at all, it must be in the country. This attack has been a serious one. Also I think he cannot in his nervous state put up with the insolence of Susan. She is indeed a heavy affliction – or infliction – the family cross. I gave [her] a lecture. She is a kind of fool – self-sufficient fool; so jealous and irritable that

she is always fancying affronts, and my good Aunt gives her
so little to do that she has learned to be idle, resumed her
gaddings, and given way to her temper. I hope I have put her
all straight for the present, and as for Aiken it is better he
should go at the end of his quarter as he certainly has not
health to keep a town place in the winter.

31. August farewell. A genial month it has been. More of
summer in it than we have had since the so called summer
season came in. In town however it is never rightly summer.
At least we can never follow summer habits. Stone walls
meet the eyes, stone ways hurt the feet, noise rings in the
weary ears. My refuge is my own little room where through
the open window, by drawing the small round table, on
which I write and at which I work, so far back as to lose the
roof of a stabling, I look over a green field and through a row
of elms to the river-like canal and beyond over fields again
to those dear mountains standing up between me and my
poor old home – that home we made, and found for many
years so happy, and that came second in my foolish loving
heart to 'the Doune' – 'Duchus'.

SUNDAY, SEPTEMBER 10. That queer little pair arrived on Saturday 2nd. They have been extremely happy; Jack is quite
brisked up. Janey has been very busy in two ways – putting
her wardrobe to rights after her travels and before the
Operas, and retailing to my Aunt all her Scotch news,
the monkey having brought a good supply of gossip back
with her, all worth listening to.

Every week brings home invalided officers and the accounts of many deaths, fully as much owing to mismanagement as to climate. These mistakes are however being
rectified and inaction having done so much mischief, it
has been determined at this eleventh hour to rise up and
be doing. The troops are all re-embarked and off either to
Sevastopol or the Crimea! very much enfeebled, very unlike
the splendid army that encamped at Varna, still reviving in
the hope of work and, one way or another, eighty thousand
strong. It is to be hoped the Commissariat will second them.
The Czar has been very busy adding to his fortifications,
concentrating his troops, and victualling them well, stores of
all kinds having been brought from all parts in fleets of boats

without masts under the noses of our gallant frigates in the Black Sea.

I am reading Mrs. Beecher Stowe's very amusing *Sunny Memories* and Macaulay's *Essays* still – not always agreeing with him, but always comprehending him. A good word that, *comprehending*, in its full meaning. It would be very satisfying to talk with a mind like that, and we must starve on rubbish generally, or feast in private and alone; so very few suit each other. After all few conversations are more enjoyable than the quiet cogitations one has with oneself: – 'communing in our own chamber and being still.'

24. A summary of the last fortnight is not likely to be written down in a minute for we seem to have had plenty to do and plenty to think of, and as this quiet Sunday evening I am not likely to be disturbed in any way, I will try and give half an hour to pleasant recollections. First and foremost we have had an opera here: nine Italians, all respectable singers, two or three the best going – Cruvelli our first soprano voice now that Grisi is gone – a very pretty graceful girl with a voice of great power and compass; a little harsh in the upper notes, too young to be a fine actress but a good one now and giving great promise. Altogether a creditable company, quite able amongst them to represent any work, *interpret* is the cant word, very effectively and certainly very agreeably. We went to the first opera, *Norma*; the pretty musick, which we all know so well, made this one of the most interesting, yet there is but one character and she not an agreeable one. Cruvelli wants dignity; the erring high priestess should be grander, severer, not a mere distracted girl; but her singing was delightful; her *sotto voce* in the 'Casta diva' very affecting. We next saw *Fidelio*; Beethoven's musick is so entirely imcomprehensible to me that I had less pleasure in this than in Norma. Cruvelli acted well but she did not look well in an very unbecoming boy's dress. We next tried *Ernani*, I never before heard any musick of Verdi's; it is a little noisy but full of beautiful airs and the chorus very spirited. The opera itself has grand situations, is imposing in scenery, dresses, pageants, and the story good enough.*

We settled to have an oyster supper on the last night. We

had the two Miss Finnemores, Sam, and John Hornidge; Matilda and Emma King were to sleep here as they had done one night before, and Miss Janey brought in her train, in addition, Edward Leeson, Tom Gardiner, and Hamlet. We had tea and sandwiches, and oysters, porter and brown bread and butter, and wine, and then a large jug of punch made by John Hornidge, Annie, Jack and I waiting on the company which grew very merry. I don't know when we broke up, and we all echoed our unfeigned regrets at having heard the last Opera.

I met two or three of the singers coming downstairs at the hotel as I was going to call on Lady Milltown and they were Italian decidedly, calling to one another in that soft language with an accent no foreigner could imitate. I have my doubts about the fatherland of the whole set, for the Fortino and Polonino part were leaving the stage entrance as we were passing it in our search for a car, and they desired their coachman who was driving off with one division of their party to return as quickly as possible for *them* in good London English that seemed to be very unmistakeably their mother tongue. After all what does it matter as long as they sing well. Tamberlik, Cruvelli and Marai are Germans, and they some of them – all of them except Cruvelli, Lucchesi and Albini – are off to Russia to sing at St. Petersburgh, the Czar being still musical these discordant times. He will need some diversion from uneasy thoughts if the fine army now landed in the Crimea proceed as we expect.

Sickness is said to be over and the troops in high spirits, as are the people at home in spite of all the distresses we have heard of, the War being really popular. At the playhouse between the Acts the gallery is always in the habit of amusing itself with allusions to passing topicks shewing the temper of the times, sometimes mischievously enough. When tired of this they cheered the Queen who used, poor little woman, to be anything but a favourite; they God blessed her and cheered the French and the Emperour Napoleon and then they sang the National Anthem and admirably well too. A bold voice one night asked a cheer for the Pope – the answer was a burst of laughter and the song 'Should auld acquaintance be forgot', all in perfect good-humour, They then began to travestie the singing *à la Liston*, shaking and holding notes and running up and down the scales and giving bits of recitative with long words meant for Italian. The temper of the Gods has improved wonderfully since the days of those frightful rows which made the rest of the audience tremble.

25. If ever, dear Jack, you have a son very dear to you, about whose welfare you are very anxious and with whom you don't on earth know what to do, you will comprehend my feelings this morning on receiving a letter from your Aunt Sally to say Major Mair will take charge of you and educate you with his son Willie for your profession. Quite a load was lifted from off me. I had so wished this and yet did not like to propose it. You will be so safe there and so happy. An affectionate domestick family, cheerful and kind and indulgent to young people though they make them do their duty. The terms are high – the College expenses greater than I expected; it will be a pull on a scanty purse, involve some sacrifice on all our parts; but we must do it for your sake, dear boy, and not grudgingly. It ought to have been there ready, the money for your two last years; your credulous mother let herself be cheated of it; the more fool she; and also my father's legacy; and my poor mother's which I was told I might surely reckon on, the indolence of Cousin Bartle has lost to us. I don't care for money, but alas! we want money's worth.

26. Having nobody to talk to, I talk to myself I see, the journal lying open as the writing materials are arrayed for business. I have been trying to make out the additional £100 for Jack's year of Edinburgh and so have been carefully going over accounts to see how we could economise without encroaching further on Baltiboys than I had agreed to, and I find it can be done by Janey giving up her gaieties and the rest us forbearing charities; for one year this must be. I can live and pay our rent with £700, without denying either Mrs. Bourne or the Colonel a single luxury; the odd £100 therefore can be Jack's. If my sister is able to continue him her £50, then we shall hardly be hampered for I find I have lent or given this last year fully that much. I must *write* again.

29. My boy went off by the *Vanguard* this afternoon in very fair spirits. They are all so kind in Edinburgh in preparing for him and are all so fond of him and he is such a domestick affectionate creature I have no doubt in the world that the plan of his living with the Mairs will answer for everybody. Their income will be so materially encreased that they will feel amply repaid for their trouble; besides they will get a good companion for their son. We may thank heaven for the chance on our part. Jane writes instantly to say she has no intention of withdrawing her £50. We therefore have but £50 additional to provide and that by good management can be effected; it is worth all we can give to have this year passed over so admirably. It is not the learning alone, the impetus given, the tutor, etc. It is the society – quite beyond any we have now the power of introducing him to here. Men with their heads full, accustomed to be busy, and to hear and see much before venturing on judging.

   Poor Paddy Dodson's deathbed and funeral; the immediate cause of the good old man's funeral was a fall from the roof of his hen house which he was thatching, but the end must have soon come some other way for he was ninety-four. He is the last of the old set nearby. The Colonel remembers him in his old father's stables. They were un-thinking times, those old times, and men were dissipated then, the stories of the Squire and his friends not exactly teaching good morals, but they were not beastly. The world seems to have gone wicked mad, in the vilest ways. Rome before she fell, the Cavaliers after the Puritans, very likely the low church bigotry is thus re-acting, but it's a horrid state of manners. The war was needed.

30. The last thing poor old Paddy did was to drink all our healths in some wine Annie had sent him – the only words he uttered afterwards were 'I thank God I bear no one envy or malice and die at peace with all'; he passed away without a struggle, nor did they know he was dead till Mary stooped over to look at him. The Colonel gave one pound towards the funeral, James King five shillings and John Byrne and James Ryan dug the grave; there was no large attendance of neighbours it being such a busy time, but respectable, and the poor old woman walked between her children behind

the coffin. Poor Paddy – innocent creature – simple-hearted and without guile. Heaven's gates will open more readily to such as you than to those of higher gifts who have misused the 'talent'. I have from Mary a most agreeable account of the school; the mistress extremely popular, much respected, and with fifty scholars. Father Germaine sent me word I had made an excellent choice. If this continue, a deal of work will have been done.

SUNDAY, OCTOBER 1. There were rumours here yesterday of an engagement or succession of engagements as our troops moved on but nothing authentick. Of course they made us successful – the two great nations fighting side by side how could it be otherwise? They say too the Russians have less than 40,000 men in the Crimea including the garrison of Sebastopol – some of them recruits – and all disheartened, and that the fortifications built by contract like those in the Baltick will be as inefficient, all being based in Russia, everybody cheating every other body and altogether cheating the Czar. Bomersund was found to be, the walls I mean, shells, outside stone, inside rubbish, filled in; they fell to pieces at every shot. It is the same system with the stores, the provisions, ammunition, etc., all 'sound and fury, signifying nothing' [*Macbeth* V ii 27 – 8]. We shall have no news to rely on till Tuesday, Sunday being our English day for inventing lies and Monday for distributing them. We must take Sebastopol, but it will be a bloody victory. We wanted war: immorality was reaching a height of such gross indecency in both services as to be revolting. Everywhere else even – in all classes and all business a reckless profligacy is consuming the vigour of the people. War has its horrours. I question whether its evils work as much mischief as the vices pursued in peace. Sloth is in fact our worst enemy. Louis Napoleon may bless the Czar: he owes his existence as a sovereign to him; the restless French would have been at *him* had no other *pièce de resistance* presented itself. Great hard man with littlenesses in that clever head.

When Sir William and Lady Craig [Betsy-Sarah, née Vivian] were in Paris in the Spring, they were to go to the Tuileries. She was cautioned against reminding either Emperour or Empress of her former intimacy with either.

She had known them both extremely well in their London days, had often sat beside the beautiful Mdlle. de Montijos at private parties, and danced, and avoided to dance, with Prince Louis whose ear was not very correct for musick. They knew her instantly: the Empress held out her hands with a beaming smile which thought seemed to check; the Emperour was gracious *but to a stranger*; however he seemed to take so much pleasure in talking to her, she is very pretty and very ladylike, that she thought she would venture an allusion to some former passages between them more to satisfy herself of the truth or falsehood of the impression given to her than out of any other feeling. 'Chut!' said he, putting his finger on his lips, but in a pleasant voice near a whisper. 'All that is locked up in the box with forgotten things. Chut.' In all the Buonaparte family there is a want of *blood*; they are not what in their adopted country is called *bien né* or 'high bred'.

One has a low opinion of human nature when one reflects on it – Lord Clive – Hastings. I am reading Macaulay's beautiful *Essays* on their career; how lamentable – *unchristian* – as I never can avoid going back to as the source of ill. Macaulay himself, so clever, so accomplished, so well informed, so eloquent, able to reason so admirably on the actions of others – and a drunkard – morning, noon and night, a slave to the bottle. He must be suffering from some painful and incurable disease, some weakness which this relieves – to encrease alas! Mr. Sheehan says there is no doubt of the wretched fact.

There has been a frightful occurrence in the North – a railway train conveying nine hundred people saved from destruction by the merest chance. It was a foolish protestant assemblage of all ranks headed by Lord Enniskillen, gone from Belfast to spend the day at Derry – peaceably, of course, in somebody's gardens where they were to have speeches and a tea dinner: absurd enough but monstrous to murder them for it. Several trains had passed that day, one a few *minutes* before this return demonstration was expected back along the line and no harm had happened to any of them. When this obnoxious one neared a village about twelve miles from Belfast, several large stones were found to have been laid on the sleepers. The engine was, of course, lifted up, turned aside, and thrown off down a precipitous embankment, for the spot was chosen well for the purpose, and only that the connecting hooks broke, were broken by the force of the upheaval, the whole of the carriages would have followed the engine and of that vast multitude how many would have been killed, how many mutilated.

As it was, fright was all they suffered, fright and discomfort, for none of the neighbouring peasantry would come near them to give assistance – not even to help Lord Enniskillen, the only person injured; he was riding for some reason on the engine, was thrown out of course, and jammed in some way between the irons so that his extrication was difficult. Great care and the strength of a powerful man seconding his own *gigantic* exertions – he is six foot four – and stout, freed him at last; the engine drivers were both of them killed, one on the spot; the other lingered two days. Eleven men are in custody on suspicion but it is supposed many more are implicated – in fact that it is a ribbon conspiracy, the act decided on here at the head Lodge in Dublin and the actors chosen by lot. A dreadful state of things if true.

4. A letter from Jack; [he] was entered in the Military College. Jane has advanced money and is prepared to advance more but it will not be necessary. After the great battle of the Alma, twelve miles from Sebastopol which our united army gained in two hours and a half, our troops are said to have fought on and gained another battle. We can have no particulars until the 6th nor dare we believe all we hear till the arrival of the official despatches.

6. We were a little premature about Sebastopol. A despatch from Lord Raglan of date the 28th only mentions continued fighting; we advancing, the enemy retreating, amid great slaughter on all sides. No official details of our bloody victories as yet. It is dreadful – but it is none the less most miserable.

James King called yesterday morning before leaving town to tell me he should certainly have the two hundred pounds ready for me after the next market, but he wished I could lend it to him a little longer; quite set him up if he could turn it over once more. As I had borrowed it myself and pledged my word to return it in November, I could not accommodate him. Would the person of whom I had borrowed it [John Robinson], lend it on to him. I knew he would not, but could not say so, therefore had to decline on my own part asking him an additional favour. Would I myself lend him a hundred pounds to buy milch cattle to make a fortune with during the winter? I who have not a hundred beyond strict necessaries, now that Jack is so expensively placed. My five pounds too which he borrowed for a week, a fortnight ago. I got Janey to get one pound for the school, and they sent me up a crock of butter and I will take some hams, which balancing of the accounts is an improvement, but the '*tottle* of the *whol*' is so unsatisfactory to me that I have written all particulars to the Doctor. He being head of the firm had better look after the hands.

7. A letter from Major Mair really quite pleased with the boy – his manners, his disposition, his acquirements – everything but his appetite; he has been found much more forward than was expected, and was even complimented by the professor of humanity on his good grounding in Latin. My sister has been so very kind, advanced twenty five pounds for him thinking it might be inconvenient for us to send over money till the rents were paid. I bid her keep half of my September money [on Kinloss] but she would not. Everybody is so considerate for us. I am quite at ease now about Jack, satisfied that he will do well in all ways.

9. We have taken possession of a fine seaport eight miles south of Sevastopol, where we are quietly disembarking our battering train, heavy artillery and relay of cavalry. Sevastopol is invested by sea and land so that we can cut off all its supplies even to fresh water; its fate is therefore settled. The defeated Russians have retreated behind its walls.

I have been quite interested in Macaulay's Warren Hastings, that great, unscrupulous and ill-used man. My Aunt says she was in London that first winter of the impeachment and that in Colonel Ironside's set, of which Sir Philip Francis was a prominent member, the ex-Governor General was quite looked on as a Pariah. She believed him to be everything that was vile, was accustomed to hear the most outrageous abuse heaped upon him as she supposed deservedly, and it was not till many a long day after that she learned to judge of him more correctly by the standard of his times, – to understand his difficulties, and the little undercurrent of jealousy of which he was the victim. Poor human nature! Without that higher support it so seldom has, how miserably it fails, and politicks seem to demoralise everyone.

11. This is war, recalling to me the days of my childhood when the mails from Spain came in with their tidings of mournful victories. A generation has grown up since in peace, and when this brush is over so will rise another, but we pay a fearful price for these breathing time. The Russian position on the Alma was, they say, a masterpiece, the officers trumps; it was the men that failed them, that shrunk from French impetuosity and the British bayonet.

13. Sevastopol blockaded. At five o'clock in the morning of the fourth the blockade began. A great fire was observed in the interiour of the town as if made on purpose and the Russians have sunk five of their ships with all their guns and stores on board at the entrance of the harbour; the masts are visible; this is their way of carrying on the War.

The servants have all begun to quarrel again, that is to say Susan has been quarrelling with them; the poor creature can agree with nobody. She is most disobliging and difficult to please and upsetting and I should suppose intolerable below, for at times she is impertinent above, after her stolen *tea*-drinkings. I am sure we shall have to part with her and, on my Aunt's account, she is a valuable attendant, when the old lady is sick. At other times she is idle enough. What plagues they are.

We had old Peggy here for a night. She is settled in a small two-roomed house in Portobello, in the way of old neighbours coming to town. Whether she will be happy in such a complete change of life we shall see. Antony lives with her, and she has two grand-children, three hens and nine chickens to look after. John Fitzpatrick wants us to provide for him, so does Mary Kelly. They declined my help when it would have benefitted them and now they must just get on without it.

16. A letter this morning from Jane on the painful subject of poor William's hopes. John is quite against power of any

sort being restored to him; he wrote and told him so, honestly; he has now written to Jane proposing that *she* should purchase William's life interest and continue to manage the property admirably on her own as the wife of the principal Trustee on that side, the side of the heirs of entail. If William's trustee proceeds with his expressed intention of selling his life interest, I suppose Jane *will* buy it. She is the principal Creditor – in every way the most proper possessor the dear old place could have. Poor William! with such abilities – so kind a heart – yet can't be trusted. Those who had the spoiling of him have much to answer for. The education of character was so little understood; how did we younger ones escape?

18. Determined to read no more details of that butchery on the Alma; the letters to surviving friends about the dead and the dying lay unfolded before my eyes the whole night. When I got to sleep, after four o'clock, I was in the battle-field among the slain, attending the wounded. What kind of nerves can I have, or do people beginning thus end by going crazy. A proper woman for the wife and the *mother*! of a soldier! How thankful I am that Jack is still at College and that we can keep him there for yet another year till all these massacres are over. Human beings rushing on to murder one another by wholesale; I can never accustom my conscience to endure it. A necessary evil it is called – in this case of Russia unavoidable. We have lived so long at peace that this 'supping full of horrours' is really agony.

James King came in to tea; his ladies don't come up till next week; they have been dining at Russborough, spending the day there, all in great spirits, my Lord being away looking after the approaching sale of his property. If he persist in declining all private offers some of which were very good, the Creditors will force a sale by auction early in November.

21. We have had poor Mrs. O'Reilly staying with us most of the week. Queer establishment hers. Eyre and the new maid, a pretty girl, and that half mad child of Pysie's keep house together – the mother here, the daughter on a visit to a particular friend, a Bride, whose marriage can be acknowledged on neither side of the house. Jos. has written at last

but says nothing that was told to me except that he should like to live and die in London. What he has been doing, how he has been existing, all these many months since the small sum he took with him was exhausted, no one seems to know or care. His mother 'thinks he must have got some employment for he has had no money from her.' Pysie 'considers him at his age the fittest to manage his own affairs'. Neither the one nor the other seems to have an uneasy thought about him. Whether they know more than they say one cannot tell; they are quite capable of being mysterious when it suits them. I only hope that he kept his two terms, and has not been misappropriating the money given him for that purpose. An uncharitable idea, but really after his meanly worded application to Lady Milltown there is no avoiding suspicions concerning him.

No additional news from the Crimea. The Courts Martial on the Arctick Expeditions are over. Captain Maclure had his sword returned to him with high and well merited compliments. We are much too much occupied with military carnages to spare a thought on that useless north-west passage. It is to be hoped that, science satisfied, there will now be an end to voyages to that dismal pole.

23. A deplorable account of John Robinson: totally unequal to business – never goes near that office of which he was once the head and soul. He had better have died of the fever, and we in our blindness were rejoicing when he was saved.

24. Poor old Peggy! The Colonel and I went to see her today. She is not happy, nor she don't look comfortable. It is not a bad little place – a cottage of two rooms with a small yard, good sized windows, one room boarded and papered and the chimnies don't smoke, but then the dreary situation – off a stable lane – one of a short double row of the same sized houses looking upon one another. She hoped to get used to it, and she knows she is doing what is kind by her children so she will try it awhile. For my part I cannot fancy her life endurable, after such a different one as she has led. She says however that without us Baltiboys was very dreary.

27. Private accounts corroborate the *Telegraph* for once. A very bloody affair is reported. Thirty thousand Russians made a sortie but were repulsed with great losses on both sides.

Steamers full of our wounded were on their way to Constantinople. Everybody one meets looks aghast. We can hear no certain news for some days, but that we shall have to mourn as well as to rejoice is pretty evident. There are rumours of the Russian General collecting men to raise the siege, and the season is so advanced. How miserably mismanaged everything has been about this expedition from the beginning all throughout; time so wasted, preparations incomplete, position of camp so unhealthy; Commissariat so scandalously faulty; no food, no covering, no tents; and neither doctors, nurses nor chaplains in anything like sufficient numbers; the cholera was as much produced by want of shelter, no beds but the bare ground often wet, and rain falling, as by improper food.

Mr. Porter was written to one day this week in a hurry to send out a hundred surgeons; he picked up the smartest young men he could get, but the pay is so inadequate no experienced practitioners except from pure patriotism would undertake the service. This is not the way to have the surgery staff of an army supplied. Benevolent women are going out as nurses on their own account, assisted by the Government certainly, but they volunteered and a large private subscription has furnished them with bandages, dressings, restoratives etc. Extremely praiseworthy in the individuals, but what does it say for the War Office? There is no doubt that thousands have been sacrificed to fever and cholera who never should have been exposed to it, and that hundreds of the wounded have died from want of care: hospitals not ready, space not sufficient and no nurses, and now they say Sebastopol is wonderfully strong, well fortified, well defended, difficult of approach and so on. We shall soon know, but people are beginning to feel gloomy.

30. At last we get quit of that disagreeable Susan – the most unpleasant servant almost without exception that I ever knew in any house. After all her promises of amendment, her tears, and her entreaties to be kept, on condition of behaving better, last night again she went out without leave and remained abroad until nearly ten o'clock. She would not have plagued me near so long but for my Aunt who I thought liked her. Susan thought so too and presumed

upon it; but we were both mistaken; my Aunt is quite tired of her pomposity and her idleness and her airs, and is longing to have Maria to wait upon her. I was therefore glad of the opportunity of dismissing this torment. She was at first in the *ask pardon* line, very humble, with excuses ready. When she found the matter was serious she got as saucy as possible. I paid no attention – merely repeated that I could not overlook such repeated disobedience and that as soon as ever I had suited myself she would go; then she wanted to be let off on Saturday – take the week and all my soap and starch to make herself smart and suit herself, but I stopt all such grandeur. Nevertheless I shall get rid of her as soon as ever I can for her temper, never good, becomes intolerable when she is crossed. She has no redeeming qualities – neither heart nor head. Certainly the lower order of protestants are thoroughly odious – so self sufficient.

31. It has quite distressed me to find that the Miss Florence Nightingale, who is making herself so absurd going out to Scutari with thirty or forty other young women in her train to act as nurses to the wounded soldiers, is a daughter of our old friend Mr. Nightingale, with whom we lived quite as a brother while he remained in Scotland. He married one of the William Smith of Norwich his daughters – a curious sort of woman with whom he has by no means lived happily. Her father was a very severe low churchman; he and all his set were outrageously puritanical. She has turned Puseyite, and this daughter, emulating Miss Sellon, has been devoting herself to doing good works in the wandering friar style. Evidently an excellent, benevolent, active minded girl. They have cherished instead of repressing her over enthusiasm; fed her vanity and so got completely round herself and into her full purse. *Punch* says the Nightingales will be turned in the East into *Ring*-doves – a very happy transmogrification. Sydney Herbert, one of the set, writes to entreat of her to prosecute her intention. Government has given her every assistance and she is off. Whether they will get good there is some doubt. Human nature retains all its contingencies in all cases; we all know the misery unto death often endured by the sisters of mercy. These are all papists in heart – limited in intellect.*

SATURDAY, NOVEMBER 4. I have met with such a loss this Saturday at e'n – my spectacles – must have drawn them out of my pocket with my handkerchief in the streets, for they were safe there after choosing a case for them in a shop. My eyes serve me better than I supposed by using them in a clear light, but I miss the help of the glasses sadly. How little we prize our hundred thousand helps and comforts and comforts and blessings till we lose one of them. What did people do before all these artificial assistants were ready for us? What would I do without a book, a pen, a needle, I who like living alone with these quiet occupations.

5. Sunday; fine rather, and warm, and the household at peace again, my Aunt having interceded for Susan now thoroughly humbled; great promises of amendment, and a proper apology, mollified my just anger! Poor creatures! Bad bringing up, no principles, vacant minds, 'tis a wonder they are as good as we find them, particularly in restless youth.

11. Mr. Sheehan gave me very bad news today; he hears they will have to raise the siege. Winter comes on so suddenly and so severely in the Crimea. We undervalued our foe, much underrated his defences, and as we all know mismanaged our own affairs so completely in the beginning that it would have required much more talented commanders than those employed to retrieve affairs. Lord Raglan from all we hear has no military reputation. Poor Sir John Burgoyne is near eighty and was never bright; and as for Admiral Dundas he's a fool. The French call Admiral Lyons *l'amiral du Fleet*, and the other stupid man [Vice-Admiral Sir James Dundas] *l'amiral du Slow*, which is a very correct witticism. And all our fine young men are sacrificed to the incapacity of these incapables and the vacillating policy of our apologies for ministers. The Militia is to be completed immediately, well drilled during the winter, and in the spring sent out to the West Indies, Canada, etc. in place of the more disciplined troops of the regular army, all of which will be wanted to crush the Czar; how differently is this miserable campaign ending from what we boastfully hoped. Still much of this may be croaking – matters may not be so bad, but the scarcity of news, the silence of the officials, and the alleged loss of despatches has filled people with anxiety; and Jane

writes in admiration of all that has been done, or rather I should say neglected to be done; so much does party spirit warp the judgement.

12. Sunday. Staid quietly in bed all the morning and felt somewhat better on getting up. Hamlet called as pleasant as usual; he affirms the reports of our cavalry being cut to pieces on 26th October by too brilliant a charge of Lord Cardigan.

15. Hamlet who has been a good deal with us since his return to town gave me his *Times* which contains the most graphick detail of that eventful 26th from the pen of their Correspondent, Mr. Russell, an Irishman, who is permitted to remain with Lord Raglan's Staff.* They were all seated on a hill watching the battle, having dismounted. The enemy had surprised and discomfited the Turks, taken their guns, destroyed their batteries, as we had formerly heard, the Turks having grossly misconducted themselves – either fled or laid down their arms or laid down themselves to pray to Alla; the heavy dragoons, 93rd, and another infantry regiment had advanced and repaired most of the mischief, retaken some of the guns and forced the Russians to retire in some confusion; it was hand to hand fighting for some minutes, very brilliant.

It was all over. The Allies had formed again, in advance; the Russians ditto, further back. Lord Raglan bade General Airey,* the Quarter Master General, to send to the Light Cavalry Brigade to advance position and remain on the defensive. General Airey sent the message by his Aide de Camp, Captain Nolan, a very dashing Cavalry Officer, whose peculiar monomania it was, poor man, to imagine the horse invincible.* He either mistook or misrepresented his message, for he desired Lord Lucan to advance and charge.

Where! What! said Lord Lucan aghast; his six hundred men to twenty thousand? There are the Russians, Sir, said Captain Nolan pointing to the mass before them. Lord Lucan rode up to Lord Cardigan, whose amazement equalled his own; however there was nothing for it; charge they did and gallantly trotting bravely a mile and a half in perfect order to certain destruction; thirty guns poured on them leaving as many gaps in the little Brigade; on they went – and were lost sight of among the mass of Russians. A *shoal* of bright scimitars gleamed over the heads of the whole and then the remnant of our glorious band were seen returning, but on the heights on either hand were batteries, in full play, and 'tis said that a troop of Russians which had pursued our men's retreat were mowed down indiscriminately with their foes. One hundred and sixty Light Horse returned out of that doomed band; a hundred came in afterwards. Only a hundred and thirty were killed outright; the rest are only wounded. Thirteen officers fell; the first among them was the authour of the butchery, Captain Nolan. The correct order was found in his pocket.

Next day another sharp skirmish ended in a more decisive victory on our part; but their fresh troops are harrassing our worn out soldiers dreadfully. Of our little army of thirty thousand not quite half are now on duty. Each week diminishes the number by about six hundred men killed or disabled; all are over-fatigued, yet their spirit is unsubdued. Our official information ends here; the French have later news. It is from them that the accounts of the sortie of the 5th November have reached us. The Vienna correspondent adds, one more such victory and the Allies must raise the siege. It has no doubt been a bloody one. The shock victory however is over. We look for nothing but grief. Victory or no victory, we lose a thousand times more than we gain.

19. A vile rainy Sunday; poor workers! your only day. My sister and I have a close correspondence just now on business matters. The Chancery suit brought on by poor half crazy Mrs. Wynch against my father's executors has been decided against her on a common rule of common law. She has diminished the fund from which all the claimants were to be paid, by the law expenses which are to be charged on it, and by the interest claimed by my mother's executors on behalf of Jane and me, her residuary legatees – two years interest the time our cause was pending. She has kept herself and others out of their rights these six years – all from temper. Her case was very hard. She had been cruelly used, shamefully used by her Trustees.* But there was no redress, and by

not bearing her wrongs patiently she has encreased them. Her sister under the same circumstances acted very differently and has been rewarded accordingly. This decision relieves me of a load – gives me my boy's commission. I had such a happy letter from him, and an excellent report from Aunt Sally. Thank God from my heart, that he is well and good and happy and not before Sebastopol.

SUNDAY, DECEMBER 10. Tuesday morning came a note by post from the Doctor to say that at two o'clock the day before he had delivered Annie of a boy [John Ponsonby] – both doing well. This was a great relief – filled our small house with rejoicing. Mother and baby thriving to a wish; even the nursing is less troublesome than it frequently is, but there is a hitch in it, which may annoy Annie for a little while. She will be a good nurse in one respect – have plenty to give her child. He is very small – born I think before his time. But he is perfect – firm, fat, hardy, lively, sleeps for ever and ails nothing; he is like his father, the head and face particularly. Poor little pet, will his heritage be one of weal or woe.

Time was, and not so long ago either, when this longed for event would have excited me almost unduly; it surprises me to feel how very little impression it makes on me; I may really say none; except that I am glad for Annie's sake that such a source of interest with never failing occupation is now attached to her, the birth of my first grandchild would scarcely move me. I am 'a'weary of the world' – the Doctor says from indigestion! Perhaps – from some cause or causes certainly. And so for fear of present consequences I'll go out to walk this fine frosty day and renovate my faculties.

11. Annie really well – awkward about nursing her baby, and baby very stupid about helping himself. We had a sad fight all yesterday – fatiguing to both. If we don't do better this morning we must just get some woman from the neighbourhood to teach both, as neither can thrive while tired out this way. We had quite an alarm last night after midnight – Garrett Doyle – his wife in labour; unfortunate woman! She lost her two first children from the length of her sufferings, Annie insisted on the nurse going to assist her and just now she has returned with the news of a young daughter amid great rejoicings.

18. Went to Russborough in the car and walked home; met my Lord at Judy Connolly's gate, grown fat and in his very best looks. Barby and Ceely with him. They left him and joined me and we all went up to the house together. My lady was at tea in her dressing-room, a very pleasant sight to me; and she was in high good humour which was pleasanter. The boys are coming home for the holidays tomorrow. Russy went up to town today about some Militia business. The girls follow him tomorrow and then go on with him to Hillsborough. A note came from Lady Cloncurry while I was there asking the rest of the family to [Castle] Lyons for the Christmas. Altogether I have seldom seen them all so happy. She gave me a warm and a pretty black cloke for Mrs. O'Reilly and desired me to send her in a ton of coals whenever the ton my Aunt gave her is expended. Poor woman, she has a good heart. I sat with her till near dark; passing the gate at Tulfarris the Doctor overtook me, popt me on his car and we had a long conversation. Ah me. Baby will be easier set to rights than the Papa.

19. Matters look a little more cheerful in the Crimea. In all the sorties the Russians are repulsed. Reinforcements have reached our troops, with plenty of provisions and necessaries of all sorts. The ladies everywhere are busily engaged in making up large parcels of warm clothing; private individuals have sent out steamers filled with stores; 'tis as if but one spirit animated the country, determination to carry on the war and in every way help those engaged in it. The fund for the relief of the women and children belonging to the Army is already very large. Miss Nightingale has done a deal of good. The Duke of Cambridge is, they say, better. His attack is called fever, nervous fever. 346 officers killed and wounded since the beginning of the campaign, some died of cholera.

Parliament has met and the Ministers don't much like their reception by it. The Duke of Newcastle very wisely admits their errors; says were it to be done over again things would be very differently managed and that their past mistakes will be a warning to them in future, which I am sure I hope; but as a cabinet they are so weak, their commanders by sea and land are so incompetent one can hardly believe them fit to bring any enterprise to a happy conclusion. The best hope is that the Russians will be starved out during the winter, a very severe season in that country, perfect tornados of wind with violent dashes of rain, and mud a foot deep. Yet our troops are in spirits and have borne a series of discomforts, nay privation, beyond the idea ever formed by any of them without losing heart in the least. Lord Rutherford dead. Lord Robertson struck with apoplexy. Poor Edinburgh.*

24. Sunday. A much more comfortable close of the week than we had almost dared to look for at one time. Annie quite herself – downstairs as usual, walking downstairs and moving about, reading, etc. Baby is certainly thriving. His nurse is gentle and careful with him; he is filling out and much more lively; there would seem to be no fear of him. James is well; low-spirited of course; it could not be otherwise, and we must let him remain so for the present – cut deep to cure, if cure we can. I will go over all his history by and bye when more fully acquainted with the means of once more setting him straight with the world. A mania for speculating seems to be the rock on which he splits. We must get him some employment that will exercise his superabundant activity and so divert it from these rash experiments, every one of which he has seriously lost by.

The Doctor saw two letters from the East the other day: one from Frank Kennedy, the other from Captain Burke, brother to Lord Mayo. For the last six weeks, they say, the Commissariat been perfectly well managed, plenty of good provisions, full rations regularly served with tea, rum and coffee, except on stormy days, or when the consequences of the storms prevented traffick through the mud – the roads being nearly impassable often from this cause. In all other respects, nothing can be more miserable than the arrangements, no preparations ever made beforehand, nothing got till long after the want has been felt, and death, disease and wretchedness been produced; no shelter thought of till winter storms set in; no forage for the horses until their numbers and their strength were reduced by starvation; no warm clothing till long after the inclement weather had killed hundreds; utter ignorance of the climate, of the country, of its resources; and a blind infatuation regarding the inferiority of the enemy. It is to be hoped that most of this being now acknowledged, much rectified, late though the amendment came, and fresh reinforcements ready, our next campaign may redeem this.

I have a very agreeable note from Major Mair accompanying the quarterly certificate of my dear Jack's College character. *Exemplary* as to general conduct and as to attention to his studies. Good, very good in ever so many branches; highly distinguished in Latin and French, but most distinguished in Mathematicks. I sent the ticket to his father so I may not be quite correct in my recollections but the sense is so. The Major like Jane and Mr. Gardiner is quite delighted with the conduct of the war – its glorious results so far and honourable conclusion at no distant time; he is in daily expectation of the fall of Sebastopol, regrets his son being younger than mine and so must miss much of the fun; congratulates me on the chance of Jack soon being ready to be shot at – in short an old soldier. I don't intend Jack to act target to Russian butchers for another eighteen months when we may trust the worst will be over; on rational physiological grounds I am averse to young growing boys having their strength unduly taxed before their constitutions are ready for work or hardship; eighteen is our Army age, and that is four years too soon say the Doctors and the Commanders, who are both of them tired out with the young recruits. The least extra duty fits the poor young fellows for the hospital; more than half die in a year after joining in war time; none can stand the strain except the highlanders and the Irish The highlanders go in wiry – all wiry; the Irish are so used to wet and want they only feel queer when in comfort.

25. Christmas Day. And as funny a one as ever was passed. A sunny morning turned to rain. Every creature left the premises excepting Mrs. Mack. Baby and Nurse were asleep at ten o'clock; they then had to be roused and I had to see baby *washed* for this essential had been neglected, and *powdered*, and then borax and honey rubbed on his sore mouth. Yes, Ma'am, says this easy-going woman but nothing she does; so Annie must look well

after her. Baby's uneasiness was quite accounted for the moment I thoroughly inspected him. I have told Annie she must be both at his dressing and his undressing and watch well that indolent woman who will otherwise give the child very bad habits. She has brought him back to life for us however.

After nursery business I went to the kitchen. Not a single preparation begun. Every article had been weighed out to Mrs. Mack on Friday that all might be ready for me just to mix up the puddings today; not a raison was stoned not a current washed, no spice ground; basins, plates, spoons, whisk, eggs, milk, etc., etc. had all to be looked for as I asked for them, and near eleven o'clock. By dint of stirring about the servants' quarters pudding was put into the pot before one and ours by two; but such a wasteful, dawdling poor body as this good old creature has no business in a poor man's house – at fourteen pounds a year wages! and help every day to do work an active girl would laugh at. So a change here must be reform the first; and I am glad to find from our conversation while picking the fruit that she has no thoughts of remaining much longer in service. A widowed sister with a large young family has a farm of twenty-six acres at a low rent, and she means to join her shortly – an excellent plan. She is quite in the way here poor woman. Really some people would seem to think money grows on bushes like blackberries, they throw it away so absurdly – fourteen pounds a year wages for any servant in a moderate house.

Annie did not do this. The Mary she has trained up as house and parlour-maid at five pounds serves her better than her Dublin fine ladies at double. She would not believe this, so lost many a good pound note in finding it out. So of her cook. She must do the nicer things herself, get a stout, active *kitchen maid* and teach her by degrees, who can care the two cows and do most of the washing; grand servants in a poor house are just ridiculous. I must speak to the Doctor for I hazard no remarks, still less advice, myself. James is much less self-opinionated than he was, much improved in that respect. Still he must be kept humble a while longer – the cork would soon rise!

31. Sunday and at home in Leeson Street. The Doctor would not let me travel on an open car after a three day's illness I had – a sort of rheumatick attack with fever from deranged liver I fancy; so they had to send up a brougham for me into which I conveyed myself and my luggage upon Thursday morning last, about a quarter of an hour after it arrived for I preferred letting the horses feed in Blesington to standing an hour or two in the yard, no matter what kind of weather it was. James went so far with me, it being market day and he, having no other valve for his restlessness, has begun to speculate in corn – buy it, grind it, ship it to Glasgow, and make a fortune by it. So long as he does not lose *much*, it is occupation. I sat an hour and a half with the Doctor and arranged all our plan of operations, in full hope of what *he* meddles with coming to good.

I have written to Jack tonight – my last letter for the year. I think I am happy about him; he is well and doing well, roused up, takes an interest in his studies, enjoys society, and is every day fonder of the abominable profession he has chosen. I ought to be content. I will try. So long as he run an honourable career I should be.

Crimea affairs look very gloomy. A stormy winter, totally unexpected by us who seem ignorant of everything, and so unprepared for it, continues to do us damage in every possible way. Men and officers die from fatigue, exposure, privation. There is no pretence at continuing the blockade, and only that the enemy is as badly off behind the walls as the Allies are before them, the end of the campaign would be the end of us. It has been a most miserable tissue of blunders – inglorious to our name, most afflicting to our feelings. All the ladies at home are sending out clothing, shirts, stockings, flannels, etc. with tons of old linen for the wounded. Gentlemen send wine, brandy, biscuits, oatmeal, camp kettles. Miss Nightingale has relays of nurses, and the Government says – Thank you all. There's a story that General Canrobert is a natural son of Napoleon's [see note 5 April 1855] and that the Army adore him in consequence; he is a clever energetick man whose ever son he be, and not too old for command, while our poor seventy-fours, seventy-sixes and seventy-eights are fit only for the chimney corner. We have a very windy 'Yule', cold, damp, stormy, disagreeable weather. The old year is going out with a hurricane. What will the new one bring us? That peace within which passeth understanding if we ask for it humbly and patiently.

1855

Another complicated year for politics finds her airing her opinions on Aberdeen, Palmerston and Russell. Jack has moved to the military academy in Edinburgh to prepare for his career in the very year that his father received his brevet promotion to general. Wicklow neighbour John Hornidge agrees to help by acting as agent for the Baltiboys estate, where Augustus West is proving a far from satisfactory tenant. She is increasingly impressed by the quality of the French leadership in the war but does comment sympathetically after Lord Raglan's death. She continues to be absorbed by the differing problems presented by the King family, the O'Reillys and sundry Baltiboys dependants. Jack's graduation in July leads the proud mother to an Edinburgh visit, and the birth of a second grandson helps to improve the chilly relations with Annie.

Illustration: New Club House, Kildare Street

MONDAY, JANUARY 8. I thought for this week back that I would give up this journal. It grows dull on my hands; age and troubles have cast a gloom over a once cheerful spirit; and the sameness of the life we lead is little calculated to revive it. But it was as the loss of a friend to me; for so many years it has been my only intimate companion, the repository of most of my thoughts, my feelings, my cares, and such pleasures as have crossed a chequered path, that the want of some such safety valve seemed an evil. So, beginning the new year here I am at the old egotistick work, not uncomfortably balancing one thing against the other.

Thank God for it, there is no change among our immediate family. My husband is even in better health of body, even his mind is at times more lively; the old Aunt is decidedly stronger, enjoying life like anyone twenty years younger, and the children are all thriving. Jack doing well, busy, happy, approved by his masters, beloved by his friends. Dear little Janey our comfort; Annie really happy, her baby all that was wanting to free us from anxiety about her.

I have been almost entirely occupied with James King's affairs, have had two interviews with his father, one with his mother, and one with Dr. Robinson, whose kindness closes my lips against all former errours. Were Annie his own child he could not do more for her. I am sure he feels he is the authour of her sorrows. The old people were dreadfully cut up by this revelation of their son's folly – the only way of helping him is to take all power from him.

His ascertained debts are at the moment £1,100; the butcher, baker, grocer, brewer, tailor, etc. all owed two years' accounts, a year's rent of Humfreystown, and large sums besides to Dr. Robinson, to me, to John Hornidge for cattle, etc. He has hay, horses, cows, harness, carriages, saddles 9 or 10 and so on; property altogether about three hundred pounds. It will be difficult to make him sell, but we must try, the remaining eight hundred pounds the father will *lend*, James repaying the interest. He is not to be trusted with it; it is to be given to the Doctor for distribution. The diminished allowance is to be paid to Annie who must undertake the charge of the household, entirely to be disconnected from him, his farming and his stable. On this point the father is imperative because he has no confidence in the honour of his son. On this same point I also am determined. I give no help to him to be squandered on his own selfish indulgences, his ostentatious absurdities; his wine, his groom, his helper, his hunters, his carriages, must come like his dress, his journeys, his pocket money and his speculations and his *Steward*! out of his twenty five acres; he shall have them rent free and may make what he can of them. We have thought of some small official situation for him, but in the evenings he would be drawn into expensive company. We gave up the Militia on this account. I believe he is safest under the Doctor's eye in that quiet country, jobbing like the little farmers for his amusement. And this is my Annie's husband – that gifted creature. Surely that cloud is a dark one. We keep the worst from her.

19. A pleasant fortnight we have been passing. We have had an immensity of troubles with James – at last, thanks to the Doctor and Annie, he is becoming reasonable; consents to give up the management of the household and the two hundred pounds a year to Annie, without interference, to sell the carriage, harness etc. And as this must be very mortifying, very humiliating to his vain, ostentatious muddling, restless, self sufficiency, we must on our parts have patience to allow for his constitutional tendencies, his educational deficiencies and the harassments of the position he is placed in. We have gained a great deal, he has made a good step in advance and we must wait. But the poor father, far behind the times, with all his son's faults and imperfections and less head, sits forlorn by the fire holding his poor worn face in his hands moaning out – 'my son, my son, my only son, unprincipled, untruthful, no confidence in him, word or deed, borrow from anyone, one system of deceit; I see it now'.

The mother took the schedule of the debts, which by the bye is encreased by another hundred and fifty pounds, remembered afterwards. She analysed it carefully, took her time – 'So,' said she. 'In four years, since his marriage, he has gone through four thousand pounds, and nothing to shew for it but a little furniture, most of it presents, three cows and five horses. The last two years no accounts have been paid for the *house*, these amount to barely two hundred and fifty pounds, and a great deal too much of that's for wine. He shan't have a penny beyond the eight hundred pounds, and he shall sell every extra he possesses that don't interfere with Annie's comfort. She has cost him nothing, poor thing. How he could eat, and drink all that wine and *sleep* and come here with his laugh and his jest and that load of debt hanging over him, surpasses my power of comprehension. Deceiving us all the while with his five or six hundred pounds worth of stock, his dairy gains, his hay and all his falsehoods. After this he may get on as he likes, he never shall be helped again.' And she seems to have made up her mind to the very severe disappointment. I am more hopeful. With Annie managing the house and the funds there will be no more tradesmen's debts, and if he can job away on his few acres sufficiently to keep himself busy and so out of her way, it will do very well. Her greatest fault, poor soul, was towards me; God knows from my heart I forgive her, though I shall never be the same woman again. From my heart I thank my God that our children are honest and upright, truthful and candid, unselfish, nay, self-sacrificing, kind, merciful and anxious to do their duty. My girls have been saved from my dangerous beauty, and their wit, their *mother* wit is well ballasted by the common sense of their excellent father, and a more carefully conducted system of education than mine.

20. Rumours are now very rife of a change of ministry; the disasters in the Crimea entirely attributable to the utter incapacity of the war department and the unsatisfactory state of the Exchequer render it indeed almost imperative to remove the whole blundering Peel section of the cabinet. Lord Palmerston has been to Paris, dined *tête à tête* with the Emperour, and it is said infused considerable vigour into our councils on his return home. And Lord John has now been over, just come back, after walking in the gardens of the Tuileries arm in arm with the Emperour for two hours. Cabinet councils sit daily – two, three, *five* hours, and all the ministers live on the rail between London and Windsor. A man has very opportunely died to leave a garter vacant for Lord Aberdeen that he may retire with the distinction of a

bit of blue ribbon and a white feather! from the scene of his blunders. A few days will enlighten us.*

The hospitals are our worst dilemma at present. The air in them has become pestilential. Miss Nightingale has done wonders, for she found incompetent surgeons and too few of them, no medicines, no cordials, no food, no soap, no lint, no linen, no fuel, no help. Beds and bedding and space were all she set out with. The Duke of Newcastle's twenty miles of lint were with his ton of tea in dreamland. *The Times* Commissioner and her father's purse furnished the funds on which she began her labours of charity, *then* the Government supplies reached her, now the overwhelming *private* assistances have given her all she wants. She has sent away most of her nuns, Miss Sellon's among them, and is getting on well though much in need of *peat charcoal* which nobody has yet thought of sending out to her.* Still we lose six hundred a week, mostly boys, poor things, quite unfit for the cruel privations and fearful amount of hard work they are thrown into. Hours in the trenches, thirty-six perhaps, wet through, without food, and under a galling fire, no shelter, no fuel. When their turn for rest has come, no change of clothes and half rations – raw. While within eight miles are piles upon piles of every requisite sent out by their pitying countrymen, to cumber a beach where there is no one to guard them and from whence there is no conveyance. The country is a bog, the horses are dead for want of forage, all the men out of Hospital are on duty in the camp, and so few in number that two nights' sleep per week is all the most of them have had this last two months. All this is no exaggeration. The indomitable spirit of the race rises over all, and will to the last man left alive of that brave devoted band. But how they have been sacrificed.

Oh for peace on almost any terms, war with barbarians is fearful. It is curious the perfect amity between our allies and us – all old sores healed. The French are fine campaigners, their paved roads made early, their troops hutted in time, every necessary provided, every contingency anticipated, order, method regularity prevailing. Work done by relays, bands playing, stoves smoking, everything at hand. In short, the wonderful aptitude for management, which amused me in small when I was in France and saw it gravely carried out in trifles, has educated the race into habits of exactitude invaluable as an element of success in every undertaking, great or small, the want of which in very truth makes half, nay, may I say not all, the misery of Ireland. The French Commanders are up to their business. General Canrobert is almost a great man; the present Napoleon seems to be a concentration of wisdom.

22. Where are the great men, even the steady men, the men of judgement. It is time for the third estate to stir itself up from the bottom, the top must plainly be skimmed off, and, with the *second*, thrown out with other used up things. It is heart rending to read of such preventable miseries, and then these idiots! ornamenting themselves with blue ribbons, trumpery as such rubbish is, a cap and bells would fit them better.

23. I am almost inclined to burn all my old journals and never write another line. I meant them to amuse my old age and to divert and to instruct my children – *disgust* them probably, I fear, that is if they are at all like the wretched, flippant, vulgar, egotistical diary of the celebrated Miss Burney.* I really never read such odious stuff. She saw a great deal of life, she met with celebrated and interesting people and yet she placed her little self so inordinately prominent that we cannot get at anybody else. So sick am I of *Evelina* and her silly childish bashfulness bursting with vanity, as she is in all the time, the fulsome flatteries she swallows, the inanity of the whole set, it is a queer and not a pleasant picture of the manners of the times, in a little clique. However, she is still very young, awoke suddenly to find herself famous and was really made a lion of – deservedly – for she was a clever girl beyond her poor day. I have read *Evelina* , but could not get on with it, the stiff manners of the polite section and the revolting vulgarity of the Branghton party are quite unsuitable to our present ideas.

By the bye, poor Miss Elphick, our very underbred governess, was not unlike Miss Burney. Her letters and journals were in the same style, her expressions the same – 'grinning and bearing it' – 'munching up her biscuit' – 'choking herself with laughter', and a thousand other elegancies of a like nature. They were of much the same rank and had in youth seen much the same class of society, had the same natural quickness and turn for style and awkward self-sufficiency. 'Oh, gin some power the gift would gie us, to see coursells as ithers see us' – we don't think half enough of Burns; he was a fine moral poet, full of true religious feeling too, charitable through all his sarcasm. This view of him would make a pretty paper for *Chambers'*, but *Chambers'* is spoiled, it has risen up to very high flights, no longer *Edinburgh*, but universal, not for the lowly, but the great, and an intolerable set of bad novels stuffed into it 'dragging their slow length along' week after week, month after month most tediously. Dickens has novels too, but such clever ones. *North and South* by Mary Barton [that is Mrs. Gaskell, the author of *Mary Barton*] is enchanting, it ends this week.

24. Much more easy about Mrs. Bourne and much better pleased with Miss Burney. In the second volume she gets into better society, and becoming used to being famous, she bears distinction better; really she was made a great deal of; her company courted by the great and the noble. *Cecilia* does not turn her head at all, though it so infinitely raised her reputation. She was a quick observer and hits off characters in a few words very cleverly. But as she never published a line worth reading after her 'Daddy Crisp's' death, I suspect we are indebted to his censorship for the finish of her two good novels.*

28. Sunday. Miss Burney improved wonderfully after her removal to Windsor* where her life, though at first very repugnant to her inclinations and always dull and constrained, was of infinite service to the ripening of her really fine mind. The mob of flatterers, fulsome flatterers, adulators, by whom she had her young head more than half turned were succeeded by a set of persons so completely occupied by the *étiquette* of the Court that intellectual superiority was in no way understood by them. She was nobody – worse – an unwelcome intruder into a place [where] there were a hundred applicants belonging to the different attendants all disappointed by her preferment. For a while she lived alone, communing with her own thoughts in her chamber and being 'very' still, her tiresome duties silently performed, her inferiour companions patiently en-

dured and the insolences of the German lady immediately over her suffered uncomplainingly. It was worth the martyrdom.

One friend she found to support her through her melancholy probation – Mrs. Delaney, and one she made herself whose intimacy lightened her servitude. This best friend was the Queen [Charlotte], a woman whose good sense, correct judgement and real amiability of temper were never sufficiently appreciated by the nation. It is astonishing how this discipline, this help, and *the journal* brought forward the mind of that clever girl, whose abilities, wonderful as they were considering the period and her defective education, were after all inferiour to her worth.

But what a life was court life then. What is it now, I wonder? Surely woman can't be made to stand five hours; gentlewomen can't be tyrannised over by Mrs. Schellenbergs; constraint and restraint and menial services can't be the lot of rank and genius and the independant born. If so, how in this free country can a place at court be sought for, kept, endured. How can our nobility who king and queen it in their own palace homes reduce themselves to slavery so despicable. I am becoming so interested in the Diary, I no longer regret the obstinate cough that gives me so many quiet hours to spend over it.

The world was thunderstruck yesterday by the announcement of Lord John's resignation. Now [this] in my judgement comes too late; by continuing so long among these idiots or lunaticks he has identified himself with them, appropriated their acts, and it don't seem manly to leave them when the mischief is done and has brought about such disastrous consequences – when they are sinking beneath the indignation of the world.*

What has damaged the ministry most is an unanswerable pamphlet by Sir Howard Douglas,* an old Peninsular hero, much looked up to in the profession. The fifth edition will be out next week. He calmly exposes the insufficiency of the preparations, the injudicious conduct of a campaign undertaken months too late in the season, the want of management, of method, of arrangement, the mistake of attacking such a stronghold with an army numerically too weak for the work, of sitting down before the wrong, the *lower* side, of no means of supply, of the fatal though inglorious error of Alma, etc., etc. The success of such an expedition was a moral impossibility. The continuance for so long in the present position of our martyred band almost a miracle. We have only seen the extracts in the *Athenaeum*, but we must get the book. Sir Howard Douglas was long in command in Edinburgh, succeeded General Wynyard, and was much respected.*

The ignorance of our ministers and the supineness of our Commanders have lost us the flower of our generation, and more than that, covered us with disgrace. The only thing to be done now would seem to be the rescuing of the suffering remnant of that brilliant army from the dreadful death hanging over it. They are found frozen in the trenches, or insensible with feet and hands bit off, and one hundred a day dying in Hospital. They have neither clothes nor food nor fire, can resist neither the weather nor the prevalent disease – dysentery, diarroea, rheumatic fever. Lord Raglan is very comfortable at Head Quarters, he don't seem to know much of what goes on around. One would suppose he did not read the lists of the dead he signs so coolly. It is true he was Aide-de-Camp to the Duke of Wellington in the Spanish war when he was a lad; he was only twenty-eight years of age at the Battle of Waterloo; here have been forty years of peace since then, which he has spent in an office with a pen in his hand.* A well trained Militia Captain would have been a fitter Commander.

31. What would have become of me without Miss Burney I know not. Poor thing! her marriage was a great mistake. She was unhappy at Court but certainly equally unhappy out of it. In fact life, bright young sunny life, was over for her. She had been shamefully used by a man she calls Mr. Fairly,* for she frequently has to give fictitious names, but my Aunt says he was a Colonel Digby, for years her shadow, advising with her, employing her to advance him, confiding in her, never easy out of her presence till suddenly he married another and then never shewed himself to her again. Her health broke completely and she had to resign, always remaining on terms of intimacy with the whole of the royal family, high in the Queen's favour.

Compassion for the Emigrés centred in a passion for General d'Arblay, who offered himself to her without a penny! or the hope of a penny! and she, with all her experience and her habits of court luxury, took him! and never, she says, repented it – writes as if thoroughly happy with him on one hundred pounds a year, *her* pension from the Queen, and a trifling annuity purchased by the price of *Cecilia*. She then wrote *Camilla* which built them a Cottage, and there they are now with one treasure of a baby boy; – he gardening, she sewing and housekeeping and writing for more bread at spare moments – cheerfully! Oh, man, man, selfish man, you do not deserve your helpmate; does not the very word teach your duty to you; the help but not the drudge. You are to *make* the money. The Scotch call the husband the 'breadwinner', the Swedes call the wife the 'bread divider'. Monsieur d'Arblay and Co. are the 'bread *eaters*'.

THURSDAY, FEBRUARY 1. All evils are thrown on Lord Raglan by the late ministry – surely far from fair. Every war department was badly managed, at home as well as in the Crimea, and if they were persuaded of the Commander in Chief's incompetency why not have recalled him, nobody would have blamed them, the only surprise was that he had ever had such a command given him. Thank God we are done with the whole set, a worse we can never suffer under.

Poor Miss Burney, she was never herself after her wretched marriage, not indeed happy from the time of her leaving the Queen, from Mr. Fairly's desertion. Eight years on her hundred and twenty-five pounds in the half furnished cottage, ten years in France on little more, separated from all her own connexions and not in any society that could replace their loss, made sad work with her mind. It seemed to fail altogether on her return to England, she had been deserted on her illstarred marriage and she never recovered caste.

2. Lord Derby can't form an administration; I fancy we shall have Lord Palmerston, but no one knows. They had far better take the head clerks out of good, well managed offices, not Government ones, these grandees don't do their work.

Finished Miss Burney; very melancholy, survived all her friends, most of her relations, her husband and her son. The son, fondly loved and very loving, did not turn out first rate, – eccentrick, indolent, yet not deficient, very delicate. She had probably failed in educating him, he was never at school. The husband she appears to have adored, to have determined to adore, and the trouble she takes to overpraise him, to exhibit her devotion to him, to drag forward every little bit of attention paid to him, every obliging notice taken of him, parading his merits as it were quite unnecessarily, gives one the feel that she was painfully alive to his inferiority. Then he was French and loved France, she all English, and she made her son English, and the father and the son did not suit. She lived to eighty-two, surviving herself, as well as her early loves.

6. Lord Palmerston successfully engaged in the construction of a Cabinet. Says Mr. Sheehan – 'So, the old pack reshuffled and a couple of knaves left out'. It won't do I think unless they quite alter their tacticks.

8. A sad patched up Cabinet. Lord Aberdeen, Lord John and the Duke of Newcastle out, Lord Panmure in as War minister, Peelites retained to a man. The country won't bear it. These people may stand a while as makeshifts but they can't alter their natures sufficiently as to become suddenly efficient after such proofs of incapacity. Sweeping reforms in all departments are talked of, they always talk thus, we'll see how they act. All the publick can make out is that everybody in authority is at sixes and sevens. Sir Edward Blakeney at last retires, he goes to Chelsea as Lieutenant Governor, (no Governor) and Lord Seaton comes here. By the bye, we've got our promotion gazetted today, and *General* Litchfield too. My General is hardly as much pleased as my Aunt is. It has quite acted as a tonick with her. We finished a bottle of champagne at dinner in honour of our Brevet rank.* One glass each to the General, another to the General's wife – large glasses as befitted the occasion.

9. Jack is working very diligently and I hear nothing but praise of him on every account. Major Mair attended the other day at the Academy while the classes were going on and was

quite struck with the way in which Jack put his whole soul in to his work, giving his answers with so much intelligence and decision, and as if he knew perfectly well what he was about. What happiness for Eliza and Colonel Smith to have such a son. Humbly and reverently do I thank God for the precious boon. To work His will, to keep His laws, carry forward His scheme, was my steady aim in educating my children. To leave no unoccupied corner for the devil *self* to enter in. I must watch to keep that root of evil from my own wearing out mind. I feel it is becoming a struggle; it shall be a silent one, no one shall ever know that I give my boy up to his inclination grudgingly. The young sanguine spirit shall be depressed by no feebleness of mine. Life is before him, and very near behind me, so quiet! foolish mother's heart. He shan't go to the Crimea, though.

10. Jos. O'Reilly writes low about the Bar. He has kept all the terms, however is very ill as before, asks advice, a thing there is no possibility of ever giving – in fine wants to know if it would offend Mrs. Bourne were he to go into the wine trade. Considering he can always go back to the Bar, I told him his best plan was first to get well, second to make diligent enquiry about the wine trade while getting well, third that both matters would go on best in Dublin, and that Mrs. Bourne was not wedded to one particular scheme by any means. She wished to forward his views whatever they were and that he need have no scruples of delicacy thereupon. His letter said that for this wine attempt he would require to borrow one hundred pounds, which part of the business I left unnoticed.

14. Such a Cabinet, as bad as the last, worse. Choke full of Peelites, all of them tractarians, the Jesuits of politicks. Hardly a man fit for his place. 'Tis like the parable of the marriage feast, where the good man getting excuses from all the respectables, sends his servants out into the highways to compel the refuse to come in – the lame, the aged, the halt, the maimed, the blind, the deaf [Luke 14, verses 16–24]. These are our rulers in times the most difficult to get through of any we have had for a generation. Lord Palmerston himself is too old, the country would have him and to all appearance will soon oust him.

18. The Queen giving the garter to Lord Aberdeen, though mistimed, may have been an old promise, but her taking the occasion of his dismissal as a minister for incompetency by the Commons to mark her esteem by permitting his retaining the Thistle is, to say the least of it, out of taste. We hermits laugh at those quite ridiculous decorations, but as these silly distinctions are by the world considered worthy of ambition, in the world they have their value.

19. There arrived from Edinburgh this morning from Jane the *Memoirs* of Tommy Thomson's life mostly contributed by her husband, I believe, and printed by the Bannatyne Club.* They were very interesting to me. Where are the clever men gone; the great men are extinct. Never was a weaker speech made than Lord Palmerston's in the House on his new position. A mere string of praises of his (proved) incapable colleagues – it was pitiable. Mr. D'Israeli withered him up in a minute, threw a torrent of well deserved ridicule over the tinkering and jugglery he had attempted, and then administered a flogging. They are really like the servants in the kitchen, quarrelling one day and making it up the next.

21. Our army is reduced to ten thousand sickly men. They are employed as a covering army, no other work. General Simpson* is off – old, but steady and active. His business is to oversee Lord Raglan! Will any Commander in Chief bear this. It is all 'too late'. What are ten thousand men. Our army is gone, our noble, glorious army, our glory is gone, our National honour is tarnished, our once proud name humbled. Miserable afflicting business, Where will it end. The *Evening Mail* stopt press to announce that the three Peelites are out. Sir James Graham, Mr. Sydney Herbert and Mr. Gladstones. Such a shout of delight as we gave.*

MONDAY, MARCH 5. Poor Lord Raglan, his indolence is excessive. Amiable man, did the work of his office well, but had no sort of capacity for active service – too old, feeble in health and no brains for such a command. Old stupid Sir John Burgoyne is ordered home, saved by pretty speeches, but really recalled. His mistake was unpardonable, sat down on the wrong side of the town, such a tissue of bungling never shamed a nation, They are all now consulting with the only head there is, the French Emperour.

14. Laid up, really ill. Alive . . . but terribly shaken, looking such a figure that it will go hard with me to play hostess tomorrow night and as for appearance! Janey will be anything but vain of her mother. The head is not up yet up to writing so all there is to say about Janey's happiness, her activity, her management, arrangements etc., must wait to be chronicled. Also a deal of fun, dear Mrs. Bourne's anxiety about the fashions, her old lace trimmings, her best blonde cap, her interest in the whole affair; the General's delight, pretending annoyance, his kind offers of assistance, and when asked to bring a man or two, overwhelming us with the whole club. Hamlet's invaluable help, here every day – *beaux*, candelabra, musick, musicians, I don't know what we could have done without him. Surely it can't be all mere kindness, and he an Irishman!

My part in the matter is to pay the expenses by and bye and keep out of the way at present, to which last request I subscribe gladly, for the house is in very uncomfortable confusion, somewhat akin to my head, and the two don't get on together. It has recalled one to the ways of the world, this little party we are giving. I have got so into the habit of living by myself in my cheerful little room with my books and my thoughts, and my journal to tell them to, that the dirty under current has rolled past unheeded, fathoms below my high philosophy. It is a good lesson for Janey who is much amused with it. People who have been passing her with a mere civil bow, all this last week, stopt her so kindly to shake hands and enquire particularly after her mother. Ladies old and young joined her walking, crowded round her at the 'Amatory'. Gentlemen became doubly assiduous, many of whom she did not know and whom her father did, suddenly took a fancy to make her acquaintance, begged the General to introduce them, etc.

20. All happily over and very satisfactorily. It was three o'clock this morning when the last of our well pleased guests took their reluctant leave. We had asked eighty, seventy came. Good lighting, attendance, refreshments, plenty of seats, all managed by that little clever active Janey and *Hamlet*. Indeed I don't know what would have become of us without his help. He suggested so many hints, lent candelabra and

musick stands and engaged the musick. The General's room was for the mufflings and there Maria reigned with a toilette table and a work-basket and her tickets. The dining room was for refreshments, the tables taken to pieces and placed end to end and covered with cloths on which were set sixteen silver dishes, glass and china. There was tea, coffee, bread and butter and cake, ices and biscuits, Claret, Sherry, orangeaid, lemonade, cakes, pastry, jellies, creams and latterly white and gravy soup and quantities of different sorts of sandwiches.

The door was not opened till the first part of the musick was over, after that the eating and drinking went on all night. Hanlon's band came in to the joy of the young people and they set to work in earnest. The musick was liked for no one spoke hardly while it lasted. The company were all very well dressed. Lady Catherine Saunderson with her diamonds took the shine out of all we elderlies. Ellen Thompson was *the* beauty among the girls, but there were many very pretty. Aunt Bourne sat out the whole. She listened and she looked and she talked and everybody was so attentive to her. She quite enjoyed it all and much admired our gentlemen, where, indeed, we shone. Hamlet and his 7th Dragoon Guards, and the General and his Kildare Street Club, having brought a contingent beyond the common. Altogether everybody found it a most enjoyable evening. Walking out today, Janey and I were complimented on all hands. Mrs. Montgomery, spirited up by our success, has already sent out cards for the 28th.

21. Yesterday evening we went to the Quartette Concert. Mozart began and was the best to my mind; Beethoven ended all, a composer I never pretend to understand. Today nobody called but Hamlet, who dined with us as he often does now. He talked very pleasantly, one of our subjects being poor good-natured Lady Stannus, who really is from her folly the ridicule of everybody. They call her the Punch of Dublin.

This was our day of publick humiliation and prayer and fasting. We neither humbled nor prayed nor fasted. Why should we. We have done nothing wrong. Lord Aberdeen might do all, and his ministry and his Commanders, and his

Commisariat, and his offices and officials, but why should all pay double for his misdeeds I am sure I don't well see. There are calamities enough, God knows, but they were the result of Ministerial shortcomings. Publick men should pray to God to help them to be honest and just in their dealing and do their duty in that state of life into which he has been pleased to call them; there might be sense in that sort of supplication.*

23. No Hamlet. At the concert his advances were drily received, at the musick party he kept aloof, and highly offended her! [Janey] surely don't expect to keep lovers at her feet to be kicked or caressed as suits the whim of the moment; not such a man as this I can tell her. I sometimes fancy she must have some secret fancy, it can be no more, she is so cheerful. Only preoccupation can account for merit so superiour being slighted. I think too she dreads poverty having had such a lesson. I much like Hamlet.

MONDAY, APRIL 2. Our dear old friend Mrs. Macpherson of Belleville died on Saturday forenoon. Jane was beside her. As Jane says, life had long ceased to be a pleasure for her, the stroke of palsy which followed the horrour of her brother's death encreased her infirmities so much that she was quite an old woman before her time. She was barely seventy, and had long spoke with difficulty, indeed there was a failure of mind, of every power. I am glad my recollection of her is of an earlier date, when she had recovered from the first attack. The kind friend of many troubled years she was. Our only neighbour for many long Highland winters; my instructor in all my household difficulties; my medium with the press in my first Authourship; kind in heart though harsh in manner – clever, active, a zealous friend.

I live my youth over when I think of her and all the happy days we spent together. Will Lord Glenelg remember to grieve for her.* She is very near the last of a band of bright spirits once walking step for step together, then widely sundered, and now gone to rest. She was only twelve years older than myself, my turn can hardly be far distant. My good friend.

3. A letter from Jane to say how very happy our Aunt has made William by her present of five hundred pounds. She had left

him double that in her will, but finding that then, before she had gone through the Insolvent Court, his creditors only would have reaped the benefit of her legacy, by a codicil she revoked it and left it to Jane, in addition to her own, as William owed Jane money. I am in hopes that next year she may give him as much more and so enable him to purchase back his life interest in dear beautiful Rothiemurchus, the wish of his heart, the dream of his waking as of his sleeping hours.

4. James was here this morning to get his money to pay Tabuteau and Cathcart. I have kept forty pounds to take up Mr. Corbett's bill in May. He will have to send ten pounds more which he can easily do having sold hay and having a young bull to sell. He is in a good temper and let me speak to him without resenting it. I therefore hope the family feud will end.

We have a curious business at home with Lord Lucan,* the man who made the unfortunate cavalry charge. Lord Raglan and he, of course, were at issue upon it. He was re-called and has twice demanded a Court Martial which has been twice refused. No imputation rests upon him. He has even been complimented on his bravery. He made a mistake – that much is certain, and the less these old sores are touched may be the better.

5. A confirmation of this Russian repulse, principally by the French, and despatches from General Canrobert* published in Paris mention that the Allies were prepared to begin the campaign in good earnest on the 3rd of this month. A pitched battle first expected, perhaps over now, and then the Assault. Sebastopol is much strengthened and reinforcements and supplies of all kinds have been pouring in, but the Garrison is not supposed to be as large as was reported, nor is money plenty in Russia, and their troops are no match for ours in the field. Oh, I wish it were all over and the world at peace again.

We in Western Europe have got beyond the fighting age. The wisest of us are far otherwise occupied, and though, particularly in France, the idle cadets of noble families are in sufficient numbers to officer our armies, the spirit of feudal days is weakened. There are better roads to fame, or ease, than through the carnage of the battlefield. I cannot fancy why we British engaged in the strife. The barbarians must advance among the civilised, they have no choice, it is the rule, and the supine must fall before the enterprising. We may for a while uphold the one and check the other, but we can't alter, though we may delay, the natural course of events. In time the unwieldy Russian Empire would fall to pieces of itself, crumble into new states to take the place of those swept away, and to be civilised by the conquered people. Why should we meddle with their foredoomed march.

Louis Napoleon is very differently circumstanced; he is confirming his own power by employing the unquiet spirits of the nation he has seized on, in an exciting war at a distance. It may be wise policy in him this expenditure of blood and treasure; establish his dynasty perhaps, if he be victorious; but for us to inconvenience ourselves, aggrieve ourselves, bring sorrow to our hearths, cripple our means, stop our progress in every peaceful art, I can in no way satisfy myself of such necessity. Good may result. We wanted a shaking up; the upper ranks were becoming luxurious, heartless, indolent, the lower were brutalising. Setting them to face danger and bear privations together may be of use so far as the influence of the army can extend itself.

16. My brother [John's] expenses about his children are enormous already, much beyond what they need be. He has large ideas and she has none, so that the galley sails in style. Young John is allowed three hundred and fifty a year, College expenses included, Trevor, *I think* three hundred pounds. Elinor, not yet seventeen, fifty pounds for clothes and pocket money. Then she is having masters of all sorts, and there are the three other children at the parsonage. Salaries had need be good in India.

My poor Annie is keeping her whole family on two hundred pounds a year, dressing herself and baby upon twenty pounds. Janey in town here has only twenty four pounds, Jack has never yet spent more than twenty four pounds, though now with full dress coats he may want more. Were we even richer I would not give expensive habits to young people; the art of spending money is easily learned, the art of economising is more difficult involving as it does so much of self-controul, and when it has to come after a career of waste, it is a hard lesson to learn. These Grant children, however, are clever, and they are going to India where want is never felt. I don't know whether I like seeing them or no, the parting is so painful, particularly to me who cannot hope to live to see any one of them again. This is morbid, not healthy feeling and must not be indulged.

No news, rumours in plenty.

The French Emperour and Empress have arrived and were met at Dover by Prince Albert and our world will be in such a whirl during the week of their visit, we shall hear of nothing but the *fetes* going forward in honour of them. The war will for a space quite fail. Dublin is very busy, with its *Levée* and Drawing-room. There will be as great a crowd as in the Eglinton days, people rushing up from all parts of the country.

18. In bed all day, very bad really, took measures to be better, and could have laughed, had it not been for the head, at the serious business of furbishing up our Major General, an expensive business as no makeshifts would be allowed. There have been great tryings on and brushings up and messages here and there. Dempsey and his master as busy as bees and so happy! The *Levée* was immensely crowded – fourteen hundred.

19. The Emperour and his beautiful Empress the delight of all eyes! John Bull mad about them. Oh! if Napoleon the 1st, *the* Napoleon could lift up his head to see the brother and sister style of Napoleon the 3rd and Victoria! James King played whist with us last night. What has brought him to town I wonder. A *Levée* of Baltiboys people today, all wanting something. Better rather, but very shaky, hardly fit for the evening.

20. Three thousand people they say at the Drawing-room last night, more or less, at any rate a crowd that was beyond measure disagreeable. The two anterooms, the withdraw-ing-room, St. Patrick's Hall, and latterly the long corridor all filled to suffocation. No moving except in masses. A poor display of nobility, the few peeresses present, however, well

diamonded. We went late, past eleven, came away at two, without our carriage, like Cinderella we had to run off and out and into a car glad to find any conveyance. It was four in the morning before all were gone. Lord Carlisle,* who was quite flushed with the fatigue of kissing, was also radiant with smiles, so pleased with his popularity.

Mrs. O'Reilly was with us half the day. Lady Milltown, her girls and Russborough, *are in London*, passed through without seeing a creature. They have taken a house in Grosvener Place for a month, after which they mean to go to Paris, in short amuse themselves while their *five hundred pounds* lasts. My Lord remains to play whist at his Club. He won above one hundred pounds the other night, and got back a cow he had sold for twenty five pounds in to the bargain.

22. A disagreeable missionary sermon in St. Anne's to which I gave one shilling. There is so much to do at home I shan't reach the missions during my length of days. If we began at home thoroughly, continued our work at home perseveringly, every one of us would turn out a missionary to whatever place we went, in whatever capacity we served. Converting the heathen of home is our duty at present, An article in *Chambers'*, a most excellent one, on ragged nurseries, has stirred me up as of old. Were there one in every parish what good might not be done. Quite true it is that such a refuge should not be wanted, but it is wanted, therefore it should be supplied. Maybe another generation may be so improved as not to need it. I have a mind to set about the scheme, it has succeeded so far as it has been tried in London, four nurseries are established already by private energy. In Paris the Government has had them in operation some time. Liberty! free institutions! the people's power! etc., must be a wonderful blessing altogether in some mysterious way, since it can make us content to go without every other. The whole nation appears to me to be in the mud, and to have every inclination to remain there. It is a well nigh hopeless task to try and pull any out, there is such a want of tools to work with; want of conscience; want of principles everywhere throughout the land.

24. Encreasing good news from Sebastopol; it almost seems as if the affair would soon be over. The Budget is not agreeable; a loan of sixteen million and encreased Income tax still leaves a deficit of seven million to meet the expenses of the year. We are therefore to be further taxed – tea, sugar, coffee and spirits, and additional Income tax. Prospects are not very cheering. But the war must be supported, would to God it were over. St. Patrick's Ball this evening.

25. Kitty Hawtayne went with us to the Ball; a perfect mob. All the rooms were open, dancing in the throne room as well as in the hall; three Drawing-rooms and the long corridor filled with well-dressed people, very few rabble, but no great attendance of the dignified. Some wits call our Irish peers the Brummagem ['counterfeit'] nobility, not ill-named, for half of them would be puzzled to make out their grand-fathers and the other half would as soon leave their re-spected ancestors in oblivion as have their pretensions blazoned in even the Castle light. Janey danced the whole night and with very agreeable partners. She looked extre-mely well. His Excellency led off the interminable country dance with the Lady Mayoress, every one of the forty or fifty couples he faithfully turned, his rather heavy partner pant-ing after him down the long room, but far from emulating the light and dainty style of his springy steps. We saw quantities of people we knew, and the refreshments were abundant, supper splendid, excellent wines, but, oh, it was a long night. Asked at nine, we went at ten, three or four hundred presentations detained my Lord until eleven, then the long, long dance, the business of the evening did not begin till near midnight. We did not get away till half after three, and we left a crowd that staid an hour later.

Poor Kitty Hawtayne was very much neglected. Ambrose Hickey told me why. She is thought both capricious and disdainful, and to a certain degree this is true. Even Janey feels it for on interceding her a partner, a young handsome Doctor, she called him *Mr*. Healy lest he should be snubbed, although the Knight who was come to the rescue of the deserted damsel. Like old Mr. King, who seeing Emma dancing with Dr. Montgomery's son, a rising barrister, and being asked by her to invite him to a party they are giving on the first of May, replied that he did not wish to extend his medical acquaintance. Those who have least right appear to me to give themselves airs. Would it not be well for the plain daughters of that silly pair to get such husbands as Leslie Montgomery, who really admires Emma, losing no occasion to pay her marked attention. How many pretty girls we saw. James King was in town, came up to get a groom, not a fine one, nobody to be had in the country, labourers getting twelve shillings a week wages and scarce at that.

29. Friday we went to the Hospital to find out the active Garrison Chaplain, Mr. Hort, from whom I wanted to hear of poor Ellen Foster, having a little money left with me for her. She is in a wretched room or closet rather, for which she pays a high rent on account of the situation being airy. I reckoned up with her the cost per annum, and she saw at once that she would be better in the country, so I went after dinner to Ogle Moore, luckily not started off to Kilbride, and I hope to get a removal arranged for her. She has lost a boy, but has another, and a baby and a big girl not quite wise with her heart affected. Poor creature, very sickly herself and no manager.

We walked home, the General calling at the Club, where of course he heard startling Sunday news to be refuted tomorrow. I finished the evening with my old friend M. Joay – *Guillaume le franc parleur*. I went through the two volumes rather amused by his Bourbonism, so very painstakingly paraded as to leave little doubt of his insincerity. I am a little bit ashamed of the politicks of my agreeable authour, although quite alive to his wit.

Jane won't allow much brains to our new Lord Lieutenant, judging of him from his book – his journal, which we all liked. It was amusing, unpretending and written in a charitable spirit. She thinks it and him ridiculous, principally on account of his dwelling with so much pleasure on his drinking tea, which little failing recommends him to me. We don't want a bright ruler; a kind manner, just dealings, an honest purpose, will do for us, particularly as all matters of moment are settled by the Council of Ancients over the water. Poor old men! seventy and upwards, every one of them, they had better stay by their own quiet hearths, go early to bed as *I do*, and leave the work for which they are not able to younger heads.

30. Lord John has returned, he and suite – six children, two stepchildren, three nieces, a nephew, the wife and four *attachés*, Secretary, Tutor, governess and a fit array of servants, all paid for by John Bull at the first hotel in Vienna. What fools we are. I can't help feeling something like the French discontents of '89 are at hand here. There must be a current of worth and sense and spirit somewhere underneath all this humbug which will break through the crust of folly and change the face of things. A quiet revolution it may be, we will hope so, it surely will be one, for such disgraceful mismanagement as we have been submitting to can hardly be much longer endured. Puseyisms, exclusiveness, unblushing jobbery all remind one of Charles and James the second and what was the end of it.

SUNDAY, MAY 6. Mr. Sheehan lends me the [March] *Dublin University Magazine*, about the cleverest of the thousand and one periodicals. A review of Lady Blesington's Life, makes me very angry with her literary executor and editor Dr. Madden. Her attractions, personal and mental, we are all aware of, as thoroughly aware of the unhappy use she made of them. There was no concealment even of the worst feature in her incorrect career, her entertaining as a lover the husband of her stepdaughter. She began her publick performances at fifteen, when old John Hornidge danced with her, and her almost equally beautiful sister, Lady Canterbury, at a picnic waterfall party at which time these ladies were under the protection of two officers belonging to a regiment then quartered at Kilkenny. Dr. Madden perhaps properly glosses over these occurrences of her youth. She had enough to answer for, certainly, in the errours of her age.*

But it is not of her reputation I am thinking. Can it strike anyone as right that all the men she held charmed in her chain of flowers should be exhibited while under the intoxication of their folly, for the amusement of the world to the distress of their connexions. Notes published that were written while under the witchery of her fascinations such as no man would write to a woman he respected, filled with admiration of her personal beauty – her hand, her hair, her eyes, her smile, all rhapsodised on by authours, wits, statesmen, whose names are held in honour. It seems to me to be as great a breach of confidence to pour into the wide ear of the publick these secrets of an ill woman's private portfolio as it would be in a priest to betray what is whispered to him in the confessional. The folly of men who have each 'written themselves down an ass' is another affair, as is their immorality which we, the virtuous *nuns* of society, are unable to exculpate from not comprehending the height of the temptation, and the poor means of resistance to evil afforded by the modern style of education to the male sex. The culprit I denounce is Dr. Madden, who writing the Life of a lady of liberal habits, might make it as entertaining as he pleased and say of her what he liked but he had no right to compromise others.

Whilst *I* am writing the clouds have passed away, the sun is shining, the air is warmed, and all the poor workers will have their afternoon holiday. Jack has given me mine in the shape of a three sheet letter, recounting his travels, admirably. What an eye for scenery the monkey has, and for all natural beauties – sun, shade, colour, moonlights, earth, water, air and sky, all delight him. His descriptions are graphick enough to sketch from. Aunt Bourne was astonished. She did not know his poetick nature as Annie and I do. He must be very strong, and Willie Mair too. They walked near upon thirty miles the first day and I should think little less than twenty every day after. They had beautiful weather, rowed on the lakes, fished, slept and ate as young pedestrians deserve to do. We were surely fortunate in placing that dear boy where he is. If I could but teach myself to view his profession with less abhorrence, to trust him to the chances of his perilous career as those do who believe in fatalism. My religion is so different. I see only a breaking of God's laws in our trained bands of murderers and can only expect such disobedience to be punished, to cause its own punishment as in the Allegory of our first parents, a lesson we never read aright and never profit by. I must just cling to the hope that this fearful war will be over and that none other will arise from its most miserable ashes. What will the telegraph tell us today.

7. The City of London met on Saturday, such a meeting. May it get rid of cliques, jobbery, and carelessness with the long list of ills our obstinate adherence to feudal habits has produced from the encreasing intelligence of all other classes not aristocratick essentially, feudalism is no longer necessary, has indeed become unsuited to our present times. It is odd that these upper classes who do not live exclusively among themselves, cannot learn that their place in the world is altered, that others once considered inferiour have now in the eyes of the 19th century equal rank. The heads of our great houses remain on the dais, but the juniors fall down among the crowd every generation and may enoble it, and should be envigorated by connexion with it. 'Tis like our Irish Brummagen peerage to ride a cock horse so ridiculously *and unwisely*.

16. Fanny Kemble* gives *Hamlet* tonight, her last reading. She has been fully appreciated here, there are few dissentients from the general feeling in favour of her extraordinary powers. I believe I have been unlucky in my two selections. Janey thinks *As You Like It* by far her best display of talent and then the play itself is so beautiful, a world of poetry in it, the action agreeable, the humour delightful, almost every character individually interesting. She herself prefers it to all other comedies, it is a treat to herself to read it. *Othello*, Janey thought a masterpiece but dreadful to listen to. I hear that *Hamlet* is her favourite tragedy.

Now for my own impressions; her manner engaging, ladylike perfectly, voice when not strained, musical, deep, and full in the lower tones, clear and sweet in the natural pitch of it, occasionally ringing out delightfully. Her pronunciation is abominable. It would require many repetitions of her readings for my ear to get accustomed to the pain of hearing words so distorted – *chember* for chamber, *hant* for haunt, might be passed as one passes in old fashioned people of high breeding too, *obleege* for oblige, but the vulgarity of her **o** is beyond endurance. In no position can she give this vowel its own sound. Own is *on*, open *oppen*, stone *ston*, close *closs*, only *onnly*, worn *wahrn*, scone *scon*. The jar is perpetual and very irritating. She sometimes croaks, quite unpleasantly because unnaturally, she speaks too fast often, and does not make sufficient pause between the two speakers in an any way animated dialogue, and occasionally her pause of astonishment is too long. I caught myself once or twice wondering when she meant to begin again.

These are the faults, the perfections are beyond numbering. In *Macbeth* she shone most in the Banquet Scene as Macbeth, in the sleeping scene as Lady Macbeth, in the witches and above all in Macduff, when he hears of the murder of his house. It was her poor father's favourite character and her version is just an improvement of his. In the other two great parts she is quite original, no copyist of either her Uncle or her Aunt [John Philip Kemble and Sarah Siddons]. It was altogether very wonderful, very good, very interesting, and yet to me unsatisfactory. I would never take the trouble to go to hear it again. The *Merry Wives* she did all well but Falstaff. I heard many admiring him above all, but I cannot join, the croak was insupportable, but Mrs. Ford, and Mrs. Page and above all Mrs. Quickly! were admirable. Anne Page was made so nice, Fenton so manly. Dr. Caius the old Frenchman himself, Mr. Ford excellent. I like the play, it is so full of humour and really a treat to hear so read, yet Falstaff spoiled it.* I wish I were easier pleased, I wish to like most things intended to please, but some unsatisfied feeling thrusts itself up into notice whether I will or no, seizing on all weak points and annoying me. Then to be sure the delight is exquisite when all goes smooth. I am glad to hear Fanny Kemble so much applauded and to know she has been overwhelmed with dinner invitations. Hamlet wrote to her for her autograph and she sent him a very pretty note in reply.

18. A quarterly return from Jack's military College equally good with the two preceding and Major Mair's report all right. No fault of disposition or habit or manner, industrious, intelligent, clear headed, advanced and advancing and 'the best mathematician they have'. This is little idle Jack. He is anxious for his commission! Were I even inclined to give it to him so young, I could not manage to buy it, not having saved the necessary sum. My mother's special legacy of two hundred pounds I have got, the rest, which Jane and I as her residuary legatees were to have succeeded to jointly, has

dwindled down to £11.5.3 between us, the lawyers, like those in the old fable, have had all else. The oyster was worth to them one hundred and eighty pounds from us, our shells being handed over to us with due solemnity quite empty.

20. A wet Sunday, so we will soliloquise. Annie is all right with us. She has an incorrect idea of their relations with the other side and so encourages James in what I think [are] disrespectful feelings, neither of them considers that they are under any particular obligation to the old man. He lent money certainly when they much wanted it and it was a great relief, but he had the sum laid by and he gets much higher interest from them than he could have got in the funds, in short he has made an excellent investment, and as to his violent offence at his son's impudence it is simply ridiculous, he may be glad the debts were not double. He brought his son up in luxury, kept a horse and a man for him, paid all his bills, and let a large amount of pocket money be wheedled out of him, and then because the son declined the profession chosen for him he was thrown upon the world to earn his bread as he pleased, permitted to marry on a very unfair annuity, the payment of which was very irregular etc.

All this is true but part of this they should not express at least. The payment of the debts was a great boon, deserving thanks at any rate, the debts were very improperly incurred for the display of an ostentatious style of living utterly beyond their well known means. It may be galling to the vanity of the young man to acknowledge this, as the father would like to have him do, but he might at least say as Annie said, that the relief was most gratefully felt. The mother, cold as she is, and miserably money loving, has tried to make peace and failed. In fact there is little affection among them. The hearts of the whole family are cramped by selfishness, so engrossing that it acts like fetters upon every generous feeling.

I have been so occupied with working there has been little reading for me this fortnight. The *Englishwoman in Russia* interesting at this time, *Revelations of Siberia* good in themselves, and the *Court of England under the Steuarts* very amusing. One does love gossip that's a fact. There is high gossip and low ditto, clever and silly, and there is scandal which is bad, but without a doubt the cream of gossip cream is palatable to all ingenious natures. Hamlet has begun to run in and out again he is a most amusing gossip. Janey calls him Sir Benjamin Backbite and he calls me Lady Sneerwell.* We have the prudence to keep our remarks to ourselves; quick-witted people cannot help seeing the ridiculous, they can, however, avoid telling what they see, and where there is good nature, good sense and good principles, there will be no scandal – promulgated at any rate.

There have been comfortable accounts of poor Jos. O'Reilly. He had let his complaint of the kidneys under which he has long suffered get to a height that brought on paralysis. A young surgical friend took him to the University hospital where he has the best attendance and the best advice. He can stand now, even walk a few steps with assistance. Eyre has gone over to bring him home and Lord Milltown sent ten pounds for travelling expenses. Five pounds was merely an advance of the mother's annuity, the other five pounds was a present; and he wrote a kind letter wishing he could do more. This will heal many an old sore.

23. Mrs. Brooks most kindly came to run over Janey's songs with her, Mr Brooks with her. He turns out to be a great critick in all matters of taste, brother to Shirley Brooks, an eminent literary character it seems, in the publick press line. For some years our Mr. Brooks did all the musical criticisms for the *Times*, and most certainly he understands good musick, for his taste and mine agree! and the merit of performance, for he thinks most highly of Janey's voice! Without a joke, he paid her and it deserved compliments, told her of her faults, pointed out the difficulties she must work against, entering upon the formation of her well-developed chest, the power of her lungs, the rigidity of muscles belonging to a voice of such compass, and then added hints for use. His wife had expected fuller praise and so was but half satisfied. I was more than content, so much has been done in these two months, the next two will show doubly. I had no idea that my pet's voice was half as fine.

24. A quiet evening at home with plenty to talk about for matters of moment are not exactly going on comfortably. General Canrobert is *very politely* superseded. General Pélissier, a very iron hearted man, succeeds. We should follow this wise example, invite Lord Raglan home to some well sounding sinecure, as was done to Sir John Burgoyne, and try and get a man of sense to head our gallant army. The disclosures of Mr. Roebuck's Committee* now over, were very startling, disgraceful to all concerned. The figure most public men are cutting in the House of Commons is of much the same stamp. Inaccuracies, to speak mildly of the general run of statements and counter statements, ill-humour, ill breeding, levity, totally unbecoming such grave circumstances, carelessness, want of *pluck*, want of principle, characterise the statesmen of thus our failing day.

All I can save must go to Jack's commission, and what can I save? This invalid establishment is so expensive. To pay our rent, servants! wages, tradesmen's accounts, market accounts, car hire, house sundries, washing, and my Aunt's carriage drives, it takes five hundred and fifty pounds per annum. I can no way do it as it must be done for less, I being so useless; were I stronger I might save the fifty pounds. Jack costs us now one hundred and fifty pounds, the General requires one hundred pounds, there is just one hundred pounds left for Janey, Annie and me, including not only dress for Janey and me but any amusements going and the twenty five pounds I promised for the future to allow towards Annie's housekeeping. There is our whole little comfortable income accounted for, and so long as those are made happy who in the natural course have but a short trip for enjoyment, and that I incur no debt to keep them so, I am satisfied.

I make Janey help me in all ways, quietly I shew her all my ways that should I be taken from them she may be fitted to supply my place. I had rather see her well married before I go, she is not so stout hearted as Annie, nor so active; she stands in need of a protector, while Annie can protect. Jack, with his good sense and thorough honesty in a profession he loves, will do well, every year will strengthen his character, and John Hornidge will look after Baltiboys; dear happy home of my happiest married years.

25. Old Mrs. King here about her son. In the conversation she had with him, he kept his temper perfectly, spoke respectfully, but firmly, not allowing himself to have been the least in the wrong, throwing the whole blame on his father and declining to make any acknowledgement for an assistance that was his due. This is quite a one-sided view of the question. The original evil will remain in the character. The mother don't see any of the philosophy of the case, she only sees a father and son at variance and longs to make peace between them. She came to me to help her and I will of course try, though having failed before I am not sanguine of success. James missed the opportunity which he had promised me to seize.

29. The electrick telegraph last night brought great news which appeared in the *Mail*. The Expedition to Kertsch has totally destroyed the town with all its stores without the loss of a man. General Pélissier seems to be at work; he has invigorated that hitherto lifeless corps; full of individual ardour it has always been destitute of a commanding head.

I have not yet seen the *Saunder's* which may contain fuller accounts. My dear General takes hours to read it, sleeping between whiles I do believe. He sends me up my refreshing cup of tea at eight, after which I get up, and before which I have commonly read an hour or more in bed glancing out occasionally these fine bright mornings to the view I enjoy so thoroughly when sitting as now at the open window with those dear Wicklow hills surrounding the green fields and well wooded foreground, which, by ingenious placing of myself, acts quite a country scene to me, no bit of town to break the illusion, and such fine fresh air comes straight from the hills, with chirp of birds and scent of flowers that I am really drawing life and drawing strength from this source and porter – a glass of which I take at dinner daily, hitherto with the best effect, having had to discontinue wine from its encreasing this strange and very annoying set of pains in my head, as I must now give up the pen though inclined to scribble, writing after a while affecting the head much. Thank goodness I am done with the brandy, my appetite having returned sufficiently to make such an odious dose unnecessary, besides, it set off the head.

30. Last night we had two parties, the General going with us to both. About fifty people at Mrs. Dr. Montgomery's, some good musick from some of the company, but no refreshments beyond tea in some room off the Statue gallery on the first landing. I did not know a soul there beyond the three members of the family and Captain and Mrs. Balfour, who being in the same isolated position were as glad to see us as we were to see them.

'Tis a magnificent house beautifully furnished, well lighted with *gas* which I abominate. Mrs. Montgomery, being one of the pious, has all of the best, amusements of any kind, romping games included, but no dancing. From this saintly assemblage we went in to our new R. Cath. friends the O'Farrells. Almost equally good house a few doors off; very dirty, very shabby and no light on their staircase and a very moderate supply in the rooms. Teas handed round and later, rather too late, a small supply of ices. Then downstairs a very shabby supper of nasty looking dishes and very little wine. Good enough for the company who were the queerest people ever encountered. Two widows in their weeds, two just out of mourning and crowned with roses; singular mannered young ladies and singularly dressed old ones. A sprinkling of strange protestants among them – Mrs. *Lieutenant Jeffcock* in blue and silver and a bacchante head.

The men with a few exceptions were of a better grade. Janey brought her own set of partners, a band of seven at the request of Miss O'Farrell, who really was a most kind hostess. Everybody in spirits with these successes in the Crimea, the forerunners 'tis to be hoped of complete victory over the barbarians of the North for this generation. It will take the space of a lifetime for the hordes to accumulate sufficiently for another pressure upon civilised Europe, particularly as the resources of the Russian Empire have in all other respects been seriously drawn upon.

31. Lady Stannus wrote in the morning to ask us to tea at nine, and to hear a little good musick. Went at ten, found seven people there, just the home dinner party, and sat talking over the discomfort of the ridiculously late hours now kept and the impossibility of getting so disagreeable a habit

changed . . . till eleven when people began to drop in. At twelve they began to drop off, half an hour later when we came away about twenty only of the forty were left. The rooms were very bright and nice. The company, mostly relations, seemed in a grave stiff way to have a good deal to say to one another. The musick was very bad, the party very slow, the attempt towards the end at dancing on the carpet to the very indifferent pianoforte playing of good-natured Mrs. Handcock was hardly successful, at least it did not wake up the sleepy spirits.

I knew few either men or women and as it has become unfashionable here to introduce persons to one another, strangers may sit side by side during the length of an evening without uttering a syllable. Now abroad, where there are no introductions and from whence we have imported this lack of ceremony, everybody speaks to everybody thus rendering the pronouncing of one another's name as an essential to conversation unnecessary. Here we have stopt short in our imitation. We have given up the old fashioned introduction without learning the ease of manner that supersedes such formality, and when any sociable creature ventures a remark to a brother or sister human being, it is really rather frequently received as an impertinence, barely replied to, an air of defence against similar attacks instantly assumed, in some cases a pointed retreat made, even rudely, for good breeding is the exception in manners here.

I often amuse myself with these airified nobodies, for fearlessly I address those near me when I see gloom settling on a row of disconsolates, certain that in a respectable house there will be no disreputable visitors. I often succeed in improving the melancholy condition of our common affairs, but I have as often been shrunk from as if I carried the plague or the cholera or, snubbed for such presumption, or civilly nodded in to silence by the dignified. 'Tis shyness very likely, the national failing, which does so interfere with the easy cheerfulness, which is the soul of society and so perfectly distinct from a hoydening [rompish, tomboyish: *Chambers*] familiarity descended into by those intimate enough to feel at ease.

FRIDAY, JUNE 1. A miserable day, not a hawthorn out, nor a lilack, a few laburnums in bloom. Annie's losses have been great, so have Mrs. Porter's. I had to consult *him* about my Aunt. She is in no danger, a real wonder she is at eighty-two; and my dear General so gay, no more like seventy-five than she is to eighty-two.

We are all quite reviving under this succession of good news from the East. General Pélissier is like the glorious marshals of old Imperial days of victory. We have entire possession of sea and shore and shall prevent men or supplies from entering Sebastopol by that route. More than all we have made the discovery that the enemy are by no means the force we had supposed, they have with consummate subtlety deceived us. Their defence has been masterly; had the *morale* of the troops been equal to the skill and bravery of their officers, we might have made hard work of it yet, but 'tis a mob of serfs, slaves, easily daunted by reverses, so they have latterly fled before us.

When I say *we*, I mean the allies. The Piedmontaise [sic] Contingent is a most efficient assistance, fine, soldierly, active, handsome men, well drilled, well dressed, well mounted with every appliance in perfection. Really it does all look brighter. We have to take not Sebastapol alone but the whole peninsula of the Crimea, and the Asiatick provinces, with command of those seas, and thus throw the barbarians back on their snows for another half century.

We went this evening to the Ancient Concert [in Great Brunswick Street]. Kitty and I on *Edward B's* tickets, Janey got hers from Mr. Sheehan whose Widow! was there on another I suppose, and a very flirting widow she is. E.B. met us and had seats for us, excellent ones, just in front of the Lord Lieutenant, who, poor man, slept during much of the first two acts, as I felt inclined to do too, for truly the musick was anything but enlivening; wretched singing [but] the Chorus's were in high order, orchestra the same, and both came out with quite a startling effect in the *Walpurgis* night, that wonderful effort of Mendelssohn's genius for which the performance seemed to have reserved themselves, their '*interpretation*' being most effective. The Lord Lieutenant and Mrs. Smith waked up! E.B. saw his Excellency into his carriage and the respected Ex-Chancellor into his, and then came back to Kitty, kept us chatting for half an hour while the crowd dispersed and then got us a car. Poor Kitty in a flutter of happiness.

2. I have been worried these few days with the discontents of Mrs. Dodson. Her daughter is really worn out, Antony having behaved most extremely ill. He has never paid anything like his proportion to the housekeeping, nor any rent at all, he keeps very irregular hours and his spoiled son in his passions endangers everybody's life. Peggy is not the woman to keep order under such circumstances. She continues to spoil the boy, and Mary's girl. She excuses Antony and permits Mary, the willing horse, to draw the team. Her own pension pays the rent and leaves one pound for clothes and tobacco, but Mary has provisioned the whole family and been at the expense of her mother's many removals. The first lodgings were too dull, the second became too hot and were always noisy, the third, really excellent, are *silent*. She wishes for a front room in a good street and on the ground floor.

It really was time to apply to me, as poor Mary at last has done. I'll soon 'regulate' matters. Step the first was to shew Mary that she had no right to squander on her relations her husband's money. All he has sent her home and her own wages, every penny gone. Step the second, told the same tale to the old woman with the addition of a severe reprimand for allowing what might end in a serious quarrel between the parted couple. Step the third, I have sent for Antony, and in the meanwhile he is left to his own resources, Peggy having another lodger in her room and he remaining in the one she vacated. He is not bad, only weak, and Irish like; while he can get himself supported will not support himself; he don't drink but I think some fair friend must take up his time and spend his earnings; he had best marry again.

5. We had a most agreeable party this evening at Hamlet's. Excellent musick, yet no professionals. Mrs. Hort, wife to the Garrison Chaplain, a handsome woman, sings well with a very fine voice, taught by Lablanche.* We found many friends, Edward B. among them, in high spirits, quite facetious, in faithful attendance – so Kitty looked brilliantly happy.

7. Went in a phaeton and pair to the park. A Garrison field day, all the troops were out, a fine day, scenery beautiful, and as we were to drive about after the manoeuvres, by following Lady Seaton's carriage, we were in the thick of all going on and enjoyed it much. James King came in, staid to tea and got his money which the father had sent here for me to give the Doctor, the Doctor told me to give it to James. I hope he will deal fairly with Annie and not ask the loan of any of her house money for his own speculations. John Hornidge also came to tea. He brought his Christmas Accounts, he has paid all demands up to this day and has recovered most of the arrears, enabling me again to buy Bank Stock to the same extent as before, so now I have four hundred pounds ready for my boy, two hundred pounds more will be required and must be thought about. The rents were perfectly well paid, all the people thriving. I must go there, however, there are several little matters requiring attention.

9. Great news we hear by the midday telegraph – the French have taken the Malakoff tower and the flagstaff battery and set London half mad with joy. Lord Milltown has gone to London at last, the ladies were getting on better by the last accounts, not much in society, but well amused otherwise, and happy. They were at the State Ball, and Lady Clarendon having most kindly held out a helping hand, they may be pushed on a bit. The father's character and the mother's manners are sadly against those really nice girls.

12. These fine summer days come so cheerily after our bleak spring, my open window is my delight, life and health and happiness, with such a lovely country view whenever I raise my eyes. All admitted friends envy my cosy room. It is not the Malakoff tower the French have taken, that has to fall yet, nor the flagstaff battery, but the Mamalon tower and the battery commanding the inner harbour. It was a very brilliant affair but it has cost dear. The allied army is in glorious spirits. All these successes rouse them into heroes and they feel they are well commanded for 'tis Pélissier and Napoleon who direct.

Certainly *we* cut a sorry figure, our *heads* I mean beside the heads of our clever allies, only the indomitable spirit of the mixed race rises up through the mud of routine and red tape and jobbery and ignorance and indolence and family interest, so that we conquer in spite of our rulers, and nourish heroes in the shade strong enough to break through this smothering. It is extraordinary that we bear it, that John Bull lies sleeping while abused by those to whom he has given his misplaced confidence. An idle *beast*, he deserves his fate since he prefers his *beef* to his reputation.

13. At half after four this fine bright morning we returned home from the Cavalry Ball. It was difficult to get Kitty and Janey away and next to impossible to drag off the General. He appeared to consider himself in his proper place, helping to do the honours, taking old ladies off to drink champaign, admiring the young, encouraging the Band. It was a charming Ball, beautifully got up, occupying every room in the Rotunda. If there is a spare half hour after coming home from our drive it shall go down here for the benefit of your generation, dear Jack, under similar circumstances.

14. These Irish girls are really queer. Marriage is with them a necessity. If they can't get the man they prefer, they set to work to attract another, systematically, as manoeuvring mothers are said to do, and they think it no harm. If Kitty's Aunts were to talk over her eligible *beaux*, and lay plans for bringing the young people together, one could forgive their indiscretion in opening their game to a friend and their matchmaking too, but for a young girl to take the whole business upon herself is something so out of all maidenly delicacy that I can't get over it. Were Janey younger or less sensible or more worldly, I really would not let her respond to her friends' wish for intimacy. As it is, she excused Kitty while blaming her and helps to keep her within the bounds of decency. Not that Kitty's manner is immodest, far from it. It is merely her regular methodical way of setting to work to make out for herself a good marriage, as her Aunt has not done this job for her, that so amazes me with my very different feelings.

Now for description. A troop of Dragoons guarded the environs of the Rotunda, every second man carrying a torch. Artillerymen were near three large guns also bearing *flambeaux*, and each side the doorway were more troopers with

torches over the light of which their helmets flashed like
gold. The long passage within was lined with the soldiery,
hussars guarded the entrance to a *tent* where all our wraps
were deposited. At the door of the Round room stood the
Committee of the officers to receive their company. One of
them advanced to take the tickets, another presented the
Ball tablets which were ornamented outside with a very
pretty etching done by Captain Chichester, a group composed of officers of the different Regiments which formed
the Brigade – the third Dragoons, the seventh Dragoon
Guards, the 11th Hussars, and the Horse Artillery. The
Band of the third flanked by two guns wreathed with laurel
and attended by the proper complement of men, played in
this room. The walls were hung with flags, standards, arms
in figures, etc., all dressed up with laurels and flowers as
were the chandeliers. The pillar room was not so military,
flowers and garlands only, plenty of light. The Band of the
7th and Hanlon's Band. The long room was a drawing-
room, the little room a tent with ottomans round it, and the
supper was in the smaller long room. Abundant and excellent and handsome, beautifully set out by the taste of the
soldiery, some of whom had painted the walls in fresco with
quaint devices.

We have all agreed to go to no more parties, none other
would be endurable after this and we none of us wish our
delightful recollections of it to be disturbed. Jane looked
very well, Kitty was dressed exactly like her, and so was
Ellen Thompson. They look so much better since they
dressed themselves in the simple clear muslin frocks best
suited to their age. The secret is to have them 'fresh and
fresh', never to wear them tumbled, and they are so cheap
that girls can afford to renew these inexpensive organdies
when they please, particularly when they go little out.
Hamlet actually thanked me for my good advice. White
was the prevailing colour at this Ball at the request of the
officers, suiting best with their uniforms, blue was bearable,
black did well, but the *pink belles* were horrours, disturbed all
eyes, looked ill themselves and spoiled the effects of their
partners' very handsome equipment. Oh, those tunicks –
very few had them and those few were frights, the hussars in

them were just like the Court jesters in the Stewart days – objects of ridicule. We hear that the Queen don't like them on cavalry officers and that they will be discontinued in that branch of the service.*

16. In the Merrion Square gardens Janey heard great news from her. Russborough is going to be married to a great Irish heiress, Miss Grogan Morgan, at least there is only our Chancellor's consent wanting, all else on all sides are agreed; how this shy young man took courage, first to pay proper attentions and next to say the awful question we can none of us understand. Lady Milltown did all that could be done by deputy, of course, but towards the close of operations, himself was *indispensable*. Well may she rejoice in her journey to London. 'Tis better for them all than the marriage of a daughter.

The Grogan Morgans are very low in birth, quite sprung, like the Leesons, from the 'people'.* I think the last generation was the first heard of; two brothers made a large fortune by trade, fisheries or something that way, and bought a deal of land along the coast of Kilkenny. One brother had no children, the other but this one daughter, heiress to both, the childless brother is dead leaving a heavy jointure to his widow, the woman so much bepraised in the pretty stories of Mrs. S.C. Hall,* and who unluckily has taken to drinking, so that reversion will soon fall in. I fancy the other man must be dead too as the young lady is a ward in chancery.

Lord Milltown had gone over to London to carry the ladies on to Paris but this agreeable affair has sent him back here to try and get the consent of the Chancellor. He may not consider the penniless Earl quite a sufficient make-weight against good acres, and this is feared, there being much against poor Russy in many ways, and she would be welcomed into the family of many a British peer more equally gifted. Then again the young people are said to be deeply in love – Russy in love! and better settlements with securities, etc. could be made now in her non age than she might make for herself if she waited. With the Leeson propensities, this is a consideration.

17. Such a sermon as has been inflicted upon us this morning. It is really monstrous to give one of the principal churches in

the city into the care of three mere lads. The Rector twenty seven, and two boy curates a year younger. Who, owning gray hairs can listen to the very meagre buddings of such intellects, there a'n't' an oz. of sense among them. The second lesson for today's morning service, the second Sunday in Trinity, being the first chapter of St. Luke, required a good swallow and little said about it. It was not the most decorous of subjects for a crowded church, nor particularly worthy of attention on any account, indeed the less noticed the better, but the new curate thought otherwise, and lest any of the indelicate illusions, or improbable fictions, or irreverent ideas should be passed over by the growing intellect of the day, he gave it us all over again in homely language. He had the cousins visiting, congratulating, discoursing on their condition. The Angel came in for his share, as did the shepherds in some round about way.

We also got to Hezekiah, God knows how, and to Jacob's well, and so to anatomy and physiology, and moral philosophy and texts brought in higgledy piggledy, prosing on for an hour in a high key and no power of articulation, for besides a hideous lisp, this poor man could neither pronounce **r** nor **b** nor **d,** nor any double consonant. 'Maiy went to Lstee full of faih, eying on e pomies of Goh out pocaynalin etc.' . . . Meaning that 'Mary went to Elizabeth full of faith, relying on the promises of God without procrastination' and so on. We really heard the people laughing, the men especially, at certain points of the tale. How any *Doctors* can listen gravely to any of it is to me a marvel. Talk of idolators indeed. We can furnish our share, I am sure, and of fools into the bargain and the provoking part is that all these fables are actual deformities. It grieves me to go to church and have to listen to the rubbish preached by authority.

20. Charles Cochrane [see *Memoirs* II, 48–9] dead, my old dancing *beau.* Mad as were all the race but very kindly and, for a small featured man, as handsome a one as could be seen. Nothing more from the Crimea. Ellen Foster, our old servant, called today with her handsome husband, the Colour Serjeant of the 21st Fusiliers, he was in all the battles and got what he called a scratch at Inkerman, a bayonet wound in the side. He has come home to recruit for the 2nd

battalion and he hopes to be back in time for the end of the war. As to 'Sebastopol falling, that there can be no manner of doubt, down it must come, and would not have been so long a doing, had we cut off supplies earlier, been awake in short. Had we pursued the Russians after Alma, all was ours; they had but few troops, no strong works, and were not full provisioned, but that poor old gentleman what commands is used up, and was most asleep the best part of winter, and uncommonly comfortable in his own quarters, had the best of everything, and didn't know much of what was going on forward, a good-natured old soul, could not bear to hear of punishment and just believed all it suited them that was about him to tell him, and so it couldn't be expected but what we must come to loss'.

And for the mismanagement, cheating, robbery, carelessness, idleness, all former sins of this class must have been a joke to it. The [Roebuck] Committee should have had a few soldiers before them. As it is, their report is sufficiently damaging to all in authority. Without mentioning any culprit individually, all are bravely censured for an amount of ignorance, inattention, dishonesty, absurd credulity, and petulant arrogance that destroyed one of the noblest armies ever sent forth, and while all praise is due to the officers and men for their heroism in every way, it is to be hoped that such an amount of suffering will never again be inflicted. They divide their report under proper heads, animadverting on each, *approving none*, nothing but the glorious endurance of the victims. So damaging a stricture on our publick men, calmly and quietly as it is done, would have upset the Cabinet had it not been upset before, not that we have got a better one, but the publick press keeps it in order. All that it advanced having been proved, the voice of the country supports it, and forces these indolent, unprincipled heads to look a little after their equally indolent and unprincipled hands. For the melancholy part of all is that there really seems to be no principle in the country. A love of ease and consequently a love of money pervades all ranks, all alike seem to forget that 'tis a working world and that we have none of us a right to bread we have not earned.

WEDNESDAY, JULY 4. Maria went away last night, Anne Fitzpatrick arriving to take her place. A tidy well grown girl; about noon comes Marianne Delaney armed with orders from her husband to stop Maria's folly and try to make her peace – luckily too late, for having got this idea of higher wages into her head, she never would have been satisfied, and as for gratitude or affection that has all died away with other old world notions. We have sent poor [brother] William back his papers. He may be able in a few years to be able to reclaim his inheritance. At present it is better in Jane's hands on all accounts. Poor dear old home, none ever was so bright or within a hundred thousand degrees so beautiful.

5. A lull in the Crimea, consequent most likely on Lord Raglan's death.* Too much befouled while he lived, he is now too much bepraised, even the *Times* his gravest accuser becoming quite fulsome in its flattery. Like other human beings his character partook of good and evil, the kindly feelings prevailing in him remarkably, as is usual in this case, energy, the iron will that makes a good commander being lacking. He was particularly useful in conciliating the French, keeping up the best possible spirit between the old rivals and ourselves. There would appear to be no better General to succeed him for our check on the 18th was principally owing to bad arrangements and the slaughter entirely the consequence of want of support for the brave few engaged, though the whole army behind them was burning with anxiety to rush forward to succour them.

16. Poor William still at work about his lost inheritance. Another long packet to my Aunt. His new plans seem not to be opposed. He has insured his life for the six hundred pounds due to Jane still. In three years he expects she will be repaid, out of the estate, the two thousand pounds she has just given for his life interests, and to pay the premiums on the insurance; he has his five hundred still in hand, the interest on which for the two years has still most of it to be provided. He expects John to lend, or perhaps our Aunt to *give* this, no great sum. There will be a couple of hundred nearly left of his five hundred pounds, a bonus probably, and the interest, now that the principal is so well secured he means to reduce to four per cent. I am surprised that Jane has all along taken

five, her husband gives her but four for what money of mine
he holds, on uncertain security too. I must make up my
mind to this hateful journey and get all these bits of business
settled.

Ellen Foster has just been here; her wounded husband is
made Colour Serjeant of the depot at Birr, with charge of
the recruits; a room, encreased pay, a pension, and no
chance of moving. So she is happy, poor soul, although
his nerves are so shattered as to make him a great charge,
very irritable all day, and at night, instead of sleeping, he is
fighting all those battles, cheering on his comrades, or in the
trenches giving orders, starting up and calling out like a man
deranged. I have bid her speak to the Doctor without delay,
there are two bullets in his body which should be seen to.

17. A little after one, left home with the General and Janey and
drove to the North Wall in plenty of time for the start of the
Herald steamer. They staid with me till a few minutes before
the ringing of the last bell. A great crowd on board, a mob of
passengers, a very heavy cargo and dogs, servants, horses,
etc. Mr. and Mrs. John Latouche were on the way to the
Highlands with two nice little girls and their whole establishment. Our ladies' cabin had every berth filled, and the
floor covered with mattresses besides, so closely fitted it was
hardly possible to pick one's way among the legs and arms
stretching out in all directions. A dozen children, two
babies, and all their maids did not make an agreeable
company – so – though we had a calm passage, the amount
of sickness all around was fearful. Luckily for me, my berth
was an upper one with a window and very airy.

18. About seven this morning we touched the quay at Greenock.
I made my solitary way among the crowd of Latouche
followers to try to ferret out my old battered trunk, which
having found with difficulty, I followed to the railway
station, thinking a little of former days when as gay a suite
attended my own movements, something like a sigh wandering towards those beautiful highlands I am never likely to
see again.

I got to York Place by three. Jane expected me, yet having
been so frequently disappointed she had remained quietly at
home, having wearied herself with running after me before

even as far as Glasgow. She had so many questions to ask about Aunt Bourne, my General, and the girls that we chattered an hour away very quickly and then went to Abercromby Place. William was in, more gossip, Sally at the Mairs where we followed her. All in but the Major and the boys who were *rehearsing*, then the Major coming in he carried Jane and me off to the Musick Hall as the cadets were still at their drill. They were doing the sword exercise, their backs turned towards us. By and bye they turned half round, then whole round and dear Jack saw me. How his colour mounted, how his eyes sparkled, but not a move he made, not the least start. Quick marching and other manoeuvres followed. At last it was over and he could come to me. He is grown a little taller, very much stouter, looks a very great deal brighter, more alive, and he certainly is as happy as possible. Captain Orr told me he was a credit to the Academy, and Mr. Scott, the Secretary, complimented me on having such a son.

20. All passed off well at the Academy. Lord Tweeddale,* who was to have presided did not come in, was ill. Lord Ardmillan, a new judge – Crauford, did very well, made a long speech about everything and then the prizes were delivered. Before all this the young men had gone through all military exercises and remarkably correctly. They marched in like a little regiment in their neat little uniform, went through the musket drill, also formed in line and file and square, etc. A military band playing all the time. Next we had the broadsword both for horse and foot, then a gun was drawn in, a small three pounder, which they manoeuvred in all possible ways, the covering party doing its duty most effectively. Fencing, the single stick, and vaulting followed, the leaps etc., were surprising, the fencing very pretty.

The prizes were then adjudged, the delivery of them to the successful pupils closed the proceedings of this day. The Directors give the four Military prizes. Each professor gives one in his own class, the Directors also give good conduct medals. The Sheriff gives a gold medal for the best answering in the Wellington Despatches, and the Superintendent, Captain Orr, gives one to the pupil whom in all respects he considers the most satisfactory. Jack got this, and a good conduct medal and seven prizes – Latin, mathematicks, drawing, fencing, gymnasticks; I forget the other two, but he most certainly did the best of all the pupils, carrying off in this his first year double honours, and being *the* favourite both of masters and students. He is reckoned very clever, not brilliant, but quick, true, reflective, with fine reasoning powers, and very hard working. As for his agility, it was quite unrivalled, as was the gracefulness of all his movements, particularly in the fencing. How proud his father would have been to have seen his boy so prominent. What I liked best was his quiet, simple manner, as if he had done nothing beyond the common, was in no way beyond his companions.

22. Leonard Horner* called, another shock, a fat, red-faced, red-nosed old man. Jane and I went first to the Deane Cemetery and then round the Queen's drive. It is a very plain but handsome monument she and James have raised to the memory of our poor father and mother. A sort of sarcophagus on a broad pediment, a strip of turf all round neatly railed in. Roses, flowers of every kind, shrubs of every size, surrounding. It is placed against the wall on the North side among the long line of tombs that face the sunny south in that garden of beauty, for it is a lovely spot, – one I should often visit were I near it, as Jane does.

23. Another hot day. News of victory crying about the streets, but one can never tell whether it be a true report or a plan to sell a paper. There are daily small sheets published here now, at a penny or even a halfpenny. Since the duty was taken off people live on gossip, a post every two hours.

Major Mair called for me and took me to the Industrial School, alias ragged school, which he assists in directing. It is small and not in fashion because not exclusive, any destitute child is admitted. On arriving in the morning, the poor little creatures are washed, get their breakfast and then attend the religious class of their own faith. At ten the school business begins by drilling and other such exercises. After this they are drafted off to their trades – carpenters, turners, tailors, shoemakers, printers or book binders, an hour both in the fore and the afternoon being devoted to reading, writing, cyphering, etc. Dinner at one, supper before leaving. The girls wash, cook, scrub, learn all sorts of useful needleworks and have their two hours of 'book learning' like the boys. Old clothes are thankfully received and patched up, new ones are occasionally made. Once a week the clothes are washed and so are the wearers in a fine warm bath. It seems to be an excellently conducted institution.

Jane called for me with William and they took me to the Agent for the kitchen range about which I have been so puzzled. I saw these grates, smoke consuming as they are, at the Exhibition, but among all the hardware merchants in Dublin could get no clew to them, so I thought I would try here, and I have found them. So Annie will be made very comfortable.

Jane and I also signed this evening the release of my mother's executors, that business being at least concluded. We have got more than we expected, a good deal; with what Bank Stock I have there is quite enough for my boy's commission. The special legacy is two hundred pounds, the half of the residue two hundred and seventy so I can buy Annie her grate, pay Jack's last quarter, and have a sufficient remainder. I do feel very much at home here among old friends, few indeed are left of them, but that makes one value those few the more.

24. Left after the usual early breakfast, kind James Craig going with me to the Terminus where we found Jack, the Major and Willie, William and Sally. James had had the thought to buy us a couple of newspapers and a great resource they were during the tedious delays we met with, for our Express train had so mismanaged as to be six minutes late in arriving. On reaching the Terminus they told us the Greenock train of twelve o'clock was just gone, none ever starts at one, 'tis the only hour in the day that no train goes. We had to wait till two, and that weary platform, for it rained too heavily for us to walk about the town. We had a luncheon of buns and lemonade. At two we were off again. At Greenock no boat for an hour and a half. When it rained we took shelter in an untidy office on the quay, between showers we paced up and down upon the platform. At half after four the pretty sight of our steamer sweeping down roused up our fainting spirits.

We were soon on board amusing ourselves by watching the arrival of other passengers, and quantities of landing. It was a fine, calm clear night, we staid on deck till quite late, past eleven, having first had an excellent tea dinner below. Toddy in plenty had followed, as we heard and smelt, sounds and sights and perfume reaching us from those regions underneath strangely discordant with our quiet moonlight walk on deck, and placid sea, starry night, looming headlands and warning watch tower lights. The company was of a very inferiour description, their manners certainly of a kind that gives a very unfavourable impression of the habits of that class; how inferiour to the same rank of foreigners.

25. Spent last night a much happier 'night at sea' than usually falls to the lot of the victims in the ladies' cabin. I was in a small state cabin holding four berths, with two portholes which we kept open; no one was sick anywhere. The *Ariel* is a steady vessel, but there was no wind to speak of, and the calmest sea. In the morning a fog turning to drizzling rain made the deck impossible, the less to be regretted as there was no view, and downstairs was very comfortable. I worked at my Tidy. We had a good Scotch breakfast, and watched our companions, not a pleasing occupation, they were most of them so thoroughly *low*. One decent looking man, after a plate of ham and eggs, devoured three herrings and paid for three glasses of toddy from overnight. An elderly gentleman, dressed young, airy, military, evidently from our own station, very conceited with careful dress, well trimmed hair and abundant moustache, both deep red; his companion was a young pretty girl, many grades below him, merry and chatting but not forward, in dress and manner like a sempstress or other young person of a respectable industrial station, not smart enough for a lady's maid. They were never apart for a moment, they talked unceasingly, were on the most familiar terms, no tenderness in the manner of either, and she called him 'sir'.

They met this morning close to me – 'How do? sleep well?' said he. A laughing reply and counter question was answered by 'berth so confounded short!' He was not himself particularly tall. 'No room hardly to dress or anything, – had any breakfast?' What she said I did not catch, but he resumed – 'Lord no, not my hours. Breakfast at eleven, dine at seven, – how'll you like that, breakfast at eleven, dine at seven, eh! What do you say to that?' 'Let's go on deck' said she – 'It's stifling here'. So up they went but soon came down again when he called for a biscuit and a glass of porter.

When the bustle of landing began, he collected all his traps in right soldierly fashion, he was quick and ready and had all neatly covered with oil cloth, his sword etc. On his head he placed a Fez smoking cap with a long tassel and then he went to help her with her poor carpet bag, her all of luggage. It was very odd, he did not seem uncomfortable, she was an innocent looking creature. They went off merrily together after the porter, who carried their effects. Jack is a capital courier, he soon had our affairs settled, and we were at home before noon, before they expected us. We have found all well, and very glad indeed to get us back.

27. The war remains in much the same state. The ministers, such as they are, likely to stand for the present, but till the grouse shooting and the Christmas festivities are over the statesmen can't be expected to attend to the affairs of the nation. The *Edinburgh* tone is much altered. Lord John dished, Lord Palmerston quite a failure. All wrong, who will set it right. Lord Derby's connexion with D'Israeli regretted, the Peelites held in horrour. Some improvement in those prejudiced minds at any rate.

29. Lord Raglan's remains were landed at Bristol with every demonstration of respect from the Corporation. None whatever from any other quarter. They were removed to the family vault and privately placed there, a few friends attending. He had better been left in the Crimea, although there was no glory to leave him with.* The Russians, it seems, valued him. Why not, he gave them what they wanted – time.

The Lord Chamberlain has given leave for Russy's marriage; he remains in town with his Bride; my lady and her daughters have come home and the girls so very kindly called here though they had travelled all night and were going off in an hour. I did not see them; Janey says they were in great spirits, delighted with London, and had latterly been out a good deal among Irish acquaintance. Miss Grogan Morgan may marry in September when she will be seventeen, have two thousand pounds a year till she is of age, then seven thousand. At her mother's death double, and Castle Johnstone.

Maria Delaney is going to leave her place and would like to be taken back again here. I should think so. Mary Ryan has had again to leave her grandmother Hipps as I expected, again all her clothes were pawned and this time no food bought, for she was actually starving. I declined giving either advice or help, but suggested! her being placed with the Uncle to whose charity she has this last week been indebted for her meals. Whiskey, what a curse. How are we to find a substitute for such ruinous excitement. The cigar in the palace and the dram in the cabin are alike indicative of faulty training. Where is the root of the evil.

SUNDAY, AUGUST 12. Most completely done up, unable even to think. It was an enjoyable though thoroughly fatiguing week. Showery weather, and intensely hot and close, so that the crowded [opera] house was a trial to health. I have not made up my mind as to the merits of this set but incline to prefer the former, to *feel* that Cruvelli and even Tamberlik were superiour to the remains of Grisi* and Mario. Mario before Garsier. Little Didier with her deep contralto stands alone, yet she utters some very unpleasing gutteral notes and is a far way off from Alboni whose parts she takes.

And now for Hamlet! who has been most truly obliging on this and indeed on every other occasion. This is so much his character to *all* that I thought little of it until lately. For his own peace, the intimacy must cease as in spite of effort he cannot now always conceal his peculiar interest in the family, and there is no response. We must slide out as he slid in, without wounding sensibility if possible

Lord Downshire paid a two hours' visit on Friday; mad about his militia regiment. Offered Jack an ensigncy! and failing that, his interest at the Horse Guards, which while Lord Combermere lives is worth having.* He looks quite handsome *en moustaches*. A letter from Annie about baby. An unaccountable home-sickness has seized the nurse; he must be weaned, poor little man, and it will be a trouble, she has so spoiled him. He is a strong child and eight months out, so that beyond a week's fret he will hardly suffer.

19. Sunday. The General has been having his photograph taken, admirable likeness, the sun is the true limner. Jack his daguerreotype for the Warden, very good too, he took it to St. Columba's yesterday, staid a few hours, was made much of, and we are all invited to the Prizes on Wednesday to meet the Lord Lieutenant, who has offered a visit! Some help is wanting as the boys gone from thence have got honours everywhere else, their numbers are sadly reduced since Jack's day, only twenty five this half. Besides the suspicion of Puseyism, the Warden being so much in Cambridge is against the interests of the College, parents will not be content with a sub. [Warden].

Soldiering has also occupied us. Lord Downshire insisted on our going to a field day to see his regiment on the ground, the whole garrison was out and all the world to look at them. Four regiments of the line, four militias, the two cavalry, and some Artillery. The South Downs are really first rate, admirably drilled, erect and firm, fine looking men, well officered, for he is most particular as to whom he admits among them. He is like a father to all, intimately acquainted with each individual. They are off to the Camp at the Curragh and on the roll being called before marching not a man was missing! He may well be proud, and Jack excused for his serious wish to join such a corps. In many respects it seems to me a desirable thing but I am so suspicious of my own motives that I have written to James and Annie to consult their less biased judgements. All *our* country wish it, in the hope of the young soldier tiring of the trade without earning his experience too hardly. I am afraid he will not tire and then he may have lost time. Two years of militia would keep him nicely out of the war.

Russy's marriage is settled, it will be in November. Nothing would induce him to tell the Chancellor he loved his bride – he liked her, respected her character, was sure he should love her as her estimable qualities became more known to him, etc. so when asked whether he were in debt, he answered – 'yes, he owed £600'. 'How incurred' –

'Betting on horses'. A friend had offered to advance this sum that Russy might call himself clear, but he said that would be a subterfuge. Now it happened that the Chancellor had been making the most searching enquiries and knew all how and about every transaction the young man had been engaged in. He must have been charmed with his honesty. They are to have four thousand a year from the beginning, three thousand more when she is of age, and the finest place in Kilkenny, Castle Johnstone. I *think* Russy will prove that he deserves his good fortune. Her name is 'Janey' and, she is short, fat and dark, pretty they all say. Lady Milltown was so kind towards everybody, her inward happiness thus shewing itself outwardly. I am very happy for her. I know she is really a better being than the half of those that abuse her.

FRIDAY, SEPTEMBER 7. Rathbally. Where I have been a week tomorrow, called by the premature confinement of poor Annie, who without warning gave birth to a second boy this day week, a seven month child, [Henry], but a fine little thing likely to live. She is recovering well herself. The cause of this was her anxiety about Johnny, who was fractious at night after losing his nurse and she foolishly carried him about in her arms for hours. There was no one with her, poor soul. James was in Dublin. Mrs. Mack. wisely sent for the Doctor, Mrs Kelly was engaged, so I had to be sent for, and so well have we done without a nurse tender, I don't think we shall ever plague ourselves with one in future.

9. Sunday. It is so impossible to find a moment in this busy house unoccupied, my private amusements are entirely given up. I have no corner to myself either. I sleep on a shake down by Annie, dress in the nursery, have no drawers nor wardrobe nor cupboard, nor even a table to myself, and between the old baby and his unskilful young nurse, and the new baby who is all my own charge and Annie who also depends on my care. Each day, however, makes the work lighter; the nursing goes on well, baby is strong and Annie is well supplied and nothing has gone wrong in any way. The first three days he was entirely fed by hand – by the bottle, a couple of spoonfulls every two hours. The Doctor thought I could not keep him alive but I did. Since he got the breast, he has been no trouble. We go regularly to bed, and now he

sleeps with his mother, waking just twice for his drink and dry linen. Johnny is getting reconciled to the new state of affairs, becoming more regular in his habits. Catherine Ryan is a nice intelligent girl, catching all hints.

14. Late in the evening, and what has not occurred since the last entry. This day week, the 7th, a wonderful fire overwhelmed Sebastopol. On Saturday the 8th the allies assaulted the town in four places. The French took the Malakoff and kept it – the key to the place. The English took the Redan but could not keep it owing to the Russian artillery. But the Malakoff did the business, covered the other assaults, and in the night the besieged evacuated the town. We have possession of a heap of ruins and dare not enter them for mines are springing up everywhere, immense stores have fallen into our hands, prisoners wounded, etc. We have, so to speak, taken Sevastopol. Our loss is great – two thousand between killed and wounded, twenty six officers killed and five hundred men, none we know much about. What next. Shall we crush the Barbarians at once and for ever or shilly shally as before and give them time to recruit. We live on the telegraph, the post being too slow. We had the news on the 11th here, 10th in London and Dublin, and we only entered the ruins on the 9th.

16. The Russians have by no means left the town of Sevastopol an heap of ruins. The quantity of material left to us is enormous, – guns, stores, accoutrements in astonishing profusion. General Pélissier was amazed, it was therefore no lack of means of defence that drove the besieged across the harbour and they had been throwing up strong works within and behind all the outer barriers. We suppose therefore that provisions failed them. The game would seem to be up with the Russians.

30. Sunday. Leeson Street, at home again at last. So now for a *résumé*. Writing time all this time I have had none though plenty to write about was not wanting. Now that I am all alone just the General and my Aunt and the little household to mind at leisure, and as it suits me, I can go back to the family transactions, for my own pleasure maybe only. I often think that those who come after me will throw these volumes into the flames unread, as perhaps would be wisest.

And here I am alone. Janey at Rathbally, Jack in Edinburgh and the rain falling heavily.

And now what can be said about Rathbally. Annie is all right. Undeceived with regard to me, enlightened as to him. He is much improved in temper particularly, in habits very considerably. Still the want of principle is there. A dreadful want overbalancing all the good there really is at the bottom of his weak character. He got two pounds from me for harvest work, and then two pounds more, very inconvenient it was to me to give it, but I knew that he was penniless, that his hay *must* be saved, that labour was very high, and the weather had been very uncertain, so I gave the two pounds on these considerations, and he spent sixteen shillings of it on a case of *eau de cologne*, eight bottles, genuine, quite a bargain. Again the Doctor had advanced to Annie her quarterly five pounds, his Godfather allowance to her for pocket money. James chose to go to town himself on the day the cart went up with my potatoes and to bring back the various purchases and presents for the babies. Some tea was wanting and, he said, coals, and there being no house money forthcoming, she having already *lent him* beyond twenty pounds of her half year, he insisted on borrowing her poor five pounds, really got cross about it. She resisted for some time. 'It's all I have for winter clothing,' in her gentle voice she said – 'But I'll pay you again, it's only a loan, I'll pay you when I sell my hay, my pigs, etc.' 'Ah, I know how you repay,' said she – 'but here it is, pay for the tea remember we have no account at Hannah's.' I believe he did pay for the tea. What else I know not, no coals came down, and a grate and mantelpiece were ordered on credit. He had got for himself a wonderful knife that was a saw and a chisel and an edge and what not, and as far as I saw there was nothing refunded. She was very grave about it, yet only remarked when called on to admire the knife – 'my poor five pounds'.

Of course there is a want of intellect where there is such folly. Our business is to keep him as innocuous as possible; we must endeavour to procure some employment that will occupy his restless nature. He has abilities to do almost anything that he likes, well. Being no reader, no thinker, having no refined pursuits, we must fill his leisure with work suited to him. It need not be lucrative, so that it be barely remunerative it will do all we want, give him something to do. She could manage most comfortably on their income were it all given to her as his father intended. This borrowing system keeps her poor. As he manages his twenty-five acres, they do not repay the mere labour on them. His Steward! and gardener, ten shillings a week, a house and firing, a lad to assist said Steward at six shillings. A groom and three horses, one of which is certainly a cart horse, and a woman to fetch the post and to weed at three shillings. All this establishment requires somewhat beyond the crop of hay to pay for it, or even the sixteen pigs, the four cows and their followers.

Annie has one extravagance in her department – poor Mrs. Mack, a wasteful servant in many respects, and from her health requiring almost constant assistance. Her wages, too, are high, yet how to counsel her being parted with, I know not. She does keep a certain degree of order in the household, even controlling some of the follies of her master, and she is a mother to Annie, so watchful of her, anxious about her, attentive to her, and, where the two other maids are mere girls, this good, honest old woman is of use. 'Tis a pity she is so untidy, so utterly immethodical, both as to time and place and purpose.

James is completely under Annie's master hand at present in essentials, and unless in a dogged fit, he adores her, is a fond husband, most affectionate father, kind in the main to all his dependants. With these half negative qualities we must be content, glad to have rescued him from the utter ruin both of fortune and fame. *Make* the best of him, habits may take the place of principles. It is hard to *un*learn, and he had to do it. He made me what he meant as an apology for his unprovoked impertinence long ago, and not badly done either. To allow of faults is a step towards amendment. I am quite content to let bygones be bygones, to sow peace and not divisions, to forgive, if I can't forget, allow, as in the case of a better man, for the faults of education.

I spent the better part of a day with Lady Milltown, listening to this marriage business. She is a year younger than they thought and can't be married until next September. Really rich, amiable, sensible, pretty enough, but totally uneducated, never has a master nor a governess, nor any good example near her, nor even a kind word since her father's death. Russy has no dislike to her, and she is very fond of him!

SUNDAY, OCTOBER 7. Yesterday's head was brought on by annoyance. Our new cook, a first class artiste, cleanliness and order personified, turned out to be a regular thief, and the receivers of all her pilferings were her sister-in-law, Mary Dodson, old Peggy and suite. Investigation brought to light Mary Dodson's equally guilty career, begun at first cautiously, perhaps thoughtlesslly; some little bits for her mother or her child. Habit encouraged freer proceedings, very skilfully managed, never a scrap from our table, only every fragment from the kitchen. Then as her funds decreased and the wants of the establishment she had burthened encreased, she grew bolder, encouraged by the ignorance of dear Janey; – cut the joints, watered the milk, overcharged the marketings, putting down a shilling for sixpence, twopence for a penny worth in the house book, and taking at least double quantities of groceries from the store closet. When I resumed the reins I was startled at the consumption. Dempsey immediately came forward before I spoke and unveiled the whole mystery. He had quietly prepared his proofs and was corroborated in every fact by Susan and Anne.

We held a Court of Enquiry which resulted in a dismissal of the whole set. The cook threatened all sorts of law proceedings, no one fears her. Mary Dodson was completely humbled. I did not see her except at a distance. They have had a grand combat at home, her face is much out and her eye blackened, probably by her husband. He had regularly sent home his spare cash, hardly earned, for her to keep lest he should spend it – twenty four pounds during the year, *all gone*, besides her wages of ten pounds, her perquisites four pounds, and her mother's pension eight pounds, Antony's earnings and her own thefts besides. It is very dreadful to meet with such wickedness, constantly to meet with it. Good conduct in this life would seem to be the exception, good principles generally wanting, and Mary was clever, active, affectionate; with these qualities she deceived, nay robbed, her husband, deceived and robbed the family who had educated her and her brother and provided for them, and had supported her own parents.

And what can be said for old Peggy. Must she not have known where all that beef and bacon and milk and eggs and sugar and butter and soap came from, to say nothing of rice, arrowroot and sago. Antony is made the scape goat; he would not work, he would be fed and clothed, and he had debts. To my mind the sin, and it is heinous, may very well be divided among them. I can't help putting a share on my own back. I ought to have looked after matters more closely, not believed in the extra large appetites of the servants, the high price of vegetables, eggs, turf, etc. A life of distrust is not the pleasantest to lead, but I fear that while the lower orders are so degraded by the evil influences that surround them, we must let suspicion rule our conduct towards them, in this country, at any rate, where the servants especially appear to be totally without principle.

I have been living very happily an hour every morning from seven to eight among my dear old friends, never to be replaced to me certainly, to the world I almost think; those brilliant intellects, so original, so acute, so full of *lore* don't seem to be in the way of begetting successors, the last quality being entirely wanting in the composition of the talents of this day. Lady Holland, the Doctor's wife, has compiled very badly the *memoirs* of her wonderful father, the good and great and learned and most truly witty Sydney Smith.* I never saw him, but did I not hear of him! often enough! and read him too with ever new delight.

14. Sunday. This is a fine bright Autumn morning for [Harry] our tiny baby to be Christened on. The General is quite pleased at having his pretty name remembered. I have had quite a treat in Sydney Smith's letters. Profound is what his mind was, foreseeing and clear judging. The wit almost obscured the nobler qualities, dazzled too much to be seen through, and yet he was vain, trifling and a glutton. *Esmond* is another charming book by Thackeray, not in his usual style, full of wisdom, 'tis its great merit, and the criticks have been so busy with the plot and the imitation of the language

and the feelings and the habits of the antiquated days of
Queen Anne, when 'tis affected to be written, that they have
overlooked all the treasures of moral thoughts clothed so
quaintly.*

22. Bartle Frere and I were very glad to meet, his affectionate
heart finding room even for an old woman. He has had my
picture taken, as I was, in bonnet and shawl; a queer picture
it will be and he shewed me at Robinson's these new
stelescopes, or some such name. Two photos together
looked at through two magnifying glasses, and having the
effect of alto relieves. People become statuettes, all objects
brought out in strong relief, to the most minute particulars.
He wants me to visit him in London to finish Janey's
'beautiful' singing with a few lessons from Crevelli. Alas!
I am bound to the soil, kept by love and duty at my post.

24. The *Times* has a furiously ungenerous article on the unfit-
ness for command of General Simpson. Quite uncalled for,
and false in many respects. He may not be up to the mark,
but he has done very well; his honours were thrust upon
him, he did not wish for the unenviable station, indeed only
accepted the office till they found a better man, and as being
on the spot and so more fully acquainted with the state of
the campaign. That paper really has become scurrilous as
well as unprincipled. It has for some time been every shade
of politicks 'by turns and nothing long', but latterly it has
been individually abusive as well, in the low style of the old
Sunday papers. He is elderly and in bad health and very
likely should be at home at ease. Yet we were right glad to
get him there, he brisked up the army wonderfully.

25. Sir William Molesworth dead. A young man – forty-five.
Always unhealthy, a most wretched sickly child as was to be
expected. He was certainly clever though flighty, surfacy
and very vain, as is mostly the case with the sort of talents he
possessed. The work of the Colonies is said to have been too
much for him. He has no child, therefore a queer younger
brother, gone I think to Australia will succeed to the fine old
place of Pencarrow.*

27. *Bleak House* brought a profit of thirteen thousand pounds
certainly. I wonder did Dickens get it all? What must the
sum realized by all his works have come to? Walter Scott

was a joke to it* and I hear this clever creature spends as recklessly as the other, in high living, his passion being for fine wines, a service of plate, etc. to entertain the nobility! and he writes so wisely. Bartle says he is quite snob, a little, handsome, pompous, conceited dandy. We'll draw the curtain over the unpleasant picture and think only of the mind he *shews* us. Probably such underbred affectation as this, added to the *Sheffield* ware, has put plate out of fashion. All great people dine off china now; it is more expensive, cleaner and prettier and can only be used when there are high class servants.

28. I went to Robinson's for my photograph. A pretty print it is, the attitude very life like, perfectly easy and natural, and of course the resemblance accurate. But oh, dear me, I look very old and very grave is the expression once so joyous. It was Bartle's fancy to have me done in my cloke and bonnet, the General is going to have another done in my home dress, cap and work in hand as he usually sees me.

29. The three great bankers, Sir John Deane Paul, Mr. Bates and Mr. Strahan, an old Etonian, friend of my brother John and John Frere, sentenced to fourteen years transportation. The Judge was painfully affected in passing sentence, yet had to call the case an aggravated one. They had been unprincipled swindlers, really bank-dupes, *selling securities* lodged with them. On this last count they were tried, and we pity them! Why! I cannot understand it, but we do. It must be a complicated feeling, – ourselves and our *class* in it. Readings of Sir John Paul's painful agitation, of the worn looks of all, one trembles. And the petty thefts and over-charges of Peggy and suite only shocked. The evil principle is the same in both cases, the sphere and the scale should not make any difference.

30. Poor Madame Giordano! Speaking of her second foolish marriage, she once told me that had her husband lived they would have been rich for his mother, a wealthy English-woman, would have left him most of her fortune although she had married again, a Dr. Reilly. They had no children, and though she had a daughter, Giordano, *Marzio* was so completely her favourite he would have certainly been her heir. The daughter was married, Madame said, and settled

comfortably in Naples, but she did not like her, they did not suit, indeed family difference was one cause why on her adored Marzio's death she had left Italy.

In the memoirs of Lady Blesington, a very ill got up regular bookseller's job, is the following passage. The Editor, Dr. Madden, is sketching the character of a Dr. Reilly, an old ship's surgeon who had gone abroad as the medical attendant of the famous lady Oxford, whose carriage full of children, when driving in the Park, Lord Nugent, (broad bottom), called the *Harleian Miscellany*. Lady Oxford and her surgeon parting, he fixed in Naples where he

married an Englishwoman in affluent circumstances; a very thrifty and money making person, but withal amiable and kindly disposed, the widow of the *maitre d'hotel*! of the Duke de Gallo. This lady, far advanced in years, had two children, a son named Marzio, a young man of good talents, fiery temperament and ungovernable disposition, and a daughter, an amiable and pretty girl who grew up to womanhood a highly accomplished and attractive person (the belle of the Chiaja), who eventually became the bride of a young English surgeon, the successor of Reilly in his professional business.

Poor Madame! with the princely descent of her Marzio. The painter ancestor might be true, but the house steward! Low as the Italian noblesse have been known to fall, I suspect they would starve on their maccaroni before they would serve as menials with their equals. There is worse to be said of poor Marzio than the fact of low birth. He was an ill living, quite unprincipled man, eminently handsome etc.

31. This evening during our whist the post came, two letters. One from Janey, very happy, all merry together and the babies thriving, wonderful pets of course. She says that Pysie had walked up to see them again to bid farewell. She is summoned home, poor Jos. is worse. Sir Philip Crampton has seen him and pronounced the death warrant. The other letter was from Pysie from Cabra Terrace. Jos. is dead, died this morning quite quietly.

Poor unhappy Mrs. O'Reilly. She never would believe in his danger, and of course she is in cruel grief; really her life has been one long martyrdom. A wretched childhood, unhappy girlhood, most unsuitable marriage resulting in misery. She never had those bright young days on which the troubled can look back as to sunshine, feeling memory to cheer the present difficulties, and after her stormy marriage ended in peace, so far as separation from her vulgar husband could ensure it, came poverty, pinching, nipping poverty, preventing the fit education of her children, precluding their advancement in life and then the murder of her son Henry, Pysie's deplorable connexion with Mr. Bowler, and now this painful end of all her hopes in Jos.

True, for most of her misfortunes, all these of latter years she is herself to blame. Her passionate temper, indolent, self-indulgent positive disposition, her idleness, want of method etc., etc., embroiled her with relations, soured her husband, spoiled her children, reduced her means; but she had never been fitted for her duties. Brought up by chance among servants, with a card playing mother and a dissipated father, always at variance and drowned in debt, what could be expected from these four thorough *Irish* daughters. They *growed* like Topsy, and for the rest had even less care taken of them. I do not like to go to them lest I should interfere with the religious ceremonies. Though the priests had little footing in the house, they will take possession of it for a few days now, Jos. having been a true son of their church, though much enlightened latterly, his poor mother told us.

Those memoirs and letters from and to Lady Blesington are really and truly utterly disgusting, revealing as they do a state of society that I would fain believe the world of our own day has too much good taste, if not good principle, to endure. Three or four women, not only of damaged reputation but of well known disrepute, handsome and to a certain extent clever, collected round them in their most luxurious homes all the celebrated *men* of the age. Respectable, so called, husbands and fathers left their honest womankind and half lived with these Aspasias,* flattering them, sending them rich presents, doing all their bidding, writing them perfect love letters, long and constantly. Lady Blesington was too notorious to have any female acquaintance, but to Holland House some wives were taken and some daughters. Fanny Mackintosh used to stay there as the particular friend of Miss Fox. And a poor peasant girl falling into errour will often have, for bread, to continue erring because no one will employ her honestly after her grievous sin. It is all so wrong, so very shocking, so opposed to the true faith we pretend to believe that it gives one a sort of turn to think of it. My dear good mother! you were very kind to 'unfortunate females' of low degree, saved many a one from greater evil and the most serious quarrel I ever remember with my father was on account of refusing to go to Raith or to call on Mrs. Ferguson or in any way notice *Mr.* Ferguson, whom she had known so well.

THURSDAY, NOVEMBER 2. Poor Eyre O'Reilly came to see me to answer my note personally that he might talk to me of his mother. They are afraid of her sinking after the great violence of her grief is over. She has been very reasonable about everything. The poor fellow is buried in Glasnevin and there was no priest craft, not one of them in the house nor any ceremonials. Four friends went with the body to the grave. Poor woman! to lose a son, one she so doted on, and though in himself, poor fellow, nothing wonderful, he was all to her, – affectionate, dutiful, and with no glaring fault. His want of energy belonged to his disease as did his strange flightiness of late – his London letters, gaieties etc. May be he was at none of these balls, just fancied it. After a while his brother and sister will be quite reconciled to the loss of such an expensive sleeping partner, and the mother, poor unhappy woman, when she is able to reflect upon all the circumstances, may be able to thank the Almighty for so soon relieving him from the sufferings he would have continued to endure had he remained longer in a world he really was no way fit for. Poor people, they are to be pitied much just now. Eyre is a plain man, but not ill-looking, with plain, blunt manners but not vulgar, no pretension. Prosy but sensible enough and mighty little of a papist.

It is the best part of Thackeray's *Newcomes*, his battle with

this odious Mammon and title worship. They say 'tis dying
out. I don't see it, the title hunt may be a little declining, but
certainly not the money hunt. We are all a great deal too
indolently luxurious, would like to eat our bread without
earning it, and have it well buttered too, forgetting that this
can't be without producing ill consequences. Nobody reads
the Bible aright, or if they do they are afraid of saying so.
While all other knowledge has spread, religion remains
much as the heathen left it. We are pagans still, groping
in the darkness yet because no bold, truthful hand will raise
the curtain of cobwebs that hangs between us and light.
When *Vanity Fair* is exhausted, a higher class of ethicks
must appear. Thackeray and Dickens are only preparing the
way.*

3. Found poor Mrs. O'Reilly less cut up than I expected. She
had been in great agony of grief, and paroxysms of violent
sorrow still return upon her, but she does her best to restrain
these outbreaks and she had exerted all her powers to gain so
much composure as 'would please me'. She will not get over
it, I think. Some cold or other change of that sort will
confirm the existing disease of the lungs. She looks very ill,
and indeed so does Pysie, who had unconsciously allowed
herself to hope. They are not without money; Lady Milltown sent five pounds and Mrs. McEvoy called with five
pounds. Mrs. O'Reilly received her and said she really
shewed kind feeling.

It was a very sad visit, as was the one I paid returning, to
old Mrs. Haughton and Mary. The old woman, half dressed,
much shrunk, very stupid, sitting mumbling by a small fire;
Mary in bed with a tattered flannel petticoat on her
shoulders looking ill enough. There is no occasion for all
this discomfort, their funds are ample, besides, a little
neatness makes no inroad on the purse, and it certainly
prolongs life, cheerfulness being an element of health. How
they have existed for so long with such melancholy sur-
roundings is a sort of marvel. They probably don't feel it,
have neither taste, nor eyes, nor *nose*, nor anything! They eat
in that bedroom, live entirely in it, without carpet, curtains,
white quilt, easy chair, or any one comfort. The washing
stands in sight, in the way even, close by the fire, and a

medley of clothes, papers, bread, bottles, shoes, brushes, etc., on all hands. Next door on the same landing is a pleasant, light, sunny room that might be made the neatest little sitting-room possible. Mrs. O'Reilly, who is by far the poorer, has her small house as neat, as clean, as pretty as could be wished with only one servant to do all, but then personally she is more untidy than the others, possessing a wardrobe of rags. Was not my mother so right, a needle is a woman's glory, the use of it her most precious possession. I think with a tear of pride of my Annie's tidy household on her such small means. Lady Milltown said, at dinner one day when some one was speaking of Annie, that she wished to God she could think her daughters would turn out as well, that she was a model. Amen, said Lord Russborough. She has indeed, dear child, won golden opinions from all sorts of people.

5. Another letter from Major Mair full of the Artillery, Jack represented as very keen for it. It is a very anxious matter, so difficult for a mother to act father; all my sympathies so antagonistick to the profession. I feel acting a part when consenting to the necessary steps for it. It is like taking all the blood from my heart out, drop by drop, on all occasions when the hateful subject is brought before me. But I suppose this is selfish and must be wrong; it is not paraded at any rate, and somehow my time seems to be nearly out here below. Warnings come pretty sharply here and there, now and then. My boy's happiness at the beginning of his career is of more consequence than my comfort at the close of mine. So hold your foolish old tongue, Mrs. Smith. I believe I never do speak of anything I feel except to my paper friend here, and let the young choose their own path through life. It's not so pleasant all through that we need place any extra thorns in it. I am glad I have got it all out, Journal won't tell of me.

11. My photo is universally despised. The general has sent his copy out of the room, Dr. Robinson has torn up Janey's and thrown it in the fire. Annie won't even allude to hers. All which of course is to be considered by me as complimentary. It is an ugly, old, sad-looking face, such, I suppose, as I wear while arranging for Jack and his artillery, though I really am

glad as he will be a soldier that he has the spirit to undertake that higher branch of the service. He has all the natural talents for it.

14. I must just mention the imprudence of Mary Dodson – came to me for her discharge! She is going to service again, her husband's earnings not being sufficient to keep them. I daresay not as they eat and *drink*. I told her I could not give her a good one, not such an one as would get her a place and that she had much better go without. She insisted, fumed up a bit, talked big, then fell to crying, said she had a clear conscience etc. All of which I answered by telling her she had forfeited my regard and I never wished to see her again, and wondered how she wished to see me.

15. Mary came again. My discharge gave her credit for her clever qualities, but said nothing of the three requisites, – sobriety, honesty, quietness, except that as far as I had seen she was sober. I added that she had left me to return to her husband. She returned me the paper to have those qualities inserted. I sent Anne to tell her that after the affair of the footstool I could not take upon me to answer for her conduct in any way, so she left the discharge as being useless and departed.

    Mary Ryan has just been here altering my gown so nicely. We have taken her from these wicked drunken relations. My Aunt, excellent woman, pays for her lodgings with a respectable woman recommended by Miss Knaggs. I have given her five shillings for present use and written through Annie to her mother to send up supplies. She is a very good little girl and will really be a clever needlewoman.

16. Mrs. O'Reilly, poor, unhappy woman behaving wonderfully well, more composed than I thought possible for one of her impulsive nature, and she will get better here from the change of scene, the quiet cheerfulness of our little family party and the good living, to say nothing of freedom from all annoyance, including the worry of the two boys, – fine, spirited little fellows, whom they have not a notion of bringing up properly. She has this morning written to her *three* sisters very proper letters of thanks, for all three have come forward upon this occasion, the two unfriendly ones proposing to renew old affectionate relations and bury

past feuds on this common sorrow, for all liked poor unoffending Jos. Mrs. McEvoy called on her twice, gave her five pounds very kindly offered and sent a dozen of old port wine for Eyre, who, poor fellow, is recovering. Mrs. Butler invited her for any length of time that suited her to her cottage near Carlow, and she has accepted the offer. Lady Milltown is just the same as ever, always kind and generous, though not always considerate. I took advantage of my guest to send her out in the carriage with my Aunt while I walked off on business. Those eternal drives hinder my work at times.

23. Wrote this morning to Mr. Fitzgerald about Ellen Foster who is too delicate to make a servant but he may in some way help the poor woman, left again with her children, three of them, the eldest an idiot, the youngest at the breast and four shillings a week to support them all. The Serjeant being recovered of his various wounds is ordered to rejoin his regiment, he is gone indeed.

We had quite a surprise this evening, Lady Milltown walked in to tea. She had come up to carry Barbara home who has been staying the week with Lady Downshire and instead of dining in state in Merrion Square she came here to see her poor sister. Very much she enjoyed her good tea with cream, sweet butter, real brown bread, etc, and long she chattered till far past the time when she was to have called for Barbara and Edward, to take them to see Buck-stone* at the Play. She is in her best looks and in high spirits although Russy's marriage is quite off. My only wonder, now that I know all particulars, is that it should ever have come on. A little, queer-looking, uneducated child, exposed for the last few years to the most demoralising influences and without sufficient character herself to rise out of the mire surrounding her. All the wealth in the world would not have overbalanced the misery to a shy, sensitive and home loving man of such an inferiour wife to say nothing of her as a future mother. Lady Milltown was full of our darling babies. Harry is a complete bundle of fat, and lovely, Johnny enchanting from his encreasing beauty and cleverness. The monkey delights in *her*, which perhaps explains much, laughs and crows when ever he sees her. She has to stop

on the road and take him up into her carriage, he makes such
a to do at the sight of her

I have succeeded so admirably in choosing a house for Lady
Downshire, I am to try my hand for Lady Milltown. She
intends coming up to town immediately. It will be far easier to
suit her as she brings a very small retinue, a house the size of
ours will quite satisfy her. London is very well to talk of, but it
was a mistake and a disappointment, and to me she owns that
Dublin suits them all better. I should think so. Mrs. Colclough had evidently intended to be bought, 'tis usual to sell
wards in Chancery. Over and over again she referred them to
her solicitor, recommending an interview between her man of
business and theirs, and they were too *thick* to comprehend
her meaning, thought too well of themselves perhaps, too
much of the *rank* they were giving in exchange for broad
lands, did not see that better could be had for the waiting – in
short, bungled it, mercifully for Russy. Lord Milltown's
Headrents will all be sold in January, and his debts paid,
leaving a sufficiency! two thousand pounds a year.

26. Some fanatick friars have been burning a pile of heretick
books in front of a Chapel at Kingstown. Ostensibly meth-
odistical tracts and such stuff with really good works,
Dickens, *Chambers'*, *Family Herald and by mistake* some
copies of the authorised version of the Bible. The excitement is furious. The act itself is illegal as is the presence of
foreign monks. Lord Palmerston has therefore given a shove
to our *Roman Catholick* Law officers, and ordered a prosecution.

30. The papers are full of the Bible burning and so are the
people, I fancy, though we ourselves are so quiet we hear
little about it all. The friars are Russian and suspected to be
spies, ignorant fools at any rate. Sir Bernard Burke [Ulster
King of Arms] and I had a deal of pleasant conversation to
which his mother-in-law to be [Mrs. McEvoy] most certainly was not up. He was <u>petrified</u> to hear one of his
Highland Legends, printed in his <u>veracious</u> *Romance of the
Aristocracy*, was spun out of my ingenious brains! facts all
true enough, but McAlister! my invention.

FRIDAY, DECEMBER 8. Sunshine again. Janey gave us last night
such an amusing sketch of Mrs. Latouche's novel. The

personages all run about after each other through the orthodox three volumes and are indebted to the electrick telegraph at the end for their ultimate disposal. This is her second and an improvement on the first. Those keepsakes, *Books of Beauty*, and so on were great safety valves for the confined abilities of the idle fashionables. They were prettily got up, so caught the eye. The engravings by true artists were good, the verse nobody read, and the prose was short. But these three volumes are trials of patience and really make their authours so ridiculous, their friends must be considerably puzzled as well as annoyed. There is quite an inundation of such rubbish at present. Between novels, biographies, memoirs of nobody cares who, by these unfortunate pretenders to name and fame, the picking out of a book worth having is a task of no small difficulty. I did not think Mrs. Latouche at all clever the day I spent with her at sea [see 17 July] and I thought her spoiled, not by her husband, he has rather harshly brought her under some controul. She herself appeared to be the principal worshipper of herself, yet good-natured withal.

10. Wrote to Dr. Eckford this morning enclosing a letter for his grandson Robert to give to Campbell Riddell, now Secretary to Government in Sydney, my dear old merry friend of Edinburgh dancing days. Bought a warm gown on Saturday for myself and one for Annie, but the road will be blocked up, we shall not get it sent. The Bible burners acquitted, rightly, I have no doubt, the speeches on all sides were most judiciously temperate. Judge Crampton directed the Grand Jury with perfect judgement. Keogh made a most proper speech as publick prosecutor. Baron Greene charged the jury without an atom of sectarian temper in his very lucid speech, but the masterly defence of Mr. O'Hagan will be long remembered by the Bar. The thing really was an act of passionate bigotry, the poor friar who committed it fully believing in the merits he was earning by making away with all that could enlighten a darkened mind, protestant version of the Bible included, so far as his little bonfire in the yard of the Chapel at Kingstown could effect this desirable end, – somewhat after the fashion of Mrs. Partington and her mop to keep off the Atlantick. But Mr. O'Hagan pretended for

his client the utmost reverence for any translation of the sacred book, the standard of the faith of all Christian men, preserved throughout ages by the R. Cath. Church in its 'beautiful integrity'. Its priests would be the last to destroy what had been their director and their charge so long; Father Peturine had collected some immoral works highly detrimental to the souls of his flock and had directed them to be brought to a place of marked resort held holy, in order to make their destruction more impressive – an unwise act – one to be regretted from many considerations, not, it was to be hoped, to be repeated, but as to burning Bibles there, or knowing they were to be burned there, or authorising any to be placed among the piles of trash he had saved the poor ignorant folk from studying, he would have been horrour struck at the bare thought, etc., etc. It was a very clever line of defence and may do good in the end. There was an utter absence of such evidence as is required by law to prove that this good friar touched a Bible, saw a Bible, or mentioned a Bible, he was therefore acquitted, and the mob, including women of the better classes made quite a triumph of his escape, escorting him home with clapping of hands, illuminating their houses, and so on, not one of them knowing on what grounds he had been set free. They have conquered the protestants they fancy and that's enough. Some of the works destroyed were by Dickens and the *Family Herald* with its useful information and *Cassell's* paper. But there were a heap of Godly tracts, which certainly I would put in the fire myself wherever I could lay my hands on them, but quietly, in the grate at home, not in a publick thoro'fare.*

11. Poor Campbell Riddell.* What merry hours we have spent together. How kind he was to us at Ceylon. Our dancing days were the days of the long country dance, a solemn affair to the English measure in triple time with three part figures, a sort of faded jig, no life in the musick. But our gay reel time, with our inspiring tunes and double figures, cross hands and back again, down the middle, up again, set to the next two couples, turn them round, set to ourselves with such a fling around, or as a change a double *pousette* to the – 'reel of Tulloch', 'Mrs. McLeod of Raasay', 'We'll gang nae mair to yon town'!, that was dancing for young people!

would cure all heartaches. By tacit consent, however much we danced together before, Campbell Riddell and I, the first dance after supper we always claimed each other as partners. 'The Devil amang the tailors', – three times down the middle and *pousette*! I wonder we had any soles left to our feet, let alone shoes and stockings. Now, here I am only happy when quiet, happiest quite alone in my own room, I believe. He is some years older than I am, he must be gray headed with the cares of that large unruly quarter of the world upon his once cheerful mind, and not, I am afraid, happily married. Such is life.

12. Good old Dempsey has had such a fall this morning, down the kitchen stairs; he is in pain and fetches his breath so uneasily that I have sent for Mr. Porter. Susan too is coughing away and looks wretched. The dear old Aunt is better, down at her whist again. My General rather croaky, still, holding on wonderfully through this most severe weather. Snow and frost are very seasonable at Christmas time though far from agreeable to elderly invalids. Arabella certainly *is* ill, more sluggish than ever, mind duller if possible, the love of stimulants of course encreasing. *She says* Dr. Stokes has ordered her two if not three glasses of port wine per day, as much bitter *ale* as she likes, and she likes a bottle, and if that don't do, a glass of brandy. She has not got to the brandy yet. Indeed she has – asked Janey for a glass about twelve to-day. Janey, however, substituted port wine. The doings at dinner resulted in a thoroughly stupifying sleep of three hours in the evening. One in the General's rocking chair, *in* the fire nearly, a chair she has quite appropriated. The other two on the sofa, packed up in shawls, a regular go to bed affair and there she lies, breathing heavily, grunting, groaning, most disagreeably. She really is an affliction and we shan't get rid of her for another ten days. Mr. Porter has taken poor Dempsey to the Meath Hospital, – compound fracture of two of his ribs.

14. Arabella is getting worse and worse – duller – more stupid, more selfish, more *sensual* than ever, and this brandy drinking is awful. Again yesterday she had her morning dram. Report says it is another love disappointment. Still, this business would be insufficient to account for the never

ending deep drawn sighs with which we are favoured during the hour she is awake after tea in the evening, nor for the extreme depression of her spirits generally. Love and brandy are both necessary to account for the melancholy state into which the poor creature is falling. I am certain those epileptick fits are at hand. The whole family would be so very much happier without her, I don't see either why I should interfere with her progress towards the travellour's bourne [*Hamlet* III i 79–80]! They would not be so ridiculous either, nor so illiberal. She is truly a monster grievance among them, and *us*. *Chambers'* has been remarkably interesting these last few weeks, good, healthy, improving articles, in the style of former times when the two brothers wrote for the ignorant, as they learned themselves. Leitch Ritchie spoiled it for a while.

15. Such happiness, a letter from Annie last night consenting to bring up the babies for Christmas. My General just as delighted as myself, pretending great annoyance. He came the more readily into the scheme as it will rid us of our wearisome guest. To see her pack herself up for her evening repose is, however, a bit of comedy. He was rocking by the fire and I was reading to him last night when she began; his amazement was charming. She quietly proceeded to examine into the condition of the window, opened the shutters, pulled down the blind, closed the shutters very carefully, then attacked the curtains, drew them closer, fastened them, removed very gently and very methodically all intervening chairs and tables, wheeling the sofa nearer the fire, collected more cushions from other parts of the room for her head, her shoulders and her back, then depositing her huge person on the soft bed, she enveloped herself in two warm shawls and almost instantly commenced grunting, snoring and breathing heavily. To all appearance she lay there dead asleep till tea time, but we know her tricks, so carefully avoided even a sign of our extreme amusement. The moment tea was ready, up she started as usual, advanced to the table, and before there was time to pour out a cup began to give her directions as to what suited her taste. The General would not have missed the scene for a game of billiards.

16. Edward McEvoy is returned for Meath by a majority of seven hundred. It was a mock election, not one gentleman even of his own faith voted for this *tenant right* and out and out radical member. He was brought in on the priests' shoulders, these reverend gentry driving their flocks to the poll, and keeping off all Mr. Merydith's supporters by every imaginable violence. There is to be a petition on account of such very evident intimidation. Mrs. O'Reilly is not comfortable in such a hot bed of bigotry. She says it is insupportable and that she must go home to breathe freely again.

20. Mr. Sheehan appeared last night! The first *visit* since last Christmas, though he has been in the passage with game or concert tickets or some other token of kindness fifty times. I was interrupted by the arrival of Mr. Porter to see Susan, who poor soul! acknowledged at last being too ill to do any work. The unfortunate temper of the poor creature broke out before him and instead of gratitude for his advice she burst out with an invective against me. It was a sad scene, poor thing, and determined me to dismiss her on the spot. Being Sunday she was to remain over the night, but do no work, indeed, one of her complaints, varicose veins in the right leg, would render any employment of her barbarous.

24. I have paid Susan, made her a present of a pound, found her very humble, so added some good advice which will be taken, and so forgave the poor creature. Her wretched health is almost an excuse for her. She will go to a sister in the country for a few weeks, lay up the leg, bind it, and then try either there or here to earn her bread as a needlewoman.

Christmas day. Everybody in church all day, or nearly so. James and Annie at Christ Church in the morning, Annie with them at St.Patrick's in the afternoon. The maids in turn once. A late dinner, plum pudding on fire! champaign, and Aunt Bourne the merriest of the party.

1856

Negotiations for the of the Crimean War are welcomed and another gleam of light comes when the enigmatic Dr. Robinson from Blessington, whose loans had helped the Smiths in several demanding financial situations, brokers a solution to the spendthrift James King's problems. Jane Gibson Craig and a family party from Edinburgh arrive for a holiday that includes a visit to Killarney, which later inspires a series of articles for *Chambers*'. A highlight of the summer is the marriage of a Milltown daughter in due splendour at Russborough House, in the presence of the Lord Lieutenant, Lord Carlisle. House-hunting takes her ménage to Hatch Street and she is promptly involved in further O'Reilly escapades. Jack's failure to pass the Woolwich examinations is another preoccupation but good news soon follows with his successful entry to Sandhurst. Tragedy strikes in the autumn with the loss of sight in one eye ('I must not journalise') but she manages to write a little each month and ends the year confidently as she proclaims that still to make out your family, friends and sunshine is not 'total blindness after all'.

Illustration: The Liffey from Usher's Quay

SUNDAY, JANUARY 13. My darlings gone; went on Thursday; Annie her maid and the babies in a covered car; James and the little maid by the van.

Annie has grown very handsome; the old most charming manner; just a little graver, poor soul, with all the cares of her struggling life. We must get him some employment, no matter what, so as it occupies his restless humour; he will do his work well so one need have no reserve in recommending him; the father *should* do this but they do nothing, neither he nor the mother.

To turn to a pleasanter subject: the Milltowns are out of all their difficulties. Russy has got quit of his odious Bride and Lord Milltown has paid his debts. The sale turned out so well that twenty three lots were withdrawn, leaving two thousand pounds a year and the house and demesne of Russborough. Her jointure is released – four thousand pounds a year – the plate redeemed and a little balance left in hands. My Lord promises to have eight thousand pounds settled on his daughters; his younger sons are already provided for, their mother having assured them a like sum by borrowing on annuity. The happiness of the whole party is thorough, and this gay winter for them: Russy, an Aide de Camp,* so many acquaintance in town: I don't suppose they any of them ever had such a true feel of enjoyment.

20. Sunday. The great news of the week is the peace. Mr. Sheehan came in with the telegraph message the moment he had received it though half doubting of its truth because of its coming from Vienna. Each day has however confirmed the report with modifications. At first Russia negatived the propositions, then accepted them provisionally, now unconditionally 'tis affirmed, but as a basis for conference, which of course may go on or go off as suits the convenience, or we should rather say, the resources of the negotiating powers.

We hear from what are considered authentick private sources that Russia is exhausted – no money – no men – enthusiasm dying away among the serfs and the nobles so unworthy in all respects as to be no stay to the nation; their luxurious habits provided for by a system of peculation on the publick. The young Empress too, a well educated Princess of Hesse, is all for peace and tries to persuade her husband to interpret the Will of the mad Czar more wisely. To extend the empire over *mind* not *matter*. Improve his subjects and let the boundaries of his enormous empire alone. It is a fearful war: must end in the ruin of Russia but at a great cost to the civilised countries of Europe.

Gaiety convulsing the town. I told Janey last year was to end hers so she was prepared for retirement and certainly bears it very sweetly. It is all the better for her in all ways; a ball now and then is excellent, but a ball every night! A series of town dissipation! out every night and all night going off when one should be going to bed! coming home when one should be thinking of getting up; the consequent lassitude of the following day, the idleness, frivolity, folly of such a life, to say nothing of the sin of it, for sin it is to destroy health and misuse time, all together the habit is the monster evil of our day. The pulpit, the mother, Charles Dickens should combine and in earnest to put such a misshapen idol down; we are only on the first step of the long flight by which we are to reach the temple of wisdom; better this generation is in some respects as compared with the last but, oh dear me, how senseless yet; and I do think this dear country and this very dear town gloom through the mist of ignorance with gigantick dimensions.

I was summoned by note to a private interview with Papa and Mama King. The old gentleman made me an apology for not having paid more attention to Annie whom without a doubt he thoroughly values; he could not have her without her husband and he positively dislikes his son whose rude, dictatorial, bullying manner he cannot abide. I know it well and do not wonder; but Oh how bitter is my grief that Annie – that splendid creature – should be thrown away on such a set. Even poor little Johnny, the old man don't take to because the baby is like his son: – 'He'll want good floggings, that fine fellow – I'd keep the chap in order.' Nicely I dare say – luckily he won't have the opportunity. Harry of course, being like his Mama is by far the prettiest, the finest looking of the two.

So little brains in any head able to hold itself up at all I never met, but the poor body has a good heart and would have been a different man differently mated; he married for money and he got it. She would never have improved under any circumstances yet she is not unpleasant. He is still in hopes through some of his influential relations of getting some small appointment for his son. We must all bestir ourselves, otherwise this idle life will have bad consequences; he is a dreadful worry too, to Annie; lounging about and interfering with everybody. Our cook and Dempsey have quarrelled. She is a stupid body and mischievous besides; *sober*, honest and economical. Really these ungovernable tempers are very troublesome and it's not the lower orders only.

21. We make our Sunday Evenings pleasanter now by my reading aloud whatever I have met with during the week likely to amuse. By sitting between the two deaf ears and speaking distinctly they hear very well. Last night we had the week's *Chambers'* and Dickens, both excellent, and though my Aunt especially don't always enter into the full meaning, she is set off upon some old tale of her own, to the point or from the point! as may happen and she gets so complacent with her recollections and he is so amused at the interminable supply of these reminiscences that it does as well as a good critique on the article. I should like to get Macaulay's two new volumes [three and four of the *History of England*] – eight years' more of English *phil.* history. One don't always agree with him but he is always most delightful. *Chambers'* had got very dull; some new writers have invigorated him mightily.

27. A fine Sunday; the talk of the week is the Peace. Whether Russia be in earnest or no who can tell? Whether this cordial acceptance of all the propositions is a basis for friendly negotiations, be but a means for gaining time or no, who can judge? An armistice is talked of during the conferences which will probably take place at Paris. In these improved times, fighting goes so against the grain with all rational intelligences that any hope of its ceasing is cordially welcomed, could we believe it would be durable, but being entered in and all the worst over, it would be better to go on and put an end at once and for ever to barbarian aggressions.

Preparations for the ensuing campaign continue vigorously and then we shall hear of the ruins of St. Petersburgh, the apprehension of which is what is so alarming the Russians.

We have had a week of thorough dissipation in Dublin, balls to no end, a *Levée* crowded beyond measure, two thousand at the Drawing-room. Russy's arm *paralysed*, his duty was to receive and present the cards with two little bows; his muscles, he says, will never recover. My Lady in spite of all this gaiety is not in good humour; there are no especial admirers and Henry de Robeck is married, a disappointment even to Cecilia who is certainly low about it.* Lord Cloncurry did his best to give her that stupid young man and how she lost him one cannot fancy, so clever she is; the want of gentleness, perhaps, and her grenadier style with other objections.

Odious weather till the last day or two. Mrs. Brooks without a spare hour! Janey singing like an artiste. My principal pleasure is that weekly singing lesson; twice a week we had it for a while till there was no time to spare, the good natured little woman giving one lesson for *love* or *vanity* perhaps as she is very proud of her pupil, her first pupil here, and I do therefore believe she is a little grateful too; Janey's fame is spreading so wide she may get vain too; I hope not. She is a dear good little thing, sits at home quite contented, is as merry as a light heart can make the young, never seeming to regret any of the gay doings we hear of. I wish I could give her more society, really good society; it is to be had even here, but how to reach at it I know not with such a house full of invalids, two of them so old, and one so odd, and money far from plenty, the income tax being heavy on small incomes.

SUNDAY, FEBRUARY 3. A little milder which to my ancient feelings is pleasant. Still the hope of Peace. Louis Napoleon finds war expenses beyond his means and having no Eastern possessions is content to keep the Russians out of the Mediterranean; his troops have won all the glories of the Campaign, sufficient laurels for the French to admire during the leisure of the next few years. Lord Palmerston pouts; he don't think we have done enough; we have 'scotched the snake not killed it' [*Macbeth* III ii 13], 'his voice is still for war', our extraordinary preparations being completed; our army drilled by sad experience and all men anxious to retrieve the reputation somewhat tarnished by the late events. Russia is done up; the Czar a quiet spirit, the Empress wife and Empress mother good enlightened women, viewing the legacy of that old Peter the madman as a curse on his country.

10. All going on here well; my Aunt and the General grown young. Our gay world taken up with an Opera Lady Downshire has set agoing, not to be acted but to be sung through at the Musick hall by all the Ladies and Gentlemen in Dublin who can be secured to aid a very worthy object, the revival of the Academy of Musick instituted for the instruction of such of the poorer classes as shew decided talent for any department of this enchanting art; and so fond are we all of exhibiting our perfections (real or imaginary) that her difficulty has been to *select* from the whirlwind of *offered* vocalists, and so modest is real merit that she has to take up with the worst going, the best having made no move, with one or two exceptions. Lady Milltown tells us the chorus will be very effective, great pains being taken with them; there are daily rehearsals, daily meetings of the Committee of Ladies which sits upon the pretensions of the claimants for tickets at ten shillings each and all this goes on at Lady Downshire's. She is to lead on the pianoforte herself, and a German living in the house to teach the children works up the Chorus. They are all as happy as possible – *busy*, the secret of happiness.*

Ogle Moore and Mr. Fitzgerald have been in town soft sawdering [flattering] us about their Church. One way or another they have made out fifteen hundred pounds for the enlargement of it; but they want to do away with the front seats in the gallery, let the organ stand free with a Hornidge pew on either side as supporters, and remove us downstairs. John Hornidge is furious, the General disinclined; we must see the plans and then think about it

Peace still the cry. It is now said that the Rothschilds insist on it; they will lend no more either to France or Russia, not liking the security, nor indeed sure of their interest from the latter magnificent power. Dickens has some admirable articles on the state of affairs and he has got some old soldier to write most powerfully on military affairs exposing so cleverly the rottenness of the system; contrasting so unfavourably with the perfection of the French management.

17. We had quite a treat on Friday! our first quartette concert, such pretty, old times musick. We met a great many friends. A good guinea's worth of pleasure for a little body well deserving of the indulgence, her [Janey's] life with us being sadly too stupid for a young person. The Society consists of a hundred and one members, meets every fortnight in the Upper room at the Musick Hall for musick and conversation, refreshed by tea and bread and butter.

We thought Mrs. O'Reilly was dying; extremely ill she was. Lady Milltown got me to go with her to see the poor woman, she was too nervous to go alone. She was better so I have brought her here where she is always happy, well cared too and gets the warmth and the nourishment necessary with no worry. Eyre is off somewhere on a speculation of employment, the Attorney business having been botched; indenture not properly made out.

Mr. Leeper took Janey and me all thro' the Kildare Place schools on Thursday, now called the Church Education, of which he has charge with a good salary and a free house. No pretension whatever, none of the magnificent formalities of Marlborough Street, no waste of money on fine buildings.* Good-sized airy school-rooms – plenty of clever teachers – every necessary requisite and a large Class of teachers in training; no appearance of cramming, no got up questions and answers. A fair attendance of very happy looking children of all ages receiving a very superiour education, so far more useful, more extended than that still persisted in with regard to those of the higher classes that if we don't look about us we shall all be pushed from our stools in another generation. I got a good many hints for my Gallery lessons.

24. Sunday. A headachy week so that my enjoyment of time can only be reckoned by moments. To make the matter better, I went to the Opera last night and am, as I deserve, suffering in consequence. It was very nicely got up indeed. A pretty little stage contrived in front of the Orchestra, pretty

scenery well managed, actors admirably dressed, perfect in their parts, and very few of them awkward. The chorus very good indeed, the ladies shining especially; in fact the failure was in the male voices. Sir Josiah Coghill, who was the King, has a good tenor voice which he can't the least manage, particularly as he used it in a baritone register.

Lady Downshire in a high morning gown presided at the pianoforte. My Lord was very busy for a while seating the company and then retired behind the scenes to his office of prompter. Lord Carlisle had a deal to do, bowing and kissing hands to every quarter, and one very good natural act characteristick of the man must not be forgotten; he sent away his high-backed ornamental chair as it certainly did obstruct the view of the back benches, and took an ordinary cane bottom, till some of the Stewards brought him a seat with a cushion on it. Edward Leeson spoke the prologue well; Lord Carlisle suppressed some lines, added others, to the extreme indignation and mortification and real downright *vain* anger of the Authoress. We have seen her almost daily, first during the composition of her verses, then in the height of her displeasure at their being meddled with.*

Also on account of poor Mrs. O'Reilly with whom she is very angry and yet don't quite give her up. Mr. Porter is most kindly attending her without the fee she could not afford to give, and we hope in a little while to see her better. But indeed they are very queer, no two of them in a story. Eyre, we were told, was in the country recruiting his health; he called here yesterday on his way to Liverpool with a friend to attend the races there where he expects to make some money, a couple of hundred pounds or so, as he has several *bets* on horses sure to win. He has left his mother for good, does not intend domiciling with her again; he also wishes her to leave her present house and take one at Booterstown to be near the sea. We think him mad, he looks very ill.

Mr. Sadleir, the M.P., a radical and a Roman Catholick, has killed himself with prussick acid; ruined; owed a million of money; had forged, sold shares fraudulently, done half the world, including widows and orphans whose *all* was entrusted to him. Just as bad as Paul Strachan, Bates and Co.

By the bye they are all working at trades in the felons' cells dressed as convicts.*

SUNDAY MARCH 10. Janey has a cold from sitting at an open window after dancing at the Gledstanes and then going in a *shawl only* this bitter weather to drink tea with Lady Milltown. To these two entertainments I accompanied her. I was wanted for dinner at the Gledstanes as they had been disappointed of some matronly guests; at the tea party I was to act musick, a set of young ones being in a very dancing mood. We were all in a very high sphere. Marquis and Marchioness of Headfort, Earl of Granard, Lord Kilmaine and Miss Browne, with other distinguisheds – guardsmen, dragoons etc. I had a great deal of pleasant conversation with Lady Headfort, a plain, kind, unaffected woman. When Lady McNaughton she knew all my people – father, mother, brothers, sisters and liked them all, as indeed she would like everybody. John was in her husband's office for some time and very much thought of. After Sir William's murder she came home, very rich, loaded with jewels and after a while bestowed herself on Lord Headfort who seems to make her very happy. The first publick appearance she made as a peeress she wore *all* her diamonds. A sight and a half – how she bore the weight of them was a marvel. She soon learned better and being really unaffectedly good natured is much liked. Lord and Lady Bective are very fond of her. That father and son have patched their ragged elbows wonderfully well. Lady Headfort has four thousand pounds a year; Lady Bective, Miss Thompson, a merchant's daughter, bought back the whole of the Headfort estates and had them settled by the wisdom of her father on her children. She was called worth two hundred thousand pounds and a very well educated amiable woman.* If poor Russy could meet with such; if he could make out Miss Palmer and give the brother to Barby. It was all moonshine that she told me. The property is partly sold. All that the English creditors wanted some ninety thousand pounds, the rest was bought in, thirty thousand pounds still owing on it; her jointure *not* relieved, income not improved a bit. Plate all gone, they borrowed ours for their little dinner t'other day. They are to stay in town another month.

11. Good Lady Milltown is here every day to see Mrs. O'Reilly who got a sad throw back from which she is only just recovering. We had her so well before; she is in a poor way, not likely to keep right when at home and home she must go some time. She requires too an amount of expensive nourishment that she will not give herself, and then difficulties are all round her – disappointments, vexations and grief that will never die, poor woman.

It is dawning on Lady Milltown that her position is little affected by this sale; no lovers appear for those very nice daughters, no heiress for the sons, and like her sister she is an idler, mistaking fussiness for employment. Dublin suits her exactly; suits them all, though the girls rave of London; their success in the third rate circle Mrs. Hatton introduced them to and where they might perhaps have found a long purse that would have liked to be attached to a title. Life, real life, is more romantick than a novel.

That wretched man [Sadleir] was a low Attorney at Cork; clever, 'cute, thoroughly unprincipled. An agitator, the priests brought him into parliament and for some dirty work he did for the Government the good Aberdeen made him a Lord of Treasury. Here was a *pied à terre* for the Irish gambler. The ruin caused by his miserable career is wider spread than is conceivable. Families mortgaged their whole fortunes on his fabulous lands. Shares in various enterprises existing but in his honied words were bought by the savings of countless hard workers; and worse – the poor, the widow, the orphan poured their mites into his Tipperary Bank, the vile paper of which is all that is left them for food and clothing. He and his brothers have failed for a million of money. It is beyond Paul and Strahan; the Sadleirs surrendered trust deeds too, and forged besides, this John did, forged the conveyances of the Commissioners of the Incumbered Estates on which his dupes would lend him money – so well done too that the signatures would have been sworn to by the men themselves. I don't like the style of the age; sensual, false, mean – better almost drink with the dirk like my Ancestors.

13. Lords Lucan and Cardigan are writing most ridiculous letters to the *Times*. All engaged in the war would appear

to have been to blame in every possible way; such carelessness, malversation,* jobbery, insolence, actual neglect and
folly never was exhibited so fully before the world; and the
Mercantile profession, emulating the misdeeds of the poli-
ticals, supplied unsound arms, filthy provisions, false
weights etc., and carried on a brisk trade underhand in
the furnishings of war with our enemies. There's many a
screw loose all through society.

20. Ellen Foster, foolish, ill-managing creature, instead of
going to her father when invited in his first gush of feeling
for her various distresses, waited for the promised remittance from her husband in order to take a little money home
and put some decent clothing on herself and children. The
Paymaster's office is slow in its proceedings; the three
pounds lodged by Serjeant Foster on the twentieth February
at Malta has not reached the poor soldier's wife yet. Neither
have two former remittances sent by him in January, half a
sovereign each time. He is surprised at her never acknowledging these letters, for he has never heard from her but
once though she has written regularly. She has been existing
with her two children on the allowance from the subscription fund given as a help to the families of the Crimean
Army – three shillings a week paid once a fortnight.

In her distress she wrote to Mr. Ritchie, the Secretary to
the fund, who gave her a letter to the Chaplain here, the
Reverend Mr. Halpin, requesting him to advance her a small
sum. She went out to Raheny where this young clergyman
lives but could not obtain an interview; she gave him Mr.
Ritchie's letter when he came in on the next Sunday to do
duty but he has not replied so she starved; she tried to work
for a slop shop, fivepence a piece for making shirts; had
finished a dozen and fell sick; days in bed, a neighbour's
daughter attending her, for Godsake. Ill, the children fam-
ishing, one by one she pawned the shirts.

We, sitting in our pretty drawing-room with fire and
lamp and tea-table and every luxury around us, may, nay
must, lecture the poor shrinking creature standing beside us,
her poor head bowed with shame, her strength and spirit
gone, telling of her evil deed to the only friend she has in this
wide city. She had lived with her two children for three days

on a pound of meal before she could resolve to break her trust. Out of these trials she must be sent down to her father's all ragged and wretched as she is. She shall go as soon as ever her three pounds come. She must repay me for redeeming the shirts even should I give her the six shillings again. She was to get five shillings for making them, on taking them home. I gave her one shilling for present use. On Saturday she will get her fortnightly six shillings and we will hope before another week the remittance through the Paymaster may come. As for the half-sovereigns, I fear we shall hear no more of them. The General got very slight help from Colonel Greaves at his Office. He was very kind, but there are such thousands of such like cases and all is so tricky, so jobby, so dilatory, so red-tapy everywhere that till some very radical reforms are insisted on by John Bull, should he ever awake sufficiently to enforce them, we must sit content under a load of misery. I will look after this poor creature, too sickly and too silly to be capable of managing herself. Mr. Halpin is much to blame; he might speak kindly to [her at] any rate should he be unable to do more.

22. So now for King affairs. James has to borrow thirty pounds more from his old friend in difficulties, Corbet the money lender. The cows not being in calf, no young cattle reared, no pigs to turn the waste of the kitchen, the dairy and the garden to profit, he hits on a scheme worthy of his antecedents; he goes to his father to beg of him for the future to pay his allowance quarterly, and begin by paying *him* fifty pounds, now. 'Luckily', as Marmontel said before me, the Doctor got scent of this pretty little speculation in the Sadleir style and 'luckily' old Mr. King had taken the resolution never to act in any way in his son's affairs without consulting me; so it was no go. So the Doctor and I had to consult.

I have bought the carriage for fifty pounds including the harness, as that relieves the stableman of most of his work and will give him those long hours of polishing etc., to employ in the garden. The Doctor lends me the fifty pounds and I shall advertise the pretty phaeton next month and probably sell it for as much as will repay him. That part being settled we find there is enough hay on hands to pay the thirty pounds. James was keeping it over in the hope of buying stock to eat it –

Sadleir fashion – a spec. with borrowed money. Summer coming on too when there is young grass for cattle. And to put him in heart he is to have forty five pounds every year cash in hand to avoid the risk of an empty pocket. Twenty two pounds, ten shillings poor Annie is to make over to him each half year; he is to pay his Club, give her all she wants from dairy and garden and the use of the car occasionally; and she is left with a hundred and forty pounds: seventy pounds half yearly to pay the house servants' wages and to keep the house. He has besides five or six pounds from us, the rent of Rathbally not coming up to Annie's annuity, and we not charging them with income tax. And she has her little private pin-money which now that she has two children, her God-father and her mother mean to encrease.

30. We have had very gay doings in our burlesque of a court. Annie, Marchioness of Stafford, is here just now with the Duchess of Sutherland, the Grosvenors, etc. All very fine and all very gay, made immensely of, at and by the Castle, to the intense disgust of the nobles of the Land!* Poor dear Lady Milltown is so furious at being overshadowed that she has been *acting* most absurdly; her foolish talking is of less consequence, those most concerned don't hear it; but to fight all precedency, to quarrel with the Chamberlain, refuse to leave a mistaken place, or to be introduced to her betters, who besides are visitors! All this is so underbred. One is really ashamed of such manners in a gentlewoman. She has been so long a triton [mythical, semi-human sea-monster] among the minnows that when more tritons come she can't abide them, and she is but a Brummagem triton after all. An Irish peerage, no British in it.

Luckily I was in my Aunt's room so was saved most of her folly. I only heard from her that these English importations were ugly, vulgar, ill-dressed yet so worshipped that no one beside them was noticed. A bad ball; she did not go to the play, neither would she go to the Oratorio; they had spoiled Dublin, bad enough at the best. Further details were given us by Mrs. O'Reilly most amusingly with witty comments worthy of the subject. Foolish Lady Milltown; this was an opportunity to have introduced her daughters to these good-natured people who might have noticed them in

London where she so longs to place them in their 'proper sphere'. Not one dinner or evening party were any one of them invited to during the stay of our distinguished strangers! She is mortified beyond expression; her girls quite annoyed, not so much at losing these attentions, but at the figure their mother cut. She is in their way at every turn; she who would lay down her life for them.

SUNDAY, APRIL 6. Jack is well, dear good boy; in despair though about the peace; they say, however, that we are to keep up our war establishment both by sea and land so that he will have plenty of work without the danger. The Peace is very unpopular. We have had very little voice in it. The French Emperor managing all the affairs of all the world. He could not continue so expensive a war and Russia being done up and sufficiently humbled and content to receive terms from the Allies, no cause of war remains. We shall see in a fortnight more on what conditions we have sheathed the sword. Anything for peace say I. I am sure I hope this is the last war our enlightening world will be cursed with.

18. Politicks very queer; the ministry four times in minority; a hundred and odd against them one night, and on the Maynooth question twenty six, so the first reading of the Bill for the abolition of that abomination is carried; so entirely has publick opinion altered. It should either have been on a very superiour scale or not at all; the cheapness of the mock education carried on there encourages the very lowest of the low to 'priest' a son; the evil feelings this vulgar being enters the college with are fostered by ill paid teachers very little beyond their pupils as to useful knowledge but deep dyed bigots; and so we are overrun with the very worst specimens of the worst of superstitions. It was a safer religion when gentlemen's sons were fitted for the priesthood on the continent; that class of men had a stake in the country besides inheriting good dispositions; these wretched poor creatures have no rallying point, they are traitors bred, at war with all that is kindly. The upper classes are certainly by degrees shoving them aside, but they are all powerful yet with those of their own degree.

20. I have another letter from Major Mair; he is fond of writing. Jack is very hard at work, making up for lost time; his illness

and a fit of idleness before it threw him back; the idleness was half caused by the illness in preparation and half by his constitutional Irish faintheartedness, he wants my 'try again'; like his father he gives all up should the least little bit go wrong. Altogether the boy's mind was unstrung. I hope he is all right again; with an aim in view he will throw his whole energies into the pursuit of it. He really must rouse out of that sort of despondency, or rather devil may care be done with it, common to all his countrymen, if a straw cross the path of the ball they are kicking. The peace may be more lasting than we suppose. Russia in earnest, the Czar has given all his subjects leave to travel, to educate their sons in the different Universities of Europe. He is inaugurating agricultural societies, relaxing the mercantile code etc.

SUNDAY, MAY 4. Here's a chasm, a whole fortnight, no less. So much has happened, a novel might be written out of the events of this fortnight. On Wednesday the 23rd of April, Jane arrived, escorted by William and accompanied by Margaret and Joanna [Craig]. During the two days they spent here, William shewed them as much of the city as could be viewed in their rather short mornings. They slept and breakfasted at the Shelburne, then wandered about with him, lunched here, started again and dined here at six. They are quite as agreeable as in their youth though much changed in looks. Margaret, who was very plain, is now a comely matronly woman, Joanna, once a beauty, is now a wreck, not even a remains of former good looks. The warm Scotch heart is in both, and the honest, clear judgement of my countrymen. It invigorates one's mind to meet again with such good sense and no frivolity.

Very early yesterday morning, soon after seven o'clock [my Aunt's] little maid Mary who had been groaning all night asked leave to go out for a *Seidlitz*,* feeling so much pain from wind. Leave was of course granted, although *Seidlitz* was an improper medicine where there was any symptom of cholick and rhubarb was advised instead, it never occurring to my Aunt to send Mary up to me, I always having a stock of common medicines at hand, and Mary herself taking good care not to come near me. Anne took up my Aunt's breakfast, nine o'clock came, Anne emptied the slops, ten o'clock, Anne tidied the room and Jane dressed the sick lady. Mary never returned. All at once it flashed across me that she never meant to return, that she was gone to the Lying Inn Hospital! But I was wrong. She could not get so far, she had to stop her car at Mrs. Daly's poor lodging and there in an hour or two she gave birth to a son! Really my astonishing blindness, both in her case and in Susan's, would be incredible to a quicker eye. I noticed the girl's strange shape, and, more than once, to herself. She said she never wore stays, she has a high shoulder and a high hip, padded the other side, had a short waist, etc. And I, delicate about annoying a modest young creature, was content. Her going to a stranger like Mrs. Daly was indefensible except from her agonies. She has no money, few clothes, no preparations for her baby. She says she is married. Why then have denied this before, taken pains indeed to pass for a maiden. Poor thing, she did her duty here, fully. She is a great loss for she could do everything and so willingly. I have engaged Mrs. Daly for the present, letting her home in the middle of the day, and we are so many now, able and anxious to wait on her, that my Aunt is put to no personal inconvenience by this unfortunate business.

11. Annie is happy with the hope of employment for her husband. He is to horse the mail coach between Dublin and Blesington by the advice of the Doctor, who advances the funds! and Mr. Owen, Ogle Moore and Richard Hornidge. It may answer and I truly hope it will. I am not myself sanguine for nothing ever yet has answered that James King has tried. He don't seem to have the knack of managing anything; this does, however, seem to be a suitable employment, and as the post office pays handsomely for carrying the mails, he may save himself. All I care for, he will leave Annie in quiet. He was very hoity toity with me about not being dictated to and so on, but had to be quiet, plague that he is.

Lady Cecilia Leeson is going to marry with a prospect of money, but with a scanty present supply. Captain Turton of the third Dragoon Guards, heir of entail to four or five thousand a year, is to sell out, and with that commission sum and three hundred a year allowed by the trustees of his father's large encumbered estates and one hundred pounds promised by Lord Milltown annually to her, they are to live on a farm in Yorkshire. He is not good-looking, he is not clever, he is gentlemanly and amiable, though eccentrick. She likes him, managed the whole business herself, nobody knowing of the intimacy till the lover wrote to my Lord, and all concerned are pleased. It is indeed a Godsend. She has only accepted him conditionally, they wait for the consent of the parents, now abroad. Russy's deserted is to be married to Lord Granard, so this happy affair comes in good time to raise the drooping spirits of my poor Lady.

A deal of talking and writing concerning this new scheme of James King's, the Doctor having been frequently with me arranging about it and above all the discovery of the Murderer of the boy Flood at Pat Farrell's gate at Baltiboys twenty years ago! What a noise the matter made at the time, immense rewards offered to an approver [informer], arrests made of all but the right man. And now after this interval an angry woman betrays the well kept secret. Lame George Quin fired the shot, every tenant in Baltiboys consenting, with two or three honourable exceptions. Phil Tyrrell was not in the conspiracy, nor Tom nor John Kelly. Whether they knew of it before or after we cannot say, but they were no movers in this foul murder. Pat Ryan was not mentioned either by name. The woman said 'twas no hidden mystery, all on the land knew of it and why 'twas done, but Jack Byrne and his father, Tom Keogh, lame James Quin, red Pat Quin and Dempsey were art and part in it. Jack Byrne slept in the bed with George Quin the murderer the night of the murder and asked how in the world he could mistake the boy Flood for Pat Farrell. So says Jack Byrne's *sister*, then a girl of twelve years of age, who slept in the same room as these wretches. She gave her testimony very quietly to John Hornidge, and Mr. Little here in our dining-room, no appearance of any incorrectness in her plain tale nor any concealment of her motive for accusing them, which was her brother's most unjust treatment of herself. If we can follow up her evidence, we shall rid the country of a set of villains.*

18. Maria Delaney, in an extasy of happiness, is installed in unhappy little Mary's place. There is no husband, this is a second child, and Irish-like all her discharges were excellent. James King is up and down about his coach, it really starts tomorrow, [sister Jane] and I in it! We are to sleep at Rathbally and return the next day in *my* phaeton which I really see no other way of getting hold of, so many excuses are sent me instead of it. Hutton, the maker, has promised to try and sell it, he will keep it a month without charge, and hopes to get sixty pounds for it. James is trying to keep back the harness but I must have all, being insatiable.

James Craig nearly ready to come for his wife, who is getting quite fat. Good kind creature, she takes Janey back with her, relieving me of infinite trouble. We three old invalids shall get along remarkably well through the summer when left quietly alone. I have almost grown out of acquaintance with everyone, Nurse tending and visiting being rather antagonistick. We have heard no more of our little business, I much fear it being followed up properly. I will remember the ill names at any rate, so will John Hornidge, and we can seize on fit occasions to get rid of the crew – quietly.

SUNDAY, JUNE 1. Monday Jane and I waited a full half hour for our coach, three outside passengers besides hangers on, no one but ourselves inside. A very comfortable coach, excellent coachman, good horses though out of condition. Kept our time well. All the well-known roads with so many familiar faces everywhere suggesting many an old memory to me. The Rathbally car met us at the head of the lane. Annie was so happy to see her Aunt, the Aunt seemed equally happy to see Annie and, like every one else who looks on those little beauties, she at once fell in love with the babies. Jane and I slept in what will be the nursery, the large room at the back of the house and chattering away at night from our several corners, we recalled the old barrack room and then other old subjects and lived over again the years of the past before she approved the present, – dear little Annie's neatness and taste and economy and propriety, and her peculiar attractiveness. James too, poor, foolish James, shines in his own house, he is so hospitable as well as orderly.

James Craig had arrived after a good passage, the only objection to his presence was his carrying off his wife to the Hibernian Hotel, where Janey had secured them rooms. We could not have put them up comfortably here but with his servant and his habits and his ways, he is happier in apartments quite his own. The remainder of the week he was busy all the mornings poking about the town into odd book shops and the College Library and other places. She went shopping, having made up her mind to a grand disbursement for her toilette. In the evenings we dined here and played whist, except one night that the dinner was at the Hibernian, the General and I attending it. James King in town about his coach, dined with us and played my cards! I was never in Mrs. Russell's most splendid warerooms till I went there with Jane. Certainly the display was sumptuous, style and taste equally first rate and prices to match.

Saturday morning Jane and her husband and I set out at noon for Killarney. Travelling by railroad is so very nearly like sitting at home at ease that incidents by the way side no one now looks for, and the run is so rapid that all the scenery, except about the station, escapes one. In this, on this occasion, we had no loss for a more dreary journey there could hardly be. A long tract of flat bare fields, or heath, or dreadful bogs, with two or three spots more civilised. One little bit of beauty and one chain of hills. The bit of beauty was at Mallow, the spots were Milltown, Port Arlington, Maryborough and Thurles. My companions were extremely interested in the eating line, always arranging, like my brother John, about the Prog. So we got gingerbread nuts at Maryborough, an excellent luncheon at the Limerick Junction, very good tea at Mallow, and so kept up the fire that we could take nothing but a drink at bedtime Killarney, – negus for two, and a brandy punch for me! The darkness had covered the earth before we left the train. We could only see some cloudlike mountains looming in the far distance dimly, and feel that we rattled through a good large town before emerging into the deeper shade of trees bordering up and down road a mile long or so. Then a lodge gate was thrown open, a pretty shrubbery appeared, the pale

light fell on a broad sheet of water and we stopt at the door
of the Victoria hotel.

Sunday morning, this day week, revealed to us all the
beauty of the situation. The Inn, a long low building, is
seated on a lawn sloping to the edge of the large Lower
Lake. The 'wide expanse' is filled with wooded islands,
surrounded by most picturesquely shaped mountains,
clothed nearly to their summits and just in front is a little
fleet of boats for the use of visitors, safely moored in a small
harbour. We could none of us leave the windows, except for
breakfast! too powerful an attraction t'other way. We
decided on a drive in an open phaeton and pair, which took
us through Lord Kenmare's most beautiful demesne, an
undulating lawn, covered with grand wooding and kept in
such order, skirting the lake all the way to Ross castle, round
that little dressed up island, on to Muckross, Mr. Herbert's
property, and so by the back of his demesne to the Tork
Waterfall up to which we had to climb by a path along the
edge of the torrent through a narrow ravine dark with
wooding, the far side a perpendicular rock hid by the rich
skreen of forest growing on the face of it. We returned
through the demesne of Muckross and by the back of
Kenmare passing innumerable villas, to the town of Killarney, and so home. It was a sunny day, the scenery looked
its best, so did the population. The town was crowded as on
a fair day, all the roads alive, a sort of holiday look over all.

Mr. Herbert is married to a daughter of the late Mr.
Balfour of Whittingham, who was married to Lady Eleanor
Maitland,* a bride won for him by a string of pearls added to
gold chains and rupees. The daughter was supposed to have
mated herself as richly, but Mr. Herbert has built a house,
Burns the architect, Elizabethan style, handsome but florid
and very large, twenty thousand pounds sunk, and his affairs
permanently embarrassed by that and other costly improvements. He is much liked, she is a pleasantly spoken lady and
seems content with the place. Lord Kenmare, an elderly
widower has just succeeded his brother, whose wife it was
laid out his grounds, dressed up his shrubberies, preserved
his ruins, her whole heart was in her work. She has never
seen the Paradise she created since her widowhood. As for

describing such scenes, 'tis out of the question, I am only recalling them, the impression they made is not likely to fade.

We were out nearly five hours, returned to a hot luncheon after which came on heavy rain, so we read, wrote, and chattered, arranging plans for the morrow, dined late, and retired early. Monday, clouds on the hills and a ripple on the lake rather prepared us for disappointment. A heavy shower brought further fears; however, matters brightened up above, and we set out for the gap of Dunloe, the opposite direction from the drive of yesterday. Different style of beauty but always beauty. One or two fine places, a clear stream, wood and mountains; Dunloe charming situation, the Gap very wild, a rugged highland pass through rocks, the brown water leaping over a stony channel where the passage is narrow, and filling it as a lake when wider – gloomy looking tarns that fish can hardly live in. The whole is an ascent of some seven miles; the last four we ladies had to ride, I concealing my feelings! and so sure-footed was my pony, so easy, so docile, I began in a few minutes to enjoy the ride, and Jane recurring to our Rothiemurchus scampers when we feared nothing and cared all and lived our gay summer days in our saddles, old veins began to glow with the fire of youth and we two old ladies trotted on as merrily as when I looked forward to twenty years instead of sixty.

Looking back from the summit of the pass was curious, a long bleak gallery with a bright peep into day light at the far end of it. The descent was fine in a different way, – a broad shoulder of the mountain down which the path zigzagged leading to a valley named the dark valley at the upper end where it is narrow, just a cut out of the hills, expanding by degrees into a wide plain dotted with trees for two or three miles before it meets the upper Lake. Here in a creek we found our four oared boat which soon conveyed us to one of near a thousand islands, where we spread our good luncheon on a stone sheltered by arbutus, cooling our porter in the lake. Between the Upper and Middle Lake is a river five miles long, the feature of the district, with its rich banks, its grand rocks, its deep bed and rapid flow, and every here and there a one arch bridge thrown between two nearing points making communication by land scarce less easy than by water. Many pretty cottages are on the banks, or among the islands, and the ruin of an Abbey on Innesfallon, where, though weary, we landed, walked round the fifteen acres! and then rowed home. Between five and six we landed. A brilliant day, only one shower throughout the course of it, and that was in the Gap where we had the shelter of a rock. Tuesday, with regret, we left Killarney and that most comfortable as well as beautifully situated Victoria Hotel.

To complete the good luck attending us, James Craig had a mob to amuse him. At the station were hundreds of the peasantry, a few emigrants setting off for America amid shoals of despairing friends. Such sobbing, shouting, howling, could only be heard in Ireland. One old woman, tired of it, and rising up from her seat in a third class carriage, she made a speech against such demonstrations thereby renewing the clamour. One or two silent mourners did look despair. At the Limerick junction we came across another mob – Tipperary gentlemen bound for some races, young and old and middle-aged of all classes. A stream of them too crowded for the refreshment room or even the platform and this a poor country! said the Edinburgh W.S. [Writer to Her Majesty's Signet]. A little further on a file of soldiers under arms marched up a poor ragged deserter. They don't shoot them now, but I am afraid they flog, except there be a truly wise commanding officer. Poor lad! I could not get his pale face out of my mind for days. James Gibson Craig, his man and his luggage went straight to their hotel, Jane and I and my carpet bag came on here, found all well, so glad to have us back. She went on to dine with her husband while I had cold meat, having, in fact, dined on most excellent sandwiches and porter at the junction at two o'clock. All met at tea, whist as usual finishing the evening. I am really glad they insisted on taking me to Killarney; besides the pleasure, the change will really strengthen me up for months to come.

2. On returning home I found all my repositories filled with Mrs. Gibson Craig's finery. Her gown from Mrs. Russell cost seven guineas, made up with blue lace and ribbon very handsomely, four guineas more, a valuable dress. A plainer, made by Miss Knapps equally well to my mind at a cost

altogether of two pounds six shillings, not silk however, but a silk dress at four guineas is to be given to her to send afterwards, which she will make for one pound well. Four, nay five, caps adorn my apartments, all pretty, and so cheap that Jane was induced to stock herself amply. I had Mrs. O'Reilly to dine with us on Wednesday. I sent for her or she might never have come though wishing it. She has evidently been in distress about Eyre, who has gone to an Uncle in the country to recover from an attack of nerves and is employed there with a hatchet and saw, thinning plantations. Janey has always thought him mad, he certainly does not seem sane.

At five in the afternoon the Edinburgh party left us. James King came to tea, played Dumby whist good-naturedly, and Saturday evening he called again. He has always to come up on Friday, it is settling day, and something had evidently gone wrong for he was quite out of sorts, cast down, in fact, and complaining bitterly of his partner. So soon to fail! there's something wrong somewhere. I was busy Friday morning with John Hornidge, our year's accounts we always settle in full in May. He has the little balance as usual but I shall not be able to buy stock with it this time. Jack may take all we have. After an early dinner came the separation, James Craig, Jane and Janey off in a car to the steamer and so ends this bit of happiness. It has been a great pleasure having her here so long, and 'tis a true boon her taking my dear good little Janey away from this hospital of a house. Wretched life this for a young, not over strong girl.

3. A long sensible letter from Major Mair. Jack is well, looking well and happy. He is behind in mathematicks, I therefore doubt these six weeks, work as he will, sufficing to prepare him sufficiently. He is quite up in Latin and French, more advanced than they expect or require in what they call general literature, but to the mathematicks I know they principally look for the Artillery. He shall not go up to fail. He has shewn the hereditary weakness, naughty Jack, gave up all work when first disappointed and now rather than work some months more, would throw his dear Artillery overboard and be content with an Ensigncy in the foot.

8. So here we are again. Another week gone. Janey quite happy in Edinburgh, already they think her looking stronger. Lady

Milltown and the girls are preparing the *trousseau*. Every-thing goes brightly, kind letters, friendly help, and the young man really desirable. An excellent marriage in all respects. Ceely is to have three hundred pounds for her wedding clothes. Two hundred she is spending here in linen and other necessaries and a few gowns, etc. The other hundred pounds she keeps for Paris whither she and Captain Turton proceed immediately after the marriage on their way to Coblentz, where his father and mother are at present, by whom the young couple have been most kindly invited. They have had the small furnished house of a cousin offered to them at a low rent, and a brougham into the bargain, close to the property in Yorkshire which will hereafter be their home. Lady Milltown gives them a jaunting car, Mr. Turton supplies them amply with plate and linen. Thus as they are both of them moderate they will get on very well with their small income of seven hundred a year. He must inherit eight thousand in the end and there are mines quite ascertained to be valuable although never yet worked which might raise him to a Beaumont fortune. They are all so happy, boys and all, and Lady Downshire has asked Barby to spend a couple of months with her in England as soon as the wedding is over. So it is quite sunshine in that atmosphere.

I have had a very satisfactory letter from Jack; he is working and he will work, he is behind only in mathematicks, alas, the one thing needful. He doubts his being able to pass, – above two hundred candidates and but thirty vacancies, and a phalanx going up from Trinity College, Dublin! Jane has sent my Aunt the *Memoirs* of Lord Cockburn, written by himself. A mere gossippy recollection of old times, but she was very much interested in it and liked the fine large type. The General has been suffering from indigestion, salmon, cheese and fifty other enormities tell in the end.

29. The last entry likely to be made in June, for writing time during the week is scarce and there are many letters, necessary business letters, which take the little time there is. Two invalids requiring incessant care, a watchfulness that must not slumber, besides an ever readiness to amuse them, leaves little space for private occupations, particularly now

that we have mere machines for servants; good creatures, willing enough, but more utterly without head than it is possible to suppose human beings could be. The fact is, I take it, the want is heart; none of them have any principle of duty, wish to do it or knowledge of it or wish to learn it. They are in service because they can't live out of it, they are quite content just to live in it, without the wish to improve themselves or their condition or the very slightest interest in their employment. They are passing the time – a little fun, a little gossip, a new bit of dress and plenty to eat, that satisfies the women, the men substitute drink for dress and then they are content, and with these tools we've to get along the best we can, happy to find no graver fault among them.

Our Janey seems to be thoroughly happy in Edinburgh among so many kind friends. She met Lord and Lady Tweeddale t'other day at Riccarton. Lady Tweeddale told her she first met me in /15!! True enough, and how very handsome she herself was then in her girlish dress at Kinrara, holding out her white arms for the poodle to jump through, all unconscious of the admiring eyes that wandered from the dog to his most fair assistant. Lord Tweeddale was very amusingly in love. A love that could not be returned, but she married him very willingly, too well brought up to demur! and she has been extremely happy.*

Ellen Foster came to take leave. She sails tomorrow for Liverpool. On Thursday for Malta. Mrs. Moore sent her one pound, I gave her another to take her clothes out of pawn and support her till she gets on board her transport, poor soul. Her husband has used her very badly – soldier like, and may be he would as soon be spared her return to him, but he must be made to support her.

SUNDAY, JULY 13. Such a busy week. Well, let me see what we have done in it. No letter from Jack on Monday nor from anyone else. We started therefore in the glums and the rain at one o'clock in a very comfortable Brougham. It cleared occasionally, giving the General glimpses of all the well remembered spots he has been so long estranged from, – fox covers and waiting places on hunt days etc. were pointed out for ever. At Blesington we drove to the Doctor's, found him, Ogle Moore and Mr. Fitzgerald and had a long merry gossip to the chime of the bells, for the ringers were practising against the approach of the Lord Lieutenant, reinforced by three from Christ Church. We went round the hill. Hal utterly amazed at the growth of his plantation. Indeed our country looked very beautiful, our own dear home the prettiest bit in it.

Annie was on the look out as I had written to her by her husband's coach in the morning. She and James and the babies were all in waiting for the old people. She had put every nice bit of furniture she possessed into the room we were to occupy. The General had carpet, sofa, easy chair, toilet, chest of drawers all as he has here and even *he* could make no annoyance for himself in any way, ingenious as he is in imagining everything always wrong. We had to wait an hour for dinner, the cook having selected this day of all days to get dead drunk. She was incapable of moving and had to be put to bed, furnishing us with a topick of conversation for the evening which, however, we ended with Dumby. Tuesday we were early astir. The parlour maid had to help in the kitchen, one nursery maid in the Laundry, I in the nursery, Annie to superintend all and deck up our toilettes besides. The drunken cook we sent away.

It was a thoroughly beautiful day, bright, warm and with a cooling breeze that quite revived the air. The whole of that fine palace [of Russborough] was thrown open. Every room filled with splendidly dressed people, a military band on the lawn, the Corridors crowded with respectable spectators, the country people in a group on the gravel. The ceremony had been performed early in the musick room, by Ogle Moore, admirably. Lord Milltown so affected he trembled violently when it came to giving his daughter away. Lady Milltown was like a corpse, so was Barby, the young men all pale as ghosts. The Bride perfectly self-possessed, her usual colour, her usual clear full voice, her eye much brighter. I never saw her look so well, all that quantity of lace softened her complexion. The company consisted of all the neighbours, the relations, the Lord Lieutenant and suite, some officers of the Bridegroom's regiment and his sister and her husband. About one hundred and fifty persons altogether. The breakfast was in the great saloon, three tables all the whole length of the room. A sumptuous collation and quantities of excellent wine – Hock, Sauterne, Claret, Champaign etc. The Lord Lieutenant took in the Bride, the Bridegroom followed with Lady Milltown who left him by the side of the Bride and seated herself opposite with Ogle Moore. Everybody else went as they could fall in. Annie had the arm of her cousin, David Charles Latouche, I only of Jos. McEvoy for I had been in a corner with the bride, *seated* on account of my toe, and so was overlooked in common with a cluster of desolates of more account than myself.

The Doctor met me and marshalled us to a very good position amid many old friends, indeed we knew almost every one in the room and it was very pleasant meeting so many well remembered faces. The speeches were quite above par. The Lord Lieutenant made three, he gave the health of the newly married pair, returned thanks for his own, and gave the host and hostess. Lord Milltown spoke thrice also, and remarkably well. Captain Turton once and surprised me. Good sense, good feeling and fun. I was far from expecting to find him really very likeable; – a tall, dark, very gentlemanly person turned of thirty, very agreeable when a strange nervousness passes away. He is very well spoken of, and has the honest air of a worthy man. Good Yorkshire stock, Lord Carlisle said, so refuting the malice of Dublin. The sister is not so well bred, very quiet, however, nicely dressed and not quite plain. Her husband is very handsome with an immense beard, but is rather snobbish.

Ceely is a strange girl – talking to Annie she said just in her straight-forward manner that she was quite surprised at his offer, never expected it; there were others she had often fancied did like her, but he had never entered her head. It was too good a thing to throw away, still, she would not marry anyone she did not feel sure she should care for, so she accepted him conditionally, and she found on better acquaintance that he suited her exactly, in fact was very agreeable, nice, sensible conversation, more in his head than you would think. She told the Doctor she considered herself very fortunate; every woman ought to marry and settle down to home duties, and she really felt she could be very happy with Captain Turton. A few years of close shaving would be followed by great wealth, and then, said she, my second son will be so well provided for – Mrs. Turton's large fortune goes to him. Lord Milltown came up to her when I was sitting beside her and bidding her draw off her glove he placed a diamond guard over the wedding ring, then looking at her various bracelets he said: – 'Why, Ceely, where did you get all these, who gave you this?' – 'Mama' – 'And this?' – 'Russy' – 'And this?' – 'My husband'! Just half an hour married, no fun in her tone, just a plain answer to the question.

The Lord Lieutenant departed about four o'clock. He had the civility to speak to me as we were standing together at the door, perhaps, because he had seen me made one of the family, for my Lady left his arm to kiss me on my entrance, and my Lord kept both my hands in his while bidding me welcome. He also said afterwards, when talking over all having gone so well – 'We only wanted dear little Janey, she should have been one of her friend Ceely's bridesmaids.' Ceely said the same, she had intended asking her, but it would have been a false compliment when she was so far away [in Edinburgh]. She and her father had arranged all, and so rightly. Minie Butler, Barby, Emy Henry, two little Lawless's and Miss Colborne were the Bridesmaids. All the neighbours invited without distinction, the near relations on both sides, Madame Giordano written to by Ceely herself, nothing omitted that should have been done, except an announcement in the papers. We have never seen a notice of the marriage in any, which has very greatly disgusted Aunt Bourne. A very pretty Brougham, Lord Milltown's present, carried away Captain and Lady Cecilia Turton, four horses, man and maid. She was radiant, in light blue, stept gaily down, thought of cloke, parasol, etc., departed with a beaming smile while Russy was totally unmanned, had to walk away to hide his tears. In the evening there was a bonfire at the gate, dancing, refreshments etc., for five hundred. Every labourer had a dinner sent to his cabin; and so has gone from her home that dear good clever, girl, the prop of the family.

Friday I went alone in a car to soft sawder [conciliate]

Mrs. O'Reilly. It would not do; she is ill, unhappy, uncomfortable, solitary, dispirited, and not to be pacified on the subject of the wedding. She would listen to no account of it, hear no messages, receive no reasonings. She wishes them well here and hereafter, but to her and Pysie they are as dead. Of course Pysie was not at home, not a word of Eyre either.

James dined with us on goose, played Dumby with a very cross partner and told us the coach had done right well this wedding week. All the neighbours seem to me to try and go by it. Yesterday my Aunt and I had a drive, my General and I another, and we sold dear Annie's carriage for forty pounds. In these *cutting* days, *two* horse carriages are not so saleable.

16. Jack's examinations all over. He is not displeased with himself all through, neither does he think he need be, evidently the boy is in spirits, but he says his admission to the practical class at Woolwich will depend on the number of vacancies, so that he don't class himself among the very best of the numerous candidates. The Dublin boys, as usual, bore the bell.

20. Sunday. My principal occupation all this week has been house hunting. Directly after breakfast several days ago I set off in a car on a tour of the Agency offices. During my Aunt's drive we called here and there where directed by our admission tickets. Dozens of pretty looking places we have seen, not one yet to suit us. We *must* be on Mr. Porter's beat, sufficiently far from the sea for the General to breathe, high enough for my Aunt to be braced by mountain air, near a railway or an omnibus that *he* may be able to get readily into town, away from any publick thoroughfare that *she* may not be annoyed by dust or noise. There must be all conveniences within the house for *him*. Strange to say impossible to meet with! Then so many rooms are required, such good accommodation for servants and a low rent and a short term! All these country houses are let by the season, we can only take one by the month because we might not be able to remain. The terrace houses which are thus let *she* won't live in – to be overlooked, as her principal enjoyment is to be sitting out in the garden, and she would hate to be seen. Also she must have her drives, they do her so much good.

I have to send Major Mair sixty pounds for my boy's London interlude, but that goes from my dear mother's legacy, all of which I am scrupulously keeping for him. What a God-send it has been. Where would he have been without it, no preparation having been made even for his proper education. Three or four times I saved up a few hundreds and the moment they were heard of they were spent. Once indeed, the *pose* [hoard] went for Annie's wedding. It was well for her and us that it was there. I have lost by her carriage just twelve pounds. It is well it was no worse. The Doctor has repaid what he borrowed from us, so I may refund that little sum as soon as I hear how Jack's affairs turn out.

He passed in all very creditably, admirably in some things. Still I must remember that he is amongst the youngest of two hundred candidates, that to win he must be amongst the first thirty, and that there are few vacancies, not above fifteen. We shall hear no news of him for another fortnight. He has gone to Mr. Sargent's, who writes thus of him to Major Mair – 'Your young friend J.G.S. is an uncommonly fine lad, the very best educated young man I have ever had under my charge.' Quite sufficient this, for me. Whether he pass or no, he deserves to pass. His character has very much come out, intellect expanded. He has always proved he *could* work, but the failing is there. Unless stimulated he lags. However shall we get this serious defect remedied. '*Toujours prêt*' – that's the motto for success. They tell me a Commission in the Line is out of the question at present, he may go up to Sandhurst for he can do nothing better. Another awakening trial, but, till the Militia officers and the supernumeraries are absorbed there will be no freshmen taken. The reductions are very large too, in every regiment. Jack will have to try for the Artillery again, and work it up here where the best education going is given, now admitted on all hands, particularly for mathematicks. Dear son of mine, hitherto you have been all I could wish; these next few years will be more trying, how I wish I were papist enough to think my prayers could help you through them.

Janey writes merrily from Edinburgh. She is not coming home yet, having to figure among the Antiquities, she says, at the approaching Archeological meeting. Her Aunt is quite happy chaperoning such a nice little niece. Annie is in gay spirits, the coach answering so well in all ways. We see her husband once a week, Friday is 'settling day' when he always has to come to town to balance the book with his partner, no accounts being longer run. The occupation is the great point, it has put him into a much pleasanter temper.

27. A curious week, let's see what has been doing. Pysie was with us – ah, dear me there's a history. Mrs. O'Reilly has at last gone to Carlow to visit her sister, Mrs. Butler, sore against the grain, for besides that they are not exactly suited, the poor woman's spirit is so entirely broken that life is almost a burden to her and now that I know all, I do not wonder at her failing health and her misery.

A young woman called on Friday and begged to see me, she declined sending up her name so I, sure that it was one of the eternal begging petitions, answered that I was particularly engaged. She then said her name was Margaret and that she had lived with Mrs. O'Reilly. Thinking it was a message from Pysie, I ran down and called her in to the dining-room. It was the old Margaret, the maid who had left them so mysteriously long ago, then returned after months of absence entreating to be taken back, this they refused, but they got her a place with a friend which she left after half a year to be married, she said. They were sure she had been married during her former escapade, and that she had found it necessary to earn a little more money. She had an exceedingly pretty child in her arms, a little tiny brunette baby girl of about two years old. 'Well, Margaret,' said I – 'so you are married, happily I hope, is your husband well off and is he kind to you?' 'You shall judge, Ma'am,' answered she in a very agitated tone, 'I have not seen him nor had one penny from him for four months. I am married to Mr. Eyre O'Reilly' – 'Good God, Margaret,' said I – 'how dreadful, his mother will never forgive you, you can't expect it, and he has nothing, he is in hiding himself. What on earth will become of you,' etc., etc.

Well, the tale is soon told, her tale. They were married at the time she asked for leave to visit her friends, or rather they had been married before and she went to a lodging for her confinement, he with her 'off and on'. The child was put to nurse, she paid for it with her savings and went to service again. A second child obliged her to leave her place. This second child is now eight months old, a boy. Eyre took a lodging in Erle Street, where he has been living ever since with her under the name of O'Brien. He went out as usual one day, four months ago, and has never returned, rent owing and she with but a few shillings.

How she has lived she can hardly tell, partly on the forebearance and the charity of her landlady. Now, having pawned almost every article she possessed, she is utterly destitute. In her despair she wrote to Mrs. O'Reilly begging for relief, a few pounds to set her up as a washerwoman, being most willing to work for her poor children, or even a few shillings to buy them bread. She never wishes to set eyes on him again, he is so thoroughly bad *now*, has been falling step by step for long, first idling, then gambling, then betting at races and *drinking*. When sober he has kind feelings, but he has been seldom sober of late. He is heavily in debt, has got his mother to put her name to bills for him, has hampered her fearfully in money matters, besides breaking her heart by his loose conduct. Receiving no reply to her petition, this poor deserted creature ventured to present herself to the incensed mother, no good resulting of course. What she wanted with me was to plead her cause with Mrs. O'Reilly, beg for the few pounds after which they would hear no more of her.

What could I say, she had brought her sorrows on herself. If unmarried, great was her sin, if married it was almost greater, to marry her master's son. She, an illiterate servant, he requiring help to succeed in life, not a drag like an ignorant wife and a set of children; and older than him too, it was very bad. She must expect desertion. He has no money, not a farthing, his mother has no money, she has had to borrow for herself and him. 'They cannot help you with money, Margaret, they have it not, you know their difficulties, you have always known them, you were not a young girl either, your marriage was inexcusable'. 'God help me,' she cried, 'I wish I were dead. Mrs. Smith, Ma'am, could you help us to Australia, it would be best for him and me.' And I truly think so. I gave her a mite, took her address and promised to consider her case.

Eyre O'Reilly, such a scoundrel, his mother's last stay, all else had failed her. I could now account for his never being mentioned, for his strange conversation with me, for her utter hopelessness, Pysie's despair about her and feverish anxiety to get her out of Dublin, the failing spirits of both. I could not make up my mind what was right for me to do. I had become acquainted with their difficulties, their condition is pitiable, and this poor woman and children can't be let to starve by those who know their state. We are not to 'pass our neighbours by on the other side' [*Luke* 10:31]. I resolved then to speak to Pysie, and during our drive laid the strange affair before my wise Aunt. How shocked she was, dreadfully. Less carried away by feeling than I am, she laid the blame where it is indeed due, on poor Mrs. O'Reilly herself, whose unregulated temper, allied to her indolent careless habits, made her quite unfit for her responsible duties. She knew no better. We who judge her may have failed in our degree as much or more.

Well, when we came in I found Pysie sitting with the General. She knew at once something had happened to annoy me and after dinner asked what it was and I told her. How she wept, the dreadful secret they had so jealously kept, discovered by the one in all the world they would have kept it from. It is true, all but the marriage. He denies that resolutely, and she, though reiterating that she has the proofs has never yet produced the certificate. Pysie therefore does not believe in it yet, but she thinks it will be, the woman is so affectionate, so clever, though she can neither read nor write, so industrious and so good. He dotes on the babies, particularly on the little 'Fanny', the image in miniature of Pysie. A few pounds they have not; her mother has so mismanaged her affairs that she is again plunged in debts, her few true friends tired of helping her, unable perhaps to lend her so large a sum as would be necessary to put her before the world, one hundred pounds at least, and for trifling sums for daily bread they are wanting in that poverty struck home. 'I am as badly off as poor Margaret if you knew all.' I believe it; it was my pound that paid Mrs. O'Reilly's journey to Carlow.

She agreed with me that Australia with or without his so called wife is the only thing left for a man so lost. He has no energy, could work his way nowhere. Money would therefore be wanting for passage and outfit. Off he should go, his mother will never see him again, his associates here are low to blackguardism, and there is no employment for such as he, in the midst of respectable connexions. How to keep the babies and their mother from starving, get rid of him and them, provide for her own daily wants, and relieve her mother might well drive a higher order of mind than Pysie's crazy. It will not so destroy *her*, though it affects her much. To add to her troubles, *her* worthless husband has been seen in Dublin, returned from America. Fortunately she has quite taken to the education of her clever boy, assists him with his lessons, has borrowed some of our old school books of me, and is reading herself for the purpose of bringing him on. But if they want food! borrowing money on their bill plan is ruinous, I often wish I were Miss Burdett Coutts, or a bit of her. Perhaps it would just encrease my distress at not being able to make all the world comfortable – good and then happiness and comfort would follow, that is were all good alike, acted on the *golden maxim*.

I have got a house close by, 10 Hatch Street, very neat and clean and as airy as this is. We shall move on Tuesday. They are really neither of them fit to go further. She is not fit to move at all with such an assemblage of essentials that must accompany her. How strange is her penuriousness. A good woman, very kind, capable of true generosity, yet bent on squeezing from us every penny possible, getting all she can, grudging sixpences, cavilling at such items as really make my cheeks burn when I shew my accounts and have to listen to them so questioned. If it were *my* money it would less signify, but it is not, it is my husband's and I feel this meanness as if I were a party to it. It must surely be old age oddity, engrafted on the enforced habits of her youth. We can get along so it don't so much matter, yet my 'budget' sometimes puzzles me.

That wretched James Sadleir, brother to the suicide, and quite as bad a man, has escaped, fled the country. There are several bankruptcies in the papers, for pretty large sums too. Fine harvest prospects luckily. I am amusing my General in the evenings reading bits of my old Journal to him. They amuse him beyond idea. He comes early home from the Club to listen, and actually considers Dumby on Friday nights an interruption, how lucky we thought of them, otherwise at this dead time of year, he would have found it dull. It interests myself too, going over those old times. Precious legacy it will be to Jack, only parts ought to be blotted out, I was in the habit of setting down my impressions too freely, compromising people by too honest strictures – not fair – might offend or even hurt feelings, never right to do. So far none of the *family* has any reason for soreness. I am sure, however, that by and bye there is much set down that had better have been omitted. It was a safety valve at the time for my own great griefs. Jack, dear, you must mind and keep my secrets should I not have been able to destroy what would vex our dear Annie to read. I am beginning to long for news from Woolwich.

31. Thursday and Number 10 Hatch Street, a nice airy, cheerful little house into which we moved Tuesday, and what a business it was. Monday I came down here, carefully looked over every room, making a memorandum of everything wanted, then got forward at home as much as possible. Arranged that the woman who was taking care of this house should remove to ours; so difficulty the first was over. Difficulty the second was to keep the General quiet. With old military habit he was up by six, fussing and packing and confusing everybody and everything. It was no use urging very gently that all would be done for him if he would but be still. No, ferret away he would, calling upon us all every two or three minutes to leave our own occupations to assist him in his. We were obliged to allow that he was method and neatness itself. Difficulty the third was to get my Aunt to move at all. She wanted to be left in the house all alone with Maria for one more day, as she had had no time to think of what she would take or what she would leave, or how she should pack or which box she should pack in or how all her various requirements were to be moved. Then when I began to work for her she altered everything I did, kindly assisted

herself to throw heavy petticoats over caps, books over rills, stuff up corners, squeeze down lids – in short half distract me.

At last came a bright thought. I went to the Colonel [sic] and told him that with her fussing about doing mischief, I should not get her away for a month and therefore I had ordered the carriage for her drive as usual and he must be gallant for once and carry her off. And to her I made up much the same speech, putting in *him* for *her* and so we got them to depart together for a two hours airing by the sea. That's grand said Maria as the pair departed and how we did get on. Each maid had her allotted task, overlooked of course, or little would have been done. Many a trot had the poor lame foot between the two houses, but all went so smooth by the help of a car and a barrow that when the drive was over and the carriage stopt *here*, the dear old Aunt found her new room just the ditto of her old. Her own easy chair and low table, her writing things, work box, medicines, pots and pans, clothes all in her drawers, stores in her cupboard, books that she was reading, all just as she had left them, and her dinner tray laid as usual, a nice country fed chicken of Annie's ready to be brought up. She was so pleased and though in the course of the afternoon she changed the contents of all the drawers, that was just amusement for her. The poor caps indeed suffered, but they are in the habit of being crushed and so don't mind it

The General's room was not ready. He never wants it at this time, so we left it in disorder rather. Unluckily he did not like his dinner, and he had very much disliked his drive. We dined in Leeson Street, Dempsey having not had leisure to pick up his things. There was cold meat, one hot dish, a *ragout*, and vegetables. James King dined with us. He had come to buy oats, and he and I made it out very well. As soon as they went off to the Club, we workers began again, – bed, chair, tables, and a hundred and fifty etcs., all moved and arranged before tea. But we had forgotten one single article, Dempsey had forgotten it, and that was quite enough to make all wrong. I, of course suffering, Avranches over again – there I cried, here I scolded, and I think this last plan the best. It does not do to spoil even good pupils.

Wednesday I made myself and the rest of the house comfortable, and went back to lock away all trifles. Yesterday that was, and Annie and I counted all the books. I had a hot drive with my Aunt in the park. We have summer in earnest. Very delightful while sitting quietly in a cool*ed* room, but in exercise in the sun, exhausting. At this back window looking over the Lefroys' large gardens, it is really pleasant. There is quite a large space of ground filled with fine trees and fruit and vegetables, and no stables between us and it, for these small houses are without that annoyance. There are no houses just opposite in the street either, so that my Aunt, sitting at her window looks over the fields to the blue hills of Wicklow. I can't think I could have managed better for them.

I had a note yesterday from poor Mrs. O'Reilly. Very happy with Mrs. Butler, and one from her daughter-in-law, Mrs. Eyre O'Reilly, whose efforts to find her husband have been unavailing. Her tone, poor, wretched creature is wrong. They have not been cruel to her, she deserves no kindness at their hands. Charity they are unable to give her, the poor house cannot expose the mother and sister, and as for Eyre, he is so exposed and disgraced as it is, this further step will hardly hurt his character. I fancy he is very weak in the head, and badly brought up, God knows.

MONDAY, AUGUST 4. We have had another charming letter from Janey; the monkey writes beautifully, I don't know where there are such letters, full of wit and fun and graphick descriptions, all in *short*. The picnics, *soirées* and lectures being over, dinners are being given to the Learned before they disperse. The Duke and Duchess of Northumberland are amongst these. Lord Talbot de Malahide was the President. Aunt Jane gave three very successful dinners, and had to buy a new gown and cap. Janey must be rather out of finery, she did not take much with her and there has been an everlasting call on every description of toilette. I have bought, as a birthday present for her, the *Life* of her most particular favourite, Sydney Smith. I shall get the former publication by the Widow for Annie on hers, and so provide myself with a yearly treat! One ought to know every sentence that fell from his wise lips by heart. Mrs. Hall's

Whiteboys is excellent. She understands her countrymen perfectly, except that I do not believe that even to carry out revenge, far less to support his character, would any Irishman of *this* day immolate *himself* along with his victim. This is carrying the 'wild justice' just a bit too far.

10. A quiet week enlivened by quantities of letters. James King was twice in town; Tuesday to buy oats, Friday to settle accounts. He is in good spirits, so is Annie, although I have made out that she will by and bye require me to visit her. She will have the baker's dozen like Mrs. Ogle Moore. I made twenty pots of raspberry jam to be divided between her and me, and what will turn out two bottles of cordial, all I mean to do in the preserving way, we use so little sweetmeats.

Pysie and I have had two more interviews, and we went together to see the unfortunate girl who has been left to starve amongst them. She persists that she is married, but has not got her certificate, neither can Pysie find any entry of the fact in the Parish books. She went, as directed by Margaret, to the Arran Quay Chapel and made a careful search, assisted by Father Dempsey. Whether the entry have been erased, or that Eyre may have had influence enough to have had it originally omitted, or that the marriage was a sham *on his part*, or an *invention* on hers, we cannot yet say. All we know is that she has been living with him as his wife for three years past, both of them under the assumed name of O'Brien; that he has now deserted her without a penny, her lodgings due, and that from the hour he rose from her side, four months ago, to this, she has never had one line from him. She did not know that he had written to Pysie to do what she could for her. Little enough, for Pysie and her mother are actually beggered through his acts. He has in some way taken his mother's name (forged it, I fancy) for a large sum, implicated Mr. Lawless, their friend, in the same transaction, someway. It may be that he had only got his weak mother to put her name for a larger amount than she was aware of. Margaret only knows that the transaction involves his character, necessitates his hiding. Pysie only says that his debts are large, that he has involved their mother and that he has had to be kept out of the way. We talked matters over well, and have agreed on the proper course of action, the difficulty will be to carry it out, but we must try.

Eyre must be got out to Australia, by himself if unmarried, with wife and children if they have really a claim upon him. In this latter case he must descend to her condition. She will make a right good poor man's helpmeet, a better wife far than he deserves. She don't wish to go with him; she is at present resenting his desertion, she also fears he would leave her again in that strange land as he has done here, she would rather separate from him entirely. This she will have to do if she cannot prove her marriage, and then we will set her up as a Laundress. She is a very nice looking, handsome woman, much more like a lady than those she served, she will pass quite as his equal at Sydney, and if she be not his wife she will do fully as well without him. Poor, unhappy creature, bitterly has she been punished for her sin. Her babies deprived of proper nourishment, for she could not give it them, and of fresh air, for neither she nor they had clothes to put on, are miserably unhealthy looking, especially the boy. They would all have died but for the charity of the landlady. She, this good Mrs. Russell, has proposed a plan likely to put poor Margaret in the way to earn her bread, and if the certificate be not forthcoming, we shall try it. We hope to get Eyre away before his unhappy mother returns to town. Pysie is an excellent little creature, not harsh at all in judgement, as so many are who have erred themselves. She had no money to give Margaret, but she gave her of her scanty wardrobe clothes that brought her twenty-four shillings, and supported the poor creature till in her despair she came to see me.

I don't really believe John Sadleir is dead. A very clever set of doubts were at the time of the supposed suicide published in the *Nation* written by either the Archbishop of Dublin or some as ingenious person in imitation of him. *Chambers'* has taken it up and very fairly stating both sides has made it very clear that the whole dead body business was deception. Money can do anything and this wretch had plenty. What a clever rogue the man must be, must have a kind of pleasure in the success of the several parts he has been acting, for his whole life has been a sham. Of course the farce has ended tragically. The mother went mad, and for the two brothers, live they or die, they are in despair for ever. It would seem as if there must be a certain quantity of crime afloat in every age, varying in degree according to the spirit of the age. In this it is forgery, bankruptcy, embezzlement of every description, why or wherefore hardly discoverable in some cases. The root of the evil lay at the infant's cradle, that's one thing certain. What was the home, what was the summer's evening, the winter fireside, the atmosphere of the family. Aunt Bourne has sent William one hundred pounds towards his recovery of Rothiemurchus; about seventy pounds more are wanting. A very good, kind woman she really is, but by no means a just one!

11. A visit from poor Margaret without a certificate. I doubt much there ever having been a marriage. Still the poor creature can't be let to starve, I at least daren't throw the stone. She is quite willing to begin her washing and try to make out her living by her own exertions. It is dismal to think of the escapades young men get into, the wretchedness of all kinds proceeding from one false step.

12. Made up a bundle of dirty curtains etc., took them to poor Margaret, whom I advised for the present to keep the name of O'Brien. She can easily resume O'Reilly if she finds she have a right to it. She has got a small cottage with two rooms for two shillings a week, none cheaper and she has all to buy, to her kettle and her bed. We are quite out of the world in this back settlement, see nothing and hear nothing, indeed I dare say there's nobody left in town and as for news there is none.

We have certainly lost caste in Europe by our conduct during war, and the peace we consented to, and our undignified haste to forget the enmity of these arrogant opponents. In fact we were just puppets in the hands of that clever Louis Napoleon, used when he wanted us, and thrown aside with very little ceremony when no longer necessary to his plans of action. He is in bad health we hear, a fear of the family hereditary complaint, cancer in the stomach.

15. Dr. Robinson surprised us yesterday and *stood* two hours with me, then half an hour with the General giving us all the

gossip of the country. That queer Doctor, such a heart the man has. Came here to offer any amount of assistance that might be required by Jack, knowing how much has been broken for this mail coach business and that these were not times for further savings. He has 'laid at my feet' three hundred pounds to be repaid, anyhow, any way, any time. I shall not want it I believe, having my dear mother's legacy as a standby. But should it so turn out that more will be necessary, I will not scruple to borrow a little, knowing that no favour I could *confer* would give equal pleasure to this receipt of one. Jane too still continues what she persists to call her mite, and offered to forestall the September payment, so we are rich in friends, though the purse be light. I find that purse, however, doing better. I have got better into the way of managing it and the house and have an honest cook (by comparison perhaps) who undoubtedly saves us many a pound.

I may be able to lend that poor Margaret a couple. She has not yet found a second security for the loan and she has four washings promised her. Two pounds would set her up in a way, but she owes so many shillings here and there she fears being obstructed by these poor debtors in her honest endeavours to earn wherewith to pay them all. I begged of her to go and speak to each and entreat their forbearance for a week or two, and bade her tell them she had found a helping friend. She persists that she is married.

The pay having come, the General and I went about paying our little bills. I seldom have any, usually giving ready money, but the dear Aunt had borrowed so heavily from me, I was near run out. Strange old woman; she has given William one hundred pounds, yet actually shrinks from giving the pound or the few shillings for her own necessary expenses, and she is wearing linen so ragged that I really am ashamed to send it to the washing, having good sets of new shifts in her drawers which I bought and had made for her.

The General all alive, so interested in the old journals. I have to continue the evening readings and at one time I kept them very carelessly, not entering half the events that occurred to us and then glancing at them as if anyone but myself could possibly understand these allusions to matters unchronicled. A deal of repetition too as if memory had failed. Still, with all its imperfections, and they are many, it is excessively amusing to us who are interested in the details, and surely Jack will find pleasure in reading it years hence. Well weeded, corrected, and names withheld, it might bring him a good penny should the present love of family disclosures remain with the idle publick.

31. I really think I must curtail the most of 1853, all at least that relates to James King. There is no need to perpetuate disagreeables. Temper had a great deal to do with his ill conduct, disease a little, and his circumstances were so desperate, he was nearly frantick. He is of late much improved. Wiser and living in pure air! has recovered health of mind in a degree. Bygones should be bygones.

TUESDAY, SEPTEMBER 2. Jack at Sandhurst, he was to go down last night, sleep there, and this morning at ten o'clock present himself at the examination hall. Poor Jack! he really was not sufficiently advanced to have tried for the Artillery, the Edinburgh [Military] Academy excellent so far not carrying the pupils forward enough without a six months' reading afterwards, and Jack did so very much in six weeks he would certainly have succeeded had he had a longer course. So I think he will do for Sandhurst. All his masters report so well of him. There's an immensity of grandeur in perseverance. He is in the hall now, under the screw, his mother's prayers all round him. Mesmerick influence! might have effect! who knows!! He will know his fate tomorrow, but we! 'Never say die'. A few minutes before seven, just as I was going down to make tea, came a letter. 'Telegraphick Despatch'. 'Immediate'. I shook so I could not open it, in a fright about I know not what. It was a message to say our boy had passed that day with credit. Thank God.

7. Sunday, after quite an eventful week. The good news of Jack on Tuesday, return of Janey Thursday, Uncle William and Aunt Sally with her. We are a very merry party, plenty to say and all in good humour. I only hope we may not fare too well and so some of us be laid up from Stilton cheese and other varieties not usually indulged in. All our letters are pleasant too. Jack and Johnny [Gardiner] dined at the

Blakeneys and Sir Edward congratulated Jack so kindly and told him he hoped it would not be very long before he held his commission. Significant, we think, particularly as Jack, who writes in immense spirits, says he is indifferent to my ignorance of the routine of the service, he has fallen among those who are perfectly up to the knowledge of it, but I'm to hold my tongue. The monkey.

Sir Edward and many others say that the Line is the best where an officer can buy himself up, that they learn their profession most thoroughly in it, and that from it all the Staff is generally taken, almost all high in command having served in Infantry Regiments. So we are content. My College plan I fear will never suit this ardent spirit. I had best cushion it, at least till we see whether the Commission be quickly forthcoming.

William's own affairs are very satisfactorily progressing. I can't quite understand the details of the business part, these being complicated of course by Deeds of Entail, and various other Deeds. What I do comprehend is that he will be 'the Laird' before Christmas, master of his inheritance, though with his land encumbered. As he fully intends hastening to pay off the debt, his income will not be materially encreased for some years. About a couple of hundreds only, still, that's a great lift, he has but three hundred pounds a year now, five hundred will make him very comfortable, and enable them, if they like, to live in Rothiemurchus.

14. A cheerful week, – William and Sally being such pleasant inmates. We have been all sufficient to ourselves, having seen hardly anyone and received but few letters. The Operas are filling the deserted town. A very good company – Grisi and Mario and fifteen more, most of them good artists. We go thrice this week, a very extravagant business. I have had to exercise no small share of self denial since the arrival of my company. No quiet hours in my own room with my book, my work, my pen. Marketing, cooking, managing half broke servants, my beloved's various jobs, and the poor Aunt's illness, have altogether completely occupied me, for we have whist every night, and Janey has been ailing, an Autumnal attack that rendered great care of her for a few days necessary. We had to apply to Mr. Porter. I think she is

all right now, but a delicate little creature, I fear. Pysie had to apply to me for one pound. She was without one penny; they have no credit, little means, and difficulties I fear encreasing round them. Whatever may have been her youthful folly, she is atoning nobly for it now, acting as confidential clerk to Mr. Lawless to support her boys. Her only grief is that this source of small earnings is but occasional.

18. *Norma*. I never heard Grisi before! Old and stiff, her beauty and her acting are wonderful, the voice gone, in the upper notes quite, is still enchanting. She had no support either, a poor set, and orchestra detestable. The getting up of the operas this season is disgraceful. No new scenery, the most abominable old costumes, courtiers dressed like beggars, and as for the orchestra! poor, yet overpowering, harsh, loud, discordant, out of time as well as tune, worse could not well be. Grisi, no longer young, has lost her high notes, the airs are so much prettier without them, it were to be wished that the profession generally would take the hint. Composers avoid them and vocalists change them to keep within the compass of sweetness. Jack went to *Don Pasquale* to hear Mr. Tennent. An excellent Ernesto, beautiful voice, carefully and skilfully managed, hardly full enough that's all. '*Come genti l'* actually well sung, the garden duett delightfully. Poor Mr. Tennent! it was his trial, had he failed the stage was closed to him who had sacrificed all to it. A second Mario, and same quality of voice, failing in quantity. The great German bass, Formes, I can't admire, too gruff, too coarse, too heavy, as if he never had worked it, indeed that's most likely true, the Germans never do practise, despise it they say, the more's the pity.*

Poor Ellen Porter has sent me such a grateful letter. She has paid Mrs. Moore, next month will pay me, and in the meantime, poor woman, she sends me a collar and cuffs of Maltese Lace. Her husband received her kindly. Now, will my laundress venture turn out as well. She is doing the clothes well any way, sweeping clean at present! All the servants have been fighting, and the cook was saucy to me! and everything went wrong, and the house full, and the sick room! Ah.

SUNDAY, OCTOBER 5. Blind of one eye! The lens had thickened and actually for a week I could hardly see. Medicine and Sulphurick ether to smart the eye have partially restored the sight and if persevered in will set all right, but I must not use either eye, therefore I read and work none, write very little, and must not journalise. Merely mention that William and Sally having been at Rathbally and much pleased there, and paid us a long happy visit, leave us tomorrow for Edinburgh.

26. What thankless creatures are we poor human beings, how desponding for little, careless of the good, unduly fretful at the evil, and how full of mercy is our common lot, did we draw the balance fairly. After all, as wise Lady Milltown once said in one of her sarcastick moods, what is there we cannot bear save and except some physical infirmity. My failing eyesight has brought this home to me. Dependant even for the news of the day on any one who would kindly read a few sentences from the newspaper for me, deprived of my happy, private reading, of my writing, my grand re-source; no needlework – all the little jobs accumulating, the maids so unskilful, that their botching shocked my neatness, I have had a weary time spite of the happy young creatures round me. Jack is back again. The General well; only the poor Aunt suffering. My eyes are better and I am using them a little, knitting the babies their warm socks and reading for a few minutes. Some writing too had to be done to further Jack's affairs. Lord Downshire has been most kind, wrote at once to General Yorke [Colonel of the 33rd Foot], so perhaps we shall not have to wait so very long for the commission. In a few days I trust to be all right again, for it is the nerve that is affected, no thickening of the lens. However I must be cautious and write no more just now.

WEDNESDAY, NOVEMBER 26. Quite done up, eyes no better, general debility encreasing. Ordered off peremptorily to the country tomorrow. A week at least at Rathbally. News of all sorts, public and private floating about. And no journal for I may not use the eyes. I have weathered on so long that I may hope to get on yet for a while, though truly I have not felt so ill since the grand break-down at Avranches. The General and my Aunt are so well just now, it is a satisfactory time to leave them. I don't well see what I write. Instinct guides the pen. A blind old age for the busy bee, a cross indeed with a thousand blessings.

THURSDAY, DECEMBER 31. A third baby boy [George] at Rathbally. I in for the fun of course, so instead of the fun in the country there was a fortnight's nursing; up all night, and again at the end, for the baby took convulsions and was all but gone. Called home by my poor General, bronchitis, and a hard matter to bring him through. He is in the drawing room again and I am quite done up. The eyes will never serve me more, a vessel which should only contain serum admits a clot of blood, this is the cobweb that hangs before the pupil and obstructs clear vision. Also the lens of both eyes is thickening, yet by care I shall escape total blindness. We are very happy. Jack and Janey read to me at spare moments and I find a number of employments that require no eyesight – dusting, sorting, messages, crochet, knitting, netting, and a sharp look out over all. We are in hopes now that James Wortley is made Attorney General,* he may be able to give a stipendiary Magistracy to his cousin James King. The old man has asked it.

And so farewell dear journal for a time. Should it never be resumed, dear children, forgive any unkind word wrote down in the heat of first impressions. There is so much love in the old trusting heart that the old worn-out frame sometimes chafes at ill requital, when more vigorous feelings would excuse poor human nature.

I shall busy myself now in putting all in order everywhere in case a sudden call should put an end to care, and try to bear with patience the great calamity, which no one can have an idea of the pressure of, till the sad lot fall on the victim.

God be thanked for many mercies, and the inestimable blessing of good children, kind friends, and a thousand nameless comforts. To see their faces still, and the sunshine, and the prospects, is not total blindness after all.

End-notes

1851

p.4: *January* 6 Joseph Leeson, fourth Earl of Milltown (1799–1866), his wife Barbara and their family were near neighbours of the Smiths in their magnificent house of Russborough. His sensitivity about his status was not matched by his financial resources and one of several themes that emerges from the *Highland Lady*, Elizabeth Smith's (E.S's) many accounts of their problems is the number of times the chances of the daughters, Barbara and Cecilia, making perfectly satisfactory marriages were sabotaged by the ridiculous pretensions of the parents. All three sons died unmarried within a quarter of a century of their father: *Russy* (Joseph Henry) of 'congestion of the lungs' in 1871, Edward Nugent 'somewhat suddenly' in 1890, and the line and title ended with Henry the following year (*Complete Peerage*).

p.5: *January* 10 The explanation for what she clearly regarded as Dr. George Robinson's bizarre and unacceptable behaviour is hard to pin down, but from what she wrote at the end of *The Highland Lady in Ireland*, where she describes what she terms his 'melancholy monomania', it clearly had something to do with his reactions to the news of Annie's wedding. She tried to explain a bit further on 23 February but the reader is not left much the wiser: 'To me, my old friend George Robinson is dead and buried. He died of brain fever . . .'. He may have been disappointed but, as the diaries for these years in Dublin show, he continued to give generous financial assistance to the Smith family. She was forced to the conclusion the following year that 'I do not believe any one has yet got at the truth regarding this singular estrangement'.

p.5: *January* 15 Colonel, later General, Smith was to die nearly ten years later at the end of 1862. He left his estate of Baltiboys and the farm of Elverstown to his son John Graydon Smith. The will stated that £5,000 was to be left to his son and £2,500 to his *unmarried* daughter Jane.

p.6: *January* 20 Brocade is a rich fabric woven with raised patterns, with added gold and silver thread; lappetts are an attached or hanging part of an item of headgear; tarletan is a thin stiff open-weave muslin used especially for ball-dresses; tabinet (sic) is a watered fabric of silk and wool resembling poplin, which according to the *O.E.D.* is 'chiefly associated with Ireland'.

p.6: *January* 20 William James Armstrong, of Kippure Park Blessington is listed in *Thom's Directory* as one of the Resident Magistrates for Co. Wicklow; amongst the others from this locality who feature in the Journals are Lord Downshire and the Earl of Milltown, for whom the duties would have been purely honorary and perhaps beneath their dignity, John Finnemore of Ballyward and William Owen, the Downshire Agent.

p.6: *February* 3 Ogle William Moore was Rector of the parish of Kilbride, which included Blessington. By 1856 he is reported in the *Dublin Evening Mail* of Wednesday 23 January as being present at the Levée in his capacity as 'chaplain to his Excellency the Lord Lieutenant', so his literary efforts contributed to his eventual preferment.

p.7: *February* 16 The Ecclesiastical Titles Bill led Lord John Russell to resign but, as she explains on 25 February in an entry in which her distaste for most of the political permutations is evident, he resumed office a fortnight later. The political complications of this period are great and it helps to know that after his intemperate letter to the Bishop of Durham, in which he lambasted the Oxford Movement, there was no possibility of any Whig/Peelite coalition being led by Lord John Russell. This is the poisonous atmosphere referred to when she maintains that Gladstone with his Puseyite views as a member of the Cabinet 'would not do in these times'.

p.7: *February* 16 Frances Trollope (1780–1863), the remarkable mother of Anthony, began writing when at fifty she found herself in straitened circumstances; she continued producing novels and travel books until 1856 by which time her total works consisted of no less than 114 volumes. Her book on Paris ('good reading for the day, but of little permanent value' according to the critical *D.N.B.*) was published in 1835.

p.7: *February* 16 *Sir Philip Hetherington, A Tale by the Author of Olivia*, was written by Augusta Louise, Lady Lyons, wife of the Crimean War Admiral.

p.8: *February* 25 Edward George Geoffrey Smith, Lord Stanley and later fourteenth Earl of Derby (1799–1869), was prime Minister of the short-lived ministry, February to December 1851, that came between the longer administrations of Lord John Russell and Lord Aberdeen.

p.8: *March* 8 *The History of Pendennis*, William Makepeace Thackeray's novel of society intrigues, combined with a didactic purpose that would have pleased E.S., was published between 1848 and 1850; he had earlier produced his gossipy and highly readable *Irish Sketch Book* (1843) – although Baltiboys is not mentioned, he must from the descriptions have passed close to the estate in his travels.

p.9: *March* 9 Patrick Fraser Tytler (1791–1849) between 1828 and 1843 wrote, with the active encouragement of Sir Walter Scott, his celebrated *History of Scotland* in no less than nine volumes. Her use of the adjective 'poor' a fortnight later, on 9 March, to describe somebody she had known since girlhood and admired as part of the Edinburgh literary establishment, might be because of his comparatively short life, or perhaps because his High Tory Episcopalian principles probably prevented him being considered for the post of Historiographer Royal for Scotland. Sir Robert Peel, however, compensated him with an annual pension of two hundred pounds.

p.9: *March* 9 Sir Archibald Alison, (1792–1867), was the son of one of the late Edinburgh Enlightenment figures who is remembered for his *Essays on the Nature and Principles of Taste*. Sir Archibald was a considerably more successful author than his father. His *History of Europe from the French Revolution*, published in ten volumes between 1833 and 1842, had sold one hundred thousand copies in the United States by 1848 and been translated into Arabic. His reputation as a public figure was such that he had defeated Lord Palmerston in the election for Lord Rector of the University of Glasgow.

p.10: *March* 11 Mother and daughter shared an interest in the fortunes of the contemporary aristocracy; Annie's cousinhood would be derived from her husband's grandmother, Lady Elizabeth Crichton, daughter of the first Earl of Erne. Henry Francis Seymour (1825–1892) was the third and last Marquis of Drogheda. According to the *Annual Register* his predecessor had been insane for forty five years; the *Complete Peerage* states that his mother's father, first Baron Congleton,

'within 10 months of his creation as a Peer . . . hung himself
in a fit of temporary insanity' in 1842.

p.10: *March* 14 John MacHale (1791–1881), baptised by a priest
who was to be hanged during the 1798 rebellion, became
Archbishop of Tuam in 1834 and, although in collaboration
with Cardinal Cullen he translated the *Iliad* into Irish, he
encapsulated the increasingly self-confident and aggressive
Church towards which E.S. was so unsympathetic. Mrs
Lynch was the niece of the Archbishop of Dublin since
1823, Daniel Murray.

p.10: *March* 14 St. Columba's College had been established seven
years previously at Rathfarnham with the aim of providing a
superior education for the landed classes, in particular so that
they might live up to their responsibilities. E.S. was somewhat more in favour of this objective than the Tractarian
sympathies of many of the school's founders and governors.
    The Rev. William James Bennet, a moderate Tractarian,
was well known as the incumbent of Lord John Russell's
church of St. Paul's in Knightsbridge, which he built at his
own expense.

p.11: *March* 15 Captain John King lived at 24 Merrion Square,
North, right in the heart of fashionable Dublin. The Downshires had a house here, and amongst the other inhabitants of
the Square well known to the Smiths' were Wyndham Goold
M.P., Sir Philip Crampton and Lord Chief Justice Blackbourne. James King's father also owned a property on the
Howth Road, St. Fintan's House, desirable enough for the
Lord Lieutenant Lord Eglinton to be interested in letting it,
at a rent of no less than '£100 a month' (see 21 September
1852).

p.14: *March* 24 The principles of the English Poor Law (no
outdoor relief) had been extended to Ireland in 1838 and
a Poor House had been built for 550 paupers in nearby Naas
in Co. Kildare by 1841. Colonel Smith was elected one of the
Guardians ('he had half a mind not to act but thought better
of it': *The Highland Lady in Ireland* p.99) and he was to be
much involved later in the year through the dubious activities
of the Rutherfurd family (see 23 May 1851), who were the
largest tenant farmers on the estate.

p.14: *March* 25 Miss Talbot's father had died in 1839 and her
mother in 1841, leaving her the heiress to a fortune of
£85,000. E.S.'s principal source of information was the
fiercely protestant *Dublin Evening Mail*, owned and edited

by her young friend Mr. Thomas Sheehan. It, or possibly he, wrote at this time of 'this dark transaction' and condemned the disinterest of one Guardian, the Earl of Shrewsbury, and as for the other, the Dr. Doyle described in the Journals as the so-called Catholic Bishop of Clifden, 'his conduct . . . was such as we should perhaps pronounce to be natural in a gentleman of his profession' (31 March 1851). This amounted to sending the girl to a convent at Taunton (where the fees at forty guineas a year were decreed to be 'modest for Squeers himself') and diverting the remainder of her fortune for the uses of the Church. 'Who could have supposed,' thundered the *Mail* 'that such an organised system of spiritual tyranny and bondage existed in England for the purpose of amassing funds for the use of *Propaganda*, by the plunder and degradation of orphans' (2 April 1851). All grist to Elizabeth Smith's mill.

p.16: *March* 30 Alphonse Louis de Prat de Lamartine (1790–1869), the poet, historian and statesman, had been a household name during the stormy days of the 1848 Paris revolution, when he had been the virtual head of the Provisional Government. His novel *Geneviève*, published in this year, was one of the many books he produced in a vain attempt to rid himself of his enormous debts.

p.17: *April* 1 Sir Frederick Shaw (1799–1876) was Recorder of Dublin for nearly half a century and M.P. for the University of Dublin from 1830 to 1848. He had three daughters and five sons, the one involved in the scandal being Wilkinson, who was to become Deputy-Assistant Quartermaster-General for China and Hong Kong. Sir Frederick had been named in the original *Plans for an Irish Collegiate College* that led to the foundation of St. Columba's as one of the 'Noblemen and gentlemen who have consented to cooperate with the Founders in the establishment of the Institution'.

p.17: *April* 1 *Mesmerism*, is named after F.A. Mesmer, an Austrian/German physician (1734–1815) who is credited with the invention and development of the system that bears his name. It is described by the *O.E.D.* as 'a hypnotic state, usually accompanied by insensibility to pain and muscular rigidity [which] can be induced by an influence (at first known as animal magnetism) exercised by an operator over the will and nervous system of the patient'. The most notorious enthusiast in Dublin was Richard Whately, Protestant Archbishop of Dublin. He was co-founder and second president of the Dublin Mesmeric Association and instituted the Dublin Mesmeric Infirmary.

p.19: *April* 6 'Aunt Bourne', her mother' sister, did indeed decide to come and spend her last years with her favourite niece in Dublin and they travelled over together from Oxford in October. Her first husband had been James Griffith, Master of University College; it was he who was noted for his 'poker drawings' some of which are still in the College archives. After his death, she married Richard Bourne, Professor of Physic and then Clinical Medicine. She was a rich lady and she was generous to her family; the expectation was that her niece would be her principal legatee. After her death, E.S. wrote on 21 January 1866 – 'she died worth forty six thousand pounds. Legacies and expenses will absorb near fifteen thousand, the rest is mine as residuary legatee. It is like the last page if a novel; the heroine through the three novels having struggled with unnumbered adversities, closes her career in comfort. Money will not restore the dead, but it will revive the living . . .'

p.19: *April* 7 Chief Justice Blackbourne (1782–1867) was to become Lord Chancellor of Ireland. His son Alfred was registered at the College in 1847 and another son was to write his father's biography.

p.19: *April* 7 George Williams (1814–1878), 'divine and topographer' (*D.N.B.*), was in 1850 appointed Warden of St. Columba's College, which he had helped to found at Rathfarnham six years before. He was a Fellow of King's, Cambridge (1835 to 1871), and before his appointment he had been Chaplain to Jerusalem (1841–1843) and then St. Petersburg (1844–1845). The school's existence in these early years depended greatly on the generosity of Lord George John de la Poer Beresford (1773–1862), younger son of the first Marquis of Waterford and Archbishop of Armagh and Primate of All Ireland from 1822, who contributed no less than £6,000 to its establishment. Amongst its aims, according to *the D.N.B.*, was the ambition 'to furnish the gentry of Ireland with a school on the model of Eton'. The Warden's controversial spell in office continued through a difficult 1853 when Beresford demanded his resignation; Williams' defiant response was to edit and publish *Correspondence relative to the Warden of St. Columba's College*, a copy of which was read by E.S. Controversy followed as he joined Pusey in protesting at the Bishop of

Jerusalem trying to gain followers from the Greek Church. There is a long commentary on these events later in the Journals on Christmas Day, 1853. He ended his career as Vice-Provost of King's, (1854–1857).

p.21: *April* 25 Edward James O'Brien, son of the landed revolutionary, whose 1848 adventures ended in 'Widow McCormick's cabbage patch', went on to Sidney Sussex where he took holy orders; this year the Warden was to spend Christmas with the family at their Co. Limerick estate. Warden Williams' successor was John Gwynn, the first married Warden; his wife was daughter to Smith O'Brien.

p.21: *April* 27 These are the words which are uttered by Wackford Squeers to one of the wretched pupils assembled at the Saracen's Head preparatory to travelling the two hundred and fifty miles to Dotheboys Hall. 'My dear child . . . all people have their trials . . . You are leaving your friends, but you will have a father in me, my dear, and a mother in Mrs. Squeers.' All of course, for the benefit of an approaching prospective parent, Mr. Snawley, who turns out to be almost as steeped in villainy as the schoolmaster himself. (*Nicholas Nickleby*, Chapter 4).

p.25: *May* 10 This is the all-important aristocratic connection for the King family. John Crichton, the third Earl and fourth Baron Erne (1802–1885), was the nephew of the first Baron, Abraham Creighton (1700–1772), whose second wife was Jane, daughter of John King of Charlestown, Co. Roscommon.

p.25: *May* 23 William Rutherfurd (sic) occupied the largest individual tenanted farm on the estate, 115 statute acres valued by Griffith's great survey at eighty pounds. Even so he was invariably in arrears and the greatest defaulter, so it was with some displeasure that E.S. noted in 1846 that she had been aware of 'his sons flying about in jaunting cars, riding races and keeping hunters'. Son William emigrated to America in 1850 with 'in my idea, a good sum of our money'. Father had been an elected Guardian since 1846 and a regular attender at all meetings. His younger son John (according to the minutes which can be consulted in Newbridge Library, Co. Kildare) had been a collector since 1843 and it is plain that, as E.S. was well aware, he had been dipping his fingers into the communal purse. The minute for 23 March, three weeks after the father's final attendance, states: 'Mr. William Rutherford . . . offered to give himself ... as security ... for the sum of £139.15.1, arrears of Poor Rates due by his son John Rutherford as Collector for the Boystown and Ballymore divisions, the amount to be repaid in two years by half yearly installments.'

p.27: *June* 17 The Rev. Henry Tripp (Fellow of Worcester College, Oxford) was the Sub-Warden of the College; according to the Prospectus for January 1850, William Francis Seymour and Maurice Thomas De Burgh (both graduates of Trinity College, Dublin) were Resident Fellows and Tutors.

p.27: *June* 17 This *cause célèbre* (mentioned for the first time on 31 March) originated in the school's response to what was regarded as the Warden's lenient punishment of a boy who had drunk a glass of sherry on St. Patrick's Day with his elder brother in a grocer's shop in Rathfarnham. He was promptly sent to Coventry by the other boys, which the Warden in his published justification described as 'organised opposition to my authority and resistance to my expressed will'. The second Earl of Ellenborough (1790–1871) was brought in to help form a judgement on the whole affair. He had family links with E.S.'s father through his father's purchase of Sir John Peter Grant's Hertfordshire property, Thorley Hall, for £30,000 in 1806 (*Memoirs* I p.73). He wrote to the Warden: 'The offence he may have committed, as he has represented it to me, would have been punished at Eton, when I was there, by the usual flogging, and then forgotten; if indeed the Head Master had thought fit to notice at all a boy being sent to Coventry'. Edward John Littlejohn, first Baron Hatherton (1791–1863) had been Chief Secretary for Ireland in 1833/1834, and he in turn was commissioned by the Primate to provide an additional judgement. He wrote that the Warden had committed 'an error of judgement ... by a feeling of Christian kindness towards a boy who was insulted and hardly dealt with by his school-fellows on account of faults which had been committed long since'. It seems extraordinary that there should have been so much activity over such a trivial offence committed in a school where there were a mere forty pupils at the time. Even more extraordinary, perhaps, was the Warden's reaction to these learned gentlemen's judgements: 'I could not desire a more complete vindication'.

p.29: *June* 17 The Rev. Christopher Wordsworth (1807–1885) was well-known to E.S. as in 1836 he had married Susanna Frere, daughter of her uncle George, one of the original subscribers at the foundation of St. Columba's to the extent of fifty pounds, the solicitor from Twyford House where she had passed part of her childhood. In 1836 he became public orator of Cambridge and Headmaster of Harrow; he only lasted until 1844 by which time, as the *D.N.B.* laconically comments, numbers had 'decreased greatly' and he had 'suffered pecuniary loss', which probably explains why his donation to the original fund to establish St. Columba's only amounted to a paltry two guineas. He ended his career rather more comfortably as Bishop of Lincoln.

p.30: *June 17* A *lien* is the right to retain possession of another's property until the owner pays a debt.

p.37: *July 22* Lord Rutherford (1791–1854) was appointed to the Court of Session in 1851; his brother-in-law came from Ramelton in Co. Donegal and is described by the *Complete Peerage* in uncomplimentary terms – 'as a public man he incurred unpopularity owing to his unconciliatory and somewhat haughty demeanor'. Lauriston Castle had been the home of John Law, the shady but convincing financier, who managed to persuade the government of Louis XV during his regency to allow him to reconstruct the royal finances with disastrous consequences.

p.38: *July 25 The Castle of Otranto*, a Gothic Story, which E.S. had been reading recently (see 15 June), has been seen as the first Gothic novel. It was written by Horace Walpole, brother of the politician and later fourth earl of Oxford, at Strawberry Hill, what he termed his 'little Gothic Castle'.

p.40: *August 7* Although their Blesssington residences may not have approached the splendours of Russborough, the Downshires were perceived as the grandest and wealthiest family in Co. Wicklow. The fourth Marquis (1812–1868) succeeded his father after he suffered an apoplectic fit in 1845. He married Caroline Frances, daughter of Sir Stapleton Cotton (1773–1870), Field Marshal and the first Viscount Combermere, Commander in Chief in Ireland. E.S. was later to have high hopes of his obtaining preferment for her son Jack in his military career.

They and their entourage had arrived that week for their annual residence on their Wicklow estates, an event which was eagerly reported in the *Dublin Evening Mail* for Monday 4 August in the *Fashion and Varieties* Column, which regularly provided obsequious accounts of the movements of the aristocracy during the social season.

> The Marquis and Marchioness of Downshire, family and suite, arrived on Saturday from England and proceeded shortly afterwards to Blessington, where their presence was hailed with undissembled joy by all classes of the people. It is the invariable custom of this nobleman to reside for a portion of every year amongst his tenantry on his estates in Wicklow, encouraging them to improve their farms and diffusing the benefits of extensive employment among the labouring population; while his benevolent lady, with un-affected heartiness, devotes herself to the promotion of their domestic comforts and moral condition.

p.44: *September* 7 James Heathorn Todd (1805–1869) was the Regius Professor of Hebrew in the University of Dublin from 1849 and Librarian of the University from 1852, whose contributions to intellectual life in Dublin and beyond were recognised by his election to the presidency of the Royal Irish Academy (1856–1861). However, for Elizabeth Smith he was perhaps more interesting as one of the four original founding fathers of St. Columba's, who is credited in the history of the College as finding and appointing all the Wardens down to his death. It was probably on his insistence that the school was one in which those intending to take holy orders might be taught Irish; he had been the founder of the Irish Archaeology Society in 1840 and he excavated the famous Mooghaun hoard (*Toisce an Mhuchain*), still one of the glories of the National Museum in Dublin. The *D.N.B.* believed 'no man has since Archbishop Ussher shown equal skill in bibliography, accuracy of knowledge or devotion to the development of Irish literature'.

p.44: *September* 7 A *post obit* is a bond given by the borrower securing the lender a sum of money to be paid on the death of a specified person, from whom the borrower has expectations.

p.45: *September* 8 This was the eighteenth Duke of Norfolk, the premier peer of England, who lived from 1791 to 1856 and married Charlotte Sophia, daughter of the first Duke of Sutherland. The *Times* commented that 'such an event is full of much significance, and may possibly be ominous of consequences more inimical to the spread of the Roman Catholic faith than any which have been dreampt of in the philosophy of our Wisemans and Cullens'. It is interesting to note that the Protestant wife of the nineteenth Duke was in turn to became a Roman Catholic.

p.45: *September* 14 It was from this Co. Kildare family that Sir John de Robeck, Bart. (1862–1928) came; he is best remembered as the Commander in Chief of the allied naval forces at Gallipoli and less well known as the first naval officer to be elected President of the M.C.C.

p.48: *October* 22 It was Robert Stephenson, (1803–1859), only son of the great George, who was the most famous bridge builder of his generation referred to here; his tubular girder bridge crossing the Conway and the Menai Straits, widely seen as his masterpiece, had been opened for traffic on 5 March the previous year.

p.54: *December* 7 The *Dublin Evening Mail* quoted on Friday 5 December 1851 from the account of the Lord Primate's visit to the school in the *Irish Ecclesiastical Journal*. 'He begged them to remember that their future welfare would mainly depend upon the habits which they formed in that place', and 'His Grace adverted to the feeling of pleasure and pride with which, even at his advanced age, he looks back to his school-boy days at Eton. He would desire to see the same spirit among the boys of St. Columba's . . .' He concluded his remarks by announcing that he was contributing no less than three thousand pounds himself towards the construction of a new dormitory.

p.55: *December* 7 Louis Napoleon, nephew of Napoleon I, made himself President for life with a practically bloodless *coup d'état* on 5 December. The fortress of Ham, from which he had escaped in 1846, was where he was consigned after the second of his seemingly pantomime attempts to seize power. A very different opinion was expressed by Victor Hugo, whose *Napoléon le Petit* was written in June 1847: 'This man of weary gestures and a glazed expression walks with an absent-minded air amidst the horrible things he does, like a sinister sleep-walker.'

p.57: *December* 21 Barbara, Lady Milltown, daughter of Sir Joshua Meredythe from Co. Kildare, was the widow of Eyre Tilson, third Baron Castle Coote. The two sisters mentioned here had married into very different circumstances. Mrs. McEvoy, an M.P.'s wife, was very comfortably off, whereas Mrs. O'Reilly, whose tale of misfortune is one that Elizabeth Smith tried in her busy life and comparatively testing circumstances to ameliorate, led a poverty-struck and singularly unfortunate existence in which the toils and tribulations of her children, Pysie, Jos. and Eyre, feature prominently at this time in the Dublin Journals. A third sister, Mrs. Butler, is a more shadowy figure.

p.57: *December* 25 Smith O'Brien himself, who had been sentenced to transportation for life after the 1848 escapade, was freed from his house arrest in Tasmania in 1854 and allowed to return to Ireland two years later. His family in the meantime continued to reside at Cahirmoyle House in Co. Limerick.

p.58: *December* 27 Sir Philip Crampton (1777–1858), one of the Surgeon Generals to the forces in Ireland, was thrice President of the Royal College of Surgeons of Ireland and is described (Alfred Webb's *A Compendium of Irish Biography*, 1878) as notable for 'the brilliancy of his conversational powers'.

p.59: *December* 31 Tom Darker the steward and his brother John between them farmed nearly 225 acres on the estate; the Ordinance Survey Field Books for the Parish of Baltiboys, which were completed in August 1838, believed that 'Mr. Darcar [sic] has the largest farm at about 16s. an acre'. According to the rough draft used for calculating the Griffith Valuation, their tenure was for seven years and the date of the lease expired this year 1851.

p.60: *December* 31 The immediate cause of the dismissal of the brilliant but maverick Foreign Secretary Lord Palmerston (1784– 1865) was in fact his precipitate recognition of the *de facto* government of Louis Napoleon earlier in the month. He was replaced by Lord Granville as Secretary of State for Foreign Affairs until February 1852 when the government fell; the wife E.S. so distrusted was a daughter of the Duke of Dalberg and, according to the *Complete Peerage*, 'a Genoese lady'.

1852

p.65: *January* 29 It was customary for the *Dublin Evening Mail* next day to publish not only a list of all who attended Vice-regal functions at the Castle, but also descriptions of what the ladies wore:

> Mrs. Colonel Smith (Baltiboys) – Corsage [bodice] and train of marone, brushed tabinet, lined with white gros and

trimmed with ruches of satin, transversed en tablier; berthe and sabots of point lace. Head dress – feathers, point lace lappets; ornaments, pearls . . . Miss Smith. Corsage and train of white poplin, handsomely trimmed with Limerick lace and ruches of satin ribbon; skirt of Limerick lace (tastefully looped with silver flower) over white glace [silk]. Head dress: feathers, point lace lappets, pearls.

(Monday, 23 January)

Gros is a type of lace, originally from Venice, worked in bold relief; a *ruche* is a frill of gathered ribbon or lace used as a trimming; *transversed* means turned upside down; *en tablier* is the front of a skirt having the form of an apron; *berthe* is a deep falling collar or small cape on a dress. Janey's *ruches* were frills of gathered ribbon or lace used as a trimming and their *lappets* were the attached or hanging parts of their headwear. No wonder, as she and her husband 'marched' around this function, attended by no less than one thousand four hundred guests, did she did she feel that she was 'most audibly admired'.

p.66: *February* 11 Thomas Arnold's *Life and Correspondence* was edited by Dean Stanley and published in 1844. This was the same year that the Reverend William Sewell, Fellow of Exeter and one of the Founders and Governors of her son's school, produced his *Journal of a Residence at the College of St. Columba's in Ireland* in which he wrote: 'I am reading the life of Arnold and it is interesting to see how entirely he accords with a number of principles in the management of the school, which has been adopted here without seeing his letters.' Anne Marsh-Caldwell (1791–1874), who started writing on the prompting of her friend, the successful author Harriet Martineau, under the first of her surnames, was very popular in her day. According to the *Dictionary of Women Writers*, novels like *Time the Avenger*, which was first published in 1851, illustrate how her principal concerns included the related themes of fallen women and redemption. Lady Emily Ponsonby (1817–1877), sister of the sixth Earl of Bessborough, had written four novels by 1852 (including *Pride and Irresolution* in 1850). E.S. also read two other novels by Mrs. Marsh, *Tales of Ravenscliffe* (28 March 1852) and *The Wilmingtons* (30 August 1852), so she was clearly a favourite author.

p.67: *February* 12 According to the *O.E.D.*, the earliest recorded use of this phrase is in Sir Walter Scott's *Old Mortality*; the next mentioned is by W.E. Aytoun in 1847 so, strictly speaking, according to this source E. S's 1852 entry in her Journal would be the third. She also used it to describe Lord Lucan on 13 March 1856.

p.69: *February* 26 George William Frederick Villiers, fourth Earl of Clarendon, (1800–1870), had been Lord Lieutenant for Ireland since May 1847 and was to be Secretary of State for Foreign affairs between 1853 and 1855, that is the period at the start of the Crimean War, which he called a 'monster catastrophe'. The thirteenth Earl of Eglinton (1822–1861) who succeeded him as Lord Lieutenant, held this office twice under Lord Derby, between February 1852 and January 1853, and February 1858 and July 1859. His wife Theresa had been acquainted with the Grant family in India, so that is why she thought they should 'get on well'. Towards the end of his first term of office the admittedly extreme Unionist and protestant *Dublin Evening Mail* asserted 'his rule has been uniform, marked by justice, firmness, wisdom and good temper'. It was very complimentary, too, about his wife's legacy: 'The influence of Lady Eglinton's unaffected kindness and warm-hearted urbanity, will be felt in Irish society long after the party connections of this day shall have been forgotten.'

p.69: *February* 29 Daniel Murray, Archbishop of Dublin from 1823 to 1852, who had been born in Co. Wicklow, was seen by her as a thoroughly moderate and responsible churchman ever since he had responded, as she saw it, so positively to her complaints about an irascible priest, Father Germaine, from Blackditches in her Barony of Upper Talbotstown, with whom there were disagreements in the early 1840s about her management of the schools at Baltiboys and his setting up hedge schools as a response.

p.70: *March* 4 Theresa, Lady Eglinton, who E.S. had seen in Edinburgh, was the widow of Commander Michael Cockerell R.N. who had died in 1843. She herself was one of the eight illegitimate children (by the same mother, Harriet Holland) of the second, and last, Viscount Newcomen of Co. Longford, whose great wealth came from his success as a Dublin banker. The Journal later compliments her for not losing sight of her background ('The Countess of Eglinton never forgot Miss Newcomen', 9 January 1853). The meaning given to the colloquial use of *pill* at this time ('an objectionable person, a bore' *O.E.D.*) contrasts both with her reputation and the impression she made on Dublin society, including E.S.

p.71: *March* 8 Lame James Quin had been involved in the 1832 homicide at Baltiboys, fresh information on which, despite a £400 reward for information leading to the conviction of the guilty parties, only emerged nearly a quarter of a century later (see 1 May 1856). It seems to have been a case of mistaken identity in a dispute over land.

p.72: *March* 8 The Eglinton style was based on lavish hospitality and her earlier veiled criticism that this was 'too racing' was probably a fair one. Although he is best remembered for the lavish extravagance of the famous 1839 Eglinton Tournament, and an obsessive interest with the turf which led him to build up one of the largest stables in the country, the *D.N.B.*'s summary strikes an accurate note when it describes him as 'a high-minded nobleman and a thorough sportsman with frank and genial manners and no particular ability'.

p.72: *March* 8 William Cobbett (1762–1835), the political journalist, reformer, farmer and army officer, used his famous *Weekly Political Register* to propagate his radical ideas. The flavour of his views on society can be gauged from one of his best known statements, in his *Grammar of the English Language* (1818), in which he defines *nouns of number or multitude* as being 'such as Mob, Parliament, Rabble, House of Commons, Regiment, Court of King's Bench, Den of Thieves and the like'.

p.75: *March* 20 Tabinet certainly was a silk and wool fabric with many Irish associations, but the principal reason for her selecting Limerick lace was that the Chamberlain, George L'Estrange, had specifically requested in an announcement of 5 March printed in *Saunder's* that at the 'Full Dress Ball in celebration of St. Patrick's Day on Wednesday evening the 24 March . . . the Ladies will appear in Irish manufacture.' Immediately underneath this announcement were two advertisements for 'Irish Guinre Lace' (Johnstones of Sackville Street) and Limerick lace 'after the most approved Designs in real Honniton, Mechlin and Brussels' (Todd and Burns).

The *Dublin Evening Mail* provided its usual list of those invited. E.S would have been pleased to note that this included the Downshires and the Milltowns, and those well-known to her such as Dr. George Porter and Sir Josalyn

Coghill, but she would have derived less satisfaction from the description of her Colonel as 'unattached'.

p.76: *March* 20 Lord Byron married Anne Isabella Milbanke (1792–1860) somewhat impetuously in 1815; they separated after just more than a year of marriage and never met again. She wrote that he had married her 'with the deepest determination of revenge avowed on the day of my marriage and executed ever since with systematic and increasing cruelty'. The connection between William Grant and Lady Byron may have originated in the family holiday described by E.S. (*Memoirs*, Volume I p.94) at the Co. Durham seaside village of Seaham which was on the estates of her father Sir Ralph Milbanke.

p.77: *March* 28 Mrs. Marsh's *Tales of Ravenscliffe* was published in 1851 and fell into that category of her novels seen by her critics as being didactic, but not without dramatic power. The Journals a month or so later saw her as 'a moral surgeon – regularly probes deep, cuts deep – so her tale leaves an uneasy impression, but is true to nature – unamiable nature, nature of a past day I hope'. Benjamin Disraeli's *Lord George Bentinck: A Political Biography* had characteristically been published in a rush in December 1851, shortly after the death in 1848 of his partner in the defeat of one of E.S.'s few political heroes, Sir Robert Peel (whose portrait is, for an inveterate political enemy, detached and accurate) over the repeal of the Corn Laws in 1846. Robert Blake, in his biography of Disraeli, calls it 'a most remarkable book, extremely readable and full of often-quoted comments and descriptions . . . as a vivid story of one of the great parliamentary dramas . . . it is unsurpassed'.

p.77: *March* 29 C. Latouche (1671–1745) founded this bank which was then still one of the wealthiest and most prestigious Dublin financial houses. Under the guidance of James Digges Latouche (1788–1826), it established an equal reputation as one of the most active philanthropic institutions in Ireland. Later, on 30 April 1853, E.S. asserted that David Charles Latouche was a cousin of James King, which might explain the origins of their business arrangement.

p.80: *April* 11 The eighth Lord Beaumont (1805–1854) married a daughter of Lord Kilmaine, whose widow converted after his death, followed by their sixteen year old son in 1864.

p.80: *April* 11 Henry Cockburn (author of the *Memorials of His Own Time*, which is regarded as one of the classic works on the late flowering of the Enlightenment in Edinburgh) and Lord Jeffrey (one of the founders of the *Edinburgh Review*, which was to thunder its increasingly influential opinions over political and cultural life in early nineteenth-century Britain), were both successful lawyers, Judges of the Court of Session and men of letters. Robert Chambers' *Eminent Scotsmen* praised Cockburn's *Life* as:

> a work so admirably written, and containing such vivid delineation of the distinguished men of a departed age, and the fashions of past Scottish life, as well as a minute record of his hero, that the work, notwithstanding the transient nature of its subject, is still a favourite with the reading public of our country.

p.81: *April* 29 Field Marshall Sir Edward Blakeney (1768–1868) was Commander in Chief of the Army in Ireland from 1836 to 1855; his wife Maria was the daughter of Colonel Gardiner of the East India Company army and her brother was the Thomas Gardiner who married E.S.'s sister Mary. Earlier, on occasion of the presentation of an engraving to the honourable and gallant gentleman, E.S.'s *Dublin Evening Mail* had described him as 'a soldier and an Irishman *sans peur et sans reproche*, who has attained the highest class of his noble profession with the perfect goodwill of his brothers in arms'.

p.84: *April* 29 She may have meant this in both senses, as she would certainly have been aware that he had been in serious trouble in June 1838 when the *Outrage Papers*, now in the National Archives, recorded that James Carney 'stonemason' had raped Catherine Bandon. According to the report sent to Dublin Castle by John Finnemor in his capacity as a J.P., 'he obtained carnal knowledge of her body in a full and ample manner'.

p.85: *May* 8 This took place in the Rotunda, where according to the *Dublin Evening Mail*, 'the company numbered about nine hundred of the nobility and gentry of the country'. It was much impressed by 'the arrangements for the reception of the distinguished assembly [which] were conducted upon a scale of great elegance', with the lecture room arranged as a drawing room and the room opposite 'filled up as a Turkish tent in flutted [sic] pillars of blue and pink colours formed into handsome fan-like arches at the top'. The Lord Clonmel she asserts to be the only tipsy person there was John Henry Scott, the third Earl (1817–1866) who was a near neighbour at Bishop's Court in Co. Kildare.

p.88: *June* 6 William Thomas Spencer Wentworth-Fitzwilliam, Lord Milton (1815–1902) was one of the M.P.s for Co. Wicklow between 1847 and 1857; he lived nearby at Coollattin Park.

p.90: *June* 16 Feargus O'Connor (1794–1855), Irish nationalist and Chartist leader, since the debacle of the last petition to Parliament of 1848 had clearly been losing touch with reality and it was on the ninth of June that he grossly insulted a fellow member of the Commons, was promptly committed to the custody of the serjeant-at-arms and next day pronounced insane.

p.91: *June* 20 *The Old Judge or Life in a Colony; Letterbag of the Great Western* was written by T.C Haliburton (1796–1865) whose claims to authorship as *Sam Slick* came from the title of the earlier *The Clockmaker or the Sayings and Doings of Samuel Slick of Slickville*.

p.92: *July* 2 Paul Cullen, who was from Co. Kildare, succeeded Daniel Murray as Archbishop of Dublin in 1852; he arrived with a reputation as an authoritarian disciplinarian and he kept a firm grip on the Church in an era of flux and change until his death in 1878. Needless to say, what E.S. perceived in them and their ecclesiastical policies was the two contrasting extremes of the Catholic Church of her day. Donald Southgate in his *The Passing of the Whigs* described him as 'subtle and tenacious' where his contemporary Archbishop in Tuam, John McHale, was merely 'aggressive'.

p.93: *July* 3 E.S.'s regular newspaper was in no doubt about the conclusion to be drawn from these disturbances. It commented on Monday 5 July: 'A prominent part of the Stockport tale is, that it has *demonstrated* to the satisfaction of the ultramontane organ [the *Times*] that the feeling of the populace of England is unmistakably English and Protestant, and that even among the Celtic helots of the Lancashire manufacturing, Popery, native or foreign, is but a poor stock for a speculator in political capital.' According to Edward Norman (*Anti-Catholicism in Victorian England*), two Catholic chapels in the Irish quarter of the town were sacked and desecrated by a mob of working class men.

p.94: *July* 4 The Queen Caroline Affair stretched from the unseemly proceedings in the summer of 1820, when the

Government tried to use sleazy evidence dredged up from her murky past to get George IV the divorce he required (E.S. remembers – *Memoirs* II, p.161 – 'skimming the rich filth of the dirt the papers were polluted with'); further embarrassments occurred next year when Caroline attempted to storm her way to the Coronation and the whole scandalous affair was, fortunately for the King, terminated by her death in August.

p.94: *July* 4 John Henry Newman (1801–1890), one of the founding figures of the Oxford or Tractarian movement which so infuriated E.S., after his move to the Church of Rome (which explains her use of the phrase 'celebrated Oxford pervert'), became Rector of the recently established Catholic University in Dublin from 1854 to 1858. The other leading Tractarian who found life impossible within the broad wing of the Church of England which E.S. so admired, was Edward Wiseman (1802–1865) who was appointed Cardinal-Archbishop of Westminster in 1850, thereby precipitating the Ecclesiastical Titles Bill which was treated with such contempt in the Journals. It was however a dead letter and was repealed later by Gladstone. They were naturally two of the leading characters in the Dr. Giacinto Achilli case about which the protestant world got very excited in the summer of 1852. However, for Theodore Hoppen in *the New Oxford History*, this former Dominican was a money-grubbing rogue.

p.94: *July* 5 Thomas Babington Macaulay (1800–1859) was the great Whig historian, who was M.P for Edinburgh on two occasions, 1839–1847 and 1852–1856, when part of his campaign was organised by her brother-in-law, William Gibson Craig of Riccarton. Although it is as a historian, many of whose finest essays were written for the *Edinburgh Review*, that he will principally be remembered, he played an important role as secretary to the East India Company Board of Control, of which Charles Grant, later Lord Glenelg, well known to Elizabeth Smith from her earliest days, was President under Earl Grey (see *Memoirs* I p.340).

p.96: *July* 12 John Reynolds,who represented Dublin from 1847 until this election, was a repealer and formerly Lord Mayor of the city, 1849–1850. Sir Edward Grogan, Bart. held one of the Dublin seats from 1841 until his retiral in 1865. John Vance represented Dublin from this election until his retiral the same year. *Dod's Parliamentary Companion* describes these Conservative M.P.s as strongly Protestant, the first being 'a firm supporter of the Established Church' and the latter as 'strongly attached to Protestant institutions'.

p.98: *July* 25 David O'Connor Henchy was indeed elected, as a Liberal in favour of tenant right, for Co. Kildare (he lived in nearby Ballymore Eustace) in July 1852 and held the seat until 1859, but the Sir Edward Kennedy, mentioned on 4 July as an 'absurd'candidate, was not so fortunate.

p.100: *August* 11 The ninth Duke of Bedford had taken the Doune when the Grant family set off to recoup their fortunes in India in 1827 and he was to die there twelve years later. His daughter-in-law, Anne-Marie (1783–1857), who was the mother of a large family, two fathered by Edwin Landseer, the painter, inherited this love for Rothiemurchus.

p.100: *August* 17 A stricture is defined as a morbid narrowing of a canal, duct or passage especially of the urethra, the tube from which urine is discharged from the bladder; she herself on 31 August calls it 'paralysis of the bladder'.

p.101: *August* 22 Father Theobald Matthew (1790–1856) was the celebrated apostle of temperance, who had successfully preached in nearby Naas on the 7th of July and the 14th of August 1840, at a time when his followers may have included half the adult population of Ireland, much to the approval of the diarist at Baltiboys. Donnybrook Fair on the other hand was an institution of which she thoroughly disapproved. For six centuries it had been a centre for trade, barter and public amusement but by the middle of the nineteenth century it had become synonymous with riot and disorder. Séamas Ó Maitiú in *The Humours of Donnybrook* (1995) quotes the estimate of John Madden, the owner of Donnybrook Fair Green where the junketing took place, that no less than 75,000 attended in 1841. Madden died in 1850 and although his nephew Joseph Dillon tenaciously attempted in the teeth of official and Church disapproval to continue the tradition, it had virtually ceased to operate by 1857.

p.104: *September* 4 E.S.'s great-great-grand-daughter (see Introduction) remembers *her* grand-mother, who was much in the company of *her* grand-mother when a young girl, maintaining that of all the sins of omission and commission perceived as being committed by James King during these early days of his marriage to the favourite Smith daughter, nothing hurt as much, or was as unforgivable, as the cutting down of these trees without any consultation.

p.105: *September 5* For details of her first romance, speculation as to the identity of her lover and the story of how she was persuaded to abandon him, see *Memoirs*, Chapter 17. The reactions of both families were so brutal that it is interesting that there was speculation amongst earlier members of the family that the rupture was caused by the knowledge that she had unwittingly fallen in love with, of all people, a natural (or, to use her own adjective, *accidental*) son of her father's.

p.105: *September 5 Passages in the Life of Margaret Maitland* was written by Margaret O. Wilson, afterwards Oliphant (1828–1897), a prolific authoress who described herself as 'Blackwood's general utility woman'.

p.108: *September 24* Dublin was extremely fortunate in the quality of the singers who came for what was clearly a biannual series of performances of contemporary operas like Donizetti's *Don Pasquale*, first produced in Paris in 1843. Giulia Grisi (1811–1869), Giovannie Matteo Mario (1810–1883) and Luigi Lablanche (1794–1858), were three of the greatest interpreters of the classic roles of Italian opera in the 1840s, when they performed in Paris in the winter and London in the summer, a routine which left room for regular annual visits to Dublin in September and October.

p.111: *October 29* There are several mentions of the ample purse of Miss Angela Burdett Coutts (for example she subscribed £56 to St. Columba's in 1849) as Elizabeth Smith contemplates the misery around her and her ability to offer only limited assistance to tenantry or friends like the O'Reillys who were facing destitution. Her mother, Sophia, daughter of the exceedingly wealthy Scottish entrepreneur Thomas Coutts, founder of the bank that bears his name, had married Sir Francis Burdett (1770–1844), the radical M.P. for, amongst other constituencies, Westminster between 1817 and 1837. Angela, who was sole heir to her grandfather's fortune, supported the social reforms of Charles Dickens that were so applauded by E.S.

p.114: *November 14* Alexander, the tenth Duke of Hamilton (1767–1852) was buried with oriental pomp on the 4 November in the mausoleum he had constructed at vast expense at Hamilton Palace in the circumstances here described. Such eccentricity need not surprise us in the Hereditary Keeper of the Palace of Holyrood who believed that he was the true heir to the Scottish throne.

p.114: *November* 21 Francois Guizot, Prime Minister of France during the reign of Louis Philippe (1830–1848) was also an important writer, the author, for example, of the *Histoire de la Civilisation en Europe* (1828–1830).

p.114: *November* 21 At first sight this is a somewhat surprising opinion and Palmerston, as Home Secretary, wrote in a letter dated 17 November – 'The Austrians have distinguished themselves by declining to send anybody to the funeral of the Duke, and I am told that our Queen is very angry with them. The papers say it is the Emperor himself who took this decision.' Queen Victoria herself wrote to the King of the Belgians (a monarch greatly distrusted by E.S.) on 23 November that 'There is but one feeling of indignation and surprise at the conduct of Austria in taking this opportunity to slight England in return to what happened to Haynau for his own character.' E.S. had speculated the day after Palmerston's resignation 26 December 1851 on the reasons without mentioning Haynau, the brutal General whose visit to London was such a diplomatic disaster. Perhaps the most measured judgement is that of Cecil Woodham Smith in her biography of Victoria: 'The Queen was much incensed that Austria refused to send any representative on the grounds of the treatment of General Haynau. She observed that the true reason was Austrian fear of displeasing France.'

p.120: *December* 12 This seems an extreme judgment on someone who was a member of a rich Quaker family celebrated for its commitment in the 1820s and 1830s to widespread social reform, in her case in particular of the prison system. She was born in 1790 and died in 1856, the third daughter of the eleven children of John Gurney of Earlham, five of whom were actively involved in the philanthropic movements of the day.

p.121: *December* 21 There were very considerable religious tensions around in this election year of which E.S. was evidently well aware. The feeling against both Rome and the Tractarians was exacerbated by the actions and words of the outgoing Prime Minister Lord John Russell and it is clear that there were a number of the Irish Liberal M.P.s (sixty three of whom were returned in all) who were prepared to act as a cohesive group, so that as Donald Southgate commented in

The Passing of the Whigs: 'The Irish masses provided prime combustible material for the Roman party. "The Pope's Brass Band" began to march, and to its accompaniment heads rolled at the election of 1852.'

1853

p.125: *January* 9 Francis Robinson (1799–1872) was perhaps the most celebrated of a succession of father and four musical sons whose contribution to the musical life of St. Patrick's Cathedral is summed up in the inscription on the north wall of the aisle: 'To commemorate an Eminent Family of Musicians whose rare Gifts and Culture were devoted to the Glory of God in this Cathedral Church and whose personal Dignity and Noble Compositions added Lustre to the Art which for upward of a Century they were foremost in providing.'

p.126: *January* 9 Edward Granville Eliot, third Earl of St. Germains (sic) (1798–1877), had been the very much Peelite Chief Secretary for Ireland between 1841 and 1845; his spell as Lord Lieutenant lasted from January 1853 to May 1855. His 'amiable wife' was Jemima, daughter of the second Marquess Cornwallis, grand-daughter of the great family friend, Jane, Duchess of Gordon.

p.126: *January* 16 Sir Thomas Nicholas Redington (sic) who died aged forty seven in 1862, was M.P. for Dundalk (1837–1856) and Under-Secretary for Ireland between 1846 and 1852; he was the permanent Joint Secretary to Sir Charles Wood at the Board of Control in Aberdeen's coalition ministry. He had been that curious mixture, a Catholic supporter of the Ecclesiastical Titles Bill, which may explain E.S.'s distaste for him.

p.126: *January* 16 William Nicholas Keogh, who was born in 1817, represented Athlone as M.P. (1847–1856) and his abilities earned him rapid preferment in the legal profession, first as Solicitor General and then with his elevation to the bench in 1856. He presided over the 1865 Fenian trials and it has been suggested that these pressures contributed to his later suicide in 1878.

p.127: *January* 23 The fifth Duke of Manchester's connection with the Rothiemurchus area is explained by the fact that his mother was Susan (third daughter of the remarkable Duchess of Gordon), who was remembered by E.S. for her 'very coarse speeches' and running off with one of the footmen (*Memoirs* I pp.100 and 198). The second wife mentioned here was Harriet Dobbs, from Castle Dobbs in Co. Antrim.

p.128: *January* 25 Julia Kavanagh was born in Thurles in Co. Tipperary and spent much of her earlier life in France, dying in Nice in 1877; her novels, like *Nathalie*, published in 1850, were praised by Charlotte Brontë.

p.128: *January* 30 Sir Thomas Askew Larcom (1801–1879) was indeed 'an able man'. His public career began with the Irish Ordinance Survey where he helped to organise numerous agents to collect what the *D.N.B.* described as 'a rich store of local information, concerning the history, the languages and the antiquities of Ireland'. These were assembled and catalogued at Mountjoy in Phoenix Park where they can still be consulted. Many of Larcom's manuscripts were handed on to the President of the Royal Irish Academy (well-known to E. S. as 'that antiquarian oddity', Dr. J.H. Todd) and, again, the *D.N.B*'s judgement helps to put his achievement into context.

> In many places it will be found that the descriptions and drawings presented in the collection are now the only remaining records of monuments which connect themselves with our earliest history, and of the folklore which the famine swept away with the aged sennachies, who were its sole repositories.

This work and his experience as a Census Commissioner made him a natural choice as one of the Commissioners who organised the public relief works inaugurated by Lord John Russell's government; his experience was also invaluable in the Poor Law Commission of Inquiry. When he was appointed Under-Secretary in 1853, a position he occupied with model efficiency until 1868, it was a measure of the respect in which he was held, at least by the governing establishment, that this was the first time the position was seen as a non-political and permanent appointment.

p.129: *February* 6 E.S. was well aware of this term although it is interesting that it was not one that readily came to her diarist's pen to describe any of what, to use the language of the day, were called 'rural outrages'. The definition offered by the *O.E.D.* is: 'A Roman Catholic secret society or league found in the north and north west of Ireland early in the nineteenth century to counteract the Protestant influence, and associated with agrarian disorder.' S.J. Connolly's contribution to the *New History of Ireland* (Volume V, edited by W.E. Vaughan) emphasises that its strongest support lay among tradesmen and that it had a strong urban bias: 'its tone was artisan and lower middle class rather than peasant or proletarian'. Moreover, he stresses that it was more than mere agrarian protest: 'Ribbonism embodied at least some elements of a political ideology.' So, perhaps E.S. was being exact when she discarded this adjective in her accounts of the comparatively rare examples of rural disorder around Blessington at this time. Later entries in the Journal describe her reaction to a Ribbon trial (18 April 1854) and her suspicion that an act of sabotage on a train full of Protestant demonstrators was a Ribbon atrocity (1 October 1854).

p.129: *February 6* 'A second Josephine', one who can be compared to the ambitious first wife of the great Napoleon, is a very reasonable point of comparison to make, especially at the time of her marriage. Marie-Eugenie-Ignace-Augustine de Montizo (1826–1920) had a cosmopolitan background. Her father was the Count of Teba and then Montizo. Her mother was the daughter of William Kilkpatrick, Scots by birth but American by nationality, and the U.S. Consul. In his speech from the throne on 21 January, to which E.S. refers, to justify what the eleventh edition of the Encyclopedia Britannica rather primly called a *mesalliance*, Napoleon III declared: 'I have preferred a woman I love and respect to a woman unknown to me, with whom an alliance would have had advantages mixed with sacrifices.'

The phrase 'mak siccar' (make certain) refers to the 1306 meeting in the Church of the Grey Friars in Dumfries when Robert Bruce and John Comyn plotted how to free their country from the domination of Edward I. Harsh words were exchanged and Bruce lost his temper and stabbed Comyn in front of the High Altar. Kennedy is, according to legend, supposed to have finished off the job. From this point Bruce had no alternative but to commit himself to what became the successful War of Independence.

p.129: *February 13* E.S's grand-daughter was to marry into the Stannus family and this explains why the opening chapter of Dame Ninette de Valois' autobiography *Come Dance with Me* is set at Baltiboys. This Lady Stannus drifts in and out of the social milieu occupied by the Smiths and their daughters in Dublin. She was related to the Major General Sir Ephraim Gerrish Stannus who became Lieutenant-Governor of the East India Company College, Addiscombe, which E.S. loathed and wished to see closed down (see, for example, 12 March 1854 when she described it as a 'contamination').

p.130: *February* 13 Mr. Sheehan, who as a regular visitor seemed high on the list of Janey's *beaux*, was such a well informed source of information ranging from Dublin gossip to political news, both of which found a receptive ear in Mrs. Smith, because he was the Editor and proprietor of the *Dublin Evening Mail*.

p.130: *February* 13 This is described by the *O.E.D.* as a biennial purple-flowered composite plant, the Purple Goat's beard, *Tragopagum porrifululius*, whose root is eaten as a vegetable. For more on Richard Whately, the eccentric Archbishop of Dublin, see 18 March.

p.131: *February* 13 She was married to John La Touche of Harriston and her correspondence during a long life (1824–1906) was edited by Margaret Ferrier Young (1908) in a volume entitled *The Letters of a Noble Woman*, in which there is only one reference to her other writing – 'she once wrote two novels, more as an amusement than for graver reasons. Perhaps because of this they were not successful and are now quite forgotten.'

p.131: *February* 13 The Marquis' second wife was Frances, widow of Sir William Hay Macnaughton, Bart. who, according to the *Complete Peerage*, had been 'assassinated 25 Dec. 1841 at Cabul'; for Elizabeth Smith's outraged reaction to the bungled Afghanistan operation ('if this be glory, it is but tinsel'), see *The Highland Lady in Ireland* 7 January 1840 and 11 March 1842.

p.133: *February* 20 Caroline Elizabeth Sarah Norton (1808–1877) and her unsuitable husband the Hon. George Chapple Norton M.P. (1808–1877), brother of the third Lord Grantley (who was to be succeeded by Mrs. Norton's second son), were the centrepiece of one of the most celebrated divorce cases of the century. He was M.P. for Guildford at the time of their marriage and in 1831, a year *after* losing his seat in the General election, was appointed a Metropolitan Police Magistrate, a position he was to hold until 1867. He was appointed by the Home Secretary, shortly to be Prime Minister, William Lamb, second Viscount Melbourne (1779–1848); in the carefully chosen words of the *D.N.B.*

because 'he was thought to be a man of easy morals . . . a very delicate situation was created'. The result was a somewhat hypocritical action by the husband against Lord Melbourne in June 1836 which ended with the 'triumphant acquittal of the accused parties' and the vindication of Mrs. Norton's character. The *Complete Peerage* noted that 'the jury, without leaving the box, found the proceedings unjustified' but chose to add the reaction of Melbourne's brother Frederick that 'no man's luck can go further'. It was after all his second appearance as a correspondent.

Caroline Norton was a grand-daughter of Richard Brinsley Sheridan, the playwright, and her third novel *Stuart of Dunleath*, which was published in 1851, came out to considerable critical acclaim; it has often been seen as containing many veiled autobiographical references, so her literary works may be said to have profited from her being so much in the public eye in the 1830s.

p.133: *February 27* Frederick Richard Chichester, an author according to the *Complete Peerage* of several works of fiction, died in his twenty sixth year. His cousin was to succeed as fifth Marquess of Donegall in 1889; in the course of a long life between 1822 and 1904 he contracted three marriages and left twenty seven pounds in his will.

p.134: *February 27* Arthur MacMorrough Kavanagh (1831–1889) was one of the most remarkable public figures of his time. He inherited the family estates by Borris, Co. Carlow in 1853 after the deaths of his two elder brothers, by which time he had travelled widely in the Middle East (1846–1848), volunteered as a scout during the Smith O'Brien insurrection of 1848, and between 1849 and 1851 journeyed through Russia to Persia (where he collected the prayer books of the recently murdered military explorers Stoddart and Conolly) and India.

What made this so extraordinary was that he was 'born with only the rudiments of arms and legs . . . and by indomitable resolution and perseverance triumphed over his physical defects' (*D.N.B.*). He was a celebrated sportsman, using ingenious methods to fish, shoot and most surprisingly to hunt. He was M.P. in the Protestant Unionist tradition for Co. Wexford between 1866 and 1868, and for Carlow 1868 to 1880, by which time even his reputation as an improving landlord with a strong personal vote was not able to stand up to his Home Rule opponents. He ended his public career as a dissenting member of the Bessborough Commission, which reported in 1881 into the land system in Ireland.

The point about the prophecy is that the Kavanagh estates were centred on Borris House in the village of Borris, Co. Carlow and that there was no issue from his marriage to his cousin Frances Mary Leathley.

p.136: *March* 18 Richard Whately (1787–1863), who became Archbishop of Dublin in 1831, features in the Journals both when E.S. came across him in his official capacity as Archbishop, when he regularly visited St. Columba's, and on the occasions when, as here, she recounts some tale about this Dublin character. With all his eccentricties, he was an important public figure, chairing the report into the Condition of the Irish Poor in 1833 and co-operating with Daniel Murray over the National Schools. His wife, who is the subject of this particular anecdote, was Elizabeth, daughter of William Pope of Hillingdon Hall, Uxbridge.

p.136: *March* 19 The *Dublin Evening Mail* of Monday 18 March certainly was impressed: 'It must be gratifying to all who wish to retain a court in Ireland to see the balls at the Castle attended by such an assemblage of rank and fashion as attended St. Patrick's ball on Wednesday night.'

p.137: *March* 20 Elizabeth Smith deeply admired *Household Words: A Weekly Journal Conducted by Charles Dickens* both for the improving aims they shared and because she so admired the editor; he himself described it as 'that great humming top . . . which is always going round with the weeks and murmuring "Attend to me!"' It sold for twopence and was therefore twice the price of *Saunder's* but it was a daily magazine. This edition was No. 156 for Saturday 19 March 1852, entitled 'Received a Blank Child; a little enquiry concerning those gaps in the decorous world'.

p.138: *March* 20 The direct line of the earldom of Westmeath died with the eighth Marquis, although he was married three times. The title passed on to his cousin Anthony Francis Nugent (described by the *Complete Peerage* as a 'staunch Roman Catholic') and he was succeeded by his son, Janey's contemporary, William St. George Nugent, (1832–1883), who became the tenth earl in 1879. He was a Captain in the 9th Regiment of Foot and saw active service at the siege of Sebastopol the following year. In the end he was to marry his cousin.

p.139: *March* 20 Wyndham Goold certainly existed and he and the Smiths were to be part of the group marshalled by, amongst others, Mr. Sheehan, who attended many of the social events of this Dublin winter season. He lived in 21 Merrion Square, had been one of the founders and original governors of St. Columba's College and was Member of Parliament for Limerick from 1850, so he was clearly an eligible bachelor. However he was to die in 1854. The funeral took place on Friday 8 December and, according to the *Limerick Chronicle*, 'the tenantry on horseback, wearing white scarfs and hat bands, led the cavalcade six abreast, to the number of six hundred' and 'the lamentations of the peasantry, especially the females, were loud and almost irrepressible, on this truly sad occasion'. The Gore-Booth family were from Lissadell in Co. Sligo, the same family that was to be immortalised in W.B. Yeats' poetry.

p.140: *March* 22 A Gaelic word with approximately the same meaning as domain; the family crest is an armed hand holding a broadsword, with the motto 'For my Duchus'.

p.140: *March* 22 The Duchess of Bedford, the fifth and youngest daughter of the celebrated Duchess of Gordon who played such an influential part in E.S.'s childhood, died at Nice on the 24 February; she had met the Grants in Flanders during their grand tour of 1819 (*Memoirs* II pp. 124–5).

p.142: *March* 25 Susan Bogert Warner wrote her novels under the pseudonym Elizabeth Wetherall and both *Queechy* and *The Wide Wide World* sold well in New York, where they were first published, and in London; it has been estimated that the latter had sold no less than half a million copies by 1860. For a comment on her sister Mrs. Winthrop's novel *Dollars and Cents or GlenLuca* ('a wise little book'), see 25 April 1853.

p.147: *April* 8 The quotation is from *Aglaura*, which Sir John Suckling (1609–1642) wrote in 1639:

> Why so pale and wan, fond lover?
> Prithee, why so pale?
> Will, when looking well can't move her, looking ill prevail?
> Prithee, why so pale?

p.149: *April* 17 This was the *nom de plume* used by the elder Ambrose Hickey, whom E.S. had met in the second part of her stay in France at Avranches in 1845 (see *A Highland Lady in France* July 1844); she had been impressed by his pamphlets on the need for agricultural improvement soundly based on a lead from the landed proprietors. His best known was *Hints originally intended for the Small Farmers of the County of Wexford; but suited to the circumstances of Many Parts of Ireland* (1828). A later edition was spearheaded by some whimsical verses:

A THIRD EDITION now attests
The value of my sage bequests.
I envy none of those who write
With empty fame or gain in sight.
With envy those alone I view
Whose pen has public good in view –
Instructive lessons who impart,
The flow of patriotic heart.
Good practice to recommend,
And be the People's real friend.
So here – I make my homely bow,
God speed the Irish farmer's plough.

p.149: *April* 17 Lady Gough's exotic costume, and her husband's title when he was ennobled in 1845, 'Baron Gough of Ching-keang-foo, China, Maharajpore and the Sutlej in the East Indies', reflected the varied highpoints of his military career in the east. Born in Co. Limerick, he was to die a Field-Marshal in his ninetieth year in 1869.

p.153: *April* 30 Spencer Horatio Walpole (1806–1898), who married one of the six daughters of Spencer Percival, the only Prime Minister to have been assassinated (E.S.'s 1811/1812 neighbour when the family were in Lincoln's Inn Fields), had been at the Home Office until December 1852.

p.154: *May* 8 The Right Honourable Sir William Gibson Craig, Bart. was sister Jane's brother-in-law; his powers of patronage would have rested on the fact that he represented the County of Edinburgh from 1837 to 1841 and the City of Edinburgh from1841 until he retired in 1852. He had been appointed a Lord of the Treasury (at a salary of £1,200 per annum) in 1846, a post he held until the demise of the government in 1852. He became a Judge of the Court of Session in 1862.

p.154: *May* 8 Edward Bulwer-Lytton, first Baron Lytton (1803–1873) sustained an expensive and extravagant social life alongside that of an ambitious politician by writing principally novels. *My Novel or Varieties in English Life* was published in 1853. He had much in common with Disraeli, whom he knew well throughout his life, and was to be portrayed in *Endymion*.

p.156: *May 22* This was the Grand Fancy Dress Ball for the Royal Hospital; the *Mail* reported on Monday 23 May that there had been 'an abundance of Chinese, Turks, Spaniards, gypseys, sailors etc.'. Vignettes, as used here, are the ornamental or decorative designs at the start of a chapter, and fardingales are a form of hooped petticoat.

p.157: *May 27* Dublin's International Exhibition, which opened on 12 May 1853 and was visited by Queen Victoria and Prince Albert, owed much of its success to the support of local businessmen, including William Dargan. He had pioneered the construction of railways in Ireland, opening the first between Dublin and Kingstown in 1831; by 1853 he had built six hundred miles throughout the country and he had contracts for a further two hundred miles. He lent £100,000 towards the costs of the Exhibition, of which he was reconciled to losing £20,000. When the Queen visited his house, Dargan Villa in Anneville (described by the *Mail* as 'a splendid mansion . . . not to be compared for grandeur, beauty and variety in the United Kingdom'), she offered him a baronetcy which he refused.

p.161: *June 13* Currer Bell was the *nomme de plume* selected by Charlotte Brontë (1816–1855) to preserve her anonymity. *Villette* was published in 1853, six years after *Jane Eyre* and four years after *Shirley*. It is based on her experiences in a school in Brussels in 1842 and in 1843 to 1844, particularly on her affection for the husband of the proprietor of the school, the Pensionnat Heger (the *D.N.B.* somewhat cautiously proposed that ' it is probable that she suffered at this time from some unfortunate attachment'). It has therefore been suggested that her heroes tended to be married or Belgians or schoolmasters or a combination (*Dictionary of British Women Writers*, edited by Janet Todd). Her two sisters Emily and Anne (who selected the names Ellis and Acton Bell to accompany that of their elder sister) did indeed die tragically before Charlotte in 1848 and 1849. E.S.'s interesting comment on the relationship with Dickens is obviously somewhat confused. He was later to fall in love with the young actress Ellen Lawless Ternan (1839–1914), with whom he acted for the first time in the summer of 1857, a relationship he was famously to deny in an article that appeared on the front page of the issue of *Household Words* of 12 June 1858 under the heading PERSONAL.

p.161: *June* 28 The facts are very much as she describes them. Wilhelm von Humboldt (1767–1835) and his brother Alexander (1769–1854) are commonly perceived as two of the outstanding intellects to emerge from eighteenth century Prussia. The younger brother is remembered as a naturalist and explorer; the elder as a philologist, diplomat and man of letters (or, as he was to E.S. 'this amiable philosopher'). Part of his reputation in this last field rests on the *Letters to a Female Friend* (*Briefe an eine Freundlin*), which E.S. and her Aunt would probably have read in the version translated by Catherine H. Couper and published in 1849. Charlotte Diede clearly shared von Humboldt's memory of that holiday at Pyrmont, probably in 1789: 'To me the remembrance of those three happy days of my youth outweighs in value all the rest of an ordinary everyday life.'

And yet she was aware that 'our's is a most extraordinary tie' (Letter II, December 1814), nowhere more so, perhaps, than when in Letter VII in 1822 the good Baron asks her for 'an exact and connected history of the development and rare progress of your mental culture'. By Letter VIII she is being addressed as his 'amiable child'. It is all too easy to read too much into personalities we know about through the survival of letters, and these were clearly meant to survive, and it is interesting to see what E.S. made of them. She makes that clear later on 4 July when she draws a direct comparison between the value of his correspondence to von Humboldt and her Journal to herself ('What Charlotte was to Humboldt, this odd journal is to me'; 'we poets must *utter*').

p.170: *August* 14 Charles Dickens founded *Household Words* to combine entertainment with a strong social message; Charles Lever the novelist was editor of the *Dublin University Magazine* between 1842 and 1845; Miss Eliza Cooke (1817–1889) started a strongly feminist Journal which she herself edited in 1849 until it closed five years later.

p.171: *September* 4 Her displeasure probably originated in the fact that the seventh Earl of Cardigan (1797–1868), who at this time was Lieutenant Colonel of the 11th Hussars, a regiment on which he reputably spent £11,000 each year of his own money, was a well-known philanderer and the third Earl of Howth (1803–1874) married for the second time in 1851.

p.178: *October* 19 The Grant brothers (from Manchester not Liver-

pool) were indeed the originals of Charles and Edwin Cheeryble, the self made merchants and kind-hearted philanthropists
who became the benefactors of Nicholas Nickleby, offering
him a job as a clerk and then a partnership. Michael Slater, in
his introduction to he Penguin Classics edition, describes
them as 'fairy-tale paragons of benevolence' and quotes
George Orwell's view of them as 'two gruesome old Peter
Pans'. However, in his preface to the original edition of the
novel in 1839, Dickens took great pains to emphasise that
where Squeers was 'the representative of a class, and not of an
individual . . . there *are* two characters . . . who are drawn
from life' and that the brothers' 'liberal charity, their single-
ness of heart, their noble nature, and their unbounded benevolence, are no creations of the Author's brain'.

p.180: *October 24* E.S. was notorious in her family for her stalwart
belief in the value of Infant Schools. It is no surprise therefore, that she should have commented with approval on the
somewhat breathless leading article in *Chambers'* for Saturday 21 April 1855, entitled 'Poor People's Children'. This
extract provides something of its flavour:

> An Infant Ragged School! What picture the name implies!
> – pictures of the very scum of babyhood, picked out of the
> gutters, alleys, reeking cellars; wretched babyhood, from
> its very birth-hour entering on its only inheritance – want,
> brutality and crime. Yet here were godly rows of small
> plants of humanity . . . tidy, clean and pretty enough for
> any rank or class of tiny girlhood.

p.182: *November 7* Valentine Browne Lawless (1773–1853), first
U.K. Baron Cloncurry, was a figure of considerable interest
in Irish and British public life from 1798 when as a United
Irishman he was imprisoned both in that year and between
1799 and 1801; within two years of his death was published
The Life, Times and Contemporaries of Lord Cloncurry by
William John Fitzpatrick. His most prominent moment in
Irish public life probably came when he was chairman of the
Dublin Mansion House Committee that raised one and a half
million pounds for famine relief by November 1845. It was
through the Milltowns that E.S. was acquainted with him,
because he had taken as his second wife Emily, the widow of
Joseph, the third earl of Milltown. It was their son Cecil
John, M.P. for Clonmel since 1846, who was so disappointed
with the practical implications of his father's will that he

expired on 5 November of what the *Complete Peerage* calls
'violent inflammation of the brain' at the age of thirty two.
The title therefore passed to the younger son; he was to
commit suicide at Lyons Castle, Co. Kildare on 4 April 1869
by throwing himself from a window. The other regular
reference to Lord Cloncurry in the Journals is in connection
with his companion during his last years, a Miss Sçavoy who
had been a governess at Russborough. She, however, is not
mentioned in the *Personal Recollections of the Life and Times of
Valentine, Lord Cloncurry* which he published in 1849.

p.188: *December* 25 There was to be a flurry of correspondence
published in the old faithful, the *Dublin Evening Mail*, next
month on this question. First was a letter dated 6 December
from amongst others Christopher Wordsworth, Headmaster
of Harrow, and the omnipresent Dr. J.H. Todd, in which the
actions of the Warden were defended and explained. Thomas Sheehan, it might have been as editor rather than owner,
wrote: 'We have seldom been called upon, in our editorial
capacity, to comment upon a document characterised by
more cool impudence than the subjoined letter to the Primate.' The commentary continued rather pointedly that
after the 'measures so properly carried out by the Primate
in the case of St. Columba's', he should 'concern himself with
the Honorary fellows of St. Columba's' who had signed the
original letter. The Primate in his reply of the 30 December
contented himself with stating that 'I cannot hold out any
promise that I will continue to give [the school] my support'.
Next month on Monday 16 January, there was a letter from
James W. Greene, the Sub-Warden, which was dismissed as
'a literary curiosity' by the Warden, a reaction which elicited
a furious response from the *Mail*. 'Our readers will, from this
glimpse behind the scenes, be able to form, or rather to
mature their opinions of the Warden's character – his want
of truthfulness, his *hauteur*, his scheming, and his identifica-
tion with that party in the English Church which boasts so
much of respect for ecclesiastical authority, and which ex-
hibits so little of it, whenever the rulers of the church do not
follow their guidance.'

1854

p.192: *January* 12 Kitty Hawtawne's father was the eccentric but
entertaining Archdeacon who was part of the newly married

Colonel and Mrs. Smith's acquaintance on the long voyage back from India in 1830. His behaviour ranged from the amusing to the distressing and it is well described in the closing chapter of the *Memoirs*. He was to commit suicide soon after reaching Ireland.

p.193: *January* 15 This passage reflects the general suspicion, if not antipathy, aroused by what was believed by many to be the role played by the Prince Consort in public affairs at this time. As Victoria's husband it would have been difficult for a prince of his background and experience not to have expected to have played a conspicuous part in the state consultation processes. By 1854, he was attacked as 'sympathising with the schemes of Russian ambitions' and seen in general 'as an evil influence working behind the throne' and even striving 'to thwart the policy of her majesty's government' (*D.N.B.*).

p.195: *January* 29 Lord John Russell's *Memoirs, Journal and Correspondence of Thomas Moore* (which the *Encyclopedia Britannica* edition of 1911 damns with faint praise by suggesting it 'contains an immense quantity of biographical material') was published in eight volumes between 1853 and 1856, years when he was a member of the cabinet as Lord President and, briefly, between February and July 1855 at the Colonial Office. He led a busy public life but this does not lead the *D.N.B.* to view his achievement as worthy of more than the dismissive comment that 'he barely realised his duties as an editor'.

p.197: *February* 12 Johan Wolfgang von Goethe (1749–1832) clearly did not make an enormous impression through his Autobiography and this is a list of some of his heroines and amatory inspirations. Gretchen is the heroine of *Faust*, Annette the subject of many of his lyrics from his student days in Leipzig, Frederika and Charlotte (which was also the name of the wife of the Weimar civil servant he loved) are the heroines of *Dichtung und Wahrheit* (Poetry and Truth) and *Werthers Leiden* (The Suffering of Werther). At the age of seventy four he married Christiane Vulpius, with whom, to the consternation of Weimar society, he had been living for seventeen years.

p.197: *February* 14 Sir John Burgoyne (1782–1871), a Royal Engineers veteran of the Peninsular War, was a distant relative of E.S. ('that old twaddle my cousin': *Memoirs* I p. 319) and their paths had crossed when he was Chairman of the Board of Public Works in Ireland, 1831–1846 and a Relief Commissioner during the Famine. He was then appointed Inspector General of Fortifications (a post he held until his retirement in 1868, by which time he was in his eighty-sixth year) and it was in this capacity that he was summoned to the Crimean army as Chief Engineer. He was recalled in February 1855.

p.198: *February* 14 This case, heard in front of the Lord Chief Justice, was one in which, very much as described by E.S., Miss Margaret Cantwell sought no less than £5,000 damages from the firm Cannock and White on two grounds, that of 'false imprisonment' and 'malicious prosecution'. The key witness was the sixteen year old Henry Campion who, according to the long account naturally printed by the *Dublin Evening Mail* on Friday 10 February, 'plainly and distinctly saw the lady take a piece of black ribbon out of a paper, turn round and throw it amongst the rolls of oilcloth'. Interestingly, it also quoted him as stating 'that he heard a sum of 53 (pounds) was offered for any evidence in the case, and that he said he could, perhaps, give as good evidence as any one else'. The damages were as stated in the journal, the jury finding for the plaintiff on the first charge but not agreeing on the second.

p.200: *March* 19 E.S.'s younger brother John Peter (1807–1893) had been chosen by Lord Dalhousie in 1848 to be secretary to the government of Bengal and five years later his fast-moving career led him to the post of permanent secretary in the home department of the Government of India and thence to membership of the Governor General's Council and finally Lieutenant Governor of Bengal. He retired in 1862, but four years later when the slave revolt broke out in Jamaica he was summoned to become Governor, which post he held until 1873, when after the death of his brother William he became the eleventh Laird of Rothiemurchus.

p.200: *March* 19 This is one of the most characteristic phrases she used to describe the volatility of the servants she had employed to bring calm, regularity and stability into their invalid household. It derived from the rocket invented in 1808 during the Peninsular War by General Sir William Congreve (1772–1828).

p.204: *April* 9 Lord Fitzroy James Henry Somerset, first Baron Raglan (1788–1855), despite his personal bravery at Waterloo, was perceived as a desk-bound soldier (he had been military secretary to the Horse Guards for twenty seven years before becoming Master General of the Ordnance in 1852) whose visits to see front-line conditions for himself were much more frequent than E.S. suggests. As Trevor Royle emphasises in his *Crimea*, like his great mentor Wellington, he was prepared to show himself to his troops in the heat of battle and led his men in person to the Alma. Sir William Francis Patrick Napier (1785–1860), who had been born in neighbouring Co. Kildare, the General and historian of the Peninsular War, seems to have been wounded and suffered dreadful privations in every campaign in which he participated in Spain.

p.204: *April* 10 This was the celebrated chop-house much frequented by M.P.s, reputedly the subject of the final words of William Pitt the Younger. According to Lord Rosebery's *Pitt*, that inveterate political gossip Disraeli used to try in his early days as an M.P. to tap 'a grim old waiter of prehistoric reputation' who was reputed 'to possess a secret treasure of political tradition'. He disclosed that the authorised version – 'Oh, my country, how I leave my country' – was 'nonsense' and should be replaced by the more mundane 'I think I could eat one of Bellamy's veal pies.'

p.204: *April* 16 Henry Hallam (1777–1859) was a barrister and Commissioner of Stamps as well as an important historian. He was the father of Arthur who so inspired Tennyson (*In Memoriam*), and as a Whig constitutional historian he was much admired by Macaulay. *Hallam's A View of the State of Europe in the Middle Ages* (1818) he described in an article for the *Edinburgh Review* as 'the most impartial work we have read'.

p.205: *April* 30 Henry Cockburn, his *Memorials of His Own Time* and the *Life of Lord Jeffrey*, appear regularly in the Journals but this is the only mention of another of that distinguished band of men of letters E.S. believed had added lustre to the Edinburgh of the Scottish Enlightenment. John Wilson (1783–1854) was the Christopher North of the Tory magazine *Blackwood's*, a prolific author best remembered for his *Noctes Ambrosianae* and as the Professor of Moral Philosophy at the University of Edinburgh; somewhat surprisingly his morals needed to be attested to for this post by another literary lady with whom E.S. is sometimes confused, Anne Grant of Laggan, authoress of *Letters from the Mountains* (1806) and *Superstitions of the Highlanders* (1811).

p.207: *May* 22 E.S. has not quite got hold of this word which properly should be, according to *Webster's*, Rhodomontade, meaning 'vain exaggerated boast or bragging speech, vain boasting, empty bluster'. It comes from the name Rodamonte, the fierce and boastful king of Algiers in *Orlado innamorata* (1487) an epic poem by Mateo M. Boiardo.

p.209: *May* 27 A *vivandière* was a suttler, a person who supplied victuals to soldiers in the field and acted as nursing assistants. She was familiar with this system of provisioning troops on the move as she had seen and commented on it when she came across it for the first time during the Smith family's year in the garrison town of Pau (see *A Highland Lady in France* p 29). In common with almost everyone who contrasted the two allies' preparations for war, she emphasised the effectiveness and urgency of the French compared with the tardy and unimpressive British efforts. As Napoleon III contrasted sharply with Lord Aberdeen, and Raglan with Saint Arnaux and Canrobert, so the *vivandières* suggested how the French had everything worked out to the smallest detail of their soldiers' comforts, possessing what she later (20 January 1855) called their 'wonderful aptitude for management'.

p.212: *July* 7 Rosalind's ironic assertion to Orlando in *As You Like It* (Act IV scene I lines 93–4) is, appropriately in this context, completed by Viola's claim to Duke Orsino in *Twelfth Night* that her father had a daughter who 'never told her love, but let concealment, like a worm i' the bud, feed on her damask cheek' (Act II scene 4 lines 110–112).

p.213: *July* 27 William Henry Ford Cogan (1823–1894) was Liberal Member of Parliament for Kildare from his election in March 1852 until his retiral in 1880. He owned houses in St. James Street in London and St. Stephen's Green in Dublin as well as a property, Tinode, in Blessington (*Dod's Parliamentary Companion*). As well as wealth he possessed considerable influence as a Magistrate for Wicklow, Kildare and Carlow.

p.221: *August* 21 Andrew Combe's *Life* (1797–1847) was published by his brother George (1788–1858) in 1849, along with a memoir by R. Cox, first published in the *Phrenological Journal* the brothers had founded in 1823 and owned until 1837. Andrew was both phrenologist and physiologist; he was appointed physician to King Leopold of the Belgians in 1836 and physician extraordinary to the Queen in Scotland two years later. E.S. was more interested, as is plain here, with the brothers' concern with the establishment of a national secular system of education. George Combe married Cecilia Siddons, the youngest grand-daughter of the celebrated actress, and so was the brother-in-law of William Grant's wife Sally. E.S. met him during her visit to Edinburgh in July 1848 ('He will produce a moral revolution as surely as the sun ripens the harvests. I could have listened to him for a century. I never spent a happier evening.' *The Highland Lady in Ireland* p.399). It is unlikely therefore that she would have agreed with the opinion of Sir Leslie Stephen, no less, the joint editor of the D.N.B. that 'his writings were for many years extremely popular with the half-educated'.

p.225: *September* 24 Jeanne Sophie Charlotte Crüwell (1826–1907) was born in Westphalia and, like all the leading singers who visited Dublin for this autumn season, she was one of the most distinguished of her generation. To write that she was 'our first soprano voice now that Grisi is gone' is misleading as the latter sang in Dublin in the 1852 and 1856 season, but in 1854 she and her husband Mario were touring America. E.S.'s kinsman Bartle Frere wanted daughter Jane to have lessons from her in London (22 October 1855). The views expressed on the three composers are interesting. *Fidelio*, first produced nearly half a century before in 1805, she found 'incomprehensible', whereas the others, the near contemporary *Norma* (1831) and *Ernani* (1844), were clearly much more enjoyable.

p.237: *October* 31 Florence Nightingale (1820–1910), 'The Lady with the Lamp', was the daughter of William Edward, a great lover of travel, which was the reason why she was named after the city of her birth. It is explained in the *Memoirs* (II p.24) how he was a friend of brother William at the University of Edinburgh and in order to inherit the second of two large fortunes he had to change his surname from Shore to 'the ridiculous name of Nightingale'. A grandfather was William Smith (1756–1835), a Member of Parliament, who was particularly associated with the movement for the abolition of slavery and, as a Unitarian, with the repeal of acts discriminating against dissenters.

When the War broke out she was superintendent of the Establishment for Gentlewomen During Illness and she was deeply impressed by the articles written by the *Times* special

correspondent, William Howard Russell (see 15 November)
on the appalling conditions in which the wounded existed
('Are there no devoted women among us able and willing to
go forth to minister to the sick and suffering soldiers of the
East in the hospitals of Scutari?'). The minister responsible
was Sidney Herbert, a near neighbour in Hampshire and a
personal friend, who had been one of the original subscribers, no less than £200, to the foundation of St. Columba's,
and she wrote to him offering her services. He replied
encouragingly ('My question simply is, Would you listen
to the request to go out and supervise the whole thing? There
is but one person in England that I know of who would be
capable of organising such a scheme . . .') and within the
week she had embarked with a party of thirty eight nurses,
mostly from religious nursing orders, as Superintendent of
the Female Nursing Establishment of the English General
Hospitals in Turkey, armed with a preliminary budget of
£1,000.

As far as her religious beliefs are concerned, according to
Cecil Woodham Smith's biography, 'in the summer of 1852
it seemed as if she might find what she wanted in the Roman
Catholic Church' but she was dissuaded by Cardinal Man-
ning (whom she had met with the Herberts in Rome in
1847); nevertheless at this time she wrote, 'If you knew what
a home the Catholic Church would be to me'.

p.239: *November* 15 Sir William Howard Russell (1820–1907) was
the brilliant journalist whose dispatches from the Crimea
invented the role of the special correspondent. A Dubliner,
he first worked for E.S.'s favourite the *Dublin Evening Mail*
and then wrote on Irish issues for John Thaddeus Delane, the
great editor of the *Times* from 1843. He was sent to the war
in October 1854, from where he wrote his *Letters* back to the
Times, which both described the shambolic organisation of
the commissariat and hospitals and delineated the appalling
sufferings of that first winter; these may be said to have
inspired Florence Nightingale to have set out for the Crimea.
It was he who first coined the phrase 'the thin red line'
describing the infantry at the battle of Balaclava on 25
October, and it is commonly accepted that his articles played
a major part in the fall of the Aberdeen coalition the
following January. The phrase about Lord Raglan is fair
as the commander-in-chief afforded Russell, despite the
critical nature of his dispatches, considerable freedom to

write his articles without either censorship or denying him use of army facilities. His Chief of Staff, General Sir James Simpson, was not so complimentary, describing him as 'one of the low and grovelling correspondents of the Times', echoing Prince Albert's opinion of him as 'that miserable scribbler'. However, his epitaph in St. Paul's describes him as 'the first and greatest of war correspondants'.

p.239: *November* 15 General Richard Airey, (1803–1880), created Lord Airey when he retired in 1876 after fifty five years' service, was Quarter-Master-General to the Crimean expedition from September 1854 to November 1855. He therefore included amongst his responsibilities the formation of troops in the field, and as such he wrote the fatal order for the charge of the Light Brigade at the battle of Balaclava on the orders of Lord Raglan. He therefore, in addition to receiving much of the blame for the appalling state of his department at the start of the war, was seen by public opinion as being bound up in the tragedy of perhaps the most notorious incident of the whole war.

p.239: *November* 15 Lewis Edward Nolan (1818–1854), captain in the 15th Hussars, began his military career in a Hungarian Hussar regiment, where he was a pupil of the instructor of the Austrian imperial cavalry. It was therefore as a cavalry expert that he was sent as aide-de-camp to the Quarter-Master-General Colonel, later Lord, Airey to purchase horses and make preparations for the arrival of the army's cavalry. He is however much better known as the headstrong and impetuous A.D.C. to Airey who conveyed Lord Raglan's written order, very much as described here, to Lord Lucan, the officer commanding the British cavalry, ordering him to prevent the Russians from carrying away some British guns. Understandably, Lucan is supposed to have asked 'Where are we to advance?' and, famously and perhaps rather impertinently, Nolan replied 'There, my Lord, is your enemy and there are your guns'. He was the first of the 107 men and 397 horse to be killed in the next twenty five minutes.

p.240: *November* 19 It is clear from *The Highland Lady in Ireland* (p. 397) that the *'joint* trustees' appointed by Mrs. Wynch's husband were in fact her father and brother William, who had promptly invested her eight or perhaps nine thousand pounds in what she described as her brother's 'abominable bank', the Union Bank of Calcutta, whose collapse was such a contributory factor in father and son's uncertain financial and legal position in the 1840s. Sir John Peter Grant in fact died at sea in 1848 returning home, and E.S. was in no doubt that had he returned Mrs. Wynch 'commences a prosecution against him the moment he lands'. No wonder, in despair at another illustration of her father and brother's financial chicanery she comments: 'there is wheel within wheel and no comfort anywhere'.

p.243: *December* 19 Patrick Robertson became a Lord of Session in 1843 at the age of forty nine. Andrew Rutherford's career was both legal and political, as he was Whig Solicitor General and then Lord Advocate under Melbourne and again under Russell (1846–1851). He was elected Lord Rector of the University of Glasgow in 1844, defeating Lord Eglinton, whom E.S. knew as Lord Lieutenant. He was appointed a Lord of Session in 1851.

1855

p.254: *January* 20 George Hamilton Gordon, fourth Earl of Aberdeen, who lived from 1784 to 1860, was Prime Minister from December 1852 to February 1855, and resigned very much under the circumstances described in the Journal. He was invested as a Knight of the Garter on 7 February 1855 and thereby became one of the few members of the Order of the Garter as well as the Thistle. It is perhaps a commentary upon his reputation as a Prime Minister, who led a worthy but uninspired ministry that found itself wholly out of its depth in its conduct of the Crimean war, that he is also remembered as the only Prime Minister who married his daughter-in-law. After the death of his first wife, Lady Katherine Hamilton, eldest daughter of the first Marquis of Abercorn, three years later he married the widow of his eldest son.

p.254: *January* 20 Henry Pelham Fiennes Pelham Clinton, fifth Duke of Newcastle (1811–1864) was Minister for War and the Colonies in Aberdeen's coalition and when the offices were separated in June 1854, he became Minister for War. He had a reputation for zealous industry tinged with unfounded optimism; he resigned office in February 1855 and went out himself to the Crimea to see for himself the real state of the army. Peat charcoal is an artificial fuel made by carbonising peat. Miss Seddon, another early volunteer who worked with Florence Nightingale and a fellow Tractarian, was earlier dismissively described as 'doing good works in the wandering friar style' (31 October 1854); there were twelve Roman Catholics in the original thirty eight strong party of nurses that went out to the Crimea that month.

p.255: *January* 23 Fanny Burney (1752–1840) was the daughter of Dr. Charles Burney, the musicologist. *Evalina or a Young Lady's Entrance into the World*, her first novel, published in 1778, was a great success. Dr. Johnson is reputed to have learnt it almost by heart and his Mrs. Thrale was her first patron. Her second novel, *Cecilia*, appeared in 1782 and the *Letters and Diaries* two years after her death.

p.256: *January* 24 Samuel Crisp, an unsuccessful poet and playwright, was an old friend of Charles Burney and clearly a very great influence on her literary progress. According to Macaulay (in his article written for the *Edinburgh Review* January 1843 about the *Diary and Letters of Madame D'Arblay*) he was 'the chief share in the formation of her mind'; further, he maintains that he regarded Fanny Burney as his daughter, calling her 'his Fannikin' whilst to her he was her 'dear Daddy'. He fits into E.S.'s description as he died shortly after the publication of *Cecilia* in 1782, on the same day that Dr. Johnson had his stroke.

p.256: *January* 28 It was her second patron who attracted her to Windsor, which was where her initial contact was made with the royal family who were regular visitors at Mrs. Delaney's home there. The Queen in particular enjoyed her company and appointed her in July 1786 to be a Second Keeper of the Robes at a salary of two hundred pounds a year. She struggled on in this post until July 1791 under the supervision of the infamous Madame Schellenberg, whom she described as 'coarse, tyrannical and ill-tempered'.

p.257: *January* 28 It certainly was not regarded at the time as a *manly* resignation. It was Lord John's fourth attempt since September and it occurred when he learned that John Roebuck had tabled a motion demanding a commission of inquiry into the conduct of the war. To have resigned from, of all offices, the Leadership of the House and abandoned his colleagues at this time cast him in a very poor light; as Donald Southgate says: 'What to him was honest scruple was bound to seem to others base desertion.'

p.257: *January* 28 Sir Howard Douglas (1776–1861) had been present at the retreat to Corunna in 1809 during the Peninsular War, after which he had served as Lord High

Commissioner to the Ionian Isles and M.P. for Liverpool 1842–1847. His record as a distinguished public servant meant that his pamphlet, published in 1855, was read the more attentively; it was entitled *Observations on the Naval Operations in the Black Sea and at Sebastopol.*

p.258: *January* 28 Major-General Robert Wynyard (1802–1864) was the son of the Lieutenant-General William Wynyard (1802–1819), whose unconventional behaviour consequent upon a social infatuation with the widow of a General Anstruther ('this ill-behaved trifling woman') is described in the *Memoirs* II p. 12.

p.258: *January* 28 Raglan's career was inextricably bound up with that of Wellington. He went out to the Peninsula with him and was appointed his political secretary in 1811; he was at his side during the battle of Waterloo and on his mentor's appointment as Commander-in-Chief in 1827, he became military secretary at the Horse Guards. Equally, there is no doubting his bravery at Waterloo. Towards the end of the battle his right elbow was shattered by a bullet and the arm had to be amputated. He bore the operation without flinching and afterwards told the orderly: 'Hallo! don't carry away that arm till I have taken off my [wife's] ring.'

p.258: *January* 31 Aunt Bourne, who through her Oxford connections had some knowledge of the world of public affairs, was perfectly correct. 'Colonel Fairley' was in fact the Honourable Stephen Digby. His first marriage had been to a daughter of Lord Ilchester, the second earl (who was to die of 'gout in the head' in 1803, according to the *Complete Peerage*.) Secondly, to the dismay of Fanney Burney, in 1790 he married a Miss Gunning, who appears in her Diaries as 'Miss Fuzilio'. The third novel was another success. *Camilla* was published in 1796 and Macaulay estimated that that she earned three thousand guineas from this one book. By this time she had married the French *emigré* General d'Arblay in 1793, and so it was that they built 'Camilla Cottage' for themselves near Mickelham. Her son, Alexander, was born in 1794 and became a priest but clearly led a deeply unfulfilled life, dying at the age of forty-three.

p.260: *February* 8 Brevet rank confers nominal rank on an officer, but without any right to extra pay.

p.262: *February* 19 *The Memoirs of Thomas Thomson* (1768–1852) were published by the Bannantyne Club, named after the sixteenth century compiler of *Corpus poeticum Scottorum*. This existed to preserve documents significant to the cultural history of Scotland which would otherwise have disappeared. He had become President after the death of its founder Sir Walter Scott in 1832. He was one of the group that founded the *Edinburgh Review* and he was appointed the first deputy Clerk-Register of Scotland in 1806. This post he held with distinction ('No man has done nearly so much to recover, to arrange, to explain, and to preserve our historical muniments' wrote Cockburn in his *Life of Lord Jeffrey*) but he was dismissed in 1839 after questions had been raised about his financial administration of his office.

p.262: *February* 21 General Sir James Simpson (1792–1868) was the half-pay Commandant at Chatham when in February 1855 he sent as Chief of Staff to the Crimea, with very much the remit described in the Journal. Trevor Royle sees him as 'a fair and sensible observer of the difficulties facing Raglan'. At the fall of Sebastopol he was warmly embraced by the new commander of the French forces, General Pélissier, a moment of weakness he later explained: 'It was a great occasion and I couldna' resist him.'

p.262: *February* 21 Sir James Graham continued in office at the Admiralty from the previous administration until replaced by Sir Charles Wood in March; Sydney Herbert made way for Sir John at the Colonial Office on February; and Gladstone continued in office as Chancellor of the Exchequer but only until succeeded by Sir George Cornewall Lewis. Personal antipathy towards Palmerston played its part in their decision, together with their suspicion that with Palmerston at the helm the war would be unnecessarily prolonged

p.265: *March* 21 A 'Day of Prayer and Supplication' for the success of the army and navy had been held on the 26 April 1854. It would have been called, according to precedent, a 'Day of Humiliation' but to this the Queen had objected in a stinging letter to Aberdeen.

p.265: *April* 2 Charles Grant, Lord Glenelg (1778–1866), Chief Secretary for Ireland (1819–1823) and leading light in the Councils of the East India Company, was, as related in the *Memoirs*, a great friend of the Grant family and patron of the extended clan. Anne Macpherson lived at Belleville, the house constructed by her father James 'Ossian' Macpherson, author of the *Fragments of Ancient Poetry Collected in the Highlands* that from its publication in 1760 was an endless source of controversy. He left four illegitimate children;

Anne died unmarried and Charles, the second son, perished in India. She seems to have been the original inspiration for the Grant sisters' literary labours that winter of 1826/1827 which provided the family's principal source of income before their hurried clandestine flight to a new life in India.

p.266: *April* 4 George Charles Bingham, Earl of Lucan (1800–1888). Surprisingly, Knight of St. Anne of Russia (Second Class), and more predictably, Lord Lieutenant of Co. Mayo from 1845 until his death. He married Anne, the seventh daughter of Robert Brudenell, sixth Earl of Cardigan in 1829, and was therefore brother-in-law to the seventh Earl who was under his command in the Cavalry Brigade, one of the elements that explains the disaster of the Charge of the Light Brigade. They returned to England at the beginning of 1855, Lucan having being relieved of his command and Cardigan an invalid. Both remained in the army, Lucan ending his career a field-marshal and Cardigan Inspector-General of Cavalry.

p.266: *April* 5 Francois-Antoine Certain Canrobert (sic) (1809–1895), after serving his military apprenticeship in Algeria, was appointed aide-de-camp to Louis Napoleon in 1850. After his distinguished contribution to the outcome of the war in the Crimea, he fought at both the battles of Magenta and Solferino in the Italian wars and was later wounded at Metz during the Franco-Prussian War. There is no suggestion, however, in the *Dictionaire de Biographie Française* to support E.S.'s earlier speculation that he might, like France's Foreign Minister Count Walewski, have been a natural son of the great Napoleon. The *D.N.B.*, however, makes a point of quoting the opinion of Lord Raglan, whose French was fluent, that he was 'a vacillating and sometimes despondent colleague'; the cynical British troops knew him as 'Robert can't'.

p.269: *April* 20 George William Frederick Howard, seventh Earl of Carlisle (1802–1864) had been Chief Secretary for Ireland (1835–1841) and he was to be Lord Lieutenant on two occasions, 28th February 1855 to 1858, and 1859 to his death. *The D.N.B.* summarises his impact: 'Without commanding abilities or great strength of will, his gentleness endeared him to all those with whom he came into contact.' He was very much a man of letters and his publications ranged from a five act verse play entitled *The Last of the Greeks, or the Fall of Constantinople: A Tragedy* (1828) to the preface for the English edition of *Uncle Tom's Cabin* for Harriet Beecher Stowe (1853). He presided over the celebrations of the Shakespeare tercentenary in the year of his death. His sister, Lady Caroline Lascelles, prepared his journal for private circulation; it is clear from the entry for 29 April that E.S. had read and liked it.

p.272: *May 6* Marguerite, Countess of Blessington (1789–1849) certainly led a life of which E.S., whose views on a decadent aristocracy she made perfectly plain throughout her journals, could never have approved, but from what she writes it seems as if it is the tinsel from the biography, the ill-advised *billets doux* from irresponsible public figures, that prompted her criticisms rather than the gross irregularities of this fascinating character's private life. She had been reading Richard Robert Madden's *The Literary Life and Correspondence of the Countess of Blessington*, all three volumes of which were published in 1855.

Lady Blessington's first husband, Captain Maurice St. Leger Farmer from Co. Kildare, in the 47th Regiment, had proposed to her when she was fourteen and a half. He was 'a man who indulged in such ungovernable bursts of passion as to suggest insanity' and she left him after three months. He died in 1817 'killed during a drunken orgy by falling from a window in the King's Bench prison' (*D.N.B.*). Four months later she married the easy-going but very rich Charles John Gardiner, second viscount and first earl of Blessington, who was quite ready to accomodate, for example, the extended continental tour between 1822 and 1828 that they undertook with her step-daughter Harriet Anne Francis Gardiner (1812–1869) and the Countess' lover Count D'Orcy. Further, his tolerance extended to D'Orcy marrying his daughter, then aged fifteen, in Naples. Blessington died in 1829 and her luxurious life was no longer capable of being supported by her own means so she turned to literature, but she and the Count were forced to flee to Paris in 1848 to avoid their debts. She died in 1849 and he three years later. He chose to be buried in the graveyard at Chambourcy (which was the residence of his sister Ida, Duchess of Gramont) with his wife's stepmother.

p.274: *May 16* Fanny (Frances Anne) Kemble (1809–1893) was the daughter of Charles Kemble, himself one of perhaps the most successful acting dynasty of the century. The uncle and aunt mentioned are John Philip Kemble (1757–1823), who like his niece is singled out for criticism of his pronouncia-tion by the *D.N.B.* ('His misuse of the letter *e* was however unpardonable') and the peerless Sarah Siddons (1755–1831), who for Hazlitt was 'tragedy personified'.

p.275: *May* 16 The *Dublin Evening Mail's* account on Wednesday 16 May of 'Mrs. Kemble's readings' reported that on 'Monday afternoon [she] entertained a crowded, fashionable and at-tentive audience', particularly singling out the *Merry Wives* for praise ('the chief characteristic in Mrs. Kemble's reading of this play is intense fun') and concluding 'the audience was kept in a vibration of unspeakable amusement'.

p.277: *May* 20 Characters from the best-known play, *The School for Scandal*, of Richard Brinsley Sheridan (1751–1816) whose brilliant and scandalous gossip as they dissect the characters all around them is one of the outstanding features of a classic comedy. Unlike the banter of E.S. and Hamlet, there was a darker side to Lady Sneerwell's malice: 'Wounded myself, in the early part of my life, by the envenomed tongue of slander, I confess I have since known no pleasure equal to the reducing others to the level of my own injured reputation' (Act I, scene I).

p.278: *May* 24 John Arthur Roebuck (1801–1879) tabled the motion for a parliamentary select committee of inquiry into the conduct of the war that was passed by 305 votes to 148 on January 28 1855, no less than 85 government supporters deserting the Aberdeen coalition. This led to the disgraceful resignation of Lord John Russell (see E.S.'s reaction 28 January) and Aberdeen offering his resignation the next day.

p.283: *June* 5 Luigi Lablanche (1794–1858), whose mother was Irish, sang regularly from 1830 in London and at the provincial festivals as well as being, according to *Groves*, Queen Victoria's singing-master in 1836–1837. Mrs. Hort had clearly been taught by one of the greatest basses of his generation ('it is indeed doubtful whether he was greater as a singer or an actor'); he was selected to be one of the thirty-two torch-bearers who surrounded Beethoven's coffin at its internment.

p.287: *June* 14 The *Dublin Evening Mail* was equally ecstatic in its description on Wednesday 13 June of the Cavalry Brigade Ball. 'The Rotunda was last evening the scene of an assem-blage such as was never excelled in brilliancy and all the accessories of enjoyment upon any of the innumerable occasions on which that building has been the theatre of

gaiety and splendour during a long series of years.' And 'For
some time past fashionable circles have been agitated to more
than ordinary degree by the current gossip in reference to the
Cavalry Brigade Ball . . . and it may be safely said that no one
of the many rumours of its contemplated magnificence went
beyond the mark.'

p.287: *June* 16 It does rather depend what is meant by 'the people'.
Joseph Leeson (1711–1783), the first Earl of Milltown, was
the son of a brewer, but rather a successful one, and his
father-in-law was Sheriff of Dublin.

p.287: *June* 16 Mrs. S. C. Hall wrote *Sketches of Irish Character*(1829) and *Ireland, its Scenery, Character etc* (1840), both
of which had more appeal for her English than her Irish
readers.

p.290: *July* 5 Lord Raglan died on 28 June in his sixty sixth year.
According to the *Times* obituary of 2 July: 'He died of a mild
form of cholera, his end hastened by chagrin at the failure of
the attacks on the Malakoff and the Redan.' Trevor Royle
speculates that it was probably dysentry or even simple exhaustion: 'those close to him felt that might even have been
from heartbreak'. E.S.'s favourite, the *Dublin Evening Mail*,
commented that 'If not a leader to be ranked with "the choice
and master-spirits of the age", he was, at least, a very valiant
and noble soldier, a pure patriot, and a truly virtuous and
Christian man', adding somewhat elliptically that 'whatever
may be his shortcomings, they were manifestly not ascribable
to any failure of the heart'. Later critics have not been so
sympathetic or generous; no public statue has ever been raised
in his memory.

p.292: *July* 20 This is the eighth Marquess of Tweeddale (1787–
1876), with whom her father had been well acquainted both
in Whig political circles in Scotland and in India when he
was Governor of Madras between 1842 and 1848. James
Crawford, Lord Ardmillan, (1805–1876) was Solicitor General in 1853 and appointed lord of the Court of Session two
years later.

p.293: *July* 22 She had been acquainted with the Horner brothers
during her girlhood days in Edinburgh. Francis (1778–1817)
achieved fame as a politician and economist and Leonard
(1785–1864), one of the founders of The Edinburgh Academy and London University, as a geologist and educational
reformer.

p.296: *July* 29 This is an ironic reference to the last two lines ('We carved not a line, we raised not a stone – / But we left him alone with his glory') of the poem by the Rev. Charles Wolfe (1791–1823), *The Burial of Sir John Moore at Corunna*. Moore, who lived from 1761 to his death in the ill-fated retreat covering 250 tortuous miles in mid-winter in three weeks to Corunna in 1809, had had his task made impossible by the unhelpful actions of the Envoy to Madrid, John Hookham Frere. He was E.S.'s uncle and she was well aware of his responsibility, as she wrote that he 'caused the retreat to Corunna and the death of Sir John Moore' (*Memoirs* II p. 180).

p.297: *August* 12 The *Dublin Evening Mail* had rather more to say about this great star. 'The series of Italian operas came to a close last evening with the benefit and final appearance of Madame Grisi – so stated the bills though we have strong doubts of it. If indeed we have taken our last look at Madame Grisi as a public singer which, we trust, we have, as it would be painful to behold such a great artist coming forward, year after year, with diminished energies – we must say that her performance last evening has left memories of such magnitude as leaves us little hope of having them effaced by any succeeding *Norma*.'

p.297: *August* 12 Viscount Combermere was Lord Downshire's father-in-law and in his eighty third year; he was to live to be ninety seven. His influence was securely based on his rank of Field Marshal and the three years he spent as Commander-in Chief of the Army in Ireland, 1822–1825.

p.304: *October* 7 Sydney Smith (1771–1845), whose life was celebrated in *A Memory of the Reverend Sidney Smith by his daughter Lady Holland, with a selection from his letters, edited by Mrs. Austin,* (published in 1855) is principally remembered as the Episcopalian clergyman on the fringe of the distinguished men of letters whom E.S. put at the heart of the last part of Edinburgh's 'Golden Age'. That he was more than a mere celebrated wit whose *bons mots* echoed through the city can be seen from the fact that he was one of the founders and early contributors to the *Edinburgh Review*. He left Edinburgh in 1828 and lived until the year before his death in the house mentioned as being so well organised by his wife Catherine; this was later to be the home of Evelyn Waugh. For, however, rather a laboured example of his wit, see 7 October 1855.

The brother-in-law, the wealthy merchant, earned his

living from the banking house of Pylus, Hyde, Dorest and Cockell; the other, Charles Small Pylus (1766–1810), was Lord of the Admiralty (1791–1797) and then of the Treasury (1797–1803). Sidney Smith's daughter Sada (he was determined that her Christian name should be unique and as he himself explained, she was so called 'merely because she must have some name and I thought that a pretty one') married Dr., later Sir, Henry Holland, a graduate of the University of Edinburgh, who was physician both to Queen Caroline and Queen Victoria.

p.305: *October* 14 E.S., who had earlier read Pendennis with enjoyment, clearly was an appreciative reader of the novels of Thackeray. *The History of Henry Esmond Esquire* contains a lot more than sublime ideas: it is a fast-moving tale that moves from an Irish background to Marlborough's Wars and Jacobite plots before the eponymous hero heads off to America, providing Thackeray with the opportunity to continue the family's history in *The Virginians*.

p.305: *October* 25 Sir William Molesworth Bart. (1810–1855) was the daughter of Mary Brown from Edinburgh and he studied at the University between 1824 and 1827; he is mentioned in the *Memoirs* and his mother was part of the Grant parents' social set. He is remembered as the editor of *Hobbes' Works* which he produced in sixteen volumes between 1839 and 1845 and as the Colonial Secretary who succeeded Lord John Russell in Aberdeen's government between July 1855 and his death in October. He was succeeded by his cousin the Rev. Sir Hugh Henry Molesworth.

p.306: *October* 27 In the six years between 1826 and 1831 when his health broke down, Scott, who had 'resolved to employ my time and talents on the production of such literary works' as would clear all debts owing as a result of the failure of his publisher James Ballantyne, earned £50,000 for his creditors and £6,000 for himself and his family (see *The Journal of Sir Walter Scott*, edited by W.E.K. Anderson).

p.308: *October* 31 Aspasia came from Miletus, the most southerly of the Ionian cities of Asia Minor, to Athens where she flourished as a courtesan, eventually settling down in what turned out to be a lasting relationship with Pericles (c. 495–429 B.C.), the statesman, orator and director of the Athenian strategy in the Peloponnesian Wars.

p.310: *November* 2 This is certainly the main theme of *The Newcomes*, which was published as a serial between 1853 and

1855. It concerns the descendants of a self-made man, Colonel Thomas Newcome, whose career had been spent in India, and the contrasting fortunes of his only son and his cousins, whose characters between them range from the other-worldy to the rapaciously ambitious.

p.313: *November* 23 John Baldwin Buckstone (1802–1879) was a celebrated comic actor, producer and dramatist, amongst whose most famous roles was E.S.'s favourite from *The School for Scandal*, Sir Benjamin Backbite.

p.316: *December* 10 The *Dublin Evening Mail* gave a graphic description of the reaction to the acquittal of Father Vladimir Petcherine in what was known as 'the Bible-burning Case'. 'The announcement was received with loud cheers and other demonstrations of satisfactions which created quite a scene in court. Handkerchiefs were waved in a vehement manner by several of the respectably dressed females who occupied seats in the front of the bench, and some of the most juvenile of these literally danced for joy.' The *Times* struck a more sombre note: 'The government of the country will no more allow these vagrant firebrands to kindle dissention and riot than it has permitted foreign demonstrators to propagate their creed by blasphemy and calls to assassination.'

p.316: *December* 11 On their way back from India in 1829, the newly married Colonel and Mrs. Smith stayed for three weeks at Colombo in Ceylon, where they discovered her old Edinburgh friend and dancing partner, Campbell Riddell. He, as she explains in the *Memoirs* (II pp. 286–7), had been sent out as a Commissioner to inquire into the misgovernment of the island and he went on to be Secretary to the Governor in Sydney. The Reel of Tulloch was clearly a favourite for, in one of the articles she had written in 1851 for *Chambers'* entitled 'A Twelvemonth in Calcutta', this is the dance she describes at a gathering of Scots:

> By way of conclusion, four of the gentlemen got up to dance the reel of Tulloch to such a tune as would have made even the lame try to move, and stirred up the paralytic. I could not sit; I was never so excited; the music and the dancing, and the shouting, altogether carried one out of one's self. So many happy people – clansmen I fancy – a great tie, all meeting on the banks of the Hoogley, so many thousand miles away from their mountain home, all well, all thriving, and all with the warm heart for the land of their birth; and the spark of

nationality awakened by the music of their country remembered in childhood. It was a moving scene.

1856

p.323: *January* 13 He is invariably referred to as 'Russy', but his full name and title was Joseph Henry Leeson, Viscount Russborough and he lived from 1829 to 1871. He was an Ensign in the 68th of Foot (1848–1851) and, according to the *Complete Peerage*, 'sometime A.D.C. to the viceroy of Ireland', Lord Carlisle.

p.326: *January* 27 John Henry, fourth Baron de Roebeck married Sophie Charlotte, daughter of William Burton of Burton Hall, Carlow.

p.327: *February* 10 According to the *Dublin Evening Mail* the opera to be performed was Vincent Wallace's *Maritana* ('one of the best specimens we possess of the modern English opera'). He was born in Waterford in 1812 and died in 1865 after a life of adventure on three continents; he composed prolifically and this opera, which was first produced at the Drury Lane Theatre in 1845, is probably his only relatively well-known work. The *Mail* continued that it would be performed at the Brunswick Street Concert Room 'under the auspices of the Marchioness of Downshire (herself a first-rate musician)'. The article ended on a characteristically grovelling note – 'We have no doubt that a crowded house will reward Lady Downshire for her zeal and energy in the cause she has undertaken; and we must say that if such zeal and energy in the cause she has undertaken were oftener found within the circle of a coronet, we should hear very few complaints about "the cold shades of the aristocracy".'

p.328: *February* 17 Marlborough Street is where the buildings of the Commissioners of National Education were situated. They had been established by Parliament in 1845 and, although E.S. in her running of the schools at Baltiboys had had her difficulties with its bureaucratic officials, it is generally seen as an enlightened body that did not deserve the severe criticisms it at first earned from suspicious critics on both sides of the religious divide.

p.329: *February* 24 The Dublin Evening Mail naturally waxed ecstatic in its review of this concert performance of the opera, describing it as a 'a complete and brilliant success'.

It also printed the text of the poem with which the Honourable Edward Leeson began the proceedings, one that argu-
ably from what E.S. writes was penned by his mother. A brief
extract provided the flavour of the whole:

> The great, good, the grateful, grave and gay,
> Combine alike to patronise this play,
> While worthy dames and modern troubadors
> Discard the cold reserve of amateurs,
> And boldly dare the stage with voice and hand.
> To aid the genius of the fatherland.

p.330: *February* 24 John Sadleir (1814–1856) was an unscrupulous
speculator who used his position as a Member of Parliament
(he represented Carlow and then Sligo between 1847 and his
death) illegally to further the interests of the Tipperary Joint-
Stock Bank, founded and managed by his brother James since
1827. He succeeded William Gibson Craig as a Junior Lord
of the Treasury from January 1853 to March 1854, a position
which gave authenticity to his issue of forged land conveyances and railway share certificates ('a *pied à terre* for
the Irish gambler') to the extent that the Bank had become
overdrawn by two hundred thousand pounds by 1856, the
year he committed suicide. Charles Lever, the contemporary
Irish novelist, Dickens (Mr. Merdle in *Little Dorritt*) and
Trollope (Augustus Merlotte in *The Way We Live Now*) based
characters on the infamous rogue. John committed suicide
(although the Journal later refers to articles in the *Nation* and
Chambers' casting doubts about his death) and James managed to flee the country.

p.330: *March* 10 The second Marquis of Headfort (1787–1870) had
first married Amelia née Thompson, and an indication of the
scale of her wealth may be gauged from the fact that her
father was Lord Mayor of London in 1828. Their son, who
died in the same year as his father, was styled the Earl of
Bective. His second marriage, to the widow of the hero of
Kabul expedition of 1841, Frances, Lady Macnaughton, has
been noted earlier in February 1853. The seventh (Irish) Earl
of Granard (1833–1889) married Jane Colclough, daughter
of Hamilton Knox Grogan-Morgan of Johnstone Castle, Co.
Wexford; this was the girl whom 'Russy' had intended to
marry the previous year ('Russy's deserted is to marry Lord
Granard' 11 May 1856).

p.332: *March* 13 This is defined by the *O.E.D.* as 'corrupt behaviour in a commission, office, employment or position of trust' or 'corrupt administration of public money'.

p.334: *March* 30 The reason explaining this descent upon what E.S. insisted upon calling their 'Brummagem', or counterfeit, Court was that Harriet, Duchess of Sutherland, was the sister of the Lord Lieutenant, the bachelor seventh Earl of Carlisle. Hugh, later the first Duke of Westminster (1815–1899) was Earl Grosvenor until 1869 and he had married Constance, the daughter of his maternal uncle, the second Duke of Sutherland. One reason explaining the Journal's slight sense of superiority, and E.S. had a very real sense of everybody's position in society even if she did not believe that these never changed, but not Lady Milltown's petulant and self-destructive behaviour, was her knowledge that the Marchioness of Stafford was Annie, daughter of the Grants' old friends the Hay-Mackenzies, whose mother was a daughter of Sir James Gibson Craig Bart., her sister Jane's father-in-law.

p.336: *May* 4 Seidliz is a village in Bohemia after which, according to rather a snooty explanation in the *O.E.D.*, the powder is 'arbitrarily named, merely on account of its aperient [laxative] powers'.

p.338: *May* 11 Although there are references to this homicide in the *Outrage Papers* in the National Archives, no one was brought to trial despite the enormous sums of money (the Lord Lieutenant added one hundred pounds to the four hundred raised from all classes in the neighbourhood) offered for information leading to the trial and conviction of the perpetrator. The time limit was even extended by twelve months on 7 February 1833. It is interesting to note that amongst the names of the tenantry contributing their shilling to the fund was Pat Quin, whom E.S. believed to be one of the leading lights in the conspiracy.

p.341: *June* 1 Eleanor, the third daughter of the eighth Earl of Lauderdale, the political and business confidant of Elizabeth Smith's father, married James Balfour of Whttingham in 1815; she was born in 1790 and died in 1869.

p.346: *June* 29 The Marquis of Tweeddale was married to Lady Susan Montague, daughter to the Duchess of Manchester, whose mother was the celebrated Duchess of Gordon. At the time of the wooing, she is described as 'a beautiful creature'. E.S.'s description of him, however, is less complimentary: 'thick set and square built and coarse mannered with that flat

Maitland face which when it gets into a family never can be got out of it, he was altogether the ugliest boxer or bruiser looking sort of common order of prize fighter that ever was seen in or out of a ring.'

p.365: *September* 18 The great Grisi was only forty three at the time but E.S. had selected just the right opera to hear her for the first time. She was very familiar with the music, as Janey sang some of the arias to her mother's accompaniment, and the composer, Bellini, had a great admiration for Grisi; he may have written the opera for the greatest soprano of her generation, Giuditta Pasta (1798 – 1865), but he recognised in the younger singer the perfect Adalgisa. Karl Johan Formes (1815–1889) was another of the fine singers attracted to Dublin at this time.

p.367: *December* 31 J. S. Wortley was in fact appointed English Solicitor General on 22 November 1856.

Index